D1738769

POPULISM and POLITICS

Peter H. Argersinger

POPULISM and POLITICS

William Alfred Peffer
and the People's Party

The University Press of Kentucky

ISBN: 0-8131-1306-7

Library of Congress Catalog Card Number: 73-86400

Copyright © 1974 by The University Press of Kentucky

A statewide cooperative scholarly publishing agency
serving Berea College, Centre College of Kentucky,
Eastern Kentucky University, Georgetown College,
Kentucky Historical Society, Kentucky State University,
Morehead State University, Murray State University,
Northern Kentucky State College, Transylvania
University, University of Kentucky, University of Louisville,
and Western Kentucky University.

Editorial and Sales Offices: Lexington, Kentucky 40506

for Jody

Contents

List of Tables

Preface

The past two decades have witnessed a historiographical debate over the nature of Populism in which participants on each side have made facile judgments based on inconclusive evidence and incomplete research. Historians have carried on their debate largely apart from the political history of the period, and their analyses of Populism have suffered accordingly, with basic questions about the movement remaining unanswered, indeed unasked. Both historical friends and critics of Populism have failed in the most elemental task of identifying their protagonists, and they have virtually ignored the time dimension in arguing that Populists believed this, or that Populism represented that. Although the life of the People's party was quite short, the party and its adherents changed remarkably during that time, and no exposition on the nature of Populism which fails to account for this will add to our understanding.

The purpose of this book is to examine precisely those changes that Populism experienced as it confronted American politics and society in the 1890s. I employ several methods of historical analysis, including quantitative techniques in addition to more traditional methodology, and I examine Populism at the personal, local, state, and national levels in an effort to review fully the transformation of the movement. Thus, although my study is broadly biographical,

I focus on William Alfred Peffer primarily to illustrate the changes within Populism. For this purpose, his career is unequaled: his six-year term in the United States Senate coincided exactly with the generally recognized birth and death dates of Populism; and with good reason, for he carried the title "Father of Populism" and was the foremost public representative of the movement in the 1890s, though historians have since neglected him. But Peffer merely illustrates the more important problems considered, and consequently much of this book finds him only distantly involved personally. I closely investigate the Populist politics of Kansas, for example, in order to suggest reasons for changes, decisions, and policy distinctions at the national level, though Peffer usually avoided any direct intervention in state politics at that time.

The essence of Populism was that it was a political movement, and the essence of the People's party was that it was a political party. This study is therefore primarily political history, and I treat the issues that have bedeviled other historians primarily only insofar as they operated politically. There are of course some reflections on the interpretive debate, but I hope that the larger work of tracing the metamorphosis of the movement will itself provide a better clue to the problem of Populism in America.

I am indebted to many people for many things. The late Professor George L. Anderson of the University of Kansas first aroused my interest in Populism and continued thereafter to encourage my work. Professor Gwen S. Argersinger of the University of New Mexico contributed immeasurably her time, assistance, and knowledge in both the researching and writing of this study. Professor Allan G. Bogue of the University of Wisconsin directed the dissertation on which this book is based and provided valuable advice and suggestions. Professor James D. Norris of the University of Missouri at St. Louis gave me reassuring advice and consistent support when I began this study. Professor David P. Thelen of the University of Missouri at Columbia gave an earlier form of the manuscript a critical reading and contributed many valuable comments and suggestions. The staffs of many fine institutions, especially the Kansas State Historical Society and the State Historical Society of Wisconsin, were helpful in a variety of ways. Portions of Chapter 2 originally appeared in the *Kansas Historical Quarterly,* and permission to incorporate this material is gratefully acknowledged. My wife, Jo Ann Eady Argersinger, devoted her time, patience, and encouragement to the completion of this work and improved it in both style and substance. If, despite all this assistance, errors still persist, they are entirely mine and deservedly so.

CHAPTER ONE

Farmers and Politics

FROM THEIR very beginnings, Kansas and the Republican party were inextricably related. The difficulties of the territorial years, the struggle of the Civil War, and the postwar influx of Union veterans sustained their mutual attraction. As a one-party state, however, Kansas still witnessed the political turmoil of the 1860s and 1870s, for all political positions found representation within an active Republican party. The state GOP, with its flexibility and responsiveness, largely controlled those reform impulses that culminated in Populism in the 1890s. Independent parties existed, but even during the economic collapse of the 1870s most reformers found it more convenient and productive to seek change within the existing party structure rather than through a third party.

William Alfred Peffer fit the pattern of these cautious reformers. Born into a distinctive rural society in Pennsylvania in 1831, Peffer inherited an enduring belief in the classical virtues and values of an agrarian way of life. A temperance and antislavery agitator in his youth, he then settled in Indiana where he farmed and helped organize the Republican party locally in 1854. Following the Panic of 1857 he moved to Missouri only to flee in 1861 because of his Unionist sentiments and to join the Eighty-third Illinois Infantry. He served in Tennessee as a foot soldier, quartermaster, and judge advocate, which provided his enduring title, "Judge" Peffer. His liberal racial and political attitudes necessitated a postwar departure from Tennessee and in 1870 he settled in Kansas as an editor and lawyer. An active local reformer, Peffer nevertheless refused to break with the GOP in 1872 over the issue of political reform, insisting that greater reform and more reliable candidates were available through regular action. In 1874-1875, a period of drought and depression, Peffer worked as a Republican state senator to produce an effective political response to the troubles of destitute farmers and burdened town-dwellers. He scorned the Independent Reform party of those years as composed of shysters and charlatans whose reform interests involved only personal aggrandizement through an irresponsible indifference to public needs. Having suffered in the past for his Republicanism, Peffer was unwilling to leave his party voluntarily during hard times and little sympathized with those who did.[1]

Other Republicans were less demanding and not inclined to punish errant party members provided they returned quickly to the fold. Samuel N. Wood, a Chase County Republican, supported Horace Greeley in 1872 and campaigned in 1875 on the Reform ticket; in 1876 he was elected to the legislature as a Republican, and his party colleagues then elected him Speaker of the House. As Republicans were ready to accept, moreover, they were equally prepared to expel in order to maintain the character of their party. Throughout the 1870s the party struggled to free itself of charges of corruption and dictation, and whole campaigns revolved about the intraparty defeat of powerful politicians, only the most spectacular being the elimination of Senator Samuel C. Pomeroy for John J. Ingalls in 1873.[2]

Receptive to new ideas as well as to new men, the Republican party in Kansas in the 1870s often seemed as reformist as third parties. Railroad regulation, antimonopoly, and free silver planks commonly appeared in GOP platforms, and in 1878 the party even agreed with the Greenbackers that national bank notes should be retired in favor of the issuance of paper money. Republicans re-

[1] Peter H. Argersinger, "William Alfred Peffer: The Early Years" (Master's thesis, University of Wisconsin, 1966).

[2] *Directory of the State Government of Kansas* (Topeka, 1877), pp. 83-84; James C. Malin, *A Concern about Humanity: Notes on Reform, 1872-1912* (Lawrence, Kans., 1964), pp. 19-20.

vealed their concern for reform tendencies most clearly in their 1876 state platform which described the GOP as "the surest hope of reform" and invited the cooperation of all "to whom 'Reform' is something more than an empty name." Under such circumstances, sincere reformers had little difficulty in reconciling their advocacy of change with their affiliation with the dominant party.[3]

By the end of the decade, however, the GOP began to turn from its willingness to tolerate diversity and became increasingly less flexible, questioning less and accepting more readily the status quo. The margin of Republican victory had constantly decreased since statehood, and apprehensive party leaders sought to stabilize the existing partisan alignment. Party regularity became the watchword of influential bosses such as Cy Leland and Samuel J. Crawford who rewarded politicians and electorates to the extent that they performed as directed. These professional leaders controlled conventions and had their slates of compliant candidates duly nominated without objection. They tolerated no independent action and opposed reform as symptomatic of irregularity and a portent of party defeat. To retain popular support they also constricted the scope of political discussion and introduced no real new issue into public debate after 1880. Emphasis upon bloody-shirt prejudices and the tariff increasingly dominated the political arena to the exclusion of the open-ended discussions of the past. Senator Ingalls, more eager for easy notoriety than for the necessary work his position required, became the nation's leading Democrat-baiter and helped turn his state party to a policy of waving the bloody shirt as a reflexive not reflective response to political challenge. With similar passion after the enactment of prohibition in 1881, party leaders made support for its enforcement the defining characteristic of a Republican. This dependence upon sectional and cultural prejudices as determining party lines kept the Democrats a despised minority, unable to mount an effective opposition, but for the GOP it was security only through stultification and servility.[4]

The economic boom that struck Kansas in the early 1880s brought

<hr />

[3] Malin, *Concern about Humanity*, p. 22.

[4] Raymond C. Miller, "The Populist Party in Kansas" (Ph.D. diss., University of Chicago, 1928), pp. 41-45; *American Non-Conformist* (Winfield, Kans.), May 31, 1888, April 18, 1889; Malin, *Concern about Humanity*, p. 26; Burton J. Williams, *Senator John James Ingalls* (Lawrence, Kans., 1972), pp. 72, 101, 119, 122.

further pressures upon the Republican party. One participant explained the cumulative effect of the boom psychology: "Most of us crossed the Mississippi or the Missouri with no money, but with vast wealth of hope. . . . Haste to get rich has made us borrowers, and the borrower has made booms, and booms made men wild, and Kansas became a vast insane asylum covering 80,000 square miles." But this description benefited from hindsight. During the boom years, Kansans gave full rein to those who viewed government as an agency for the stimulation of private wealth and personal power. Republican leadership became first the spokesmen and then the puppets of business enterprise and, assuring the public of an increasing and endless prosperity, they promoted and pursued the compelling material vision that an untrammeled business society promised. Fearful of antagonizing the goddess of commerce and her handmaiden, credit, and thereby checking the state's economic development, Republican leaders failed to respond to unfolding abuses and disorders and ignored alternative proposals. As they muffled criticism of the course of the state's economic development, it too became part of Republican orthodoxy. Those who questioned the wisdom of public funding for railroads and other private enterprises, of grand schemes and overexpansion, were denounced as impediments to progress and gradually forced out of the GOP. Sam Wood again left the party, this time for good; Peter Percival Elder, former lieutenant governor and Speaker of the House, followed, as many of the reform Republicans of the 1870s joined the independent third-party movements. The more such men left the party, the less responsive to popular needs and new issues it became, and the smaller became the possibility of substantive reform through the Republican party.[5]

There remained some Republicans still committed to both reform and their party, however, and among these William A. Peffer was perhaps the most important and influential. In 1881 he became the editor of the Topeka *Kansas Farmer,* the state's foremost agricultural journal and circulation leader among papers of any type, and thereby assumed a natural leadership of those who objected to

[5] See James C. Carey, "People, Problems, Prohibition, Politicos, and Politics, 1870-1890," in *Kansas: The First Century,* ed. John D. Bright, 4 vols. (New York, 1956), 1: passim; O. Gene Clanton, *Kansas Populism: Ideas and Men* (Lawrence, Kans., 1969), pp. 22-27, 30-31; Miller, "Populist Party in Kansas," p. 22.

the party commitment to business enterprise. The agrarian tradition offered a useful alternative to the commercial values that seemed to distort society, and by reaffirming the basic importance of agrarian ideals Peffer hoped to bring the developing industrialism into harmony with traditional democratic values. He firmly believed in the necessity of establishing popular control over the commercial and industrial system to insure a political democracy, and he considered the Republican party the only practical vehicle for such reform hopes.

To argue the economic validity of the specific complaints of the discontented agrarians of the time ignores the basic point they were trying to make. Essential to each grievance was the charge of the misuse of public power and the exclusion of agrarian representation. The complaints about financial oppression led directly into the accusation of power as the agrarians probed the relationship between economic might and political influence. As much as anyone, Peffer helped frame the farmers' critique:

The government's land policies fostered monopoly and privileged wealth by encouraging "the rapid absorption of public lands by corporations" rather than promoting democratic settlement by actual "poor farmers."

A system of taxation upon real property discriminated against the agricultural classes in favor of those "that deal in stocks and bonds and money," while it also provided special exemptions and light assessments for railroads.

The banking laws promoted urban, commercial interests rather than rural, agricultural interests and enabled the wealthy "to dictate the amount of money the people may use" by creating an unnecessary intermediary between the people and their government in the issuance of money.

The government's financial policies benefited the creditor classes through currency contraction while the people at large thereby suffered from appreciated interest charges and depreciated values of property and produce.

Tariff laws injured farmers by forcing them to sell in a free market and buy in a protected one, designed to benefit industrialists "to the extent that they ask it."

As for interest rates, usury penalties, and foreclosure provisions, "creditors have had the laws their own way a long time," resulting in a system designed to benefit the lender not the borrower.[6]

[6] *Kansas Farmer* (Topeka), November 1, 1882, November 19, December 3, 1884, December 15, 1886, January 12, November 24, December 1, 1887, January 17, October 2, 1889.

A correlative principle of this system that operated so consistently against agrarian interests was the farmers' inability to use the government to remedy such abuses or to gain advantages for themselves. Peffer and the Kansas farmers watched helplessly, for example, as a bill to reduce legal interest rates was referred to a committee composed entirely of bankers that unanimously recommended indefinite postponement. Nor were they able to secure effective railroad regulation from a legislature that held itself "in readiness to do . . . service" for the railroads, as one legislator phrased it, in exchange for free passes and other favors.[7] Their attempt, however, well illustrated the plight of agrarian reformers in the 1880s.

As editor of the *Kansas Farmer,* Peffer led the agrarian outcry against railroad combinations and rate discrimination and manipulation as cheating farmers in "a most gigantic robbery." Despite the language, it was clear that Peffer was more interested in political justice than simple economic reform. Indeed, he complained more of the arbitrary and unrestricted power of the railroads and their potential for oppression than of excessive tolls in themselves. The issue, he believed, was whether corporations or people were to be represented in the government. Insisting that the people were sovereign, Peffer urged farmers to "compel your party leaders to listen to your appeal, or put them behind you and take the reins into your own hands." He outlined what was needed: the destruction of railroads' independent power of discriminations, the effective prohibition of pools and other combinations, public participation in establishing rate scales, and the exposure of "respectable, christianized robbers." He specifically opposed the appointment of railroad commissioners merely to oversee the carriers, for "railroad commissioners amount to no more than a clerical force of respectability to make reports to the legislature." Peffer forced reluctant candidates of all parties to declare themselves in favor of railroad regulation and was instrumental in having the GOP make it a principal platform plank in 1882.[8]

Success in the campaign was more than balanced by frustrations

7 *American Non-Conformist* (Winfield), March 24, 1887; *Topeka Daily Capital,* January 22, 1887; Joel Moody to O. E. Learnard, January 28, 1885, in O. E. Learnard Papers, Spencer Research Library, University of Kansas.

8 *Kansas Farmer,* June 7, July 26, September 6, 27, 1882, January 3, 1883; *Topeka Daily Capital,* August 7, 9, 11, 1882.

in the legislature. Despite their campaign pledges, the legislators refused to approve any fundamental regulation and enacted instead a weak bill allowing the railroads to set their own rates and appointing railroad commissioners with advisory power only. As a spokesman for Cy Leland later admitted, "Republican legislatures of Kansas simply obeyed the orders of the railroad companies. The Railroad and other committees were made up largely of railroad attorneys. Nothing could be done without the consent of the railroad companies. The Railroad Commissioner law, that is supposed to be for the purpose of maintaining justice between the people and the railroads, was really got up by the attorneys of railroad companies, in order to ward off the enactment of laws regulating freight rates."[9]

Peffer recognized at once the nature and purpose of the law. He railed that "the people's cause has been surrendered," assailed the legislature for fathering "this miserable mixture of meaningless sections," and urged farmers to remember their betrayal at the next election. Even that was fruitless, for many less perceptive Kansans welcomed the law while at the next election, as Peffer explained at another time, the politicians would simply deal "in generalities about the iniquities of other parties, the pauperism of other nations, and the barbarism of past ages" rather than responding "to matters in which their constituents are most directly and most vitally interested." Even a regular Republican described his party's policy as to pass partisan legislation and then "pound on the side of an empty barrel."[10]

Thus the primary agrarian objection became directed against the association between politicians and business interests and the methods used by each, for, as Peffer wrote, "these things mean the still further concentration of power that comes from concentrated wealth and political influence." The question ignored in such an arrangement, he declared, was "what of the people's side?" To assure that the people's side would be considered, Peffer wanted to encourage popular participation in a political system made more directly

9 *Weekly Kansas Chief* (Troy), December 31, 1896; *Senate Journal: Proceedings of the Senate of the State of Kansas. Third Biennial Session* (Topeka, 1883), pp. 431-45, 627-38.
10 *Kansas Farmer*, March 7, 14, November 7, 1883, June 6, 1889; Malin, *Concern about Humanity*, p. 33.

responsive to the wishes and needs of the majority of the people, which, in an agricultural society, meant farmers.[11]

Peffer began his career on the *Kansas Farmer* with a series of editorials on "Farmers and Politics." As the largest and only essential class in society, he argued, farmers should be actively involved in the direction of society. But instead "they are in the meshes of the bosses and managers, and they are not ignorant of the vicious methods used by those fellows in manipulating party machinery." Denouncing this passivity, Peffer urged farmers to organize themselves, for acting together they could control politics and thereby correct social and economic abuses as well. "They could purify politics, and then the way would be clear for permanent reform." Peffer's concern for local self-action reflected his democratic instincts that the people should participate in social and political decisions, but it had an awkward corollary. Arguing that organization could be successful only if the people and not the politicians arranged it, and that "the people will never be ready until their reason is convinced that such organization is necessary," Peffer was placed in the position of instructing those who were to lead. The essential precariousness of such a situation troubled him for nearly a decade and left him, alternately, ahead of and then behind the developing consciousness and capacity of Kansas farmers for independent action.[12]

To convince the farmers, Peffer pointed out abuses of social, economic, and political power in state and nation and campaigned for reforms in the farmers' interest, thereby increasingly attracting a general agrarian support for his larger plan. To remedy those abuses required organization, and thus throughout the 1880s Peffer's reform agitation and farmers' organization proceeded apace. By the end of the decade the two would carefully coincide to explode into Populism.

Peffer early broached the subject of general political reform in such didactic editorials as "How to Oppose Monopolies." His objective was to create an effectively democratic society, with public restraints on arbitrary private power in those areas where the individual was virtually defenseless. Here he added to the previous

[11] *Kansas Farmer*, May 17, 1882, September 29, 1887.
[12] Ibid., November 2, 16, December 28, 1881, February 8, 1882.

agrarian grievances demands for government action against trusts, fraudulent insurance companies, and speculative trading in grain options and futures.[13]

The ultimate answer, however, was for farmers themselves to enter politics. Especially, then, did Peffer seek to promote the creation of a strong agrarian organization which would replace impotence and frustration with political and economic power for farmers. He applauded both the Grange and the National (or Northern) Farmers' Alliance but considered them limited in both numbers and outlook and lacking the vigor required to advance the farmers' interests and political power. He therefore personally attempted to establish a more effective league of farmers. In 1882 Peffer suggested the formation of a Kansas Farmers' Association to oversee the legislature in its railroad regulation efforts. In 1884 he proposed holding annual farmers' conventions to "exert a good influence over political conventions and party candidates." In 1885 he recommended the creation of a state association of farmers to go beyond the Grange and Alliance and to protect "farmers' interests in their relation to business and government." In 1887 he once more advanced his plan for a statewide organization which would purify politics and give agricultural regions the control of their own affairs.[14]

This very persistence indicates Peffer's lack of success. The conditions he attached to his own proposals may have worked against their implementation as much as agrarian alienation and apathy. While advocating reforms which required political control and encouraging organization to engage in politics, Peffer constantly urged that all activity be nonpartisan. To be nonpartisan in Kansas was to be Republican, and Peffer wanted reform activity kept within party lines. Accordingly he described his proposed 1882 association as one that "would deal with subjects only, not with parties"; his 1884 conventions as political but "in no sense partisan"; his 1885 association as "wholly free from party politics"; his 1887 organization as a pressure group only.[15]

13 Ibid., May 24, 31, November 16, 1881, July 30, 1884, February 23, June 23, 1887.
14 Ibid., November 15, 1882, October 1, 1884, March 18, 1885, December 15, 1887.
15 Ibid.

Peffer believed an avoidance of partisan activity would promote more effective organizations by allowing farmers to act together "without being subjected to party discipline or to suspicions of treason to their particular political party." Frequently the *Farmer's* readers, however, pursued Peffer's own arguments to their logical ends while he refrained. All too often Republican leaders either had ignored or scorned his reform efforts or when forced to commit themselves, as in 1882, had afterwards violated their campaign pledges. The more daring of his readers implored Peffer to support third-party action or write-in campaigns directed against those regular candidates who rejected his reform program. One correspondent criticized Peffer's aversion toward an independent farmers' party and declared, "We have the voters; we can make our strength felt if we are only supported by the 'old reliable' *Kansas Farmer.*"[16]

The *Farmer's* editor responded that at the very least such a movement was premature, but even more fateful for its chances of success in Peffer's eyes was the strength of party bonds. Describing party loyalties as second only to patriotism in emotional intensity, he asked his questioner to "look at the men in your own vicinity that have dared the old parties, and note their apparent seclusion. Such is the prejudice in this matter that these men are covered with opprobrium, and made to endure insult, suspicion, and sometimes even violence." Rather than organize a new party, Peffer concluded, the farmers could accomplish more by "taking hold of the old ones and cleaning them out."[17]

As much as any Republican, Peffer felt personally the prejudices from the Civil War along partisan lines, and he especially abhorred those who opposed prohibition in Kansas. Clearly he wanted to work within the party to which he had given his allegiance since its founding and which had rewarded him with recognition and respect. Nevertheless, Peffer refused to rule out categorically the possibility of his renunciation of the party if it failed to meet his standards. It would be, he believed, more a case of being forced from a party that rejected his principles than of leaving voluntarily. As often as he declaimed against third-party action, then, Peffer added the important qualification: Having organized thoroughly, if the farm-

[16] Ibid., July 5, August 9, November 15, 1882, January 26, 1887, July 26, 1888.
[17] Ibid., December 28, 1881, January 18, February 1, March 22, 1882.

ers "cannot then control existing political parties which they have aided and supported willingly so long, they must cut themselves loose from all parties and organize one that they can control." "The important matter," he concluded, "is not the maintenance of political parties, but the redress of wrongs."[18]

The economic condition of Kansas farmers largely dictated their response to such calls for reform crusades. The fantastic boom of the early and mid-1880s with its good weather, large crops, high prices, rapid land-value appreciation, and blind confidence in the future made farmers oblivious to the calls of Cassandras such as Peffer. But such prosperity was bought by mortgaging their future, and when the mortgage came due in times of drought, poor crops, low prices, plummeting land values, and despair, they were ready to listen and learn.

The collapse of the boom came in the winter of 1887-1888 when signs of poor weather, falling crop prices, and a general slowdown in development interacted to break that confidence which had increasingly become the primary foundation of the boom. Artificially stimulated and maintained by public bond issues and private mortgages to increase land values over those actually warranted, the boom left in its wake a state burdened with an overwhelming debt, both public and private. The public debt increased during the decade from $15 million to $41 million, the largest increase in the nation and, excluding four sparsely populated far western states, the largest per capita public debt. The per capita private debt was nearly four times that of the nation as a whole. Sixty percent of the taxed acres were mortgaged, a figure unmatched by any other state. The state auditor reported the assessed value of all property in Kansas at $348,459,943 against a total indebtedness of $706,181,627. The collapse of land values left many farms mortgaged for more than their adjusted worth, and the drop in prices further lowered farm values while requiring an increasing amount of the farmer's products to pay his debts.[19]

[18] Ibid., January 11, February 1, 1882.
[19] Raymond C. Miller, "The Background of Populism in Kansas," *Mississippi Valley Historical Review* 11 (March 1925): 469-89; W. P. Harrington, "The Populist Party in Kansas," *Collections of the Kansas State Historical Society* (Topeka, 1925), 16: 407-8.

Shaken from their apathy, Kansas farmers moved toward organization. The dormant Northern Alliance revived and, with nearly 700 local charters, in August 1888 formed a State Alliance which selected the *Kansas Farmer* as its official paper. Peffer also encouraged the new Southern Alliance and other minor farm groups. Still others joined Peffer in his campaign for political consideration for agrarian interests. In particular, the onset of hard times prompted the reestablishment of an independent political party, whose leaders believed that the Republicans, having proudly claimed responsibility for prosperity, could not escape liability for the calamity that had overtaken Kansas when the boom turned to bust. The spokesmen of this Union Labor party made the state's mortgage indebtedness a major focus of their effort to break old party political dominance and thereby turned the issue into a partisan one. The *Kirwin Independent,* for example, as early as April 1888 reprinted advertisements revealing Senators John J. Ingalls and Preston B. Plumb as officers of major financial firms and then declared, "These are the sort of men who make laws for Kansas farmers. Result— Two-thirds of the farms of the state under mortgage. Remedy—Let farmers stop trusting usurers to make laws."[20]

Such appeals had their natural constituency and together with the demands of agrarian Republicans such as Peffer alerted the GOP to the necessity of an accommodation with the hitherto ignored demands for change. State senator C. H. Kimball urged the party to steal the reformist thunder from the partisan storm. Prior to the Republican state convention, Kimball issued a circular letter to all delegates advising, in view of the rapid growth of the Union Labor party, the adoption of a platform pledged to reduce legal interest rates and provide stronger penalties for usury. Other Republicans applauded Kimball's efforts for their political value to the party: "It does certainly seem that there is a great opportunity here to prevent the Union Laborites from gaining very many Republican votes by the insertion of such a plank."[21]

Thus inspired, the Republicans adopted Kimball's planks and then added others demanding remedial labor legislation, destruction

20 *Kansas Farmer,* June 7, July 5, August 9, October 18, 1888; *Girard Herald,* April 19, 1888.
21 *Topeka Daily Commonwealth,* July 25, 1888; *Girard Herald,* August 17, 1888.

of the dressed beef trust, and protection for farmers from excessive railroad charges. The convention refused to be stampeded, however, and the mildly reformist agrarian ticket headed by A. W. "Farmer" Smith for governor lost to a more conservative one led by Lyman U. Humphrey, an Independence banker. The progressive platform provoked conservative criticism, but Peffer warmly defended it while other Republicans praised it more for its potential political appeal than as an earnest program to be followed. One of these described Kimball's convention success as "only another evidence of the fact that no Republican need leave his party for the purpose of accomplishing any needed reform." If any voters still wavered, the Republican *Topeka Commonwealth* assured them that the platform "amounts to an instruction from the party to each Republican member of the next legislature to favor the proposed legislation."[22]

Peffer had been pressured to help form the new party but had insisted the effort should be to make existing parties "more responsive to the people's wishes." The Republican platform now reinforced his belief that reform could be accomplished more effectively through the existing party structure than by starting out anew. Despite his Republicanism, however, his personal position did not dictate great hostility to the Union Labor party, which had declared itself not only for interest reduction but also for programs dealing with other issues he had consistently advocated in the *Farmer*. Accordingly, Peffer expressed his respect for and confidence in P. P. Elder, the Union Labor gubernatorial candidate, and encouraged local voters to select the best man for legislator, regardless of political affiliations, declaring that "the interests of the people are far above the interests of a party."[23]

The Union Laborites, in turn, often accepted Peffer as one of their own in principle if not in political practice. John Davis, venerable reformer and editor of the *Junction City Tribune*, often cooperated with Peffer despite their partisan differences, while Elder praised Peffer's editorial positions and the *Farmer*'s influence. Other third-party men commended Peffer's stands, and one sent

[22] *Topeka Daily Commonwealth*, July 27, August 3, 1888; *Kansas Farmer*, September 20, 1888.
[23] *Kansas Farmer*, July 26, August 16, October 4, 1888.

him a copy of a Union Labor platform, asking for his opinion of it. Peffer responded that he "heartily" endorsed "almost every word" of the detailed, radical document and in fact mentioned no disagreement. Union Labor newspapers in the 1888 campaign frequently reprinted *Farmer* editorials, urging their own readers to study them well, and asserted that only the election of Union Labor candidates would bring about the conditions advocated therein.[24]

But if Union Laborites praised Peffer's analysis of existing problems and his proposed reforms, most of them bitterly arraigned his officially nonpartisan approach. His immense influence with the state's farmers made his opposition to independent political action a deathblow to Union Labor hopes for any significant success. Radical newspapers like the Winfield *American Non-Conformist* attacked reformist Republicans such as Peffer and Kinball as hypocritical in advocating change through the agency of the GOP, a course that they allegedly knew to be self-defeating. Elder, among others, early recognized that Peffer's announced nonpartisan position on the *Farmer* often represented merely a defense of the Republican party.[25]

The dominant party, however, did not require much defense after it pledged relief and reform, and it was further aided by the ineptness of the Democrats. They were even less equipped to deal with the new issues than were the Republicans, and their readiness to agree on prohibition and the tariff as the major issues prevented their capitalizing on the discontent of the state by encouraging the traditional partisan alignment which assured GOP ascendancy. More ominous to Republican success was the Union Labor party, which interpreted the old-party emphasis upon the tariff as an attempt to divert attention from the real issues and which itself stressed crop failures, low prices, and mortgage pressure as political weapons. Republicans united to condemn such "senseless howls" about poverty and mortgages as more injurious to the state's credit and economic growth than droughts, grasshoppers, and tornados combined. But, as always, the bloody shirt figured most prom-

24 *Girard Herald,* October 19, 1888: *Kansas Farmer,* December 8, 15, 1887; *Junction City Tribune,* October 29, 1885.
25 *Girard Herald,* August 17, 1888; *Kansas Farmer,* October 13, 1887.

Brendan and toffee
in Methards

inently in the Republican campaign. So effectively waved in the past that the word "Democrat" itself connoted treason and treachery to most Kansas farmers, the bloody-shirt style of campaigning merely made it necessary to contend that the Democratic party was the beneficiary of the Union Labor movement. This Republican orators and papers did with a vengeance, branding the new party as "the stub tail of the Democratic dog," and the GOP swept to an awesome victory at the polls.[26]

Republican success was so complete that the party proudly acclaimed Kansas "the banner state" of Republicanism for carrying national, state, and local tickets so overwhelmingly. The voters placed thirty-nine Republicans in the forty-seat state senate and 121 Republicans in the 125-member house. Far from repudiating the GOP because of economic distress, Kansans had given the party its greatest victory. Success in 1888, however, came only by mortgaging the party's future, and the debt had to be paid in January 1889 when the legislature convened. The voters had granted another chance to the dominant party when it promised consideration of agrarian interests and matters of popular concern, when it promised a readjustment in the distressing economic situation without the necessity of seeking redress outside existing political organizations. The Union Labor party had been buried in November's ballots, but the issues it had raised remained alive.[27]

Judge Peffer was determined to exact legislative compliance with the Republican platform, which he regarded as the result of his own work through the *Kansas Farmer*, and he accepted for himself the leadership of those similarly inclined. He emphasized in December 1888 that the *Farmer* had a circulation of four times that of its nearest rival and that it peculiarly voiced agrarian opinion in politics as well as in agriculture. With "an army of toilers" behind him, Peffer confidently prepared to place his program before the legislature. That program included demands for legislation relating to railroad regulation, prohibition of the beef combine, radical reformation of taxation to redistribute tax burdens, and the general land and mortgage problem. This last formed the crux of the

26 *Atchison Daily Champion*, September 26, 28, October 2, 9, 24, 1888; *American Non-Conformist* (Winfield), February 23, 1888.
27 *Atchison Daily Champion*, November 17, 1888, February 19, 1889.

agrarian economic program and embraced interest-rate reduction, prohibition of alien land ownership, and a redemption law.[28]

In proposing these measures, Peffer expanded the reform demand upon the legislature from that imposed by the 1888 Republican state convention. Yet, as soon as the ballots were counted, many Republicans were prepared to renege on those campaign promises. The *Hutchinson News,* for instance, declared that the party platform was for the campaign, not the legislature. The *Kansas City Gazette* agreed, announcing that the platform was never intended to be enacted into law but was only "a little sop thrown to a half dozen who were howling so loud as to make everybody believe the woods were full of howlers." The state's leading Republican paper, the *Topeka Capital,* concluded that enacting the party's platform "would put Kansas back seventy-five years." Liberal Republican newspapers such as the *Atchison Champion* and the *Emporia Republican* vigorously disagreed, writing that "party principle is party law" and that the party "is morally bound to make such changes in the present law as are demanded by the explicit declarations" of the platform. Even these papers, however, shrank from Peffer's proposed redemption law as inexpedient, admitting the need for popular relief but unwilling to support positive government action to that end.[29]

The farmers of Kansas, however, generally supported Peffer's program. The alliances endorsed it, most farm papers seconded it, and various ad hoc groups resolved in its favor. Peffer himself called a convention of farmers to meet in Topeka to press for relief measures when the legislature convened. The virtual unanimity of agrarian spokesmen and organizations for the various proposals made it clear that the legislative response would reveal the actual influence of farmers in Kansas.[30]

The disposition of the legislature was soon evident. When the outgoing governor urged the enactment of the Republican campaign pledges, conservative legislators protested and even opposed the printing of the governor's message. Though numerous bills

---

[28] *Kansas Farmer,* December 6, 27, 1888, January 24, 31, 1889.

[29] *Atchison Daily Champion,* December 20, 28, 29, 1888, January 23, February 13, 1889.

[30] *Kansas Farmer,* January 3, February 14, 1889; *Atchison Daily Champion,* December 12, 1888; Miller, "Populist Party in Kansas," pp. 72-73.

were introduced embodying the reform proposals they were usually referred to the conservative Senate Judiciary Committee. This committee in particular and the senate in general throughout the legislative session prevented the enactment of meaningful financial reforms.[31]

The financial interests of Kansas counted on just such a performance. Alarmed by the public demand for changes in the interest and mortgage laws, many bankers spoke out against the recommendations, and representatives of various loan companies organized "to take such steps as . . . necessary" to protect their interests. The loan agents generally believed, one of them wrote privately, that they "can defeat almost any adverse legislation in the senate—it only remains to determine what is most advisable to encourage or what to defeat."[32] With expected results, the loan agencies promptly threw their influence against what they termed "granger legislation." A moderate bill deferring the time in which a mortgage could be foreclosed, for example, was "vigorously assailed" by the senate, wrote one newspaper correspondent. One senator read on the floor a letter from a loan agency announcing that it would refrain from lending money in Kansas while the bill was pending. Having already tabled by a vote of 31–2 a resolution respecting mortgage foreclosure in order "to soothe and allay the anxiety of capital," the senate struck out by a three-to-one majority the enacting clause of the condemned bill. "The loan agency was needlessly alarmed," confirmed the reporter. "There never was a day when there was any danger of Senate Bill No. 1 becoming a law. There will be no 'debtor class' legislation at this session."[33]

As such an outcome became increasingly obvious, Peffer used the editorial and correspondence columns of the *Farmer* to defend the farmers' program warmly. Endorsing the agrarian demands as a popular attempt to inject "a little justice and mercy" into a system

[31] *Senate Journal. Proceedings of the Senate of the State of Kansas. Sixth Biennial Session* (Topeka, 1889), pp. 45-48; *Kansas Farmer,* February 14, 1889.

[32] *Atchison Daily Champion,* January 22, 1889; W. J. Patterson to J. B. Watkins, January 18, 1889, Patterson to T. B. Sweet, January 18, 1889, J. B. Watkins Land Mortgage Company to C. B. Northrup, February 1, 1889, all in J. B. Watkins Papers, Spencer Research Library, University of Kansas.

[33] *Atchison Daily Champion,* February 14, 1889; *Senate Journal* (1889), pp. 297-98, 457-58.

biased against the farmer, Peffer sharply questioned the politicians in a manner that revealed the underlying agrarian complaint. If railroads were permitted to reorganize, decrease their interest rates, and save their property when in financial distress, why should the farmers be refused an equal right? "Is the debtor to lose all, the creditor nothing? Are laws for the protection of creditors only? . . . Is it not better that the people have opportunity to save their homes after paying their debts, rather than that they should be turned out homeless? As a matter of public policy, can the State afford to pauperize its own people? Is it not the first duty of the State to protect its own citizens?"[34]

Readers of the *Farmer* strongly backed Peffer, and he printed many of their letters in an effort to influence the legislature by countering the lenders' lobby. The letters invariably commended and encouraged Peffer, denounced the inaction and infidelity of the legislature, and provided examples of usurious or unethical practices of local banks and loan agencies. Peffer editorialized on such letters that "the people are speaking out in their own interests. Farmers are getting to be desperately in earnest about these things. . . . They expect the present session of the Legislature to do something to relieve the people."[35]

The legislature, however, overlooked Peffer's questions, ignored the pleas of his readers, and overwhelmingly rejected the agrarian reform program. Its members did pass a law in the closing hours of the session reducing interest rates as promised but providing no effective penalty for usury. One senator declared that he lent money at 24 percent and was assured that he could continue to do so under the new law. Another senator described the law as a victory for the opponents of usury legislation. The legislature rejected the redemption bills as unconstitutional; indefinitely postponed taxation reform; failed to approve the alien land ownership bill; took no action on the promised legislation granting the State Board of Railroad Commissioners the authority to prevent rate discriminations; and maintained rather than restricted municipal authority to vote bonds. In short, Peffer complained, there was "no remedial legislation of any kind," a result he blamed on "the party leaders and the party press."[36]

34 *Kansas Farmer*, January 17, February 14, 1889.   35 Ibid.

Denunciation of the legislature was widespread. Liberal Republican newspapers such as the *Atchison Champion, Wichita Eagle,* and *Emporia Republican* censured every action of the legislature and arraigned its members as "vicious demagogues and corrupt shysters." The *Champion* argued that the GOP had betrayed the people but would not have a chance to do it again. These three papers felt such revulsion that they took the lead in what they termed a "rebellion" against the leaders of the GOP for the next two years. Others would not be so easily satisfied.[37]

Individually and in groups farmers expressed their anger and discontent even before the session concluded. No one better stated the agrarian complaint or made clearer the link between the legislature and the future of Republicanism than did a rustic correspondent of the *Farmer:*

> No legislative body was ever elected for a more specific purpose than this one, and every one of its members swore solemn allegiance to the party platform. . . . The people at large believed the platform was made in good faith, the candidates pledged themselves to carry it out to the letter in good faith, and the people, believing their words, elected them with a wonderful majority. . . . [Now the legislature is attempting] to fill poor, simple Republican eyes with dust . . . [and money lenders urge the legislature to] commit a political infamy. Will they prove successful? . . . Our Republicans here, with coats of blue and heads of gray, fear they will and are hot with indignation. Their eyes are fixed upon Topeka, and woe to the man that sells them out. . . . If these money-loaners compass our defeat look out for the future. The air is full of lightning.[38]

Peffer saw the lightning and feared it, yet he kept the storm building. He repeatedly warned politicians that "a day of reckoning is coming" and asserted that if the legislature failed to enact what the Republicans had demanded in their platform and the voters had endorsed at the polls, the third-party vote would triple to 100,000 in 1890. His concern for the GOP, however, was surpassed by his fury over the outrageous conduct of the legislature,

---

36 *Atchison Daily Champion,* January 20, February 21, March 3, 6, 7, 16, 1889; *Kansas Farmer,* February 14, 21, 28, October 2, 1889; *Senate Journal* (1889), passim; *House Journal. Proceedings of the House of Representatives of the State of Kansas. Sixth Biennial Session* (Topeka, 1889), passim.

37 *Atchison Daily Champion,* February 19, March 6, 7, 16, 1889.

38 William Kibbe to W. A. Peffer in *Kansas Farmer,* February 14, 1889.

and he wrote so vigorously that the *Kansas Farmer* was threatened with an advertising boycott unless its editor relented. Peffer brushed aside the threat and increasingly addressed farmers in person as well as through his paper. Speaking to a Farmers' Institute, for instance, he arraigned the legislators "for their refusal to give farmers the promised relief from unjust laws." Partially through his assistance, the first state convention of the Farmers' Alliance met in Topeka in February, and he spoke by special invitation on the work necessary to secure the needed legislation in the farmers' interests.[39]

The legislative defeat of the agrarian program, however, made a mockery of Peffer's advice. The nonpartisan program of the farmer, for which Peffer had labored a decade, resulted in total failure. The plan had been to capture the GOP for reform, and it had apparently succeeded in the campaign of 1888. In the legislature of 1889 it at last became clear how the party viewed reform, even in mild measures. The demand for the reform laws had been as nearly a mass demand of the farmers as any request for decades, and it was completely ignored.

Now Peffer and the farmers confronted a difficult choice: either they must abandon their legislative reform program or they must undertake positive political action to gain direct participation in political parties and genuine representation in lawmaking bodies. The agrarian emphasis upon legislative relief was not so much a distortion of the predicament of agriculture as it was a simple recognition that the political system *was* responsive to some interests, that the instruments of public power were directed toward satisfying narrow private ends rather than achieving popular demands. Farmers reasoned that a usurpation of political power had occurred at the direct expense of the common masses, and private corporate wealth had secured control of the legislature, the railroad commission, and other political agencies. Nor were the alienation and suspicion of the agrarians necessarily symptoms of political paranoia or conspiracy-mindedness; rather the farmers were realistic in their perception that those without economic power were without political power as well. It was not economic distress but political

[39] *Kansas Farmer*, January 31, February 14, 28, 1889; *Girard Herald*, February 16, 1889; *Topeka Capital-Commonwealth*, February 7, 1889.

alienation that would cause popular revolt. But depression conditions had provoked among normally apathetic people a heightened political consciousness which coincided with the realization of their loss of political power. And the revolt would come, for a challenge to private power thus entrenched would have to come through public power, a political mass movement. Only the most radical argued immediately for independent political action while most listened to Peffer's summons to more militant agrarian activity within the old parties. The final decision between the two courses was not yet clear to those like Peffer who clung to partisan traditions, but it was certain that the political system would be challenged as never before.

CHAPTER TWO

The People's Rebellion

THE FAILURE of the agrarian reform program in the 1889 Kansas legislature revealed the political weakness of the state's farmers and encouraged a movement among them to promote their own interests. William A. Peffer and other agrarian spokesmen had long agitated unsuccessfully for thorough agricultural organization, but in this period of political frustration exacerbated by deepening depression farmers began to organize spontaneously at the grass-roots level. Farm organizations were not new to Kansas, but they had been weak and ineffective, and when Kansas farmers actively turned to one in 1889 they joined the militant National Farmers' Alliance and Industrial Union. Known better as the Southern Alliance to distinguish itself from the less contentious National (or Northern) Farmers' Alliance, this organization entered Kansas in 1888 prepared to mobilize isolated farmers into a cohesive group to advance agrarian interests.

Peffer delightedly welcomed the order, seeing in its spectacular growth the promise of rural influence. He began a "Farmers' Alliance Notes" column in the *Kansas Farmer* and then added an "Alliance Department." He encouraged the two Alliances to unite and applauded their efforts to voice agricultural discontent. He promoted the Alliance on the rostrum as well, traveling across Kansas with various Alliance officials, including John H. McDowell of Tennessee, the national vice president.[1]

Peffer's active support had made his paper the official organ of the Northern Alliance, and he hoped that the Southern Alliance would similarly recognize the *Farmer*. McDowell even suggested that it might serve as the official paper of the organization in the entire West. While many local subordinate alliances resolved in favor of the *Farmer*, however, others supported the *Meriden Advocate*, a militant new paper edited by Dr. Stephen McLallin. As a result of this division, the Alliance did not recognize any paper as official, although it agreed to use the *Farmer* for publishing its correspondence.[2]

The resistance to Peffer stemmed from his continued opposition to independent political action and a fear that his *Farmer* might therefore not be sufficiently aggressive. McLallin and other Alliance leaders commended Peffer's analysis of the agrarian problem but contended that his hopes for a conversion of the old parties were unwarranted and that ultimately a new party would have to be formed. "I have little faith," Benjamin Clover, the state president of the Southern Alliance, wrote Peffer, "in a politician who is 'good' because he is afraid of being kicked out of office." Those already committed to third-party action, largely the Union Laborites of 1888, also criticized the "Peffer stripe of statesmen" for being unwilling to face the realities of the Kansas political situation. "It is an axiom," declared one Union Laborite, "that reforms do not come in state affairs by consent of those in power; that 'reform within a party' is out of the question; but that reforms come through new party organizations. . . . Every utterance of the old party leaders on the subject of new parties is but a repetition of false promises to reform."[3]

Both Peffer and McLallin worked to secure favorable nominations and platforms in the old parties during the off-year election campaign of 1889. Their lack of progress by September caused McLallin to advocate third-party action. Peffer's plan of nonpartisan, pressure-group politics, McLallin argued, had been tried unsuccessfully for years; a new tactic was necessary. He believed that reformers could not effectively use the old parties because

1 *Kansas Farmer*, March 21, April 11, June 6, 27, August 7, October 2, 1889.
2 Ibid., April 25, May 2, August 21, 1889.
3 *Meriden Advocate*, August 24, 1889; *Kansas Farmer*, June 27, July 31, 1889; *Girard Herald*, September 7, 14, December 28, 1889.

memories of the bitter political past prevented former partisan enemies from affiliating with existing parties. The creation of a new party, therefore, was both logical and necessary. McLallin, however, was as far ahead of most alliancemen as he believed Peffer lagged behind, and no widespread third-party movement developed.[4]

In some areas alliancemen did attempt to control the Republican party, but they were outmaneuvered by party leaders and forced to form local independent parties. Few of these achieved any measure of success. In Jefferson County, for example, the Republican convention rejected alliancemen's credentials, denounced their political ambitions, and defeated their resolutions by a six-to-one margin. The rebuffed alliancemen met hurriedly on the eve of the election and nominated an independent ticket over which the established Republicans won easily. The uneven entry into partisan action imperfectly revealed potential third-party strength, but it did alarm some discerning Republicans. "There are not many more Democrats than there were last year," observed one, "but there is no use undertaking to disguise the fact that the Republican discontents are a very numerous and growing body." For the most part, however, the off-year elections had little relevance to the Alliance program, and few attached great importance to the results.[5]

Peffer himself devoted most of his efforts to publicizing the agrarian reform position. To explain the discontent he published a brief history of agricultural organization in the December issue of the *Forum* under the title "The Farmers' Defensive Movement." In this article he discussed the organization and objectives of the Alliances, Grange, Farmers' Mutual Benefit Association (FMBA), and other rural groups that would seek consolidation in the St. Louis convention of December 1889. The origin of this movement, he wrote, lay in the powerless position of the individual and the injurious activities of railroads, middlemen, and banks, which were aggravated by preferential governmental policies. "By reason of his isolation and the smallness of his individual business," Peffer declared, "the farmer found himself paying tribute to men and

4 *Meriden Advocate*, September 21, October 5, 1889.

5 *Topeka Mail*, October 25, November 1, 8, 1889; George L. Douglas to L. U. Humphrey, November 9, 1889, in Lyman U. Humphrey Papers, Kansas State Historical Society, Topeka (hereafter cited as KSHS).

corporations who had control of the money and markets of the country." It was to redress this imbalance of power that the nation's farmers had organized and were "now conducting the greatest revolution ever peacefully inaugurated."[6]

Remarkably, Peffer scarcely mentioned agrarian political activity in this article, but concentrated largely on social and economic aspects of organization. Written in October just before the election, it suggested his continuing belief in the possibility of reform within the existing political alignment, yet in its national outlook it revealed how far Peffer and the Kansas farmers had traveled from strictly state demands in early 1889. This increasingly national outlook, moreover, made independent action more likely, for the farmers could not be satisfied with the relief a state could provide, even were it willing, a fact emphasized by the resolutions demanding congressional action adopted by the St. Louis meeting.

Accordingly, Peffer turned his attention to the nation's capital in December 1889. Declaring that the *Kansas Farmer* spoke for every farmer in the country, he announced that the "time has come for action. The people will not consent to wait longer. The present Congress must act, and act in good faith. The future is full of retribution for delinquents." He then presented a reform program for Congress to follow, as he had for the state legislature earlier. And while there was a struggle over the course of the farmers' movement, McLallin and Clover assented to Peffer's statement of principles: the abolition of national banks and the direct government issuance of paper money to the people; suppression of trusts and combines; railroad regulation; equitable taxation; market regulations; unlimited gold and silver coinage; tariff reductions; "rigid enforcement of public rights in every special corporate franchise"; and, most important and basic to all other demands, the acceptance of effective popular participation in political decisions.[7]

In addition Peffer developed an extraordinary proposal which he published as *The Way Out*. The agrarians had rejected private control of money as dangerous and undemocratic, thereby accepting the necessity for government control of money and interest rates and the direct issuance of money to the people without such inter-

6 *Forum* 8 (December 1889): 464-73: *Kansas Farmer,* November 6, 1889.
7 *Kansas Farmer,* June 13, December 4, 1889.

mediaries as national banks. The remaining problem was to devise a method whereby the money could be distributed. Peffer's solution, and "the way out" of financial troubles, was to allow farmers to borrow short-term money on warehouse or elevator receipts at 3 percent. Government warehouses would be constructed to store the security for short-term loans, and government loan bureaus would be established to lend money on real estate security.[8]

In December 1889 Peffer began to publish *The Way Out* serially in detailed form in the *Farmer,* and in early 1890 he issued it as a booklet. Phenomenally popular, it went through thirteen printings in that one year and formed the nucleus of his book, *The Farmer's Side,* published in 1891 as the fundamental Populist economic discussion. *The Way Out* represented the combination of agrarian self-interests and monetary reforms; farmers who had rejected inflationist ideas in the past were now, under their heavy indebtedness, attracted to the ideological position held as central by post-Civil War radical political movements. Developed concurrently with, yet independently of, the less sweeping subtreasury proposal of Charles W. Macune, which it resembled in expanded form, *The Way Out* culminated the popularization of radical financial ideas first proposed in 1849 by Edward Kellogg and provided the discontented farmers with a specific plan promising to relieve their economic distress.[9]

The publication of *The Way Out* also marked a decisive shift in the focus of agrarian reform agitation in Kansas. Arguing that only national government action could alleviate the plight of the farmers, *The Way Out* clearly required congressional rather than state legislative approval. Peffer continued to agitate for immediate state action but only as a tactic to "sustain ourselves until we can secure favorable Congressional action." He requested a public statement on these matters from every Kansas candidate for national office and advised his readers to pledge every candidate to support the desired legislation. Kansas congressmen provided no more satisfaction than had state legislators. All except Senator Preston B. Plumb ignored Peffer's request or replied evasively.[10]

8 *The Way Out* (Topeka, Kans., 1890); *Kansas Farmer,* December 18, 1889.
9 *Kansas Farmer,* February 26, March 5, April 16, 1890; Peffer, *The Farmer's Side* (New York, 1891), pp. 272-75. For Edward Kellogg, see Chester McArthur Destler, *American Radicalism, 1865-1901* (Chicago, 1966), pp. 7-8, 50-77.

Peffer was especially concerned about the position of Senator John J. Ingalls, the state's leading Republican. Ingalls had declared that legislation could not relieve agricultural distress, directly contradicting Peffer's position. Stressing again the agrarian conviction that legislation was a sign of political power as much as it might be beneficial in itself, Peffer replied sharply: "The Senator knows, we assume, that when banks, and railroads and classes on the creditor side of the line want legislation, they ask for it and get it." Farmers, he continued, had not requested the federal credit strengthening act of 1869, the funding act of 1870, the coinage act of 1873, the resumption act of 1875. "It must be," Peffer concluded, "that our public men do not understand the situation. . . . Relief can come only from legislation, and statesmen are blind not to see it. Farmers, in self-defense, will employ new agents. The times will raise up new statesmen having eyes and ears."[11]

In addition to his public request, Peffer also wrote Ingalls personally in February 1890 asking him to outline for publication his views on the Alliance demands and agricultural relief. Ingalls replied that he would make public his opinions on such questions later and through a medium other than Peffer's *Kansas Farmer*. Peffer took Ingalls's impolitic reply as a rebuff to the state's farmers and reported it in the same issue with an editorial letter from "Farmer" advocating the replacement of Ingalls with a farmers' candidate in 1891. Peffer was not alone in his dissatisfaction with the course of Ingalls. The Union Labor party had denounced him in its 1888 state platform, Democrats regarded him as their greatest enemy, and several liberal Republican newspapers opposed his reelection.[12]

Nevertheless, Ingalls represented so completely Kansas Republicanism that Peffer's misgivings exposed a practical modification in his stance against partisan activity. Indeed, from the end of 1889, Peffer increasingly demanded positive action regardless of partisan consequences. In January 1890 he declared, "It is better to be right than to belong to a party." In February he cautioned his readers against politicians who attempted to divert attention from the real

---

10 *Kansas Farmer*, February 12, 19, 1890.
11 Ibid., February 5, 1890.
12 Ibid., February 26, 1890; *Topeka Daily Capital*, August 30, 1888; *Atchison Daily Champion*, January 21, 1890.

issues of political and economic reform to the false questions of the tariff and sectional prejudices. Already anticipating the coming campaign, he demanded the election only of men pledged to the farmers' cause. "No matter about parties; throw party to the winds if necessary to success." "We have," he concluded, "gone too far to stop."[13]

These views alarmed Republican leaders who feared that Peffer might commit the influential *Farmer* to independent action, and they attempted to force him back to orthodoxy. The *Topeka Capital* and *Fort Scott Monitor,* in particular, led the Republican attack on Peffer. His widespread speaking tours combined with his editorship of the *Farmer* and his authorship of *The Way Out* gave him a public prominence that enabled his conservative critics to accuse him of seeking personal political preference from the farmers' movement, a charge that gained strength from the frequent grass-roots suggestions that Peffer should be elected to replace either Ingalls or Governor Lyman Humphrey. The criticism soon devolved into personal abuse.[14]

As the partisan press increased its verbal assault on him, Peffer announced that he would not be silenced: "*The Kansas Farmer* is on the side of those who need help, and there it expects to remain until relief comes. If leaders of parties cannot come up to this standard we shall have the satisfaction of knowing that we ourselves are there." In encountering political opposition to his reform proposals, Peffer increasingly recognized the relationship between politics and social and economic abuses and the consequent necessity for political reform. And remembering his defeated efforts of the past years, Peffer wrote, "We have asked for consideration to which our constituency is entitled, but no attention was paid . . .—they laughed at our impertinence. Now that the storm is approaching, they would avert its effect by crying out against the *Kansas Farmer*."[15]

While Peffer and the *Farmer* acted as the public lightning rod for critics of the farmers' movement, other agrarians sought to increase the political strength and effectiveness of the Alliance. Many Al-

13 *Kansas Farmer,* January 1, February 5, 12, 1890.
14 *Lawrence Daily Journal,* March 11, 16, April 2, 1890; *Topeka Daily Capital,* March 11, 1890; *Kansas Farmer,* February 26, March 12, April 30, 1890.
15 *Kansas Farmer,* March 19, 1890.

liance leaders had become convinced that if the organization functioned only as a pressure group, making endorsements, it would
create suicidal splits in the order, composed as it was of Republicans,
Democrats, and old third-party men. More could be gained, they
decided, through independent action. On March 5, 1890, an Alliance committee met with representatives of the Grange, the FMBA,
and the Knights of Labor and adopted mutual political platforms.
The Alliance state president, Benjamin Clover, then issued a call
for a state convention of the presidents of the county alliances to
meet in Topeka on March 25 to consider the possibility of organizing a new party based on Alliance strength.[16]

In secret sessions, the convention devoted itself to political discussion. The resolutions that emerged asked Governor Humphrey
to call a special session of the legislature to provide mortgage relief;
requested that farmers be represented on the Board of Railroad
Commissioners by the appointment of P. B. Maxson; and demanded
the implementation of other Alliance proposals, including the direct
popular election of United States senators and railroad commissioners. The final resolutions challenged the political order. Denouncing Ingalls as having rarely supported a measure in the interests of
farmers or workers, the convention resolved to oppose any candidate
for the legislature that favored his reelection to the Senate. And,
clearly anticipating some form of direct political action, the alliancemen resolved "that we will no longer divide on party lines,
and will only cast our votes for candidates of the people, for the
people, and by the people." They then made arrangements to
organize "the People's state central committee."[17]

The Alliance leaders had taken the decisive step to form a new
political party, but they recognized the necessity of winning over
the cautious Peffer, the key to the state's farmers. Led by Stephen
McLallin of the *Advocate* and B. E. Kies of the Wichita *Kansas
Commoner*, these men earnestly besieged Peffer for his support and
gradually he granted it. Indeed, as early as February, Peffer had
responded to a probe of the *Commoner* by asserting that the people

---

16 *Topeka Advocate*, August 22, 1894; W. F. Rightmire, "The Alliance Movement in Kansas—Origin of the People's Party," *Transactions of the Kansas State
Historical Society* (Topeka, 1906), 9: 1-8.

17 *Lawrence Daily Journal*, March 26, 28, 1890; *Topeka Advocate*, August 22,
1894; Rightmire, "The Alliance Movement," pp. 1-8.

themselves could quickly create any political machinery needed. Perhaps an even more important influence upon Peffer was the continued hostility and arrogance of Republican leaders toward the grim efforts of the farmers to gain influence. Following the March Alliance convention, Peffer complained of the imperious manner in which the Republican press served notice "on the Alliance that no attack upon the policy of the Republican party will be tolerated" without indicating even a willingness to listen to agrarian complaints. Replying to criticism of the convention's resolutions, Peffer declared of the Alliance that "this movement has grown so great that it cannot be checked by rehearsing patriotic memories, reviving buried prejudices, or appealing to old party associations." He warned that the question of a new party would be answered by the reception the old parties gave Alliance principles: "Nothing can save the parties and party leaders but prompt and earnest response to the popular will." The GOP, in particular, would have to reverse itself, he argued. "It is the party that is wrong, not the people."[18]

Following this editorial, the *Atchison Champion* observed that the *Farmer* was "out this week with a double coat of war paint" and clearly did "not propose to have any more monkeying—the issues of the campaign must be met squarely by Kansas politicians or they will be compelled to take the consequences." Yet Peffer hesitated to make the final break. While he struggled with himself in such editorials as "Whom Will Ye Serve?"—the Alliance or the party—Ingalls himself forced the issue.[19]

Interviewed in the *New York World* in mid-April, Senator Ingalls responded to a question of political reform with the blunt assertion:

The purification of politics is an iridescent dream. Government is force. Politics is a battle for supremacy. Parties are the armies. The decalogue and the golden rule have no place in a political campaign. The object is success. To defeat the antagonist and expel the party in power is the purpose. The Republicans and Democrats are as irreconcilably opposed to each other as were Grant and Lee in the Wilderness. They use ballots instead of guns, but the struggle is as unrelenting and desperate, and the result sought for the same. In war it is lawful to deceive the adversary,

[18] *Kansas Farmer*, February 12, April 2, 16, 1890; *Topeka Advocate*, May 7, 1890.

[19] *Atchison Daily Champion*, April 18, 1890; *Kansas Farmer*, April 23, 1890.

to hire hessians, to purchase mercenaries, to mutilate, to destroy. The commander who lost a battle through the activity of his moral nature would be the derision and jest of history. This modern cant about the corruption of politics is fatiguing in the extreme. It proceeds from the tea-custard and syllabub dilettantism, the frivolous and desultory sentimentalism of epicenes.[20]

Regardless of the senator's efforts to explain this statement, Alliance leaders pronounced it his true attitude and reprinted the interview in all friendly newspapers. It sustained the growing Alliance belief that the Republican party was indifferent to the wishes and needs of the people and contemptuous of the cry for reform. And, in particular, it repelled Judge Peffer. Above all a highly moral man, whose conscience had driven him since he was a young antislavery agitator in Pennsylvania, Peffer could have believed only that Ingalls, the symbol of Republicanism, ridiculed his very life. In the wake of this interview, Peffer announced that the *Farmer* would henceforth oppose Ingalls and support any "competent man upon whom the opposition shall unite."[21]

Peffer thus crossed the Rubicon to join Clover, McLallin, and the state's farmers waiting on the far shore. The Republican press exploded in denunciation of Peffer, the last link to past partisan stability, often alleging that his opposition to Ingalls stemmed merely from a desire to replace the senator in Washington—a "Senatorial bee" placed in his bonnet, declared the *Kansas City Journal,* by those enemies of Ingalls who realized that "the only hope of defeating his re-election lay through uniting the agricultural classes of the State against him. . . . Recognizing the influence which the *Farmer* has among the agricultural classes," the *Journal* continued, "and the esteem in which Judge Peffer is held by them, it was thought that he combined in the largest degree those qualities which would solidify and head this opposition."[22]

Peffer replied to such charges with more anguish than anger. His critics, he announced, misunderstood the motivation for his political course. Carefully distinguishing between politicians and the people, Peffer pointed out that his position had not changed, but merely evolved.

20 *New York World,* April 13, 1890.
21 *Kansas Farmer,* May 14, 1890.
22 Ibid., June 4, 1890.

We have been on this road a long time, and at every signal station gave due and timely warning. Time and again we have called attention to the growing discontent among farmers, have pointed out particularly the imperative need of some remedial legislation. . . .

Now the farmers, acting in line with the advice of this paper, many times uttered, have organized in their own interest and have set forth their demands. What would these party men expect of us but that we would stand by the people who are doing just what we have constantly urged them to do? Would they have us betray our friends? Did they not, long ago, see what our course would lead to?[23]

The reelection of Ingalls provided a splendid issue for mobilizing the political discontent of Kansas for the coming campaign of 1890. Ingalls represented both the methods and the policies of the old Kansas Republicanism—acts and ideas in sharp contrast to those of the Alliance. His election to the Senate had twice occurred under shady circumstances and his "iridescent dream" interview confirmed many people in their belief in the corruption of existing political parties. His aloof manner easily aroused criticism from a mass movement rebelling against being ignored, overlooked, and spurned: Ingalls, Judge Peffer complained, "holds the masses at arms' length and does not enter into the joys and sorrows of the common people," discuss affairs with them, or believe in their intelligence. Ingalls had disputed the Alliance contention that legislation itself could improve the depressed condition of agriculture. His public career illustrated that party regularity which the Alliance had to break to achieve success, and his personal policy of "skinning Democrats" diverted attention from pressing issues. Benjamin Clover pointed out that Democratic "skins are the thinnest clothing a shivering family was ever wrapped up in." The Alliance wanted a new Kansas operated on new issues; Ingalls personified the old Kansas and the old issues, and he became the first object of attack.[24]

Most Republicans expressed little public alarm over the announced opposition of the Alliance. Beyond bitter denunciations of such apostates as Peffer and Clover, the Republican press exhibited a partisan assurance. The *Fort Scott Monitor* admitted

---

23 Ibid., May 21, June 4, 1890.
24 Raymond C. Miller, "The Populist Party in Kansas" (Ph.D. diss., University of Chicago, 1928), pp. 117-18; Burton J. Williams, *Senator John James Ingalls* (Lawrence, Kans., 1972), pp. 73-76, 92-95, and passim; *Kansas Farmer*, May 21, 1890; *Topeka Advocate*, May 21, 1890.

that farmers comprised two-thirds of the state's voters, but it believed most were good Republicans who would do little to hurt party candidates. Moreover, "the politicians express great confidence in the re-election of Senator Ingalls." A correspondent of another paper blithely announced that the Alliance had "no grievance as far as known" and predicted that Republican farmers would stay with their party and support Ingalls. Ingalls himself sarcastically expressed his gratitude to the March Alliance convention "for being the first to formally announce my candidacy for a fourth term" and confidently proclaimed that the anti-Ingalls resolution would hurt its authors more than its object.[25]

More discerning Republicans harbored private doubts about the effect of the Alliance's course upon their party. "Some how I fear," Governor Humphrey wrote to Republican Congressman Bishop W. Perkins, "that you, in common with our Republican friends in Washington, hardly realize the real condition of public feeling in Kansas." A nonpartisan demand existed, Humphrey explained, for congressional action to increase the currency supply and to prohibit trusts. "While I am not easily panic stricken, and am not given to unseemly haste in yielding to public clamor," he assured Perkins, "yet the demands respecting these matters are so firmly rooted in the public mind, and with all so apparently just, that I almost feel that Republican supremacy is entirely dependent upon some substantial legislation on these questions." To Ingalls Humphrey confessed that "the feeling is so intense that I do not very much covet a re-nomination for governor" and warned that "your eggs and mine are in the same basket." As the GOP controlled all branches of the national government, the governor pointed out, it would be held responsible; and if no satisfactory action resulted, the third-party movement would be greatly strengthened and "the question will be, what shall we do [to] be saved? in the next . . . election."[26]

There was a limit to Humphrey's concern, however. Although willing to urge congressional action on agrarian complaints, he refused to accede to them himself on the state level. Admitting that

[25] *Fort Scott Daily Monitor,* June 6, 1890: *Atchison Daily Champion,* April 1, 1890; J. J. Ingalls to M. M. Beck, April 6, 1890, M. M. Beck Papers, KSHS.
[26] L. U. Humphrey to B. W. Perkins, March 21, June 25, 1890, and Humphrey to J. J. Ingalls, June 25, 1890, Humphrey Papers, KSHS.

"some things demanded by the farmers' organizations are just," Humphrey still determined to "draw the line and fight." He refused the Alliance petition for a special session of the legislature to provide mortgage relief, declaring that the 1889 legislature had settled the question. Like most Republican leaders, he denied that the farmers' troubles resulted from or could be relieved by legislation. Moreover, Humphrey, a banker himself, maintained that enactment of Alliance proposals would adversely affect the state's credit. Although he criticized the farmer for relying on legislative relief, he did suggest that a congressional committee investigate agricultural conditions, a proposal Peffer denounced as an attempt to mislead, divert attention, and postpone action. Finally, the governor rejected the Alliance request for the appointment of P. B. Maxson to the Board of Railroad Commissioners. He declared his opposition was to Maxson personally and that the Alliance should have asked merely for board representation. When the Alliance suggested another candidate, however, Humphrey described its action as "only inclined to complicate matters" and retained the objectionable commissioner.[27]

The rejection of Alliance demands with such transparent duplicity merely strengthened the determination of farmers to break away from the old parties. In an editorial entitled "The People's Rebellion," Peffer demonstrated that it was this political discontent, not simply economic distress, that was the essence of what would become Populism, for it had become obvious that political purification was a prerequisite for not only immediate economic reform but also the assurance of popular participation in future political decisions. "An open rebellion on the part of the masses," Peffer declared, had begun "against existing methods of politicians and party leaders in their treatment of just demands set forth by the people." In every instance, politicians and parties had failed to respond sincerely or effectively to the demand for action in the public interest: the legislature had rejected the agrarian program of remedial legislation; the governor refused to reconvene the legis-

---

[27] Humphrey to Levi Ferguson, April 22, 1890, Humphrey to T. J. Jackson, February 26, 1890, Humphrey to J. Crans, February 14, 1890, Humphrey to L. M. Briggs, April 5, 1890, Humphrey to John Kelly, April 5, 1890, Humphrey Papers, KSHS; *Topeka Daily Capital*, January 29, 1890; *Kansas Farmer*, February 5, 1890.

lature or to recognize agrarian interests in his appointments; Ingalls disdained to answer the public's questions; Congress not only ignored the St. Louis demands but actually contravened them in such legislation as the McKinley Tariff. Politics, then, had failed the people. "Nothing short of a rebellion of the people will regain the power they have lost and restore justice in public administration," Peffer concluded. "The political work must be done by the people acting in large masses."[28]

Mass political action became every day more a reality. By late spring the Alliance claimed 100,000 members in nearly 2,000 local suballiances, with up to fifty new suballiances being established each week. The demand for Peffer's presence was so great that he proposed holding mass meetings in order to save time, and he soon estimated that he spoke to almost 2,000 people a day. Beginning in April, county alliances prepared for independent political action in local contests and demanded independent tickets on the state and congressional levels as well. Then on May 14, Clover issued the authorized call for a June meeting of the People's State Central Committee, elected by alliancemen in district meetings, and urged other rural and labor organizations to participate in joint action.[29]

The convention assembled in Topeka on June 12 with forty-one Alliance delegates, twenty-eight Knights of Labor, ten members of the FMBA, seven Patrons of Husbandry, and four single taxers. The delegates unanimously agreed that full state and congressional tickets, pledged to Alliance principles, should be nominated. The convention encouraged suballiances to nominate county and legislative tickets responsive to their local interests, though it recommended the creation of a separate organization to avoid the transformation of the Alliance directly into a partisan body. It then decided that the proper name of the new party would be the "People's Party" and called a state nominating convention to meet in Topeka on August 13, 1890.[30]

Before that nominating convention met, however, the fledgling People's party had to withstand a Democratic attempt to assume command of the movement, a struggle that set the pattern for the

[28] *Kansas Farmer*, June 25, 1890.
[29] *Topeka Advocate*, March 6, May 14, 28, June 4, 11, 1890; *Fort Scott Daily Monitor*, March 14, 1890; *Kansas Farmer*, May 14, 28, 1890.
[30] *Topeka Advocate*, June 18, 25, 1890; *Fort Scott Daily Monitor*, June 13, 1890.

future course of the third party. The Democrats throughout the 1880s had been willing to cooperate with reform parties, not out of any sympathy in political principles, but because no success was possible on a separate basis. The question of campaign "fusion" between the two secondary parties, then, figured in each election but scarcely troubled the triumphant Republicans. Although fusion was rarely successful, it did frequently assist the Democrats who were able to operate the plan more to their own advantage than to that of their less-established and transient allies.[31] The Alliance-People's party movement of 1890, however, was less a definite partisan entity composed of men with common durable partisan attachments than a mass demand for political action. As such, it was subject to disruption rather than stabilization by the introduction of partisan appeals or controls. Certainly such leaders as McLallin and Peffer recognized this potential for disintegration and so did Republican politicians who sought to exploit it. Moreover, the Alliance, drawing so heavily upon the state's largely Republican agricultural class, needed to avoid any taint of collusion with the traditional and bitter enemy of the GOP, the Democracy. Alliance leaders who joined the reform movement from the Republican party—such as Peffer and McLallin—thus attempted to prevent obvious collaboration with the Democrats while those from the background of Democratic-Union Labor cooperation generally tried to foster fusion.

As early as April Peffer complained of Democratic pressure upon the Alliance to enter politics as a Democratic adjunct, but the major Democratic effort to capitalize on the strength of the Alliance came only with the creation of a new party by the June convention. Led by John Martin of Topeka, Democratic politicians maneuvered to secure for Charles Robinson the gubernatorial nominations of both the new party and the Democracy. Robinson, the state's first governor, had become a Democrat during the 1880s because of his intense hostility to the Republican policy of prohibition. Well-known throughout the state, he had acted in the past with third

---

[31] Walter T. K. Nugent, *The Tolerant Populists: Kansas Populism and Nativism* (Chicago, 1963), pp. 47, 52; *Girard Herald,* December 8, 1888; *Topeka Daily Commonwealth,* August 23, 1888; Elizabeth N. Barr, "The Populist Uprising," in *A Standard History of Kansas and Kansans,* ed. William E. Connelley (Chicago, 1918), 2: 1125-29.

parties and seemed a logical choice to lead the opposition to victory over the GOP. By July Democratic newspapers had created a boom for Robinson's nomination by the People's party, and they gained the enthusiastic support of several men perennially active in third-party agitation who believed in Robinson's nomination out of expediency. W. H. T. Wakefield of Lawrence, the 1888 vice-presidential candidate of the Union Labor party, declared that Robinson's nomination by the People's party would assure Democratic cooperation in a united effort to defeat the Republicans.[32]

The issue of Robinson's candidacy dominated the political scene two weeks before the state convention after Clover, the natural choice of the alliancemen within the party, announced that he would not accept a nomination. Many Republicans contemplated with pleasure the selection of Robinson, for they were convinced that such a step would split the new party and ensure continued Republican supremacy. They anticipated a quick return of alliancemen to the Republican fold if the reform leaders grafted onto the new party a Democrat favoring an end to prohibition. Indeed, as the possibility of Populist cooperation with the Democracy increased, the Farmers' Alliance of Harvey County resolved to remain Republican if it had to align with an old party. Nevertheless, most Democrats and some Populists believed that Robinson's nomination would assure the defeat of the GOP, and they worked to secure his selection. Prominent Democrats solicited the *Farmer*'s support for Robinson by suggesting that Peffer would then be the logical choice to replace Ingalls in the Senate.[33]

The Alliance's antipolitical doctrine that the office must seek the man rather than the reverse meant that the politicians' boom for Robinson went largely unchallenged. McLallin's *Advocate,* for example, refrained from commenting on possible candidates, lest it be accused of attempting to dictate or manipulate nominations. Peffer, however, regarded the Democratic advances precisely as dictation, and he countered them with his own suggestions that, given the nature of the constituency to which he must appeal, the

---

[32] *Kansas Farmer,* April 2, 1890; John Martin to Charles Robinson, June 16, 1890, Charles Robinson Papers, KSHS; *Lawrence Gazette,* July 10, 1890.

[33] Humphrey to W. R. P. Dow, June 27, 1890, Humphrey to E. H. Crawford, June 7, 1890, Humphrey Papers, KSHS; *Kansas City Star,* August 12, 1890; *Atchison Daily Champion,* August 1, 1890; *Chicago Tribune,* June 4, 1899.

party's gubernatorial candidate should be an old soldier, of Republican antecedents, and in favor of prohibition. Some observers thought that this was a bid by Peffer for his own nomination. Robinson himself, however, recognized the objective of Peffer's editorial and angrily denounced its author for attempting to rule him out.[34]

It appeared, however, that Peffer's challenge had come too late to stop the Robinson bandwagon. Although admitting that Peffer had disturbed the "calculations" of the professional politicians, newspapers generally agreed on the eve of the convention that the Democrats and Populists would combine on Robinson. To insure the success of the fusion plan, it was alleged, the Democrats had promised to support Clover in a race for Congress in the Third District. Edward Carroll, the Democratic state chairman, and John A. Eaton, Democratic leader of the Third District, arrived in Topeka "to complete the deal" on August 11, 1890. As the convention opened on the thirteenth, Republican leader A. W. Smith flatly predicted Robinson's nomination, and the *Topeka Capital* maintained that Democratic manipulation of the People's party had already determined the results of the convention. Such observers admitted the existence of Populist opposition to fusion with the Democrats but considered it too weak to overcome the arrangements made. The *Kansas City Star* reported that "Judge W. A. Peffer's name will be presented by those who decline to be led into the Democratic camp," and the *Capital* speculated that John F. Willits, a farmer, prohibitionist, former Republican legislator, and president of the People's State Central Committee, might also be nominated to stop Robinson. "If Judge Peffer was to be nominated for governor a coalition with the Democrats would be impossible," the *Capital* explained, "and it is not likely that Mr. Willits would be acceptable to the Democrats."[35]

Peffer had frequently been mentioned as a possible gubernatorial candidate since early spring, but he had repeatedly asserted his noncandidacy. On the eve of the convention he claimed to have no interest in the position and left for central Kansas to address

34 *Topeka Advocate*, July 23, 1890; *Kansas Farmer*, August 6, 1890; *Kansas Democrat* (Topeka), August 14, 1890; *Topeka Daily Capital*, August 10, 1890.

35 *Kansas City Star*, August 12, 1890; *Topeka Daily Capital*, August 10, 12, 13, 1890.

an Alliance meeting. Such a disinterested attitude reflected not only the Alliance doctrine that the office should seek the man but also Peffer's natural emergence as the implicit candidate of the People's party for senator. He denied any personal ambitions, but both friends and enemies considered him the unspoken nominee because he had unrivaled prominence within the reform movement and because the Alliance had focused its campaign on replacing Ingalls. One preconvention rumor held that if Peffer would drop his opposition to Robinson, the fusionists would acquiesce in the party's explicit recognition of Peffer as its senatorial candidate.[36]

The People's party state nominating convention opened amidst vigorous struggles for party control, with the Peffer-Willits-McLallin group of radical prohibitionists, woman suffragists, Greenbackers, and antifusionists arrayed against the more moderate and pragmatic faction represented best by Wakefield and William A. Harris. The latter group generally prevailed in framing the platform, which merely reiterated the St. Louis demands while avoiding a prohibition plank, and it seemed that the nominations might be similarly controlled. Eight men were nominated for governor and all but Robinson, Willits, and Peffer withdrew. Peffer was out of town but the others made short speeches. The balloting revealed the Populist contempt of politicians' schemes, opposition to Democrats, and support for prohibition by awarding Willits the nomination by a four-to-one margin. Peffer attracted only a scattering of votes, as the antifusionists concentrated on Willits. The convention, however, did declare Peffer its choice to replace Ingalls, although it avoided an explicit nomination because of a technicality. The other nominations also reflected the strength of the antifusionists, as only one nominee, John Ives for attorney general, had Democratic antecedents. The People's party respected its name by further designating a woman, a Negro, a minister, a farmer, and a schoolteacher for its candidates.[37]

The results of the convention brought different reactions from the older parties. Though Robinson's rejection in favor of Willits surprised Republicans, they were certain of victory over the polit-

---

36 *Kansas Farmer,* February 26, May 7, June 11, 1890; *Topeka Daily Capital,* June 12, August 12, 13, 1890.
37 *Topeka Daily Capital,* August 13-16, 1890; *Fort Scott Daily Monitor,* August 14, 1890; Nugent, *Tolerant Populists,* pp. 72-73.

ically unknown Alliance leader. "The nomination of Peffer," admitted the *Atchison Globe*, "would have caused alarm in the Republican party," but Willits was a weak nomination. Democrats, on the other hand, raged over their rebuff by the Populists. Robinson again denounced Peffer and Willits. Carroll believed that "the nominations show a plentiful lack of political wisdom," and other Democrats satisfied themselves that Republican interests controlled the new party. One wrote to Robinson that "the only adverse criticism of you that I have heard is that you are a Democrat!"[38]

Leading Democrats agreed to nominate a separate state ticket rather than support the People's party candidates. Robinson and several other prominent Democrats even foresaw success for a straight ticket, believing that the People's party would split the normal Republican vote. There had been few important Democrats who had aligned themselves with the new party (as opposed to those who were merely willing to fuse with the Populists), and after Robinson's repudiation they returned to their old allegiance. The politician who had presented Robinson's name to the Populist convention, for example, then took a conspicuous role in the Democratic state convention that began in Wichita on September 9, 1890. Resubmission Republicans, so-called because they favored resubmitting the constitutional amendment imposing prohibition to another vote of the people, met simultaneously and joined the Democrats in a coalition ticket. Robinson predictably received the gubernatorial nomination. The Democrats did fuse on Ives, but this was the only instance of fusion with the Populists on the state level in 1890.[39]

Opposition to continued Republican control, however, led the Democrats to accept Populist candidates for other offices. Most importantly, they implicitly fused on three Populist congressional candidates by not making nominations opposite Clover in the Third District, John G. Otis in the Fourth, and Jerry Simpson in the Seventh. On legislative and county offices Democrats even more willingly cooperated with Populists, but again it was largely a case of Democratic initiative and decision after the Populists had

[38] *Topeka Daily Capital*, August 16, 1890; Ruth [?] to Robinson, September 8, 1890, Robinson Papers.

[39] *Topeka Daily Capital*, August 10, 16, 1890; *Fort Scott Daily Monitor*, September 10, 1890.

made independent nominations. The Democrats, moreover, made no pretense of acting with Populists out of agreement on principles. Rather, they looked upon fusion, even with unwilling allies, as a traditional political tool to accomplish real, if limited, political goals. The defeat of Ingalls was a platform objective of Kansas Democrats and would cause Democratic rejoicing even if achieved by Populists. Most Populists, on the other hand, necessarily rejected explicit fusion, for they had repudiated both old parties out of principle and could not consistently cooperate with one against the other. The June state convention creating the People's party had in fact resolved that "we will not support for office any member of our organization who will accept a nomination from either of the old parties, but will consider such member a traitor to our cause."[40] Generally, then, any fusion in 1890 resulted from Democratic fusion *on* Populist candidates without Populist solicitation and regardless of Populist wishes.

Indeed, the Populists in 1890 made clear that they opposed the methods as well as the policies of the old parties, and in their insistence upon real participation and self-determination they adopted a number of innovations. In making their conventions effective nominating devices, for instance, the Populists frequently employed the Phillips County Plan. Each suballiance elected its most qualified members for the various offices, as a sort of primary contest which assured a candidate's commitment, and from the men so chosen the Populist county convention then elected its nominees. The Phillips Plan functioned well in local affairs, for it guaranteed faithful candidates not encumbered by promises to special interest groups for political expenses or support. It was difficult to extend this system to the nomination of state candidates, however, and there Populists sought to secure the same results by requiring candidates to deliver short speeches to the convention, giving the delegates the opportunity to judge the men and their commitment personally.[41] Time would unfortunately prove that Populists, when severed from local sources of information and with their limited

40 W. P. Harrington, "The Populist Party in Kansas," in *Collections of the Kansas State Historical Society* (Topeka, 1925), 16: 407-8; *Smith Centre Pioneer-Bulletin*, September 4, 1890.

41 *Topeka Advocate*, April 23, 1890; Miller, "Populist Party in Kansas," pp. 130-31.

access to reliable media, would be susceptible to misleading appeals and candidates and succumb to political manipulation despite their condemnation of it.

By early September the Republicans had also completed their campaign preparations. The state convention renominated virtually the same ticket that had carried the state by 80,000 votes in 1888, and congressional incumbents generally won renomination as well. Ingalls warned against complacency, however: "In my opinion success will depend more on hard work and organization from this time on than anything else."[42]

Hard work and organization typified the campaigns of all three parties, and each added more specific strategy to meet peculiar needs. The Populists were in the most precarious position, attempting to gloss over the traditional and divisive issues of prohibition and party loyalty as irrelevant and to emphasize the necessity for new action to meet new issues. Clover illustrated the basic approach of the People's party when he announced, "The issue this year is not whether a man shall be permitted to drink, but whether he shall have a home to go to, drunk or sober."[43]

Judge Peffer, as closely identified with the GOP as any Populist, led the effort to blunt Republican appeals for partisan loyalty. His common response to these pleas, which were often publicly directed specifically at him, was to deny the efficacy of old-party reform, pointing out the repeated rejection by both old parties of popular reform requests for the past decade. Clearly, he concluded, "the independent political movement of farmers and laborers is necessary." Peffer also attempted to appropriate Republican tradition for Populist advantage. He compared the new party to the early GOP, for example, and declared that the Republican party had abandoned its original position and vision. He less wholeheartedly accepted the irrelevance of prohibition, but he did recognize that other issues were more important, and he urged Populists to resist all attempts to divert attention from the major questions of political and economic reform. "Let all side issues alone. Stick to the text."[44]

42 *Fort Scott Daily Monitor*, September 4, 1890; Ingalls to P. I. Bonebreak, August 18, 1890, John J. Ingalls Papers, KSHS.
43 *Girard Western Herald*, November 1, 1890.

Peffer was only one of many who followed the Populist text. Mary Elizabeth Lease, a restive firebrand who practiced law and preached rebellion; John Davis, Peffer's only rival in producing dry statistical speeches; "Sockless Jerry" Simpson, a natural politician and splendid speaker; Benjamin Clover, sometimes a foolish but always a determined worker; John G. Otis, as serious and sober as Peffer but less politically oriented; William Baker, a farmer and minister of solid persistence; John Willits, a forceful agitator who rejected compromise; Annie L. Diggs, a diminutive suffragette who realized that Populism necessarily meant woman's rights—these and others preached the new gospel of Populism. Through the influence of the Farmers' Alliance they were joined by outside speakers including Leonidas L. Polk of North Carolina, the national president of the Alliance. The Populist rhetoric was stern and unyielding but few repudiated it. If the calm Peffer could speak of revolutionary times and "the people's rebellion," Mrs. Lease could promise "to win this battle with the ballot if possible, but if not that way then with the bayonet." All campaigned against "politicians," and Willits especially operated on an antipolitics theme.[45]

Republicans countered with their own rhetoric and traditional political appeals and avoided any real discussion of the Populist program. They obliquely replied to the Populist stress on economic depression by foolishly asserting that prosperity dominated the scene while maintaining that bountiful crops were on the way. Sheer ridicule and abuse formed a major part of the Republican strategy, culminating in outright fabrications of public records and a sordid attack on Willits as a perjurer, swindler, and defaulter. Most importantly, however, Republicans emphasized the issue of prohibition and waved the bloody shirt. On both issues the two old parties held sharply divergent positions, and if prejudice could replace discontent the former bifurcated partisan alignment with Republican dominance should follow. Republicans announced, then, that if the People's party split the prohibition vote with the GOP, the whiskey Democrats would triumph at the polls. Governor

---

[44] *Kansas Farmer,* June 25, August 20, 27, 1890; *Topeka Daily Capital,* September 24, October 12, 1890.

[45] *Kansas Farmer,* June 25, 1890; *Smith Centre Pioneer-Bulletin,* September 11, 1890; *Atchison Daily Champion,* October 9, 1890.

Humphrey, privately no prohibitionist, feigned concern to a member of the FMBA that "efforts will be made to divert the attention of farmers from the question of prohibition, anti-prohibition and resubmission this fall, and induce them to indifference concerning these questions." And, Humphrey continued, "while the members of your order are earnest in their efforts to secure their just rights, and to remedy existing and past wrongs, they should not . . . forget their duty to themselves, their families and the state, on this subject of prohibition." The following day Humphrey confidently explained to a fellow Republican, "There are thousands of Republican Alliance farmers in the state, who will hesitate very long before doing anything to aid the Democratic party in its fight to re-open the question of prohibition in Kansas."[46]

Republicans hoped that cultural conflict would fortify the old partisan cleavage. The Democrats obtusely helped their opponents by proclaiming resubmission the major issue. The Populist rejection of Robinson removed the possibility of driving "every temperance voter in Kansas" back to the GOP, as one old politician had hopefully anticipated, but Republicans continued to associate independent voting with a Democratic triumph for whiskey. They denounced third-party nominees as "creatures of the rum-soaked Democracy" and professed to be incapable of believing that Republican alliancemen would consent "to be led off into the ranks of the enemy" under such leadership. And when a court decision in October weakened prohibition enforcement, Humphrey refused to deemphasize the question of resubmission as a campaign issue because "it would probably be detrimental to our candidates."[47]

Republicans also employed the old-soldier appeal and revived sectional prejudices in their attempt to force the recalcitrant farmers back to the GOP. Polk's presence among the Alliance speakers gave a semblance of truth to Republican charges that Southern Democrats controlled the Alliance in an effort to divide the GOP in the North and thereby gain Democratic ascendancy in order to

46 Humphrey to W. R. P. Dow, June 27, 1890, Humphrey to S. J. Stewart, June 6, 1890, Humphrey to E. H. Crawford, June 7, 1890, Humphrey Papers, KSHS; *Topeka Daily Capital*, May 6, 10, 18, 1890; *Fort Scott Daily Monitor*, October 21, 23, 1890; *Topeka Advocate*, November 19, 1890.

47 *Topeka Daily Capital*, August 13, October 12, 1890; *Fort Scott Daily Monitor*, November 1, 1890; Humphrey to W. R. P. Dow, June 27, 1890, Sperry Baker to Humphrey, October 24, 1890, Humphrey Papers, KSHS.

undo the results of the Civil War. Polk's Civil War service as a Confederate officer also provoked such outrageous Republican allegations as that he had "murdered in cold blood a number of [unarmed Union] prisoners of war." Newspapers contrasted Humphrey's war record with Willits's lack of one and implied that the Populist had no sympathy with the Union in 1861 or with old soldiers in 1890. Even Peffer, whose war record was well known, suffered from "the current political gossip," he complained, "that I was unfriendly to the soldiers, that I was disloyal to their interests, and that in every way I was incapable of serving them." The Republicans climaxed their campaign by welcoming President Harrison to Topeka to address a huge gathering of Union veterans while the city's newspapers carried articles headlined "The People's Party Is the Scheme of Ex-Rebels."[48]

Such appeals only partially succeeded. Several Republicans did withdraw from the Shawnee County Farmers' Alliance declaring that they "would no longer affiliate with an organization which was officered by southern brigadiers and run in the interest of the Democratic party." More frequently, however, the alliancemen held ranks and announced that they would not be diverted from the real issues by bloody-shirt tactics. One suballiance recognized such intolerant appeals as a product of "the extremity of party position" and another reason to leave the corrupt old parties. This determination inspired Populist optimism as the campaign drew to its close, and the Populists were further encouraged when Ingalls refused the party's challenge to debate Peffer. Clover then provided his followers with advice before the polls opened: "Remember the interests at stake. Remember the homeless, the sorrowing, the discouraged, the weary, and the heavy laden. The decalogue and the golden rule must have a place in the great uprising; the great J. J. to the contrary notwithstanding; reform must come from the heart of the common people where the 'higher civilization' always comes from."[49]

The old parties expected victory too. The Democrats thought

48 *Fort Scott Daily Monitor,* October 4, 11, 16, 1890; W. A. Peffer to F. H. Hathaway, March 7, 1892, KSHS Archives; *Topeka Daily Capital,* July 23, 27, October 7, 8, 12, 1890.
49 *Fort Scott Daily Monitor,* July 13, 1890; *Kansas Farmer,* July 30, August 13, October 1, 1890; *Leoti Western Farmer,* July 31, 1890.

that Robinson at least would triumph, though the Democratic state chairman admitted that the party could not afford many defections to Populism. He therefore concentrated on convincing the former Democrats in the third party to return to the Democracy and leave the Populists to split the old Republican majority. The Republicans conceded that they would not overwhelm the opposition as in the past but foresaw no trouble in winning handily. They were also certain of Ingalls's reelection, wrote a correspondent for the *Chicago Tribune.* Of the forty state senators, all holdover, thirty-nine were Republicans. Of the 125 members of the lower house to be elected, the Republicans needed only forty-four to assure Ingalls's reelection. The Republicans, he continued, were claiming sixty-five and were certain of fifty. To defeat Ingalls the opposition would have to elect eighty-two representatives and unite behind another candidate, clearly an impossibility, and the Republicans confidently went to the polls.[50]

"The election in Kansas," declared the *Kansas City Star* the following day, "has been a Waterloo to the Republican party." Even the *Topeka Capital,* after having predicted a crushing Republican victory, admitted "the landslide has slid."[51] The Populists elected five congressmen and ninety-one members of the legislature and stripped the 1888 Republican plurality by 90 percent. The only state-level candidate the Populists elected, however, was John Ives, who also received full Democratic support. The People's party had become the other major party in Kansas, doubling the vote of the Democrats and nearly matching that of the Republicans.

The reactions to these startling results were predictable. Peffer rejoiced, "When the people move together they are invincible." Joseph K. Hudson of the *Capital* sullenly retorted that the Populists had "trusted for victory to the ignorance of the people and to the shame of Kansas their confidence was not misplaced." The McKinley Tariff and increased pensions may have caused the election reversals elsewhere, he added, "but what did it in Kansas

50 W. C. Jones to W. H. Sears, [early November 1890], and Chairman of the Douglas County Democratic Central Committee to Sears, October 11, 1890, William H. Sears Papers, KSHS; *Kansas City Star,* October 30, November 1, 1890.
51 *Kansas City Star,* November 5, 1890; *Topeka Daily Capital,* November 6, 1890.

was 'The Way Out.' " Hudson consoled himself by noting that "while the People's Party controls the house by a very large majority, the senate is still Republican by 38 to 1, and a governor's veto also stands in the way of radical legislation of which businessmen and capitalists might have stood in dread."[52]

There still remained the imminent contest for the Senate, and the results of that struggle over Ingalls were anything but predictable. Reporters and correspondents of the country's leading newspapers and magazines crowded into Topeka to cover the election by the legislators in January 1891. *Harper's Weekly* explained the remarkable national interest in the contest by pointing out its extraordinary characteristics: first, Ingalls was a major political and public figure and permanent president pro tem of the Senate; second, "Kansas is the State in which the revolution wrought by the Farmers' Alliance is most conspicuous"; third, there existed a possibility that the Populist legislators, despite their majority, would be unable to elect a candidate and that Ingalls might triumph because of factionalism within the People's party.[53] One thing was certain: whoever emerged from this political struggle was assured of national prominence.

Many observers foresaw sure defeat for Ingalls. Democratic leader George Glick assured an anxiously inquiring Grover Cleveland that "Ingalls is now eliminated from our politics," and a Leavenworth politician declared, "I don't see how Ingalls can make it. The farmers have got it and will certainly elect their man." But Peffer, while also expressing a judgment against Ingalls's chances, pointed out the weakness of the Populist position: "People's Party members are all pledged *against* Ingalls, though not pledged *for* any other man.[54]

Peffer, of course, was the leading candidate to succeed Ingalls, and many felt that the party had already implicitly nominated him, first by its action in the state convention and then by designating him to face Ingalls in public debate. Republicans also regarded

52 *Kansas Farmer*, November 12, 1890; *Topeka Daily Capital*, November 6, 11, 12, 1890.

53 *Harper's Weekly* 35 (February 7, 1891): 103.

54 George Glick to Grover Cleveland, November 27, 1890, and W. A. Peffer to George Innes, November 29, 1890, Grover Cleveland Papers, Library of Congress; *Topeka Daily Capital*, November 13, 1890.

Peffer as the Populist senatorial candidate and had acted accordingly during the regular campaign. But after the November election, as the possibility of success became greater, so did the number of Peffer's challengers. Most formidable of these appeared to be John Willits, who most Populists believed had been counted out in the gubernatorial contest and now deserved some recognition.[55] P. P. Elder, just elected to the legislature, Charles Robinson, and a host of others also attracted public support before the legislature convened.

Peffer had three important advantages over his rivals: recognition as the party's original choice; control of the influential *Kansas Farmer;* and the support of the National Alliance. L. L. Polk, the national president, had pledged his support to Peffer during the regular campaign and now reaffirmed it in an attempt to center Alliance strength before other candidates appeared to create division. When the Farmers' Alliance elected Willits national lecturer of the order at its annual convention at Ocala, Florida, in December, it was alleged that Polk had arranged the election "to get Willits out of the way of Judge Peffer for the United States senate." Although Peffer opened the *Farmer* to letters and resolutions supporting all candidates, for weeks the paper printed hundreds of endorsements of Peffer from local suballiances. He also used the *Farmer* to answer questions and campaign charges, but he did not editorially advocate his own election, and maintained he was making no active canvass and had not conferred with legislators on the matter.[56]

The major Populist objection to Peffer involved his history of Republicanism and his relatively recent conversion to independent political action. The Winfield *American Non-Conformist* believed that "to overthrow Ingalls and elect a nine-months old convert would sound to the world as a very mediocre type of reform." Other long-time third-party men expressed reservations about the permanency of Peffer's loyalty to Populist principles and feared that as senator he would act with Republicans. These former

[55] *Atchison Daily Champion,* August 27, September 9, October 8, 1890; *Topeka Daily Capital,* November 8, 9, 13, 1890; *Kansas Farmer,* December 3, 1890.

[56] *Topeka Daily Capital,* November 11, 13, 19, December 11, 12, 1890; *Bird City News,* November 20, 1890; *Kansas Farmer,* December 3, 24, 31, 1890, January 7, 1891.

Union Laborites demanded the selection of one of their own, as a reward for their persistence in the cause of reform, and generally favored either Elder or John Breidenthal.[57]

Democrats within and without the People's party also feared a latent Republicanism in Peffer and opposed his election. Many Democrats believed that the defeat of Ingalls was vital regardless of his replacement and though a Democratic successor would be preferable, wrote one, "we propose to beat him with *any sort of a man if we must.*" Other Democrats, however, insisted that if the Populists "want our support they must select a candidate that will at least be unobjectionable" and warned that they would support neither Peffer nor Willits. Democrats suggested either Robinson or William A. Harris. When Democratic and Union Laborite sentiments combined, as in the editorial policy of Wakefield's *Lawrence Jeffersonian,* Peffer was sharply proscribed. But, according to one observer, nearly all Populists of Republican antecedents suffered from "the suspicion that they have too much Republican blood in their veins to be up to the wild-and-wooly standard of reform."[58]

Another objection specifically to Peffer involved his age and health. Already nearly sixty years old, he was frail and frequently ill. Indeed, a severe attack of bronchial asthma confined him to bed most of December. Opponents exaggerated his illness, moreover, and brutally predicted his rapid demise if elected senator, adding that Governor Humphrey could then appoint Ingalls to the remainder of the term and cut short the political reformation.[59]

In responding to his critics, Peffer reminded the *Non-Conformist* that he was a charter member of the People's party; it was not merely the old Union Labor party but a new and distinct organization made up of former Republicans, Democrats, and Prohibitionists as well as Union Laborites. Moreover, Peffer pointed out, he had advocated the Alliance position before either the Alliance or the *Non-Conformist* had even been established in Kansas. And while the third-party papers had encouraged the Union Labor and

57 *American Non-Conformist* (Winfield), January 15, 1891; *Girard Western Herald,* January 17, 1891; *Topeka Populist,* December 3, 1892; *Topeka Daily Capital,* January 6, 1891.

58 Nelson Acres to Cleveland, November 13, 1890, and Edward Carroll to George Innes, November 29, 1890, Cleveland Papers; *Topeka Daily Capital,* January 6, 9, 14, 15, 24, 1891.

59 *Kansas Farmer,* January 7, 1891; *Chicago Tribune,* January 28, 1891.

Greenback elements, he declared, the *Kansas Farmer* had delivered the bulk of the new party's voters by attracting the decisive converts from the major parties. He further insisted that his break from the GOP was permanent, that he supported a national third-party movement, and that he had not actively sought the nomination but that the people and the party had denoted him the rightful recipient in the state convention, in the campaign, and in local endorsements since that time. Others deemphasized the issue of Peffer's age and health by noting that Elder was even older, that the robust Willits had been unable to match Peffer's pace in the regular campaign, and that although the "Judge" was not strong, he had a mental and moral courage that fortified him.[60]

Such explanations apparently satisfied the party's rank and file. Even while Peffer lay ill in Topeka, unable to fill his speaking appointments in the special election in the Thirty-second Senatorial District, the Populist party of that district instructed its successful candidate to vote for him. When Chase County farmers heard that their representative favored another candidate, they called an emergency meeting of the county alliance in which they unanimously declared Peffer their choice and instructed their representative to vote only for him. As other suballiances and local Populist clubs continued to endorse him, it seemed clear that Peffer was the popular favorite.[61]

But others retained support from the politicians who gathered in Topeka. Some still pushed Willits as a compromise candidate who could attract votes from the Union Laborite faction without alienating those former Republicans that composed Peffer's strength. Frank Doster, one of the most brilliant of public figures in Kansas, also attracted former Republicans but did not have Peffer's personal popularity. Elder's hopes received a boost when the Populist legislative caucus agreed to elect him Speaker of the House. Behind these major possibilities appeared nearly every other figure of Kansas Populism as a local or group favorite.[62]

The debate over the Populist candidate obscured the fact that Ingalls had not conceded and, indeed, provided him with reason

60 *Kansas Farmer*, January 7, 1891; *Kansas City Star*, January 28, 29, 1891.

61 *Atchison Daily Champion*, December 23, 1890, January 2, 1891; *Topeka Daily Capital*, January 13, 20, 1891.

62 *Topeka Daily Capital*, January 3, 11, 13, 14, 1891.

not to do so. The division within the People's party might prove so bitter, Republicans hoped, that the Populists would be unable to unite on a candidate, and Ingalls might be able to win. The ease with which each side of any Populist dispute accused the other of being "Ingalls's fixers" delighted the Republicans, who confidently expected the People's party to break into its constituent parts. As William Buchan, Republican state chairman, explained, "Eight out of every ten men elected to the legislature are [or were] Republicans, and there will be a division in the ranks and Mr. Ingalls will be reelected."[63]

Ingalls and his backers actively tried to produce just such a division. In particular, they relied upon their traditionally successful political weapon—waving the bloody shirt to incite partisan and sectional animosities to conceal their narrow demands for Ingalls's reelection. Republican newspapers hammered at the theme that the Southern Confederacy directed the People's party, that unfrocked but unrepentent Confederate officers controlled the Farmers' Alliance, that the People's party opposed the flag and old soldiers, while needlessly pointing out that Ingalls was a national leader in keeping the traitorous Southern Democrats under control. The decision of the Ocala conference to postpone the formation of a national third party made plausible these charges against the People's party as an arm of the Southern Democracy, for it seemed to restrict the effects of political discontent to the Republican states of the Northwest while the Democratic party continued to profit from the unaffected South. Republicans especially appealed to the sentiments of the old soldiers. They distributed printed petitions to the Kansas posts of the Grand Army of the Republic with instructions to flood the legislature with these demands for the reelection of Ingalls. In a few days hundreds of these pro-Ingalls petitions descended upon the lawmaking body. Veterans staged mass meetings and in sanguinary language described how the South viewed old soldiers and Ingalls or how the irreconcilable traitors had welcomed the Alliance at Ocala as a friend of the Democracy. Three thousand Topeka veterans enthusiastically greeted Ingalls and resolved that "the election of any other person to fill his present position . . . will be regarded by us as a direct blow to the defenders of our country in the hour of her greatest need."[64]

In a last effort to divide the Populists, Republicans promoted a late senatorial boom for William A. Harris, a former Democrat and Confederate officer and a conservative leader of the Leavenworth County Alliance. Democrats had avoided any public statements of their intentions but had maneuvered to dictate the selection of the Populist candidate. They preferred a straight Democrat but, recognizing the Populist ability to elect a senator without their help, determined to press for a Populist with Democratic tendencies. In conjunction with some Democratic Populists, then, the straight Democrats urged the selection of Harris. Ingalls's supporters quietly encouraged the Harris boom, expecting that combined with bloody-shirt passions a Harris nomination would split the People's party. However, Democratic influence upon the Populists was lacking strength, and when Populists also perceived "Buchan's handiwork in the Harris candidacy," as one reporter described the Republican interest, the Harris boom faded rapidly.[65]

But the possibility that Ingalls might indeed achieve a victory through Populist dissension activated Populist preparations for the election. To ensure Populist solidarity and success, Peffer proposed a three-part plan as early as December. He advocated the instruction of legislators by their constituents, the holding of a caucus to prevent a division on the final vote, and the presence in Topeka of as many Populists as possible in order to bolster confidence and enforce obedience to the caucus decision. Peffer also warned Populist legislators, many unfamiliar with the world of Topeka and its politics, to be wary of strangers and to bring with them several "strong men" selected by the party from their district. Republicans derided Peffer as an "old fogy" for this suggestion, but Populists readily assented to it, as it corresponded with their emphasis upon popular participation and local control.[66]

[64] *Topeka Daily Capital*, December 5, 12, 1890, January 24, 25, 1891; *Senate Journal* (Topeka, Kans., 1891), pp. 126, 140-42, 151-56, 160-62, 166-68, 176; *House Journal* (Topeka, Kans., 1891), pp. 138-40.

[65] Carroll to Innes, November 29, 1890, Cleveland Papers; *Atchison Daily Champion*, January 27, 1891; *Kansas City Star*, January 21, 26, 1891.

[66] *Kansas Farmer*, November 19, December 3, 10, 1890; *Fort Scott Daily Monitor*, November 25, 1890; *Topeka Daily Capital*, January 9, 1891.

The record of previous senatorial elections seemed to warrant all but the most extreme fears of the Populists, and those earlier elections had involved merely intraparty struggles and nothing so convulsive as the overthrow of the GOP. Members of all parties expected Ingalls to attempt to bribe legislators, and many were convinced that violent tactics including assassination had not been ruled out. In Topeka, one reporter noticed that three bodyguards escorted each legislator to prevent Ingalls from practicing his feared "amoral tactics to secure his reelection." The Populists avoided the major hotels, crowded together in cheap rooming houses, and absolutely refused to talk to anyone about anything. They held all their meetings secretly, behind locked and guarded doors, and in order to keep a united front agreed to make no move on any question without caucusing first.[67]

Ingalls and his supporters certainly had no intentions of obtaining his election through violent means, but apparently they did not completely rule out extralegal tactics. Republican boss Cy Leland arrived in Topeka "to remain a few days in the interest of Senator Ingalls," as a newspaper delicately phrased it; actually, as William Allen White later wrote, Leland carried $10,000 and a list of legislators to be bought. Several third-party leaders reported that bribes were offered to Populist legislators, though these offers may have been without Ingalls's authorization. Ingalls, however, did give $250 to John Livingston, president of the New York State Farmers' Alliance, to go to Topeka in an effort to influence Alliance legislators for his election. There, on the basis of his official position, Livingston persuaded Annie Diggs to introduce him to a Populist audience, whereupon he "revealed" how the goals of the Confederacy were to be realized through the Alliance, declared that Alliance leaders intended to punish Union veterans, proclaimed that Southern brigadiers dictated to Kansans, and announced his support for Ingalls. Finally, Republicans considered adjourning the senate to avoid holding the required joint ballot with the Populist house and thus perhaps allow Governor Humphrey to appoint Ingalls to the Senate.[68]

[67] Williams, *Ingalls*, p. 123; *Kansas City Star*, January 13, 21, 1891; *Chicago Tribune*, January 26, 1891; *Atchison Daily Champion*, January 30, 1891; Acres to Cleveland, November 13, 1890, Cleveland Papers.

[68] *Topeka Daily Capital*, January 13, 21, 28, March 21, 1891; *The Autobiog-

All such actions merely intensified the suspense that enveloped Topeka and intrigued the nation. Both the Populists and the Republicans scheduled their decisive caucuses for the night of January 26, 1891. Amidst confidence and harmony, the Republican legislators quickly pledged themselves unanimously for Ingalls. The Populist caucus offered a striking contrast. All possible candidates were required to speak briefly and to pledge their support for the eventual nominee. The caucus balloting revealed the variety of positions and personalities within the People's party and the dominant status of former Republicans, particularly Peffer. Seventeen aspirants split the ninety-three caucus votes on the first ballot with Peffer receiving thirty-five—as many as the total of the next four candidates: Willits, twelve; Elder, ten; Breidenthal, eight; Doster, five. Generally eliminating the candidate with the fewest votes on each preceding ballot, the caucus struggled through five hours of debate and voting before declaring Peffer the party's nominee for United States Senator. Peffer led on every poll, but the persistent strength of Willits and Elder required eighteen ballots before he secured a majority.[69]

Only superficially had the contest within the People's party been a struggle between moderate and radical factions, and few Populists genuinely viewed the choice as an ideological decision or a victory for the moderate wing of the party. Instead, the reaction among Populists to Peffer's selection was nearly invariably governed by their previous party affiliation. Ex-Republicans such as William Baker admired Peffer and expressed pleasure at his selection. The opposition of the former Union Laborites arose from partisan prejudice and pride at least as much as from any theoretical disagreements. These critics simply wanted recognition through senatorial honors for their generation of reform agitation as they saw it come to fruition. Indeed, Elder, the national chairman of the Union Labor party, ascribed his rejection to the influence of the radicals, and others added that between Willits and Peffer the radical Pop-

raphy of William Allen White (New York, 1946), pp. 190-92; *Atchison Daily Champion,* January 18, 19, 20, 1891; *Topeka Advocate,* October 28, November 4, 1891, October 2, 1895; John Livingston to Benjamin Harrison, February 6, 1891, and enclosed clippings, Benjamin Harrison Papers, Library of Congress.

69 *Kansas City Star,* January 27, 1891; *Topeka Daily Capital,* January 27, 1891; *Kansas Farmer,* February 11, 1891.

ulists favored the latter.[70] Moreover, former Republicans usually proved the most militant in arguing for immediate implementation of sweeping reform proposals, in the time-honored fashion of converts; whereas most Union Laborites exhibited a practical moderation approaching fatalism produced by a life of defeat and a custom of compromise through fusion with that other political minority, the Kansas Democracy. Democrats and Democratic-Populists also rejected a true ideological approach to the contest, except insofar as such practical political issues as prohibition influenced their viewpoint. They were willing to accept Elder or another Union Labor candidate from the "radical" faction of the party but were adamant against a "moderate" former Republican such as Peffer. Years of deliberately inflamed prejudices and exaggerated hostility separated Democrats and Republicans on principle, as well as principles.

The following day in the legislature the ranks of the People's party held firm, resulting in a strict party vote: ninety-eight Populists for Peffer, fifty-eight Republicans for Ingalls, and six Democrats for Charles Blair. There remained the necessity of the official ballot in joint session on January 28, but the demonstration of Populist solidarity made it a formality, and all involved conceded Peffer's election. The only change stemmed from the maneuverings of the Democrats. Displeased with Peffer's nomination, they had voted for Blair on the first roll call. Some, however, felt that by voting for Peffer on the official ballot they might be able to exert more influence upon the course of the People's party. Others such as Senator Edward Carroll steadfastly opposed supporting Peffer, and a final caucus left the votes up to the individual Democratic legislator. Three Democrats did change their votes to Peffer, and he was declared senator by a vote of 101–58 over Ingalls. The Populists erupted in a paroxysm of shouts, songs, laughter, and tears. Representatives danced on their desks in their excitement over Ingalls's defeat. The senate quickly dissolved the joint session and left the chamber before Peffer was brought forward. In tears, pale, and nervous, Peffer spoke only briefly, promising to promote the

70 *Kansas City Star,* January 27, 28, 1891; *Topeka Populist,* December 3, 1892; *Fort Scott Daily Monitor,* January 28, 1891. Compare David Rothman, *Politics and Power: The United States Senate, 1869-1901* (Cambridge, Mass., 1966), p. 173.

People's party through which a new society could be created.[71]

Populists continued their celebrations all day and into the night. Alliancemen and reformers throughout the country joined them in welcoming Peffer's election. The National Farmers' Alliance considered the election "the beacon light that will lead to better times," and L. L. Polk regarded the defeat of Ingalls as "the greatest blow at sectionalism that has been struck for twenty-five years." The Knights of Labor exulted over the first Knight senator; countless local reform groups across the nation praised their rejoicing Kansas counterparts, who heard, somewhat needlessly, Elder describe Peffer's election as "the victory of the people."[72]

Peffer's election also demonstrated several things about Kansas politics. It revealed the continuing domination of the People's party by former Republicans, the persistent factionalism of the party and the distrust each faction had of the others, the lack of Democratic influence on Populist decisions but the repeated Democratic efforts to control the party, and the Republicans' unbroken reliance upon traditional sectional and partisan prejudices in their effort to destroy Populism.

But the Populist legislators did their job well; the "people's rebellion" had succeeded. Peffer's election not only overthrew a national symbol of Republicanism, corrupt politics, and sectional and partisan hatred but also provided a national leader for the new forces of political reform. *Harper's Weekly* pointed out the impact of the contest: "The election of Mr. Peffer has been enthusiastically welcomed by Alliancemen in all parts of the country, and has greatly encouraged them in their political action. It is one of the greatest purely political victories they have won, and will doubtless tend to strengthen the third-party movement in that body." The intense national interest in the Kansas senatorial contest also guaranteed Peffer a vast audience and immense publicity for his reform plans. The *Philadelphia Evening Bulletin* concluded,

---

[71] *Kansas City Star*, January 28, 1891; *Topeka Mail*, January 30, 1891; *Topeka Daily Capital*, January 28, 29, 31, 1891; *Chicago Tribune*, January 29, 1891.

[72] *Topeka State Journal*, January 29, 1891; *Topeka Daily Capital*, January 29, 1891; Stuart Noblin, *Leonidas LaFayette Polk, Agrarian Crusader* (Chapel Hill, N.C., 1949), p. 228; *National Economist* (Washington, D.C.), February 7, 1891; *Atchison Daily Champion*, January 29, 1891; *Journal of the Knights of Labor* (Philadelphia), February 5, 19, 1891.

"There has been no senatorial election this winter which has attracted more attention from the country than the one which has just been decided in Kansas. . . . Whether Peffer is a cunning demagogue or whether he is an honest dreamer remains to be seen, but his election to the senate is one of the most curious results of the political upheaval of 1890."[73]

Whether demagogue or dreamer, Peffer had become the first national figure of Populism and, as he told one reporter, "I shall not be the last."[74]

[73] *Harper's Weekly* 35 (February 7, 1891): 103; *Topeka Daily Capital,* February 3, 1891.
[74] *Topeka Daily Capital,* January 30, 1891.

CHAPTER THREE

The Partisans of Politics

WHAT KIND of people were these Populists who so jolted and threatened the established order in 1890 and 1891? For most of the first half of the twentieth century, scholars regarded Populism with an approving eye and pen; as Walter T. K. Nugent has phrased it, the Populist was a Saint George in American historiography and his opposition was a dragon. Historians took their cues from such sympathetic students as Solon Buck and John D. Hicks and viewed Populism as a movement of economic and political protest in the rural areas of the West and South during the 1890s, and Populists as an injured, democratic citizenry possessing foresight concerning important issues of the time. By the mid-1950s, however, a new generation of scholars, political scientists and sociologists as well as historians, sharply reversed the images, and the resultant Populist dragon was a scaly one indeed: anti-Semitic, nativistic, irrational, reacting to nonexistent economic difficulties, and even protofascistic. C. Vann Woodward concluded that the critics threatened to establish "a new maxim in American political thought: *Radix malorum est Populismus.*"[1] Clearly, Populists seemed to torment many historians in the 1950s and 1960s as they had tormented John J. Ingalls in 1890 when he described them as "an enemy whose strength is unknown, a secret organization based upon discontent, bound by oath, led by malevolent and vindictive conspirators, who have everything to gain and nothing to lose in the conflict."[2]

The judgment of the historians, moreover, was no more well founded than that of the partisan Ingalls. With few exceptions, no direct and thorough investigations supported this transformation of the Populist stereotype. It derived from more general studies dealing with Populism only obliquely. The implicit methodological approach seemed to be one of making broad generalizations based on scattered observations of a very few Populists. Though the critics proudly claimed to have "detected and described" the "dark side of Populism" that earlier students had missed, they made no systematic inquiry into the subject that would have resulted in a real understanding of Populism, leaving at least one scholar to wail that "basically, historians know very little more about the Populists today than they knew" thirty years ago.[3]

This impasse has resulted at least in part from a failure to consider seriously the approach conducive to an analysis of a popular movement. Both the "attempt to purge the American past of dissident elements," as Norman Pollack has described recent historiography, and "the tortuous apologetics of the Populist defenders," as Oscar Handlin has characterized the even more recent rebuttals, have emphasized Populist rhetoric. But like all major popular movements, Populism included many different people with many divergent attitudes and ideas and had different factions dominant at different times. In short, today's scholar can find some support for nearly any claim he may care to make.[4]

The failure to acknowledge explicitly the diversity of Populists and its implications or to consider the time dimension in discussing Populism has obstructed the understanding of the contours of the

1 Walter T. K. Nugent, *The Tolerant Populists* (Chicago, 1963), pp. 3-32; C. Vann Woodward, "The Populist Heritage and the Intellectual," in *The Burden of Southern History* (New York, 1960), p. 147. See also Theodore Saloutos, "The Professors and the Populists," *Agricultural History* 40 (October 1966): 235-54.

2 John J. Ingalls to P. I. Bonebreak, August 18, 1890, Ingalls Papers.

3 Norman Pollack, "Fear of Man: Populism, Authoritarianism, and the Historian," *Agricultural History* 39 (April 1965): 61; Irwin Unger, "Critique of Norman Pollack's 'Fear of Man,'" ibid., p. 78; J. Rogers Hollingsworth, "Commentary; Populism: The Problem of Rhetoric and Reality," ibid., p. 81; Oscar Handlin, "Reconsidering the Populists," ibid., p. 68.

4 Pollack, "Fear of Man," p. 65; Handlin, "Reconsidering the Populists," p. 69.

movement and prevented the construction of an accurate Populist model. Much of this book will suggest the variations in Populism over time that might have given rise to the contrasting historical interpretations. Since this is a study of internal Populist politics, traditional methodology can be effectively employed, but methods of data quantification can also permit the historian to make legitimate generalized statements about the Populists as a group. Theodore Saloutos has written that, in the 1890s, "there wasn't anything mysterious or secretive about who the Populists were," but the recent debate over Populism has obscured even their identity until the questions to be answered have become the elementary ones of who and what kind of people were the Populists.[5] In this chapter I will attempt to provide some tentative answers to such basic questions for the Populists of 1890 through an aggregate data study of electoral behavior in that year's election in Kansas, the center of Populism.

Quantitative history, of course, has certain limitations of its own. Its applicability is sharply restricted by the kind and amount of historical information available. Thus the major technique used here is that of ecological correlations, simply because the data necessary for individual correlations are not available. The following discussion is therefore generally relevant only to the behavior of electorates, usually at the county level, and not to that of individual voters.[6] Similarly, neither the data nor the methods avail-

---

[5] Saloutos, "Professors and Populists," p. 254; Hollingsworth, "Commentary," pp. 81-85. There have been several recent and notable attempts to explicitly identify Populists and to suggest some statistically valid characteristics. Unfortunately, thorough consideration of the time dimension is generally absent even in these accounts of some statistical sophistication. See Stanley B. Parsons, "Who Were the Nebraska Populists?" *Nebraska History* 44 (June 1963): 83-99; Walter T. K. Nugent, "Some Parameters of Populism," *Agricultural History* 40 (October 1966): 255-70; and Sheldon Hackney, *Populism to Progressivism in Alabama* (Princeton, N.J., 1969). Other recent and more generalized attempts to determine political characteristics and explain political change during this period, the assumptions and conclusions of which are not all in agreement with this book, include Paul Kleppner, *The Cross of Culture: A Social Analysis of Midwestern Politics, 1850-1900* (New York, 1970), and Richard J. Jensen, *The Winning of the Midwest: Social and Political Conflict, 1888-1896* (Chicago, 1971). In light of their emphasis upon the religious background of political behavior see my earlier "Pentecostal Politics in Kansas: Religion, the Farmers' Alliance, and the Gospel of Populism," *Kansas Quarterly* 1 (Fall 1969): 24-35.

[6] W. S. Robinson, "Ecological Correlations and Behavior of Individuals," *American Sociological Review* 15 (June 1950): 351-57; Austin Ranney, "The

able are appropriate for testing such theories as political alienation as independent factors. The conclusions necessarily follow the recorded measurable statistics of economic and demographic information. Here published census data and voting statistics from the primary basis for comparative analyses of Populist, Republican, and Democratic voting behavior. In order to test the validity of some of the Populist rhetoric and some of the claims of historians, I used a stepwise regression program to consider the influence on voting behavior of those variables originally regarded as important and for which data were available:

a) The previous partisan preferences of each county;
b) The percentage of the resident farm-owning families on mortgaged farms in each county;
c) The percentage of families residing on farms in each county;
d) For encumbered acres, the proportion of the acre-value under mortgage in each county;
e) The average interest rate in each county;
f) The percentage of the population engaged in manufacturing in each county;
g) The voter turnout in 1890 in each county;
h) The average farm-acre value in each county;
i) The per capita assessed valuation in each county;
j) The average value of farm products per farm in each county;
k) The percentage of the improved farm acres planted in corn in each county;
l) The percentage of the improved farm acres planted in wheat in each county;
m) The percentage of the population of foreign birth in each county;
n) The percentage of the population of Protestant religion in each county;
o) The percentage of the population of Catholic religion in each county.[7]

Utility and Limitations of Aggregate Data in the Study of Electoral Behavior," in *Essays on the Behavioral Study of Politics,* ed. Austin Ranney (Urbana, Ill., 1962), pp. 91-102.

[7] These variables were calculated from data in the *Eleventh Decennial Census of the United States* (1890) and the *Biennial Reports* of the Kansas secretary of state. As a contest for a state office of low visibility, the secretary of state

While the Republicans tried to destroy the popular coalition formed by the People's party by appealing to old-party loyalties, waving the bloody shirt, and emphasizing the divisive issue of prohibition, the Populists rejected these as irrelevant issues during a depression and focused much of their campaign on economic questions. At the August state convention, Mary Elizabeth Lease stated the Populist position: "Forget party affiliations of the past, forget moral issues of the present, in this great struggle for our homes."[8] The election results as tested reflected this campaign concern. No other variable was as important in predicting a county's Populist vote as the percentage of its resident farm-owning families that lived on mortgaged farms. The correlation between this ratio and Populist vote was a highly significant .526: mortgaged Kansas farmers evidently were much more likely to vote Populist than were those unencumbered. The impact of the mortgage issue was so overwhelming that this was also the most important variable in predicting a county's Republican vote, even more important than knowledge of the county's Republican vote in previous elections. The correlation between the mortgage ratio and the Republican vote was −.546: the more a county's farmers had mortgaged homes the less it voted for the GOP, and the converse.

That the Populists staggered under the heaviest, most onerous mortgages, as they claimed, is not so clear. Indeed, the simple (Pearsonian) correlation coefficient between Populist vote and the proportion of the county's average acre-value under mortgage was negligible (−.076) and of no significance in predicting Populist vote. In the stepwise regression program, in fact, this variable reflecting the degree of mortgage indebtedness was the least important of the fifteen variables in the prediction of Populist vote. It was no more related to a county's Populist vote than to its Democratic vote (−.077), but it was significantly and positively correlated (.235) with the Republican vote. Apparently it was more likely for a county with heavily mortgaged farms to vote Republican.

---

election was the best indicator of party strength, and the partisan division of votes for that office was used in this study. Correlations with census data involve 106 counties in analysis; correlations with other voting statistics involve only 105 counties, the transient Garfield County being aggregated with Finney. Unless otherwise stated, the significance level used is .05.

8 *Fort Scott Daily Monitor*, August 14, 1890.

TABLE 1

Mortgage Variables and Populist Voting, 1890

Variable	25 counties with Populist majorities	25 least Populist counties
% of resident farm-owning families on mortgaged farms	median 42.52 average 39.66	median 25.66 average 23.93
% of average acre-value under mortgage for encumbered acres	median 47.01 average 49.13 (with Seward County excluded	median 42.58 average 50.59 42.31)
Average interest rate	8.80	8.77

The nature of the data, however, undermines that conclusion. The data indicate the extent of mortgage indebtedness for only those acres that were mortgaged. Thus it was possible for a county with only a small proportion of its farms mortgaged, but those heavily, to appear greatly encumbered as a whole, while in actuality it might have been in relatively favorable financial shape. Gray County in the Republican area of southwestern Kansas might be an example of such a county. A comparatively high 54 percent of the average acre-value of its encumbered acres was under mortgage while it cast only 12 percent of its vote for the People's party. Countering the superficial conclusion is that scarcely more than 7 percent of the county's farmers had mortgaged farms. If voters did in fact split along economic lines, such counties would obscure the result. Another difficulty is that the correlation coefficient is highly sensitive to a few extreme values of either variable. The inclusion of Seward County, with a small 9 percent Populist vote and the extremely high figure of 207 percent of its average acre-value under mortgage, may have produced an importantly lower correlation than that existing among the other counties (See Table 1).

Further restricting the reliability of the proposal that heavily mortgaged counties were not significantly more likely to vote Populist are the contingency table and chi-square statistic relating the two variables. They indicate a strong (positive) measure of association, with a probability of less than .005 that the Populist vote is independent of the index of mortgage indebtedness. That the simple correlation was quite small and negative suggests a non-linear relationship between a county's Populist vote and the proportion of its average acre-value under mortgage for encumbered acres.

To clarify this relationship and to reduce the influence of extreme values without excluding them, I determined the rank-order correlation (Spearman's r_s) between the two variables for each of the three subregions of the state. I divided the state into subregions because the pace of settlement created a pattern of regional development and because there was, broadly, a geographical distribution of Populist and non-Populist counties, with Republicans and Democrats predominating in both the older, better-settled, and developed eastern third and the sparsely and recently settled western third. Under these conditions all three correlations indicated a positive relation between the variables, though that of the western subregion, the locus of most of the extreme values of both variables, was not significant (.151). The correlation within the eastern subregion was .388, significant at the .05 level, and that of the central third, the center of Kansas Populist strength, was .521, significant at the .01 level.

Closely linked with the mortgage issue was that of interest rates. The Populists repeatedly contended that the moneylender and mortgage broker charged exorbitant interest on loans, perhaps in an attempt to gain the borrower's land. Although the reported interest rates may not be adequate to test the Populist contention accurately, the available data did not really support the Populist position. Support for none of the three parties was associated significantly with interest rates, nor did the variable aid importantly in predicting any party's vote. Because the greater risks of lending in frontier areas caused interest rates to increase in a westward progression, generally regardless of political conditions, regional rank-order correlations were again made with the Populist vote. The same broad pattern prevailed as before, all three coefficients being positive, with the highest (.293) being in the Populistic central region and those of the eastern (.168) and western (.108) thirds being somewhat lower. The first verged on insignificance at the .05 level while the others were clearly not significant. In addition to all the above, the interest rates under consideration, varying from 7 to 11 percent, were not the oppressive charges of which the Populists complained, though a partisan might reasonably argue that any usurious rates would not be reported.[9] It might be further noted that historians, in evaluating the Populist contentions concerning interest rates, have not always carefully distinguished between farm mortgages and chattel mortgages nor recognized the full role and importance of the latter. In order to meet payments on farm mortgages, debtors often had to arrange chattel mortgages, thus entering a business with little regard for law or adversity. In 1887 the state labor commissioner reported the average annual interest rate on chattel mortgages in Shawnee County to be 156 percent. In predominantly agricultural counties the average rate was generally lower, though still at least twice the maximum legal rate of 10 percent.[10]

Thus a county with a relatively high proportion of mortgaged farmers was more likely to vote Populist, though the influence one way or the other of the extent of individual mortgaging and of interest rates is not clear. Perhaps these served more as a rallying cry of Populist orators to convince the farmer that any mortgage was ipso facto evidence of impotence and oppression. Just as likely, however, is that in a deflationary period all mortgages, even if initiated for land speculation or machinery, represented a burden and especially so psychologically if entered into during an inflationary time with a promised future. One historian, moreover, has convincingly demonstrated that Populists more often mortgaged their land from necessity than from entrepreneurial ambitions than did members of the old parties and that the responsibility for the general financial collapse lay disproportionately on the shoulders

[9] In a situation of generalized usury, however, the face rate of interest charges should be at the legal maximum, which certainly was not the case in Kansas in 1890. For a general discussion of the whole mortgage problem, see Allan G. Bogue, *Money at Interest: The Farm Mortgage on the Middle Border* (Ithaca, N.Y., 1955).

[10] *Second Annual Report of the Bureau of Labor and Industrial Statistics* (Topeka, Kans., 1887), pp. 99-108.

of the latter.[11] In any case, those who were mortgaged rejected overwhelmingly the political party that had sponsored such improbable dreams until the dreamers and the yeomen had been trapped in a nightmare.

The percentage of families residing on farms was the second most important variable in predicting a county's Populist vote. Other variables had higher simple correlations with Populist vote, but its .241 was significant and, with the first variable held constant, the partial correlation between Populist vote and this measure of rural population was .461. This variable was not significantly related to the Republican vote, suggesting the broad nature of Republican support in Kansas, while its simple correlation with the Democratic vote was a significant −.433, indicating that rural counties were distinctly not Democratic counties. The Democratic vote centered in counties with relatively large urban populations: Leavenworth, Atchison, Wyandotte (Kansas City), and Shawnee (Topeka) in the northeast and Sedgwick (Wichita) in south-central Kansas.

Counties did not report precinct returns for the 1890 election to the Kansas secretary of state, but vote tabulations as irregularly published by newspapers of individual counties further revealed the relation between voting and residence. Not surprisingly, the Populists achieved their greatest strength in rural precincts, attracted considerable support from mixed precincts, and languished in the urban precincts.[12] This pattern remained fairly uniform regardless of region. For example, the Populists polled only 17.1 percent of the vote in rural Grant precinct of Douglas County in northeastern Kansas, but they garnered a scant 1.9 percent of the vote of the county seat, Lawrence. Where they did attract more substantial town support, their rural vote generally increased correspondingly, as in Ellsworth County in central Kansas. There the town of Kanopolis cast more than a quarter of its votes for the third party, and the rural township of Ash Creek delivered an overwhelming 96.4 percent of its votes to the People's party.

Table 2 indicates the approximate division of the three-party

---

11 Nugent, "Some Parameters of Populism," pp. 261-70.

12 As used here, "rural" simply means a precinct (i.e., a township) with no communities large enough to be listed separately in the census. "Mixed" refers to any precinct with both farmers and villagers in residence.

town vote according to community size. The major strength of the Republican party was apparently concentrated in the small and medium-sized towns where its share of the vote far surpassed its percentage of the state's total vote. The Populists usually cut sharply into the Republican rural poll and the Democrats were dominant in the largest cities, though even there the Republicans retained only a slightly smaller proportion of votes than their share on the state level because of the very low Populist percentage.

TABLE 2

Voting Distribution by Town Size, 1890

Community size	Republican vote	Democratic vote	Populist vote
To 2,500	56.7%	32.1%	11.2%
2,501-5,000	57.6	24.7	17.7
5,001-10,000	52.2	32.0	15.8
Over 10,000	38.9	52.2	8.9
State totals	41.3	19.1	39.6

The Democrats attracted at each level of community size a considerably greater following proportionately than they did in the state as a whole. In the important urban centers the Democratic party even achieved majority status, but its very poor showing outside the cities greatly reduced its share of the state total vote. The negative association between rural dwellers and Democrats has already been noted, but even more significant was the highly positive correlation (.508) between a county's Democratic vote and the percentage of its population engaged in manufacturing. This measure of urbanization was the most important variable in predicting a county's Democratic vote.

Unlike the Democrats, the People's party collected at each level in Table 2 a considerably smaller vote proportionately than it did in the state as a whole. Clearly, the Populist stronghold was among the farmers, so much so that Populist congressional candidate L. C. Clark felt constrained to speak in Atchison on the eve of the election "to correct the impression that it [the People's party] was against the towns."[13]

This interest in the election outcome encouraged high voter

[13] *Atchison Daily Champion,* October 9, 1890.

turnout throughout Kansas, and 76.7 percent of the state's age-eligible males voted in 1890. Voter turnout was regularly high in the late nineteenth century, but the 1890 rate represented nearly a 10 percent increase over the rate of the 1886 state election.[14] Of the ninety-three counties that voted in both elections, the voter turnout of sixty-one increased in 1890. The vast majority of those counties that experienced a decrease was in the western half of the state, from which a great exodus took place following the onset of hard times, deflating turnout statistics and perhaps removing the discontented who, had they stayed, might have voted for the third party and thereby increased the recorded association between Populists and interest rates. As one western Kansas paper phrased it, "White covered wagons are carrying [Populist congressional candidate William] Baker votes out of this district by the hundred every day."[15] The closeness of the vote also apparently affected turnout, drawing voters who sensed the marginal value of an additional vote. Forty-two counties carried by only a plurality vote by one of the three parties had greater turnouts and only fifteen had lower turnouts than in 1886. Those counties carried by a majority vote divided much more evenly: nineteen had higher and seventeen had lower turnouts.

Political scientists like to puncture the venerable (and vulnerable) notion of the independent farmer as the backbone of American democracy by pointing out the well-established fact of low political involvement and high political indifference among farmers. Such,

[14] Comparable figures as to age-eligible males were not available for the earlier election, so the crude measure of total votes as a percentage of total population was used. The data bias in this approach, however, was usually to increase turnout percentages for the 1886 election and to decrease them for the second campaign, and thus it is not unreasonable to accept the 10 percent figure as representing a real increase in voter participation. (Because the population was determined and reported in early spring, and because voting requirements were often both easy and loosely enforced, boom years with their high rates of immigration would make available for November voting more citizens than indicated by the population report, which of course formed the base for calculating turnout. In years of depression and emigration the process would be reversed.) The population figures used in this discussion are from the *Biennial Reports* of the Kansas State Board of Agriculture. The election of 1886 was the nearest previous, nonpresidential year, state election to that of 1890 and occurred before the collapse of the state's economic boom that precipitated Populism.

[15] *Glen Elder Herald* quoted in *Atchison Daily Champion,* October 16, 1890.

however, was not the situation in Kansas in 1890. There was a positive association on the county level between voter turnout and the percentage of families residing on farms, although the simple correlation of .193 was just below the .05 significance level.

TABLE 3

Turnout and Residence, by Counties, 1890

% Rural	% Average turnout rate
Over 80	76.27
70-80	77.45
60-70	82.35
50-60	80.54
40-50	74.02
Under 40	62.74

Table 3 further illustrates the relation between turnout and residence. There is no direct linear progression, yet the statistics indicate a reversal of the usual findings: voter turnout was by far the lowest in urban areas and the highest in heavily rural counties. In fact, the only true metropolitan county in the state at that time, Wyandotte (Kansas City), recorded a turnout of but 43.7 percent and was the only county that did not surpass the 50 percent level. The slight depression in turnout figures in the highest ranges of rurality on Table 3 reflect those counties in the western part of the state where the contest was not so close as to generate the feeling common in other places, where extremely sparse settlement and long distances made it physically more difficult to vote, and perhaps where emigration affected turnout as in the 1886–1890 interval.

With turnout higher in rural areas, it was of course linked to Populist voting. At the county level there was a significant simple correlation of .296 between voter turnout and Populist voting behavior. This did not merely reflect the association between Populism and rural residence, for it was a higher correlation than that between those two variables and there was a distinction between rural counties that went Populist and those that did not. Rural counties captured by the Populists had higher turnouts on the average and far more often experienced increased voter turnouts than those rural counties won by the old parties, and when turnout decreased it was proportionately more frequent in non-Populist counties. Considering all counties, the relationship between turnout and Republican vote was negative but of negligible importance. Turnout was much more negatively correlated with Democratic vote (−.363) and, of course, with manufacturing population (−.417). Evidently, Populist concern for increased political participation took real as well as rhetorical form.

The other variables important in predicting Populist vote suggest the economic marginality that characterized Populist counties. Populist vote was negatively correlated with average farm-acre value, the coefficient of −.209 just significant at the .05 level. With the variables measuring rurality and mortgaged farmers held constant, however, the importance of this connection sharply dropped. This reflects the geographical position of the Populist counties between the high land values about the eastern cities (there was a correlation of .803 between farm-acre value and the manufacturing population index of urbanization) and the low land values in the sparsely settled, arid western region.

The variable measuring per capita assessed valuation for each county was the third most important factor in predicting Populist vote. It had a negative simple correlation of −.352 with Populist vote, and even with the first two variables controlled it had a partial correlation of −.239. High per capita assessed valuations did not occur in the urban counties of eastern Kansas but were most common in the western subregion. Indeed, per capita assessed valuation was negatively associated with the manufacturing population index and significantly positively with the index of rurality. Despite this, Populist counties were more likely to have lower per capita assessed valuations. This tends to support both the Populist claim of being among society's have-nots and the hypothesis that emigration removed the discontented and left the more prosperous in the western subregion, thus partially explaining the low Populist vote in that area.

The fourth and last variable of major importance in predicting a county's Populist vote was its average value of farm products per farm. With mortgaged farmers controlled, the partial correlation between the two was −.352, again suggesting the relative privation of Populist voters. These four major variables produced a multiple correlation coefficient of .699, indicating that they explain nearly one-half of the variation in Populist votes in 1890.

Historians and social scientists have recognized that specific farm movements are generally confined to specific types of farming areas, and they have traditionally assigned Populism to the wheat growers. Some historians have made a bald equation that "as the area of wheat production moved westward, so did farm protest." Social scientists have generally been more circumspect, pointing out the vulnerability of farmers who produce for national and world markets and the natural tendency for such insecure agricultural groups to support radical parties which champion their interests.[16]

This association apparently did not hold in 1890 Kansas. At the county level, Populist vote was more closely correlated with the proportion of improved acres in corn (.285) than in wheat (.069). Though both correlations were positive, that with wheat became negative when the major variables reflecting mortgages and rurality were held constant and certainly was not statistically significant itself. Since corn was the pioneer crop on the Kansas frontier, perhaps the Populists were more recent arrivals who had not yet adapted to an area well suited for wheat production, or perhaps they were less commercially oriented than their non-Populist neighbors. Evidently, however, there was at least a grain of truth in the Populist political exhortation to raise more hell and less corn.

The data available here also failed to support some of the recent claims of historians about the nature of Populism. This analysis at the county level particularly did not sustain the charge against Populism of nativism. The proportion of foreign-born in a county's population bore little relation to its Populist vote. Both old parties, however, had significant correlations with the foreign-born. Democratic counties were more likely to have higher proportions of foreign-born in their populations (a correlation of .258) while Republican counties were more likely to have lower proportions of foreign-born (−.282) than Populist counties.

None of the three parties was significantly correlated with Prot-

16 Samuel P. Hays, *The Response to Industrialism, 1885-1914* (Chicago, 1957), p. 28; S. M. Lipset, P. F. Lazarsfeld, A. H. Barton, and Juan Linz, "The Psychology of Voting: An Analysis of Political Behavior," in *Handbook of Social Psychology,* ed. Gardner Lindzey (Cambridge, Mass., 1954), 2: 1124-37.

estant population, and knowledge of it was of negligible importance in predicting either a county's Populist or Democratic vote. It was of greater importance in predicting Republican vote and was positively correlated with the Republican vote when the variable reflecting mortgaged farmers was held constant. Of even more importance in predicting a county's Republican vote was its Catholic population. There was a simple correlation of −.296 between these two variables, and the stepwise regression program considered the knowledge of a county's Catholic population second in importance among the socioeconomic variables to only the knowledge of its mortgaged farmers in predicting its Republican poll. Neither Catholics nor mortgaged farmers supported the GOP. Catholicism was positively correlated with Democratic vote (.360) and was more important in predicting a county's Democratic vote than all other socioeconomic factors except the variables indicating the mortgaged and the manufacturing populations. Populism once again occupied an intermediate position, with a weakly negative, but far from significant, correlation with Catholicism. Thus, if any party in Kansas in 1890 deserved the epithet of nativist, it was not the People's party. A more deserving candidate was Populism's fiercest opponent, the Grand Old Party.

In general, then, counties that were carried by the People's party were more likely to have large proportions of their populations turning out to vote and living on farms which were mortgaged, which had lower land values, and which raised more corn than wheat. Republican counties were less rural, had fewer mortgaged farms and fewer Catholics, and had higher assessed valuations. Democratic counties were more often urban, engaged in manufacturing, and had relatively more Catholics and foreign-born. Though the evidence is not yet conclusive, apparently the Populists of Kansas generally recognized their position better than have many subsequent scholars.

Soon after the election in November 1890, Republican Governor Lyman Humphrey informed a correspondent that the votes of the People's party were "mostly taken from us, of course." A week later Democratic leader Thomas Moonlight explained to Grover Cleveland that Democrats had overwhelmingly entered the Populist ranks in Kansas.[17] It remained for Populist Senator Peffer to attempt to gauge accurately the relative strength of the various factions within his party, and appropriately so, for the composition of the People's party with respect to the former partisan affiliations of its members was crucial to the party and its political course. Peffer estimated that the Kansas Populists of 1890 included 45,000 normally Republican voters; 35,000 former Democrats; 33,000 Union Laborites; and 2,000 ex-Prohibitionists.[18] By determining the difference between each party's actual vote and its expected vote, given its 1888 vote and the voter turnout differential of the two years, an estimation of partisan composition remarkably close to Peffer's is obtained. On this basis the Kansas Populists of 1890 consisted of 41,667 Republicans; 35,867 Democrats; 34,024 Union Laborites; and 4,375 Prohibitionists. These groups provided, respectively, 35.94 percent, 30.94 percent, 29.35 percent, and 3.77 percent of the total Populist vote.

Correlation coefficients further clarify the nature of the party's membership. With the county again as the unit of analysis, the Populist vote of 1890 correlated positively with the Republican vote of 1886 at .201 and negatively with the Democratic vote of the same year (−.244), indicating the relatively greater similarity between 1890 Populist counties and previously Republican counties than between Populist and formerly Democratic electorates. The disruption within the GOP caused by the new party is also evident in the correlation between the Republican votes of 1886 and 1890: .249, a figure not greatly more significant than that of the Populist-Republican correlation. The different impact of the People's party upon the Democracy is evident in the correlation of .514 between the Democratic votes of 1886 and 1890. Correlation coefficients between the 1890 returns and the voting results of 1888, which reflect the reintroduction of a third party into the political arena, reveal not surprisingly a strong positive relationship between Union Labor and Populist strength (.417) and again a closer Populist relationship with Republicans (−.257) than with Democrats (−.423),

---

17 L. U. Humphrey to George W. Moore & Co., November 19, 1890, Humphrey Papers, KSHS; Thomas Moonlight to Grover Cleveland, November 27, 1890, Cleveland Papers.

18 Peffer, *The Farmer's Side* (New York, 1891), p. 157.

though both are negative. The swath cut through politics by Populism left the older parties positively if weakly correlated with each other (.126) in 1890.

The greater absolute strength of the ex-Republicans within the People's party is thus reflected in the correlations between the 1890 Populist vote and earlier election results. Another indication is the change in vote shares held by the parties between 1888 and 1890. The Republican share of the state's poll declined by 14.17 percentage points (55.30 percent to 41.13 percent) and the Democratic share by 12.19 points while the third-party share increased by 27.85 points from the Union Labor 1888 figure of 11.57 percent.[19] Thus the People's party clearly drew more Republicans to its ranks than any other group of ex-partisans. And yet, the common assumption that the People's party was overwhelmingly ex-Republican in composition is clearly inaccurate. The former Republicans held only a small plurality of the party's strength and could be outvoted by the Democratic and Union Labor elements—which had a tradition of cooperation.

Despite the absolute greater numbers of ex-Republicans within the People's party, the movement clearly appealed disproportionately to Democrats. If the Democrats lost only 12.19 percentage points to the GOP's 14.17, that represented a loss of 39.08 percent of their 1888 vote compared to a Republican loss of 25.62 percent of its 1888 membership by 1890. This relative difference in the effectiveness of the Populist appeal is further indicated by the correlations at the county level of analysis between the increase in the third party's share of the vote and the decrease in the shares of the two old parties between 1888 and 1890. Both figures are naturally strongly positive, but the Democratic loss/Populist gain correlation is somewhat higher (.801) than the corresponding Republican figure (.729).

Again, of the state's 105 counties, only one witnessed a loss of 50 percent or more in its Republican share of the vote between 1888 and 1890, and that county (Sedgwick) was the center of Resub-

---

[19] The difference came from a Prohibitionist decline of 1.49 points. A party's "share" of the vote here refers to its proportion of the total vote expressed in percentages, and "percentage point" here refers to 1 percent of the total vote and not of the party's vote.

mission Republicanism and as such one of the few counties in which Republican loss did not necessarily mean Populist gain. But fifty counties lost 50 percent or more of their Democratic share of the 1888 vote by 1890, ranging upward to an incredible decline of 98.11 percent in one county. This impact upon their own party would further prompt Democratic politicians to attempt to manipulate the People's party to accomplish their partisan objectives.

The decision of voters to enter the People's party, however, seemed, except for the Union Laborites, not without reference to their expectation of the election outcome within their particular counties, indicating a high degree of mass political knowledge and involvement. The stronger the Republicans were in 1888, and thus ostensibly the more certain of 1890 success, the more willing the Democrats were to leave their correspondingly hopeless party for the new People's party in 1890. A tetrachoric correlation coefficient of .252 existed between the 1888 Republican vote and the proportion of the 1888 Democratic vote lost by 1890. Consistently, the stronger the Democratic party in 1888, and thus the greater the possibility for a Democratic victory in 1890, especially if the People's party could split the formerly Republican vote, the greater was the tendency for Democrats to remain steadfast in their partisan allegiance. In those nine counties that had Democratic votes of 40 percent or more in 1888 (no county had a Democratic majority), for example, the Democratic vote declined by only 19.34 percent from 1888 to 1890, compared to a decrease of 50.32 percent for all other counties. Those nine counties contained 22.03 percent of the state's Democrats in 1890 compared to only 14.82 percent two years previously, and the Democratic share of the total vote of those counties varied only from 43.80 percent in 1888 to 40.78 percent in 1890. Table 4 illustrates the Democratic disposition.

Republicans also considered the probable actions of their traditional opponents before casting their ballots. A Populist victory over the GOP might be necessary, but a Democratic victory would be a catastrophe. Republicans generally proved more stable in their affiliation when the apparent chance for a Democratic victory was greater, and less constant in counties with little likelihood of a Democratic triumph. In contrast to the Democratic practice, then, the stronger their party in 1888 the more Republicans deserted it

TABLE 4

Strength and Losses in Democratic Voting, 1888-1890

Democratic voting 1888	Number of counties	County average proportion of 1888 Democratic vote lost by 1890
0-25%	21	59.43%
25-30%	21	51.97%
30-33.13%	21	50.52%
33.14-36.99%	21	46.40%
37-49.09%	21	30.42%

in 1890 to enter the People's party. In the nine most Republican counties of 1888, for a comparative example, the Republican share of the vote plummeted from 66.60 percent to 51.52 percent between 1888 and 1890. This Republican tendency was less clear than its Democratic counterpart because of the strength of Resubmission Republicans in such urban areas as Wichita, Leavenworth, and Kansas City which also had above average Democratic concentrations; and because the massive exodus of the less-established from the far western counties permitted the retention or expansion of the Republican percentage of the vote.

If Republicans kept a wary eye on the Democrats before committing themselves it was not without cause. The marginal value of a Republican convert far surpassed that of a Democratic adherent to the new party. The Kansas GOP had frequently demonstrated its capacity to defeat easily a fusion coalition of Democrats and third-party voters, and the People's party therefore necessarily required substantial numbers of normally Republican voters in order to achieve any success. A Populist vote taken from the Republicans counted twice, once for the Populists and once against the Republicans; a vote acquired from the Democrats counted but once. The importance of this distinction is obvious. Of the twenty-five counties which returned a Populist majority in 1890, only one could have been carried without the assistance of those Populists of Republican antecedents; but eleven of those counties could have been carried without any support from Populists of Democratic antecedents. One other county won with a plurality would still have remained

Populist without the assistance of previously Democratic voters.[20] Indeed, strictly speaking, the third party could have captured every county in the state through Republican converts alone, and not a single county with only former Democrats voting its ticket. Thus it was more realistic for Populist leaders to appeal to discontented Republicans rather than to seek expedient-minded Democrats; and any policy or tactic which threatened to drive former Republicans from the Populist ranks, even if directly replaced by Democrats thereby attracted, would be suicidal. Peffer and McLallin understood this if Wakefield and Harris did not.

Correlation coefficients calculated between the Populist county pluralities and the percentage-point losses of the two old parties also indicate the greater importance of Republican-derived Populist strength.[21] Both coefficients were strongly positive, of course, reflecting the general movement of increased third-party strength and decreased support for the old parties, but that with the Republican figure was significantly stronger than that with the Democratic figure (tetrachoric correlations of .753 and .501), again revealing the Populist dependence upon ex-Republicans for actual victory.

The absolute necessity of winning Republican votes placed former Republicans in prominence among the Populist leadership in 1890, even out of proportion to the number of ex-Republicans within the ranks of the People's party. Peffer was only the prize of the Republican catch which also included Benjamin Clover, Stephen McLallin, Frank Doster, William Baker, Percy Daniels, and many others. Ninety-three Populists were elected to the legislature in November 1890, and of the eighty-three that disclosed their previous party affiliation fifty-four had been Republicans, only fifteen Democrats and fourteen Union Laborites.[22] This pattern also held on the local level. In Brown County, for example, which had nearly equal Republican and Democratic contributions to the People's party, sixty-seven of the 134 delegates to the 1890 Populist county conventions could be identified by previous party affiliations, and

20 The Republican loss in percentage points between 1888 and 1890 is here taken to represent Populists of Republican antecedents; similarly Populists of Democratic antecedents are estimated from the Democratic loss over that period.

21 "Plurality" as used here indicates the difference between a county's Populist vote share and the larger share of the two older parties.

22 *Kansas Legislative Blue Book* (Topeka, 1891).

of these forty-one had been Republicans, twenty-one Democrats, and five Union Laborites.[23] The prominence of these former Republicans arose from the Populist reliance upon the heavily Republican Farmers' Alliance and from the rebellion among Republican partisans against the deceptions of their leaders. This prominence, however, did not go unchallenged. From the initial steps toward third-party action, there existed a struggle for leadership among the factions of the new party. Union Laborites believed the laws of primogeniture entitled them to leadership of the new party; former Republicans claimed it as their representative right; and ex-Democrats asserted their abilities as traditional and accomplished manipulators of anti-Republican coalitions. All wanted power for its own sake. But practical policy distinctions were at least as important to these men who had already rejected one party for ideological reasons. Former Republicans and Union Laborites agreed on the need for an active government with a social and economic vision of positive and national scope—to the horror of the Democratic-Populists; the demand of the former Democrats for an end to prohibition filled the Republican-Populists with revulsion and the Union Laborites with indifference; and the insistence of the Democratic-Populists upon the continued relevance of the tariff as a major political issue astounded both Union Laborites and the regenerated Republicans; the Union Laborites doubted the sincerity of the reform conversion of both their new allies and feared they would accept half a loaf to feed the hungry radicals. Above all, the prejudice of years of violence and ridicule brought profound distrust into the People's party, and especially between former Republicans and ex-Democrats. Each worked more easily with the Union Labor faction than with the other.

In many counties the People's party explicitly nominated candidates on the basis of their partisan background in an attempt to unify the party and balance its ticket. Reports of the outcomes of factional struggles commonly appeared in the press, as did this

[23] Previous partisan affiliation was determined by delegate attendance at previous county conventions during the 1880s in Brown County. That fully half of the Populist delegates had never before attended a political convention in Brown County again reveals the increased popular political participation that was an essential element of Populism.

description of the effects of one Populist county convention: "After the meeting adjourned the [former] Greenbackers and Union Laborites were very jubilant, the [ex-]Republicans looked careworn, and the [erstwhile] Democrats were not as jubilant as they have been in times past." Mutual distrust also encouraged vote trading and scratched tickets. Democrats within and without the People's party pressured the organization on both candidates and tactics, and both groups frequently announced their intention to vote for only the former Democrats on the Populist ticket.[24]

Thus the People's party in 1890 was more an uneasy coalition of former opponents temporarily united through dissatisfaction, distress, hope, and hard politics than a unified and cohesive political party. It had achieved substantial success through suppressing such divisive issues as prohibition and partisan traditions and muffling the attempts of old party leaders to activate the jealousy, suspicion, and distrust which they had carefully encouraged for decades and which now lurked within the People's party. To maintain its advantage, its own leaders would have to avoid antagonizing the various factions. And fusion with unrepentant Democrats made as much sense to the decisive Republican-Populists as fusion with the GOP would have pleased those Populists of Democratic background. Fusion would not be, as some Democratic-Populists in 1890 and some historians since believed, the salvation of Populism, but its destruction.

24 *Erie Republican-Record,* August 8, 1890; *Atchison Daily Champion,* July 25, August 24, 1890; *Lawrence Gazette,* July 24, 1890; *Topeka Mail,* August 15, 1890; W. C. Jones to W. H. Sears, [early November 1890], Sears Papers.

CHAPTER FOUR

The National Crusade

KANSAS POPULISTS learned much from the turbulent campaign of 1890 and the subsequent senatorial election. To maintain momentum and deprive the Republican party of its major political argument, the Populists had to increase the scope of their activities. They had to launch a national third party, both to push their reform goals and to prevent Kansas Republicans from charging that their independent action would result only in the national triumph of an unregenerate Democracy, entrenched as it was in the Solid South, where political independence was not permitted. The Populist effort in 1891, then, had to be primarily an attempt to convert the South from its traditional Democratic allegiance to an acceptance of the new party they would organize. Senator-elect William A. Peffer, as the most conspicuous spokesman of the People's party, would play a major role in this dual effort in national politics.

The task of organizing a national party received first priority. Various independent state parties based on Alliance strength had conducted reform campaigns in 1890 throughout the Northwest. Though the People's party of Kansas proved the most successful, these independents elsewhere elected numerous legislators, three congressmen, and one senator, James H. Kyle of South Dakota. In the South, alliancemen had carefully avoided such third-party action, but working through the Democratic party they elected four governors, gained control of the legislatures of eight states, and pledged as many as forty-four successful congressional candidates to Alliance principles. Now the Kansas Populists hoped to consolidate this mass unrest into an integrated political party. As early as June 1890, Peffer had predicted that the People's party would not remain strictly a Kansas movement but would develop into a major national party. Repeatedly he advocated the unification of the nation's reform organizations as a step toward that objective. He particularly urged Southern alliancemen, at their December conference in Ocala, Florida, to follow the Kansas example of renouncing partisan prejudice in order to unite on new issues.[1]

Others took a more direct role in organizing a national party. Led by William F. Rightmire, John H. Rice, and the Vincent brothers of the Winfield *Non-Conformist*, these men were almost invariably prominent in the Citizens' Alliance, a group formed by those ineligible for the Farmers' Alliance. These activists generally were more politically knowledgeable and experienced than their agrarian associates and frequently had a traditional third-party background. Together with C. A. Power of Indiana, they drew up a call for a national conference of all reform organizations to meet in Cincinnati in February 1891 and, after securing signatures from many Northern reform leaders, took it to Ocala. There the entire Kansas delegation, headed by Benjamin Clover, Rice, John Willits, and Stephen McLallin, attempted to commit the Farmers' Alliance to the third-party movement. Southern delegates, however, coldly rebuffed the Kansas effort, convinced that their political successes within the Democratic party in the 1890 elections portended eventual Alliance ascendancy without threatening white supremacy in the South. Charles W. Macune, editor of the Alliance's *National Economist*, proposed deferring decision on the third-party issue until 1892, and the outnumbered Kansans reluctantly agreed. Perhaps as compensation, Clover was then elected national vice president and Willits, national lecturer.[2]

When Republicans seized upon the Ocala decision as proof that

[1] John D. Hicks, *The Populist Revolt* (Minneapolis, 1931), pp. 152-85; *Kansas Farmer* (Topeka), June 25, November 5, 26, 1890.

[2] W. F. Rightmire, "The Alliance Movement in Kansas—Origin of the People's Party," *Transactions of the Kansas State Historical Society* (Topeka, 1906), 9: 6-7; Hicks, *Populist Revolt*, pp. 207-9; *Topeka Advocate*, December 24, 1890.

the Alliance served the interests of the Southern Democracy, Kansas Populists quickly renounced any intention of delaying action until 1892. The Populist State Central Committee soon officially endorsed a national political organization and Peffer and other leaders announced their concurrence; Willits declared that his Alliance speeches would naturally reflect his Populist sentiments; and the Kansas Citizens' Alliance agreed to push plans for a national third party. On February 7, 1891, Rightmire, as secretary of the National Citizens' Alliance, reissued the call for the Cincinnati Conference, rescheduled for May 19, 1891, and now signed by Senator-elect Peffer, as the People's party's nominal leader; P. P. Elder, as the national chairman of the Union Labor party; most members of the Populist Kansas House of Representatives; and such customary third-party supporters as Ignatius Donnelly and James B. Weaver.[3]

To ensure an appropriate response, Peffer and his fellow Populists now actively promoted the cause of independent action. He pledged to avoid the caucuses of both old parties in the Senate and promised that the political cataclysm that had struck Kansas would soon sweep other states. He joined the five Populist congressmen to provide financial backing for the debt-ridden *Advocate* in order to have a vigorous Populist paper in Topeka. He and McLallin then helped organize the Kansas Reform Press Association (KRPA), which, like its national counterpart, would publicize and promote the cause of Populism. The new senator was elected the KRPA's first president and McLallin became secretary. Finally, Terence V. Powderly, Grand Master Workman of the Knights of Labor, visited Topeka to confer with Peffer and John Davis, the first Knights ever elected to Congress, on the subject of organizing the third party nationally. To their disappointment, he expressed his unwillingness to commit the Knights as an organization to any party, though he assured them of his personal cooperation.[4]

In late February Peffer went to Washington to observe Congress and consult with other reform leaders, including Henry George,

[3] *Girard Western Herald,* January 10, 1891; *Topeka Daily Capital,* December 12, 1890, January 24, February 8, 1891; *Topeka Advocate,* December 17, 1890; *Kansas City Star,* January 14, 1891; *Kansas Farmer,* January 7, February 18, 1891; Rightmire, "The Alliance Movement," p. 7.
[4] *Topeka Daily Capital,* January 29, 30, February 17, 25, 1891; *Kansas City Star,* February 25, 1891; *Journal of the Knights of Labor* (Philadelphia), February 19, 1891.

Laurence Gronlund, Macune, Kyle, and Polk. Together with Congressmen John G. Otis, Davis, and Jerry Simpson, he spoke to the National Citizens' Alliance, the Nationalist Club, the Federation of Labor, and other reform groups. Peffer attracted a great deal of attention when he visited the Senate, for neither old party was ready to accept his claim to independent status and each sought him for its own caucus. Peffer's repudiation of the GOP encouraged the Democrats, who invited him to attend a celebration of Democrat John M. Palmer's election as senator from Illinois. Already annoyed because Simpson had encouraged Illinois's independent legislators to vote for Palmer, Peffer brusquely declined, saying he had no reason to rejoice at a Democratic victory. His subsequent prohibition speeches also dismayed the Democrats, who had been originally elated over his election.[5]

The persistent Populist effort to promote the formation of a national third party also irritated Democrats, especially Southerners. Peffer, Otis, and Simpson found little Alliance support of their intentions in Virginia and Maryland, while M. W. Wilkins of the *Non-Conformist* was rebuffed at the Texas Alliance state convention in his effort to line up delegates for the Cincinnati Conference. Indeed, the Kansas Alliance was not joined in its official endorsement of the Cincinnati meeting by any other state body in the Southern Alliance. Macune and Polk announced their opposition to the conference and argued that action be postponed until 1892 with the interval spent on an educational campaign. Other Southerners were even more adamant and warned Peffer against ever forming a new party, declaring, "We are Democrats first and Alliancemen next."[6]

This Southern reluctance revealed the tenuous position of the Populists in Kansas, for as it takes two to argue it takes two to be reconciled. Kansans could not be expected to renounce partisan and sectional loyalties lest Southerners did likewise; their fear was that Southern resistance lay in a desire for the Democracy to reap the advantage of political independence in the North. That this

---

[5] *Washington* (D.C.) *Post,* March 3, 14, 27, 1891, April 8, 1891; *Topeka Daily Capital,* March 29, 1891; *National Economist,* March 14, 1891.

[6] *Washington Post,* March 6, 11, 12, 1891; *National Economist,* February 21, April 4, 25, 1891; Robert Cotner, *James Stephen Hogg* (Austin, Texas, 1959), p. 257.

belief was more than a Republican stratagem was evident in repeated Populist statements, none more so than that of the new Alliance state president, Frank McGrath. Reacting to the pronouncements of Southern Alliance spokesmen, McGrath specifically urged Southerners to attend the Cincinnati Conference and be prepared to act with a third party, and he scarcely veiled a threat that Kansas and other Northwestern states would swiftly return to the GOP if the Southern alliancemen did not join them. For McGrath, a major objective at Cincinnati would be to determine whether the South was ready to unite with the Northwest "or whether the South is working to divide the North and place the Democracy in unlimited power in our national affairs in 1892." McLallin attempted to soothe the situation in his *Advocate,* but he too believed that the South "must be held responsible for any further delay of the results of the conflict in which we are engaged in common."[7]

For their part, the Kansas Populists would tolerate no further delay, and the Cincinnati Conference clearly depended upon them for its direction and motivating force. Of the 1,443 delegates, moreover, 411 were from Kansas. Both the Farmers' and the Citizens' Alliances sent delegations, as did the Knights, the Farmers' Mutual Benefit Association, the Kansas Reform Press Association, the People's party, Union Labor remnants, and other organizations. Nearly all anticipated the immediate formation of a national third party. Peffer, a delegate of the Shawnee County Farmers' Alliance, outlined his plan for the conference. He wanted an unequivocal declaration of a new party, the adoption of a platform and a public appeal, and the selection of a national committee to supervise the party's campaign, deferring only the nomination of candidates pending a conference of all reform organizations scheduled for St. Louis on February 22, 1892.[8]

Most delegates agreed with Peffer not to postpone the decision, but often for McGrath's reasons. Former Republicans from the Western states, one reporter noticed, "urged that this is the time to make the South show its hand. If the convention was postponed

---

[7] *Kansas Farmer,* April 15, 1891; *Washington Post,* April 15, 1891; *Topeka Advocate* quoted in *National Economist,* May 16, 1891.

[8] *Topeka Advocate,* May 27, June 3, 1891; *Topeka Daily Capital,* April 4, May 19, 1891; *Kansas Farmer,* November 26, 1890; *Washington Post,* May 13, 1891.

till '92," he continued, "it would then be too late to organize a third party, and the Southern farmers would find an excuse to stick to their own party, but at the same time encouraging the Republicans to vote for an independent ticket. Some of the Western men say they do not intend to be used to elect a Democratic president, and unless the South shows up at the Conference many of the Republican farmers in Kansas and the West will return to their old party allegiance until the South is ready to join with them with an honest purpose to elect independent party men."[9]

Though the Southern states were indeed poorly represented, Kansas Populists seized control of the convention from its beginning and directed it toward the creation of a national party. The immense Kansas delegation arrived in Cincinnati before any other group and immediately caucused. Declaring their intention to overwhelm any opposition to the new party, the Kansans shouted down Simpson when he argued for a discretionary postponement and then unanimously passed a resolution favoring the third party. "As goes Kansas, so will go the convention" was a popular expression at the conference, and other delegations in their own caucuses quickly agreed with the Kansans.[10]

Kansans remained dominant when the National Union Conference opened officially on May 19, 1891. Rightmire called the meeting to order, Sam Wood helped direct temporary arrangements, and even the entertainment was provided by the Kansas Glee Club. Peffer was elected permanent chairman of the conference, pleasing proponents of an immediate third-party declaration. After an afternoon devoted largely to committee sessions, a mass meeting was held in the evening with Peffer as the principal speaker. Responding to a thunderous ovation, he spoke movingly of the conference. "We come here as harbingers of a revolution . . . to reestablish the authority of the people," he declared, and he urged the formation of a new party as their instrument of revolution.[11]

Despite such appeals, many delegates were swayed by more conservative advice offered by Weaver, Simpson, and Polk. These men

[9] *Topeka Daily Capital,* April 21, 1891.

[10] *Cincinnati Commercial-Gazette,* May 18, 19, 1891; *Topeka Daily Capital,* May 19, 1891; *Washington Post,* May 19, 1891.

[11] *Kansas Farmer,* June 10, 1891; *Topeka Daily Capital,* May 20, 1891; *Cincinnati Commercial-Gazette,* May 20, 1891.

hoped that by delaying action they could ultimately attract greater Southern support. The resolutions committee, chaired by Ignatius Donnelly, devised an acceptable compromise: The conference created a national People's party with an executive committee composed of three members from each state and directed this committee to attend the proposed St. Louis conference and promote a union with those reform organizations there assembled. If the St. Louis meeting objected to a third party, this committee was authorized to call a national nominating convention.[12]

Although this decision pleased both factions, Kansans left no doubt that they regarded it as having established a national party. McGrath expressed his displeasure with Simpson's dilatory efforts but applauded Peffer for his constant third-party advocacy. "Everyone opposing the third party," he grinned, "was run over."[13] Presiding over the birth of the party Peffer exulted, "We have started and there is no such thing as stopping us [A voice: "That's it!"], and the right thing to do is to keep in the middle of the road [A voice: "That's right!"] and to go ahead [More applause]."[14]

With the organization of the national People's party accomplished, Kansas Populists turned to the second phase of their campaign plan, the extension of their political revolution throughout the nation, with a special emphasis upon converting the South. The poor Southern attendance at Cincinnati greatly concerned Kansans. Levi Dumbauld, Populist state chairman, had repudiated McGrath's pronouncement before the conference, declaring "the People's party of Kansas is in the field to stay," but the real anxiety had scarcely been concealed by the repeated assurances that the popular fear of Southern nonattendance was unwarranted. When such hopes proved unfounded, Populist leaders were urgently

---

12 *Cincinnati Commercial-Gazette*, May 21, 1891; Rightmire, "The Alliance Movement," pp. 7-8; Hicks, *Populist Revolt*, pp. 214-15.

13 *Topeka Daily Capital*, May 23, 1891; *Kansas Farmer*, May 27, 1891.

14 *Topeka Advocate*, May 27, 1891. Previous students of Populism have found the term "middle-of-the-road" used no earlier than 1892. In fact, it was not an uncommon term before then, used to indicate an avoidance of both the Republican and the Democratic parties (which were considered to be in the gutters of the political system—on each side of those who kept clean and honest in the middle of the road). Clearly, however, Peffer must have been the first to apply it to the People's party, doing so at the very conference that organized the party, and to suggest the policy that later came to be identified as the mid-road position within the party.

questioned as to the intentions of the South. Again they assured their followers with optimistic statements, maintaining that the South would join the Populist coalition and thereby guarantee victory in 1892. With such expectations, then, the Kansas Populists launched what the newspapers dubbed "the Southern crusade" of the "Kansas missionaries."[15]

These third-party advocates scattered over the South during the summer of 1891. John Willits, as national lecturer of the Farmers' Alliance, had already begun his canvass of the South and, though circumspect, was, one observer noted, "gently leading the farmers to the point where a grand rush and a pull all together by the Kansas publicists would throw them clear over in the third party camp." Now Willits used the National Alliance's lecture bureau in conjunction with the Kansas Populist State Central Committee, the Populist National Executive Committee, and the Kansas Alliance lecture bureau to place Populist spokesmen throughout the South, and to a lesser extent in the important political pivot of the Old Northwest. After making a few speeches in Kansas and such Eastern forums as New York's Cooper Union in early June, Peffer began a great swing through the South from West Virginia to Texas by the end of July. Simpson made two sorties, one into the Deep South of Alabama and Georgia with Mary Elizabeth Lease and Annie Diggs, and one into Arkansas and Texas. Otis concentrated on the border states, B. E. Kies on the Southwest. Innumerable minor figures of Kansas Populism joined these acknowledged leaders in their attempt to convert the South.[16]

The political faith of the South was rooted in devotion to the Democratic party and its traditions. Leonidas F. Livingston, Georgia Alliance leader and congressman-elect, explained his section's position. Southerners, he declared, "are naturally Democratic, and before organizing a third party want to wait and see what the Democratic party will do. If that party will recognize the Alliance demands, they will take no step toward a third party."[17]

15 *Topeka Advocate,* April 22, May 6, 1891; *Girard Western Herald,* May 30, June 13, 1891; J. C. Ruppenthal Scrapbooks, 1: 427, KSHS; *Topeka Daily Capital,* July 18, 1891.

16 Ruppenthal Scrapbooks, 1: 427; *National Economist,* June 13, 1891; *Kansas Farmer,* July 1, 1891; *Topeka Advocate,* July 8, 1891.

17 *Cincinnati Commercial-Gazette,* May 19, 1891.

Such a course, however, would leave Kansas Populists in the predicament Republican alliancemen would have faced in 1890 had Kansas Democrats endorsed Alliance demands. That intolerable situation had forced the creation of a state party and now drove Populists to construct a national third party for their own survival. O. B. Deane of Meyers Valley, Kansas, explained to Southern alliancemen why their Northern counterparts rejected the proposal to control the existing parties: Southern alliancemen were primarily Democrats, whereas Northern alliancemen were more evenly divided as to political affiliation and had been unable to control either old party. To carry out the Southern proposition, Deane added, "We in the North would require a majority of both the old parties, because you can't make Republicans out of Democrats, nor Democrats out of Republicans, and to divide up is just what they both want us to do." Thus a separate, third party was necessary for success in the North, he concluded, "and if the South goes with us it will strengthen our hand, as it will put an end to the cry of Democratic aid society in the North and Republican aid society in the South." Another Kansan further described the tactical reasons behind the Southern tour of the Populists. The question that faced Kansas in 1890 now confronted all the states, J. T. Howe told the Bell Spring, Virginia, Alliance. How could Alliance principles be put into operation?

Democrats say there is but little difference between Democracy and Alliance principles, and we had better fall in line behind their banner and march on to victory. Well, Brother Democrat, that seems to be a fair proposition. Of course you extend this invitation to the large number of Republicans who belong to the Alliance? Do you expect them to accept it? Try the boot on the other foot. Suppose the Republicans would accede to our demands and extend the same invitation to you; would you accept? Of course not; [you] never can go into the Republican party. Well, then, what you will not do yourself you ought not expect them to do, because they feel that they make as great [a] sacrifice in leaving their party as you do in leaving yours. They have already made sacrifices by leaving their party and say they are willing to meet you halfway. Are you willing to go the other half?[18]

Most observers predicted a negative answer. The *New York Saturday Globe* believed that "whatever else may come, the Dem-

18 *National Economist*, July 4, 1891.

ocratic party has nothing to fear from this [People's party] movement. It draws its independent support from states in which only the Republican party can be injured. In the Democratic states of the South," it continued, "no power can, for the present, detach the sympathizers with the Alliance and its ideas from the Democracy."[19] It was this very task that the Kansas Populists set for themselves.

There were two parts to their effort. First, as they had in Kansas, the Populists had to nullify the emotional prejudices that bound people to the old parties; second, they had to confront the Democracy directly on the issues. The bloody shirt and prohibition found their Southern counterparts in the Lost Cause and white supremacy, and the Populists hoped to deal with them as effectively. From Maryland to Texas, they celebrated the defeat of the hated Ingalls— the man, Simpson declared, "who had kept the Republicans of Kansas together by pleading sectionalism." They appealed to their Southern listeners to strike similarly against "sectional agitators," whose object, wrote Clover, was "self-aggrandizement and the service of an oppressive and unscrupulous combination of public robbers." Thus, he continued, "sectional hate and its other self, party prejudice, have been the means by which monopoly has been enabled to bind the people." It was in the South's own interests, then, to help the West bury the past and unite in pursuit of common goals. Indeed, Simpson wrote, it was to "set an example to the rest of the country, particularly to the South," that the Kansas Populists had "resolved to cast aside the chief apostle of this doctrine of hate, John J. Ingalls," after having discovered for themselves "that for long years they had been blinded to their own interests by designing politicians, who kept alive the old war issues and prejudices."[20]

The emphasis upon the defeat of Ingalls gave Peffer a natural leadership in the Kansas effort to influence the South. Even before his election, however, Peffer had begun to develop the Populist indictment of sectionalism which he repeatedly used thereafter. Sectional prejudices, inflamed by politicians for partisan purposes,

19 *Washington Post*, May 25, 1891.

20 *Washington Post*, March 6, 1891; Cotner, *Hogg*, p. 257; Benjamin H. Clover, "Sectionalism," and Jerry Simpson, "The Political Rebellion in Kansas," both in N. A. Dunning, ed., *The Farmers' Alliance History and Agricultural Digest* (Washington, D.C., 1891), pp. 253-56, 283; *Dallas Morning News*, August 8, 1891.

he charged, divided the West and South to the injury of both sections. The Populists, he maintained, opposed any effort to incite sectional animosities and instead sought Southern cooperation in solving pressing political and economic problems. The effort would require sacrifices, he admitted, especially the renunciation of partisan loyalties, but more than 100,000 Kansans had already rejected such restraints, he pointed out, and Southerners must be equally committed.[21]

The issue of white supremacy presented greater problems. Peffer assured the South that Populists would never support legislation motivated by sectional hatred, and he felt that hypocritical "Northern lecturing" served no useful purpose, but he also believed that all citizens, black and white, must have equal protection of the laws. He maintained that the Kansas Alliance and Populists made no racial distinctions and urged the South to act likewise, realizing that the interests of the oppressed transcended color.[22] Such words often fell on deaf ears. When Josephus Daniels interviewed Peffer in June 1891 about his intentions for the People's party in the South, for instance, his major concern was simply that the Populists would insure Negro domination by dividing the Democracy. Persistently Peffer declared Daniels's anxiety an irrelevancy, for the People's party could not consider the effects of disrupting the Democracy in the South except insofar as it related to the triumph of Populist principles. Populists, he added, opposed as much the politicians' attempts to incite racial prejudice as sectional hatred, and they hoped to destroy both old parties. Daniels retorted that Democrats were not responsible for the wrongs against which Peffer inveighed and that the Democracy in control would solve the nation's troubles.[23]

This refusal to accept the inclusion of the Democracy in the Populist indictment of politics formed the dominant Southern response to the third-party proselytizers. But while most Alliance leaders were announcing their Democratic commitments, there

21 *Kansas Farmer,* November 5, 26, 1890: William A. Peffer, "The Farmers' Alliance," *Cosmopolitan* 10 (April 1891): 699; *Atchison Daily Champion,* January 29, 1891.
22 *Kansas Farmer,* November 26, 1890; Peffer, "Farmers' Alliance"; *Topeka Mail,* May 9, 1890; *Atchison Daily Champion,* January 29, 1891.
23 *Washington Post,* June 10, 1891. See also *Kansas Farmer,* November 26, 1890.

were some hopeful signs. The Atlanta *Southern Alliance Farmer* proclaimed, "Our Western brethren have shown the faith by their works, and Southern Alliancemen should now meet them halfway." "With what consistency," it wondered, "can Alliancemen in the South ask their brethren of the North to throw the mantle of oblivion over the dead past, and still keep aflame the old war feeling themselves?" Even this paper, however, reported Southerners reluctant to leave their party and willing to give it every opportunity to accept Alliance principles. L. L. Polk, increasingly inclined toward independent action, also considered the relationship between the new party and the Southern Alliance in his *Progressive Farmer*. "The new party has adopted the Alliance demands in its platform. Does anyone suppose intelligent Alliancemen will vote against the party that adopts these demands, and in favor of a party that not only fails to adopt, but resists these demands?"[24]

The Populist obligation, then, was to demonstrate the incongruity of Democratic and Alliance principles and the inability of the Democracy to respond effectively to the new issues. Throughout the South, county alliances met in July to elect and instruct delegates to the state Alliance meetings in early fall which would in turn determine the position to be followed at the National Alliance conference in Indianapolis in November. The Populists focused on these July meetings in their campaign to commit the Alliance as an organization to the People's party.[25] Before these audiences they repeatedly pointed out that the Democrats often agreed with the Populist description of existing difficulties but could only blame Republican legislation and vaguely promise relief under a Democratic government. Peffer hammered at the inability of the Democrats to promise specific and realistic remedies. They had only two suggestions to relieve economic depression and social polarization, he told his Alliance listeners in the South: tariff reduction and free silver. These promised measures of relief, he declared, "if they shall be forthcoming, which is doubtful, are wholly inadequate to the needs of the people." The Democratic Mills tariff bill had proposed only small reductions in tariff duties, he argued, while even free trade would produce a per capita net

24 *National Economist,* June 13, 1891: *Girard Western Herald,* July 4, 1891.
25 *National Economist,* July 4, 1891; Ruppenthal Scrapbooks, 1: 427.

savings which would be insignificant in lightening the popular burden.[26]

Peffer and his fellow Kansans equally arraigned the Democratic free silver stand. The amount of money free silver coinage would add to circulation, he declared, "is a mere bagatelle in comparison with the sum needed," and free silver would neither reach the core of the trouble in American society nor provide permanent relief. In 1890–1891 silver was of distinctly minor importance to Populists, and they were emphatically hostile to it as a political or economic panacea. Free silver was a common demand in the West and even Ingalls was an eloquent champion of it. Indeed, Nevada Senator William M. Stewart had pled for the reelection of Ingalls because of his importance in the cause of silver, a plea the Populists plainly rejected. They demanded more fundamental changes.[27]

Still, free silver often proved a popular issue on their Southern tour, as long as many of their listeners regarded themselves as silver Democrats. In such instances the Populists pointed out the inconsistency of silver men supporting such Democrats as Grover Cleveland. Indeed, Cleveland's public opposition to free silver, admitted the president of one Southern state Alliance, encouraged alliancemen to view more favorably a third party because of the likelihood of his renomination in 1892. Populists also believed that between Cleveland's intransigence and the silver declaration of the Cincinnati Conference the Southern Democrats would be unable to retain Alliance support. Peffer's usual speech, then, not only emphasized Alliance and Populist demands for thorough reforms, especially financial reform involving greenbacks and banking, but also asserted that the Democracy dared not put even a free silver plank in its national platform and ridiculed the Democratic tariff position as "a fraud and a delusion." He invariably closed with a pledge that when Southern alliancemen failed to have their demands answered in the Democracy, they would then find the People's party "in the middle of the road."[28]

<hr />

26 *Kansas Farmer*, July 29, 1891; *Dallas Morning News*, July 31, 1891.

27 *Dallas Morning News*, July 31, 1891; *Kansas Farmer*, July 29, 1891; Peffer, *The Farmer's Side* (New York, 1891), p. 128; *Topeka Daily Capital*, January 28, 1891; O. Gene Clanton, *Kansas Populism: Ideas and Men* (Lawrence, Kans., 1969), p. 104.

28 *Girard Western Herald*, August 1, 1891; James H. Davis to Ignatius Donnelly, June 3, 1891, Donnelly Papers; *Washington Post*, March 30, June 10, 1891;

More important than either the tariff or free silver as a wedge to separate alliancemen from the Democracy was the subtreasury proposal. An ingenious plan, not dissimilar to Peffer's *Way Out,* the subtreasury promised farmers short-term credit for agricultural products stored in government warehouses and offered the nation an increased and elastic currency supply. It was endorsed by the Alliance at its 1889 St. Louis national meeting and became the favorite demand of Southern alliancemen, who anticipated breaking out of the crop-lien system through its adoption. Involving centralized authority and government competition with local business interests, the subtreasury naturally provoked strong opposition from conservatives, especially on the traditional Democratic grounds of "paternalism." Democratic politicians, elected on Alliance platforms in 1890, had promptly denounced the subtreasury once in office. Now in the summer of 1891 the subtreasury became the primary target of Southern critics of the Alliance and its third-party tendencies.[29]

Democrats encouraged the more conservative alliancemen to reorganize their order on an anti-subtreasury basis. Led by the president of the Missouri Farmers' Alliance, Uriel S. Hall, an ambitious politician who wanted to manipulate the Alliance to promote Democratic interests, these men held a special Alliance convention in Fort Worth in July to repudiate the subtreasury. Those in attendance who supported the subtreasury plan were not permitted to speak and ultimately were forced out of the convention. The *Dallas Morning News* found the speeches more "in the line of a political Democratic speech than a non-political alliance speech" and that the delegates cheered every reference to the necessity of remaining within the Democracy to remedy agrarian distress. One delegate told a reporter, "The truth of the matter is that there is a political split in the alliance. This [anti-subtreasury] wing is composed of Alliance Democrats . . . and the other wing is crystallized into an adjunct of the People's Party."[30]

Indeed, an adherence to Alliance principles came necessarily to

---

Dallas Morning News, July 27, 1891. See also Peffer, *Farmer's Side,* pp. 124-30: "Partisan Remedies Proposed."

29 Davis to Donnelly, June 3, 1891, Donnelly Papers; C. Vann Woodward, *Origins of the New South* (Baton Rouge, La., 1951), pp. 239-40.

30 Uriel S. Hall to Grover Cleveland, May 19, 1891, Cleveland Papers; *Dallas Morning News,* July 11, 12, 1891.

include an inclination toward the third party. Although a few Populists such as William A. Harris, himself a former Southern Democrat, opposed the subtreasury, most agreed with Peffer's strong endorsement of the plan and his determination to force the issue in the South. Frequently they regarded opposition to it as a Democratic scheme to destroy the Alliance's political influence. Moreover, as one newspaper reported, "The Kansas leaders fear this is but the beginning of a movement that will disrupt their organization in Kansas, as thousands of Republicans who affiliated with the People's Party last year will follow the course of their Southern [Alliance] brethren and go back to their old party." At the July Alliance meetings throughout the South, then, it was usually a Kansas Populist who advocated the full Alliance program while Southern Democratic leaders argued for the abandonment of the subtreasury. In Arkansas, for example, Willits and Simpson traveled the Alliance circuit supporting the subtreasury while the state's Democratic congressmen attacked the plan and urged the farmers to remain inside the Democratic ranks and not join the third-party movement. In Texas, too, the subtreasury was the basic issue which aligned Peffer, Willits, Simpson, and "a Mrs. McCarty of Kansas" against prominent Democrats in a series of debates before Alliance encampments across the state. Peffer was especially popular, for "everybody wanted to listen to the man who beat Ingalls, and he pleased his audience."[31]

The Populist success in advocating the subtreasury in these debates with Democrats led one state Alliance after another during the summer of 1891 to endorse the full Ocala platform, causing Populists to expect ultimate Southern support. By the end of August eleven Southern state Alliance conventions had overwhelmingly subscribed to the subtreasury. Another attempt by Hall to organize an anti-subtreasury Alliance in September was a total failure.[32]

In response to the Populist campaign in the South, Democrats relied less on rational argument than on the dogmatic reassertion

[31] *Topeka State Journal*, July 10, 1891; *Kansas Farmer*, August 5, 1891; *Dallas Morning News*, July 12, 22, 23, 27-31, August 5-7, 1891; *Topeka Daily Capital*, July 30, 1891.
[32] *National Economist*, August 29, 1891; *Dallas Morning News*, July 12, 1891; Woodward, *Origins of the New South*, p. 239.

of the old political ploys that the Populists had characterized as irrelevant to the needs of the people: sectional, racial, and partisan appeals. Arkansas Democratic congressmen replied to Simpson's discussion of the subtreasury by attacking the traditional Southern bête noire, outside agitators, and declaring that Arkansas would pursue its own course without any interference from Kansas. Peffer's interview with Josephus Daniels provoked both sectional and racial prejudice against the Populist. Demanding to know who had asked this "black republican" to invade the South anyway, a Raleigh paper urged its readers to "Send Him Back Wiser."

Are the honest, manly White Southern farmers ready to receive their lessons in political science from such sources[?] Can they acknowledge as their leader a foreign-born fanatic like Peffer, or any Southern White man who hears his degrading race principles and still associates with him? We answer no. The farmers of the South will not follow such men. The chivalry of Anglo-Saxon manhood, reverence for the virtue of Southern women, and respect for ancestral and race pride, all condemn and repudiate such self-confessed demagogues.[33]

The final admonition of the *News and Observer* was for Southern farmers to stay Democratic. This appeal to partisan loyalty formed the essence of the Democratic counterattack. The Democracy, its supporters argued, had always done what was best for the South, was able and willing to remedy social complaints, and alone preserved the integrity and protected the special interests of the South. "The advent into Georgia of Senator Peffer, Congressman Simpson, and Mrs. Mary Ellen [*sic*] Lease, apostles of the third party, is a serious matter," editorialized the *Augusta Chronicle*. Their intention was "to gain converts to the People's party, and thus impair, if not destroy, the unity and strength of the Democratic party." The possibility that the People's party might disrupt the GOP in the North provided another Southern argument to remain within the Democracy. "Our people should not play the fool now and throw away upon mere abstractions and distractions the only chance the Democratic party will probably have in many years to regain possession of the Federal government."[34]

[33] *Dallas Morning News,* July 28, 1891; *Raleigh* (N.C.) *News and Observer,* June 27, July 1, 9, 1891.
[34] *Kansas Farmer,* July 22, 1891; *Louisville Courier-Journal,* July 14, 15, 1891.

The Populist threat and the Democratic defense appeared most clearly in Kentucky. The People's Party National Executive Committee decided in June to campaign extensively in Kentucky and Ohio where full state tickets were to be elected. Kentucky's election would reveal the willingness of Southern alliancemen to commit themselves to the third party and Ohio's would indicate how the important Midwest viewed the People's party. Kentucky in particular was vital to Populist hopes, for its election occurred in August, and a good showing there would presumably influence the later elections in Ohio, Iowa, and Nebraska. But if a good showing would encourage the People's party, many feared the reverse would also be true. A Kentucky Populist reported that a decisive defeat for the Populists "may belittle the reputation of the movement in this state as well as elsewhere and give the assertion strength, that you can't get the Democratic farmers in the South to support it." Another Populist campaigner admitted that the effort to poll a large vote in Kentucky was being made "in order to show members of the party in the Northwest that the Third party movement was taking hold in the South, as well as in that locality." He declared, moreover, that "the future growth of the party depended largely upon the results in Kentucky," because a failure there would give the movement "a black eye, and it would demoralize the party's strength in the West."[35]

Led by John G. Otis and M. W. Wilkins, Kansas Populists actively organized the People's party in Kentucky. They used the same techniques they had employed in Kansas—"pic nics, Barbeques, Mass meetings of every description in every county and precinct in the state." Peffer entered the Kentucky campaign in mid-July with extensive publicity. Here he advocated the Alliance principles, emphasizing the subtreasury; but with a state People's party already in existence, he was also able to champion more openly the People's party qua party. Closely connected in the public mind with the party, he was more effective in Kentucky while others such as Simpson, who had opposed immediate formation of the People's party at the Cincinnati Conference, remained in the Deep South on

[35] *Girard Western Herald,* June 20, 1891; Robert Schilling to Donnelly, June 26, 1891, Taubeneck to Donnelly, June 27, 1891, Blanton Duncan to Donnelly, July 7, 1891, Donnelly Papers; *Louisville Courier-Journal,* July 15, 1891.

speaking tours where he emphasized strictly Alliance principles.[36]

Populist-Democratic debates in the Kentucky campaign resembled those elsewhere in the South. Peffer reported that Democrats were "quite as hard on us because of our alleged connections with the Republican party as our Kansas Republicans in Kansas were last year because of our supposed connection with the Democratic party. We are pounced upon and hammered by the predominant party, whatever it is, in the particular locality which we visit." In debate with Peffer, Democrats also denied that their party had any responsibility for the nation's distress, declared that his proposals were paternalistic, castigated the Kansan for interfering in Kentucky's affairs, and contended that only through Democratic ascendancy could the nation's ills be remedied.[37]

Such traditional appeals proved persuasive, and Democrats even encouraged the disbanding of suballiances to prevent defections. Lack of time and money also severely hampered the new party in Kentucky, and difficulties in organization and disagreements over procedures further weakened Populist chances. Herman E. Taubeneck, the Populist national chairman, went to Kentucky personally to manage the campaign, but the superior resources of the Democratic party easily prevailed.[38]

The Democratic victory was not unexpected, of course, and while Southern Democrats and Western Republicans rejoiced that the new party was practically moribund, Populist leaders expressed pleasure at their showing: thirteen legislators elected and a state poll of 25,631 votes (about 9 percent of the state's total) for their gubernatorial candidate. The Northern Republican press considered the election proof that Southern alliancemen would never desert the Democracy for the People's party, but Taubeneck asserted the Populists had gained a great victory, considering their limited time and funds. "The 'Solid South' is broken," he maintained. Kentucky Populists were also cheered by the results. One argued that the People's party had exceeded expectations: "Its

[36] Taubeneck to Donnelly, June 27, 1891, Duncan to Donnelly, July 7, 1891, Donnelly Papers: *Topeka Advocate*, July 22, 1891; *Louisville Courier-Journal*, July 14, 16, 18, 1891.

[37] *Kansas Farmer*, July 29, 1891; *Louisville Courier-Journal*, July 14-19, 1891.

[38] Schilling to Donnelly, June 25, 26, 1891, Duncan to Donnelly, July 7, 1891, Donnelly Papers; *Louisville Courier-Journal*, July 13, 1891.

friends felt that if twenty thousand votes were cast for it, it would make a respectable showing, and let the People's Party men in Kansas, Nebraska, and other Republican states know that the Democratic farmers in Kentucky were willing to forsake their old party and take up with the new." The 25,000 votes, he contended, were 15,000 more than their enemies had expected and 5,000 more than Populists had hoped for.[39]

Populists, in fact, expressed a general optimism about their party in the South, for they were convinced that their Southern crusade had achieved a success which would be soon visible at the November national meeting of the Farmers' Alliance. Peffer announced that he and his fellow Kansas Populists had received a friendly welcome from all but the politicians, and he believed that both white and black Southerners were flocking to the People's party: "It is wonderful how men are breaking away from the restraints which have held them. Our presence inspires courage among the doubting people." McGrath also anticipated that the People's party would receive the full black vote in 1892 and that by controlling the Alliance and neutralizing Democratic appeals the party would carry at least six Southern states in 1892. Even Simpson reported himself delighted with the results of his Southern tour and, convinced that the South would support the third party, reversed his earlier opposition to the national movement. From Mississippi Willits exulted: "I want to tell you that the old bosses can no more hold the Alliance men in the south in the Democratic party in 1892 than they held them in Kansas last fall. They are kicking over the traces and giving them a world of trouble everywhere I go in the South. I have been having big crowds and they have voted me thanks everywhere, and I have given them *straight goods*. . . . I know where they will stand in 1892."[40]

With such confidence in the South, Populists turned their attention to the Northern states where fall elections would be held.

39 *Cincinnati Commercial-Gazette,* August 4, 1891; *Chicago Tribune,* August 13, 1891; *Kentucky Journal* (Newport), August 4, 5, 1891; *Appletons' Annual Cyclopaedia* (New York, 1892), p. 408; *Journal of the Knights of Labor,* September 17, 1891.

40 *Kansas Farmer,* July 29, 1891; *Indianapolis Journal,* September 7, 1891; *Atlanta Constitution,* July 14, 1891; *National Economist,* August 8, 1891; *Dallas Morning News,* August 8, 1891; *Topeka Advocate,* August 5, 1891.

Willits had already canvassed Ohio in early spring and with Polk and Otis had helped organize the Iowa State Farmers' Alliance in March. In June, Simpson and Polk made a quick swing through Wisconsin, Illinois, Indiana, Ohio, and Pennsylvania, organizing alliances, encouraging local reform groups to align with the larger movement, and gauging potential Alliance political strength. That strength the Kansans sought to transform into Populist votes.[41]

Ohio was the first target of the Populists. Senator John Sherman, one of the architects of the nation's financial policies against which the Populists argued, faced reelection, and they hoped to " 'Kansasize' Ohio" and send him the way of Ingalls. They also hoped to disrupt the presidential ambitions of William McKinley and James Campbell, opposing candidates for governor in the important state, as well as to test their own strength. Peffer opened the Ohio campaign with a speech in Cleveland on July 30, 1891, before the People's party was even officially organized in the state. He continued to emphasize the necessity for sweeping reform and stigmatized free silver, half-heartedly supported by Ohio Democrats. "Free coinage of silver," he declared, "is but a drop in the bucket which must be filled." Willits, Otis, Rightmire, Wilkins, and Mrs. Diggs followed Peffer through Ohio in early August and helped organize the Ohio People's party at Springfield on August 5. Peffer's speaking engagements prevented his attendance, but he wrote a letter to the convention, advising the endorsement of the Cincinnati platform and the nomination of a full state ticket. The convention applauded this letter and proceeded to follow his advice.[42]

Though Peffer was optimistic about Ohio's prospects, the Populists made little impact upon the campaign. Their ticket did frighten Republicans enough to import a Kansas Republican, Governor Humphrey, to counter the appeals of the Kansas Populists, but in general the old-party response to the new was familiar. Democrats self-righteously demanded the support of those who sincerely favored free silver; Republicans denounced the Populists as Democratic allies and even raised the outside-agitator clamor.

---

41 *Washington Post,* March 21, April 7, June 8, 1891; *Topeka Daily Capital,* June 11, 1891.

42 *Cincinnati Commercial-Gazette,* August 1, 5, 6, 1891; *Chicago Tribune,* August 3, 1891; *Topeka Daily Capital,* August 6, 1891.

Outside agitator Humphrey conceded that Peffer had some success in organizing the People's party "here and there in the country districts," but the Populists, despite their initial promise, hardly out-polled the Prohibitionists in the November election.[43]

In the Iowa election, too, the Populists suffered disappointment. A state convention on June 3, 1891, with Willits and Otis playing prominent roles, had organized the Iowa People's party and nominated a full ticket. Iowa Populists planned extensive use of Kansas speakers and sent a representative to Topeka to arrange for speeches by Peffer and all five Populist congressmen plus Willits, Rightmire, and others. Peffer campaigned through Iowa for two weeks in August and September, but found surprisingly little interest. As in Kansas, prohibition was a divisive issue, and when the Iowa Populists proved unable to neutralize it there were virtually ignored in the election, capturing only two legislators and about 3 percent of the vote. Dissension between the established, more conservative Northern Farmers' Alliance and the new Southern Alliance also hurt the Populist cause, while Republicans worked the sectional ploy, emphasizing that the People's party was "a stool pigeon trap of the Democratic party, in Iowa and all other Northern states," and that Populists were merely Democratic agitators.[44]

From August through October, Kansas Populist leaders campaigned extensively elsewhere outside their state. They helped organize state People's parties in other midwestern states and even arranged the transference of the *Non-Conformist* from Winfield, Kansas, to Indianapolis to advocate Indiana's new People's party. They urged alliancemen to align with the new party in still other states. Peffer debated Senator Palmer in Illinois, a Republican congressman in Pennsylvania, and minor politicians of both parties in Indiana. He addressed a Labor Day crowd in Indianapolis, urged Missouri alliancemen to repudiate Hall by endorsing the subtreasury, traveled to Nebraska and back to Ohio and made

43 *Indianapolis Journal*, September 7, 1891; *Cincinnati Commercial-Gazette*, August 12, 1891· *Topeka Daily Capital*, September 25, 1891; *Appletons' Annual Cyclopaedia* (1891), p. 693.

44 *Iowa State Register* (Des Moines), August 22, 26, 1891; *Topeka Daily Capital*, June 10, 1891; *Topeka Advocate*, August 12, 1891; Herman C. Nixon, "The Populist Movement in Iowa," *Iowa Journal of History and Politics* 24 (January 1926): 55-57.

plans to visit North Carolina and Alabama before winter. Peffer was most in demand, but other Populists were nearly as active in spreading the new gospel of political independence.[45]

Exhausted by his rigorous schedule, Peffer was unable to return to the South in the fall of 1891, but Jerry Simpson did so, speaking for the People's party in North Carolina and Louisiana. He returned even more certain that the People's party would dominate the South in 1892, that "the Southern bloody shirt, fear of Negro domination, can no longer be waved successfully to hold the white people of the South solidly in the Democratic party," and that the Populists would absorb the black vote as well.[46]

Simpson also expected that alliancemen, after having spent the year vigorously fighting the Democracy over the subtreasury and other reform demands, would insist upon strict allegiance to Alliance principles by Southern politicians. Many believed that Democrats dependent upon Alliance support had deceived the farmers by opposing Alliance demands in their debates with Populists. These politicians had repeatedly argued that Southern alliancemen owed primary loyalty to the Democracy and not to their Alliance principles. After his fall canvass, Simpson believed that the Alliance would repudiate such narrow partisanship by requiring its congressmen to caucus separately on the basis of adherence to the Ocala platform, thereby testing their sincerity. Support for this view came from the South too. Thomas E. Watson, a newly elected Alliance congressman from Georgia, launched the *People's Party Paper* on October 1, 1891, to defend the entire Ocala platform, denounce any compromise with temporizing Democrats, and support a strong West-South concord. Watson also wanted Alliance congressmen bound not to the Democratic party but to a caucus defined by observance of Alliance principles. Both Simpson and Watson attended the Indianapolis meeting for that purpose.[47]

45 *Chicago Tribune,* August 5, 7, 9, 10, 14, 22, 1891; *Topeka Advocate,* August 26, 1891; *Indianapolis Journal,* September 7, 8, 1891; *Topeka Daily Capital,* September 1, October 6, 13, 1891; *Topeka State Journal,* September 1, 1891; Ernest D. Stewart, "The Populist Party in Indiana," *Indiana Magazine of History* 14 (December 1918): 353.

46 *Girard Western Herald,* September 26, 1891; *Journal of the Knights of Labor,* September 10, 1891; *Washington Post,* November 6, 13, 1891.

47 *Dallas Morning News,* August 8, 1891; *Washington Post,* November 13, 1891; *Girard Western Herald,* August 22, 1891; C. Vann Woodward, *Tom Watson,*

The Populist crusade of 1891 culminated in success at the Indianapolis meeting in November. Kansans flocked to the conference and of those of prominence only Peffer was absent, his poor health preventing his attendance, though he had been scheduled to deliver an address. His son, Elwood S. Peffer, however, an editor of the Indianapolis *Non-Conformist,* reported the conference for the National Reform Press Association and kept the senator informed of events. The active purpose of the meeting was to determine the attitude of the Alliance toward the People's party. The party's executive committee met in Indianapolis at the same time and worked to secure the Alliance's endorsement. Third-party sentiment among the Alliance delegates revealed itself in Polk's unanimous reelection as president of the order. Polk was considered a third-party man by this time, and his election came without opposition after the delegates learned that his potential opponent, L. F. Livingston of Georgia, opposed independent action. Populist leaders hailed Polk's election as a victory, but their success did not end there. A member of the People's Party National Executive Committee was elected vice president of the Alliance, and Willits, after a year campaigning for the People's party as national lecturer, was reelected. The delegates, in accordance with their instructions from the local Alliance meetings of the summer, reaffirmed their faith in the entire Ocala platform, including the subtreasury, now anathema to leading Southern Democrats. Simpson and Watson's Georgia supporters argued for a resolution instructing Alliance congressmen to shun any party caucus unless the principles of the Ocala platform were made the test of admission. The delegates enthusiastically passed the resolution, thereby, as Elwood Peffer believed, "drawing the party line on our Southern [Alliance] Congressmen." Finally, the FMBA, also meeting in Indianapolis at the same time, moved toward unification with the Alliance by revising its platform and constitution. Altogether, the results of the meetings assured the existence of a third-party ticket in 1892 supported by the Alliance and other farmers' organizations. Tom Watson declared in Indianapolis that the Alliance congressmen would hold their own caucus and present their own candidate

---

Agrarian Rebel (New York, 1938), pp. 182-87; *Topeka Advocate,* September 9, 1891.

for Speaker. "Georgia is ready for a third party," he added, and, to the delight of his Populist listeners, he predicted the movement "will sweep the state."[48]

Certain that they had committed the Alliance to their party, the Populists looked forward to the campaign of 1892 with optimism. Six months after the organization of their party in Cincinnati they had broadcast its principles throughout the nation, established numerous state party organizations, and attracted implicit pledges of support from major agrarian and reform groups. The Kansas Populists also believed they had strengthened their position at home through their 1891 activities. By establishing a national party they weakened the Republican charge that a Populist vote in Kansas was ultimately counterproductive of reform as it merely strengthened the Democracy. Moreover, their Southern crusade convinced them that the Southern farmers would stand with them in opposition to the two old parties in 1892, and this was crucial for success in Kansas and the nation. The *Topeka Advocate* expressed the Populist conviction: Southern alliancemen were being swept into the reform movement, and "it will be absolutely impossible for them to avoid the support of a new party. . . . The refusal of the old parties to support Alliance measures will force them to make a stand, and there is absolutely no shadow of doubt as to what that stand will be."[49]

48 *Topeka Advocate*, November 4, 1891; Stuart Noblin, *Leonidas LaFayette Polk, Agrarian Crusader* (Chapel Hill, N.C., 1949), p. 271: *Indianapolis Journal*, November 18, 20, 1891; *Topeka Daily Capital*, October 23, 1891; *Kansas Farmer*, December 2, 1891; Woodward, *Watson*, p. 187.

49 Quoted in *National Economist*, May 16, 1891.

CHAPTER FIVE

The Betrayal of the Promise

As THE Kansas Populists confidently awaited the election of 1892, others were preparing to deliver a series of blows which would cause great changes in the composition and direction of the new party. Before beginning their campaign to gain full control of the state government, the Kansans turned their attention to Washington to observe proudly their representatives in the national government and to witness the expected signs from Southern alliancemen in Congress that the Populist Crusade had converted the South.

Senator-elect William A. Peffer left the 1891 campaign circuit for Washington and recuperation in November. The *Washington Post* announced his arrival with the observation, "Perhaps the most extensively advertised Senator that ever came to Washington is Hon. W. A. Peffer, of Kansas." Indeed, Peffer had burst into the public spotlight with his defeat of the famous Ingalls, and he remained a popular figure for interviews, articles, editorials, and cartoons. Not only his summer campaign for the People's party but his lectures in Washington, New York, and Boston had given him national exposure. He was so largely associated with the third-party movement in the public mind, in fact, that for a time he lent his name to it. Before the People's party movement became designated as Populism it was popularly referred to as Pefferism; and Populists were frequently termed Pefferites or Peffercrats. Gradually the term "Populist" became accepted in late 1891, and

"Pefferism" came to mean less the political movement and more the lamentation of distressing social and economic conditions—from the apocalyptic language of Peffer and other leading Populists. In this sense the term survived a number of years.[1]

Peffer received added publicity and further identification with the People's party when admirers and enemies combined to give him a presidential boom during the summer of 1891. Kansas was so vital to the success of the new party that many assumed a Kansan would lead the ticket in 1892 and Peffer was the natural choice to lead the Pefferites. The *New York Sun* complained "the boom of Peffer Longbeard has been let loose already" and thereby indicated another aspect of Peffer's new notoriety: his appearance. He was tall and very thin and always dressed in black, wearing boots and a hat, but no collar or tie; above all, he had a beard that reached nearly to his waist. His general appearance, it was invariably noted, was "ministerial," but his beard attracted most attention, and "Whiskers" became his nickname, an appellation so compelling that Peffer is known even to historians almost solely as the possessor of his beard. His appearance naturally lent itself to caricature, and he became the political cartoonists' symbol of the People's party more consistently than either the donkey or the elephant served the major parties. Never commented upon before the senatorial election, his beard became the subject of political ridicule, and while his appearance suggested to his followers a patriarchal biblical figure, it encouraged his Eastern opponents to dub him a "new Visigoth."[2]

The press observed at the time of Peffer's election that the People's party had disappointed those who had hoped for a senator who would bring derision upon the movement. Peffer, all conceded, was a respectable, honest, sensible man above reproach. Six months later he was regarded as the most bizarre of a collection of crazed fanatics that included "Sockless Jerry" Simpson and "the Milkman" John Otis. Such unfair criticism, arising from fear and hatred of

---

1 *Washington Post*, December 8, 1891; *Topeka Daily Capital*, July 1, August 11, 29, 1891, February 17, 1895; *Cincinnati Commercial-Gazette*, August 10, 15, 1891; *Topeka Advocate*, November 13, 1895, February 5, 1896.

2 *Topeka Advocate*, June 3, July 22, 1891; *Topeka Daily Capital*, February 1, June 5, 1891; *Dallas Morning News*, July 23, 30, 1891; Peffer Scrapbooks, 3: 17, KSHS; *New York Times*, March 5, 1891; Hamlin Garland, "The Alliance Wedge in Congress," *Arena* 5 (March 1892): 447-57.

Populist principles as much as from the appearance and expressions of their advocates, has continued to affect adversely the historical portrayals of men who were, by and large, perceptive, shrewd, and extraordinarily able. A *Washington Post* reporter observed the Populists in their early days in the national capital and then concluded that "no set of men ever merited less the ridicule that has been heaped upon them." Another newsman met Peffer "to describe the peculiarities of his personal appearance" for the paper's eager readers. From advance notices the reporter expected "a political dime museum freak" but was astonished to find "a gentleman of a mild and benevolent countenance, of engaging manners, and of a gentle and persuasive voice." In looking for the celebrated beard, he continued, he saw "a patriarchal cataract of rippling hair instead of a tangled mass of coarse, straggling and unkempt locks in the wild man of Borneo style." Peffer may have had unorthodox ideas about society and finance, but he was an erudite, gracious, and sensitive individual.[3]

Once in Washington, the newly elected Populist congressmen made their plans for the organization of Congress. Peffer repeated his pledge to avoid both the Republican and the Democratic caucuses and joined Senator James H. Kyle of South Dakota, who still considered himself an Independent rather than a Populist, to request proper recognition on the committees of the Senate. Peffer wanted to be named to the committees on finance, agriculture, and interstate commerce to advance Populist proposals, but he failed to win a seat on any of these. Although initially both parties courted Peffer, his determination to gain the People's party recognition through the organization of Congress caused the older parties to agree to ignore his specific requests and show him no particular favor. He was roundly denounced in the Democratic caucus, in fact, for "his anti-Democratic actions and speeches." Eventually the Republican caucus assigned him to the committees on claims, the census, railroads, and civil service, and the Democrats accommodated Kyle.[4]

3 *Kansas City Star,* January 27, 29, 1891; *Topeka Mail,* January 30, 1891; *Washington Post,* March 4, 1891; *Topeka Daily Capital,* March 8, 1891, February 25, 1892; *Washington Evening Star,* October 12, 1893.

4 *Topeka Daily Capital,* December 13, 16, 1891; *Washington Post,* December 10, 1891.

Populist representatives in the House faced a different problem, and one more important to their party, that of securing adherence to the Indianapolis resolution instructing Alliance congressmen to avoid the old party caucuses. The five Kansas congressmen met at Peffer's apartment and decided to hold a caucus and nominate a candidate for Speaker, regardless of the action of others. Simpson expected at least four others to join the Kansans: Omar Kem and William McKeighan of Nebraska, Kittel Halvorson of Minnesota, and but one Southerner, Tom Watson of Georgia. Other Southerners, Simpson commented ruefully, "had talked quite independently during the summer" but now appeared to be solidly Democratic. Benjamin Clover and other Kansans remained optimistic and hoped for at least twenty-five Southerners to join their cause.[5]

A conference of the Alliance congressmen quickly shattered their illusions. The meeting broke into two bitter factions over the question of an independent caucus. Otis precipitated the uproar by reproaching the Southerners for their obvious reluctance to place principles before party, and Simpson arraigned the Democratic party while urging independent action. Led by Leonidas F. Livingston of Georgia, the Southerners retorted angrily that the Democracy represented the best hope for securing relief and should be supported. Watson denounced Livingston as a betrayer of the farmers' trust, and after a few tense moments the conference adjourned in such an acrimonious atmosphere that Watson spoke of an "irrepressible conflict between factions." Indeed, with the exception of Watson, all Southern alliancemen entered the Democratic caucus on December 5, 1891, and were pledged to support for Speaker, Charles F. Crisp of Georgia, a conservative politician who opposed the subtreasury and other Alliance demands. The Kansans and their four allies then met again at Peffer's apartment where he called the first Populist congressional caucus to order. They unanimously endorsed the Indianapolis Resolution and chose Watson as their party's candidate for Speaker: the Populists still hoped to split the Solid South.[6]

Other events soon added to the Populists' disappointment. The

5 *Washington Post,* November 28, 1891; *Girard Western Herald,* December 12, 1891; *Topeka Daily Capital,* December 4, 10, 1891.

6 C. Vann Woodward. *Tom Watson, Agrarian Rebel* (New York, 1938), pp. 190-93; *Topeka Daily Capital,* December 10, 1891.

Alliance's official newspaper, the *National Economist,* edited by C. W. Macune of Texas, an opponent of the third party, praised the Southern Alliance congressmen for not respecting the Indianapolis Resolution and described the election of Crisp as an Alliance victory. In mid-December, Stephen McLallin arrived in Washington to attend a meeting of the National Citizens' Alliance. The Kansas delegation accompanied him to a stormy interview with Livingston, whom McLallin upbraided for deserting the Kansas alliancemen. Livingston ridiculed the Kansans for ever imagining he or any other Southern allianceman intended to leave the Democratic party. In the Senate, Peffer approached John L. M. Irby, leader of the Tillman political organization in South Carolina and elected by Alliance votes, and expressed his hope that they could work together. Irby stiffly replied, "Well, sir, we Alliancemen in the South are all Democrats." Alliance congressmen continued to meet for several weeks, but the split between the two factions widened. Livingston criticized the Kansans for attempting to force reformers into a party movement. The Populists responded that by subjecting themselves to the Democratic caucus the Southerners obviously had a different conception of the importance of the Alliance demands, and they refused to attend any more meetings called by Livingston.[7]

Among the Populists in Congress, Peffer took the lead in proposing legislation to enact Alliance demands. He announced his intention of ignoring the custom that freshman senators should not speak, and the prominent and the curious packed the galleries when he made his first speech. This initial effort was a superb discussion of the Populist financial position and an argument for the passage of a bill embodying the land-loan principle, and Populists afterwards distributed copies of it as a major campaign document. Peffer also introduced bills and resolutions to prevent dealings in options and futures, to prohibit the formation of trusts, to increase the circulating medium through the issuance of paper money, to establish a bureau of irrigation, and to increase popular participation in politics.[8]

[7] *National Economist,* December 12, 1891; *Topeka Daily Capital,* December 15, 1891, February 7, 1892; *Chicago Tribune,* June 2, 1899; *Washington Post,* January 22, February 5, 1892.

The Kansas congressmen were also active in introducing bills in the House based on Alliance demands, but they received little real support from the Alliance congressmen of the South. Neither did Irby or Senator John B. Gordon of Georgia, also elected by an Alliance legislature, indicate any interest in joining Peffer in promoting Alliance principles in the Senate. In particular the Southern alliancemen renounced the subtreasury and rejected the pleas of Otis to have a Southerner introduce a bill embodying the proposal. But, as one reporter observed, "they have cut loose from their Kansas brethren on everything. With the exception of Watson," he added, "the Southern alliancemen have agreed to act with the Democrats in everything; in fact they declare they never had any other intention. The Kansas men feel bad about it, and some who thought the Southern alliancemen would be with them in everything are really mad about it. They declare openly that the Southerners have gone back on them." Simpson explained further the Populist indignation: "When we went through the South last summer the meetings were large and enthusiastic. . . . [But now] These Congressmen since they have got to Washington have forgotten the pledges they made the people and have forgotten the people, too."[9]

Chagrinned to find the Southern congressmen "disposed to be Democrats first and alliancemen afterward," as one Kansas congressman expressed his disappointment, the Populists turned their attention to the St. Louis conference of the Confederation of Industrial Organizations in hopes of there gaining an explicit endorsement of their party by the nation's reform organizations. Peffer and Watson remained in Washington on congressional business, but the other Populists and their Southern adversaries in the Alliance all attended. The Kansans were again optimistic, but once more Livingston dampened their spirits. "We don't care what they do in Kansas and other western states," he declared. "They can have a third party if they want one; in fact, a third party in Kansas is

---

8 *Congressional Record*, 52d Cong., 1st sess., vol. 23, pp. 35, 107, 357, 470-78, 1171, 5443; *Kansas Farmer* (Topeka), January 20, 1892; *National Economist*, January 30, February 6, 1892; *Topeka Advocate*, January 6, 1892; *Topeka Daily Capital*, January 13, 22, February 3, 1892; *Washington Post*, June 14, 1892.

9 *Topeka Daily Capital*, December 26, 1891, January 20, 1892.

probably a good thing with which to overthrow the Republican party, and in that good work we wish them success; but in the South we want no third party."[10]

The Populists achieved mixed results at St. Louis. Those delegates favoring independent action won every contest over officers, credentials, and resolutions, and the convention appointed a committee which met with the Populist National Executive Committee to call a People's party national nominating convention for Omaha, July 4, 1892. This had been the Populists' objective since Ocala, but their joy was tempered by the large minority, overwhelmingly from the South, that opposed the third party. The declaration of the third party had been repeatedly delayed in order to gain Southern support, and now that support was not forthcoming. Southern Alliance leaders denounced both the People's party and the St. Louis convention, and entire Southern delegations refused to accept the convention's decision. One Tennessee delegate, however, welcomed the decision for a third party because, with the South certain to remain Democratic, "I think the Republican party is the sufferer."[11]

Following the St. Louis convention, the Populist hopes for Southern backing were less optimistic than desperate. Southern Democrats refused to temporize with the Alliance in 1892 as they had in 1890. Democratic officials in at least Texas and Tennessee required alliancemen to renounce their Alliance principles before permitting them to enter party conventions and primaries; elsewhere alliancemen were simply outmaneuvered or outvoted. One state after another rejected Alliance platforms and candidates and selected delegations to the Democratic national convention pledged to Grover Cleveland, who had repeatedly expressed his hostility to Alliance demands. South Carolina Democrats, under the dictation of Ben Tillman, did adopt an Alliance platform, but carefully promised to support the party's eventual nominee, even if he were Cleveland.[12]

10 Ibid., January 20, February 9, 1892.

11 *Kansas Farmer*, March 2, 1892; *Topeka Daily Capital*, February 24, March 20, 1892; John D. Hicks, *The Populist Revolt* (Minneapolis, 1931), pp. 223-29.

12 *National Economist*, February 20, May 28, 1892; Roscoe C. Martin, *The People's Party in Texas* (Austin, Texas, 1933), pp. 39-40; J. A. Sharp, "The Farmers' Alliance and the People's Party in Tennessee," *East Tennessee Historical*

Despite these rebuffs, however, few Southern alliancemen were willing to leave the Democracy, fearful that such action would only permit Negroes and Republicans to triumph. Alliance leaders Frank Burkitt of Mississippi and John H. McDowell of Tennessee did declare allegiance to the new party, but any real chance that Southern voters would follow ended when L. L. Polk suddenly died on June 11, 1892. Almost certainly he would have been named to the People's party national ticket and had the support of Peffer and many others for the first position, because, as Colorado Populist leader Davis Waite wrote, "in order for the People's Party to succeed, WE MUST BREAK THE SOLID SOUTH." Peffer, Otis, and Baker were among Polk's pallbearers in Raleigh, North Carolina, and with Polk the Kansans also buried their hopes for a Populist victory.[13]

None of the Populist congressmen attended the Omaha national convention because important legislation was pending in Congress. Instead, they joined together to send a telegram, signed first by Peffer, an honor always accorded him as the party's ostensible leader because of his position as its first senator, urging the convention to "select for our great party of the people standard bearers worthy of the time and occasion." There was some support for Peffer's nomination at the convention, but his repeated refusal to be a candidate, his continued delicate health, and the important position he already held kept his name from serious consideration. Willits and Davis of Kansas also attracted some interest, but the nomination eventually went to James B. Weaver of Iowa. James G. Field of Virginia received the vice presidential nomination as another move to engage Southern support. Embodying the Alliance principles on money, land, and transportation and advocating the expansion of responsive governmental power to promote the public

---

Society's Publications, No. 10 (1938): 99-100, 104; Francis B. Simkins, *Pitchfork Ben Tillman* (Baton Rouge, La., 1944), p. 206; *Girard Western Herald,* April 29, May 6, 1892.

13 *Girard Western Herald,* April 16, 1892; *Washington Post,* July 18, 1892; John Willits to L. L. Polk, April 21, 1892, and Paul Van Dervoort to Polk, April 12, 1892, L. L. Polk Papers, Southern Historical Collection, University of North Carolina Library; Stuart Noblin, *Leonidas LaFayette Polk* (Chapel Hill, N.C., 1949), pp. 284-94; John R. Morris, "Davis White: The Ideology of a Western Populist" (Ph.D. diss., University of Colorado, 1965), p. 260; *National Economist,* June 18, 1892.

welfare, the platform and its ringing preamble attracted much more enthusiasm than the candidates.[14]

Indeed, the Populist disdain for politicians also expressed itself in a unique resolution which repudiated politics in favor of populism. The Omaha Ordinance for the Purification of Politics established as "fundamental party law" the principle that "no person holding office . . . federal, state or municipal . . . including senators, congressmen and members of legislatures . . . shall be eligible to sit or vote in any convention of this party." Populists were determined that the people and not the politicians should control their movement.[15]

Certainly they felt the opposite held true at the Democratic convention. The nomination of the stubbornly obtuse Cleveland, although expected, caused many Southern alliancemen finally to consider seriously the call of the third party. So obviously hostile to their principles, Cleveland provoked revulsion among many alliancemen. A Virginia Alliance leader declared that Cleveland's nomination had "snapped the last cord which binds free men to the Democratic party," and in some places in the South, notably North Carolina, there was a chance of Democratic defeat.[16]

The Democracy aggressively responded to the Populist challenge by ignoring even the tariff and financial issues to emphasize the sectional theme. "The old issue of sectionalism is confronting the South," declared the *Atlanta Constitution,* "and White Supremacy is more important than all the financial reform in the world." The *Richmond Dispatch* argued that "the present Democratic party in Virginia was formed . . . for self-protection against sectional misrule—and without any reference to economic questions." Support for the People's party, Southern politicians insisted, would cause a Democratic defeat, the passage of a force bill, and the establishment of Negro domination—issues upon which all Democrats could unite. The Populist attempt to play down race as a political issue and to create a popular front between black and white farmers merely reinforced Democratic racist charges against the People's party.[17]

14 *Topeka Advocate,* July 6, 1892; *Topeka Daily Capital,* April 10, June 30, 1892; *Washington Post,* July 4, 1892.

15 *National Economist,* July 16, 1892; Hicks, *Populist Revolt,* p. 236.

16 *National Economist,* July 2, 1892; C. Vann Woodward, *Origins of the New South* (Baton Rouge, La., 1951), p. 243.

Republican encouragement of the third party throughout the South, moreover, added to the Populist difficulty in attracting support from Democratic farmers. Eager to cooperate with the People's party in order to hurt Southern Democrats and offset the inroads the new party was expected to make in the Republican Northwest, Republicans actively entered into Southern Populist conventions, appeared on many Populist tickets, and sometimes avoided making separate nominations. This Republican activity prompted dissident Southerners to return to the Democracy, preferring the lesser evil of a conservative party hostile to economic reforms to the greater evil of "negro domination," and the third-party movement never adequately expressed the extent of the Southern farmers' disaffection from the Democratic party.[18]

Added to the rhetorical attack on those Southerners who threatened to be "traitors to their race" as well as to their party was a Democratic campaign of open violence. Mobs attacked and intimidated Populist leaders and meetings and even forced Weaver, Mrs. Lease, and others to cancel many of their Southern speaking engagements. Democratic politicians, Mrs. Lease complained, encouraged the lawlessness, intolerance, and violence that Populists had to face in the South.[19]

In the face of such pressure, Populist strength in the South suffered a serious decline following the mid-summer peak after Cleveland's nomination. By the end of September, the Virginia Democratic state chairman was able to report that "the Third party is rapidly resolving itself back into the Democratic party from which it was mainly drawn." But as early as April the outcome was clear. The Populist gubernatorial candidate received

17 William DuBose Sheldon, *Populism in the Old Dominion* (Princeton, N.J., 1935), pp. 72-73; Stanley P. Hirshson, *Farewell to the Bloody Shirt* (Bloomington, Ind., 1962), pp. 238-40; *Washington Post*, July 10, 18, 1892; *National Economist*, May 14, 1892; Woodward, *Watson*, pp. 222-23; Tom Watson, "The Negro Question in the South," *Arena* 6 (October 1892): 540-50.

18 John D. Hicks, "The Farmers' Alliance in North Carolina," *North Carolina Historical Review* 2 (April 1925): 182-84; Sharp, "Alliance and People's Party," pp. 105-9; *National Economist*, May 6, 1892; Alex M. Arnett, *The Populist Movement in Georgia* (New York, 1922), pp. 150-51; Hicks, *Populist Revolt*, pp. 245-47; Sheldon, *Populism in the Old Dominion*, pp. 72-73; Albert D. Kirwan, *Revolt of the Rednecks* (Lexington, Ky., 1951), pp. 95, 101.

19 Fred E. Haynes, *James Baird Weaver* (Iowa City, 1919), pp. 324-25; Woodward, *Watson*, pp. 216-43; *National Economist*, October 1, 8, 1892.

fewer than 10,000 votes in Louisiana's state election on April 19, and only one Populist legislator was elected. In other state elections before November, the Populists were also easily defeated. In Arkansas in September the People's party ran third behind the Republicans, and in Georgia's state election in October the Democrats nearly tripled its vote despite Republican assistance. Arkansas's election had been expected to reveal the strength of the People's party in the South, and the easy Democratic victory was surprising. The election in Georgia, considered one of the best hopes of the new party, confirmed the observation that, since the summer peak, "the strength of the people's party [in the South] has gradually dissolved and disappeared until now the organization is but a shadow of its former self." Indeed, in November, the South voted overwhelmingly for Cleveland, and the Populist ticket frequently ran third, even in Texas where the party made its best showing. The champion of Southern Populism, Tom Watson, was rejected by his neighbors in his bid for reelection, and despite frequent fusion with Republicans no Southern Populist was elected to Congress. The Populist hope that the Southern people would repudiate their political managers had failed utterly.[20]

The Louisiana People's party had issued an address to the public, praying that its vote might "break the 'solid south' and greet our great toiling brethren of the North and West with the cheering hope of industrial reform in the near future."[21] Populists outside the South had depended upon that reassurance and anxiously had observed their movement in that crucial section. The full impact of the South's inability to overcome its special fears and frustrations and accept a new compact responding to real and pressing issues would be felt in Kansas and the Northwest only after the revealing election, but earlier signs of apprehension and doubt were only too obvious, even when couched in words of confidence.

The possibility that the South might refuse the Populist overture

---

[20] Sheldon, *Populism in the Old Dominion*, pp. 88-92; Lucia Daniel, "The Louisiana People's Party," *Louisiana Historical Quarterly* 26 (October 1943): 1082-91; *Topeka Daily Capital*, September 17, 1892; *Frank Leslie's Weekly*, October 20, 1892, p. 275; *Appletons' Cyclopaedia for 1892* (New York, 1893), pp. 5, 20, 308; Kirwan, *Revolt of the Rednecks*, p. 96; Sharp, "Alliance and People's Party," pp. 105-12.

[21] Melvin White, "Populism in Louisiana during the Nineties," *Mississippi Valley Historical Review* 5 (June 1918): 11.

attracted great comment long before the elections of 1892. If the obvious Southern reluctance before the Cincinnati Conference to countenance the third-party movement disturbed Frank McGrath and other Kansas Populists, it delighted the Republican press, which reported every announcement of a Southern Alliance leader's intention to remain with the Democracy. Editorials explained Southern abstention by emphasizing the allegation that the People's party existed only to assist the Democracy: "Peffer will discover that it is one thing unconsciously to lead the farmers of Kansas into a southern Democratic trap, and another thing to turn that trap against its very makers. There will be no third party in the south." The Cincinnati Conference itself, argued papers throughout the Northwest, was part of a scheme to divide the North so that Southern Democracy might prevail. And in Kansas, Populist and Republican papers engaged in editorial debate over both the number and the significance of Southern delegates at the conference.[22]

The press also followed the Southern crusade of the Populists closely. The *Chicago Tribune,* for example, detailed a reporter to dog Jerry Simpson's steps throughout the summer of 1891. Northern Republicans declared that the split over the subtreasury indicated that Southern Democrats would refuse to support the new party and thereby doom it to failure. The *Cincinnati Commercial-Gazette,* for instance, warned "Republican farmers in the North" to "look well into the situation in the South before consenting to give aid to the Third Party movement." Southern threats of violence against Peffer, Simpson, and other Populists received wide publicity as did "events occurring from day to day which plainly prove the loyalty of southern alliancemen and of their leaders to the Democracy." The 1891 Kentucky election particularly convinced Republican spokesmen that, as Southern Democrats obviously refused to renounce their old party, "Republican farmers in the North with Alliance tendencies" should not remain in the third-party movement.[23]

The disputed impact of the People's party on the South became

22 *Topeka Daily Capital,* March 20, April 11, 21, May 20, 1891; *Cincinnati Commercial-Gazette,* May 19, 1891; *Girard Western Herald,* June 13, 1891.
23 *Cincinnati Commercial-Gazette,* August 3, 4, 1891; *Topeka Daily Capital,* July 18, August 15, 16, 29, 1891; *Chicago Tribune,* August 13, 1891.

an important issue in the Kansas off-year elections of 1891. The Republican emphasis upon the expected ultimate failure of the Southern crusade provoked Populist leaders to extravagant predictions of their imminent success. Peffer toured Kansas, reporting on his Southern trips and assuring his Populist listeners that the South would stand by them in 1892. In another effort to embolden their followers, Populist leaders arranged to have Polk travel with Peffer and Willits in September to address party meetings in Kansas. This visit, some commented, was to "stiffen up the backbone of Kansas Populists who had about concluded that there was to be no Third Party in the South."[24]

One remarkable feature of the Kansas elections of 1891 was Republican-Democratic fusion to defeat Populist candidates, revealing both the hypocrisy with which party managers manipulated partisan appeals and the practical problems faced by the Populists in trying to create a coalition of two sections, each strongly dominated by one party. Kansas Republicans were eager to regain their local political control and to strike the Populist heresy a deathblow before the 1892 national elections. Moreover, at stake were largely judicial offices, and conservatives were aghast at the prospect of a Populist judiciary. Democratic support for fusion with Republicans was more inspired by national politics. Georgia Congressman Charles Crisp declared in the fall of 1891, "If the damned Alliance, or the People's Party should carry Kansas this year, all hell can't hold the Alliancemen of the South; therefore it is necessary to break up the People's Party of Kansas, in order to preserve a solid South." Kansas Democrats thus agreed to cooperate with Republicans in hopes of discouraging third-party tendencies in the Democratic stronghold of the South. Republicans continued to denounce the People's party as an adjunct of the Democracy while cooperating with Democrats in a move designed to insure continued Democratic strength. Southern Democrats who denounced the People's party as an ally of the GOP urged Democratic cooperation with Republicans who wanted to regain their regional ascendancy.[25]

24 *Girard Western Herald*, September 19, 26, October 31, 1891: *Topeka Daily Capital*, September 12, 15-17, 1891; Hicks, "Farmers' Alliance in North Carolina," p. 180. *Kansas Farmer*, September 2, 1891.
25 *Topeka Daily Capital*, August 18, 30, October 20, 22, 1891; Woodward,

The meaning of the 1891 election returns was clouded. The Populists, who had vigorously rejected any suggestion of fusion, welcomed the union of the old parties as a sign that there was no essential difference between them and that the new party was necessary for political and economic reform. But that combination reversed the 1890 outcome, and the Populists carried only 127 of 404 local offices. Republican newspapers declared that the Populist defeat ended the Kansans' influence in other states and represented the repudiation of "the whole train of anarchistic schemes that belongs to this new party." Republican partisans were even more enthusiastic. In celebrating the apparent Populist defeat, a mob at Emporia dragged, shot, and burned effigies of Peffer, Polk, and Mrs. Diggs. The actual Populist vote, however, had increased 11 percent. Defeat, Peffer and Willits maintained, stemmed merely from distortions by the partisan press and from old-party collusion, which could only help increase the Populist vote again in 1892.[26]

Popular attention in the Northwest remained riveted on Populist overtures to the South. The failure to attract Southern supporters in Congress during the winter of 1891–1892 produced considerable comment. "If the Southern Alliancemen are sincere they must then cut their Democratic hawser and come into the Kansas People's Party," one newspaper asserted. "On the issue whether this will be their course or not hangs the future existence of the new party in Kansas." The campaign and various elections in the South in 1892 bred further charge and countercharge, promises and predictions in the Kansas press. Populists rejoiced at every report of Southern gains, but the obvious general Southern reluctance to break away from the Democracy introduced a fretful note in their appeals to that section. "Are you going to cringe under the crack of a party whip? . . . Why should the South . . . hesitate any longer? The fight has to be made." Northern Republicans used this Southern resistance in 1892 in an effort to draw former Republicans out of the People's party and back to the GOP. In May a Southern conference of the state presidents of the Farmers' Alli-

Watson, p. 186; *National Economist,* August 29, 1891; *Girard Western Herald,* August 29, 1891; Hicks, *Populist Revolt,* p. 223.

26 *Topeka State Journal,* July 10, 1891; *Topeka Advocate,* November 18, December 9, 1891; *Topeka Daily Capital,* November 5, 7, 1891; *National Economist,* December 5, 19, 1891.

ance rejected pleas for an endorsement of the People's party by reaffirming the order's nonpartisan policy, and the Kansas Republican press trumpeted "the final judgment of Southern alliance leaders" as proof of the failure of Populist ambitions.[27]

The aborted campaign trip of Weaver and Mrs. Lease through the South was also used in the Republican attempt to win back voters from the People's party. Mrs. Lease had told Southerners that the Kansas Populists were "depending upon the people of the South to join with them in their revolt," and her forced withdrawal from the platform indicated the Populist dependence was misplaced. The *Topeka Capital* believed "this settles the people's party campaign in the solid south. . . . Gen. Weaver's abandonment of the south is the most sensational incident in the campaign and a matter worthy of the serious consideration of his followers in Kansas. It must now be apparent to them that his election as president is out of the question. To give him the electoral vote of Kansas would result only in . . . the election of Mr. Cleveland . . . [and] the continued supremacy of the solid south, procured by fraud and violence in contempt of free institutions." When Peffer attempted to minimize the significance of Weaver's Southern treatment, the volatile Mrs. Lease assailed the senator and denounced the South in an interview widely circulated by Republicans. But other Populists pointed out that their speakers suffered violent attacks in Kansas, too, and assured their fellows that the party remained strong in the South. "Let no Populist in Kansas be discouraged by these things nor by the use that Republicans are making of them."[28]

Kansas Populists had to keep up a brave front. From the first they had staked their eventual success upon Southern cooperation. If the South refused, declared the party's leading paper, McLallin's *Topeka Advocate,* "we confess, nothing but failure and defeat await us." Thus they continued to forecast sweeping success, perhaps in belief, perhaps merely hoping to shore up their local

[27] *Topeka Daily Capital,* December 26, 1891, January 19, 20, May 8, 17, 1892; Stephen McLallin to Polk, April 26, 1892, Polk Papers; *Girard Western Herald,* April 6, 23, May 6, 1892; *National Economist,* September 24, 1892.

[28] *National Economist,* September 24, 1892; *Topeka Daily Capital,* September 27, 28, October 7, 19, November 4, 1892; *Kansas City Star,* October 6, 1892; *Girard Western Herald,* October 7, 14, 1892.

followers. When the Democrats overwhelmed the People's party in Louisiana's April election, Kansas Populists dared the Republicans to tell how wonderfully their party was doing elsewhere in the South. They denied that the defeat of an independent ticket in Alabama's August state election indicated actual Populist strength there. In late September Peffer still predicted that his party would carry a number of Southern states. The crushing October Democratic victories in Georgia and Florida brought a Populist response that the party had never claimed it would win either state. Simpson, for example, valiantly told a reporter: "That Democratic majority in Georgia is not going to have the least effect on the People's Party vote in Kansas. They can't get the People's Party men in Kansas to go back into the Republican party by telling them that People's Party men in Georgia went back to the Democratic party. Because one man makes a mistake it is not an argument why another man should make one."[29]

For all their bravado, however, Kansas Populists were downcast at their repeated Southern disappointments. "The people's party leaders in this community," noted one local observer, "have been thunderstruck at the result of the Georgia election and the effect it is having on the old time Republicans in that party. Quite a number here renounced their allegiance to the people's party in the last four days and came back to the Republican fold." Though there were such defections, however, more Populists agreed to postpone judgment until the general election. "Although the Republicans are trying to make us believe that the people of Georgia are not with us," one wrote, "we still have confidence in the intelligence and fidelity of the people of Georgia, and feel confident that they will be found with the people of Kansas, in the middle of the road next November."[30]

"Next November" made it clear at last that the South would not join Kansans in the middle of the road. The sweeping Democratic success in the South made a mockery of the efforts and hopes of the Kansas Populists and placed a Democrat in the White House. That

29 *Topeka Advocate,* November 11, 1891; *Topeka Daily Capital,* May 17, 1892; *National Economist,* September 24, October 29, 1892; *Girard Western Herald,* May 27, August 12, October 14, 1892.
30 *Topeka Daily Capital,* October 18, 1892; *National Economist,* October 22, 1892.

Democrat, moreover, was the hated Grover Cleveland, who opposed everything the People's party stood for. James G. Field, the Populist vice presidential candidate, added to their misery when he asserted that Cleveland owed his election to the existence of the People's party, which enabled him "to secure electoral votes by pluralities north of the Ohio which he could never have secured by majorities" in a two-party election.[31] The Republicans and not the Populists had understood the South. The full impact of this upon the People's party would appear after November 1892.

If the action of the South seemed to make the People's party in Kansas an ally of the Democracy as the Republicans had predicted, other events in Kansas during 1892 strengthened that opinion for many people, including for perhaps the first time substantial numbers of Populists. A series of political maneuvers engineered by small groups of Democratic and Populist politicians placed the two parties in an explicit partnership that began first to undermine the ethics and weaken the ideological justification of the new party and then to change its composition and modify its direction.

Immediately after the 1890 election, Democrats began planning with the assistance of several Populists of Democratic antecedents to employ the new People's party to further Democratic ambitions in 1892. Several of these men discussed their thoughts with Grover Cleveland. George Glick, former Democratic governor, and Thomas Moonlight, 1890 Democratic congressional candidate, assured Cleveland that Kansas Democrats stood solidly behind him and were eager to do "all things that will best insure your election." That could best be accomplished, they maintained, by fusion with the Populists. "In four or five of the Western states it is possible to beat the Republican party in 1892 by uniting all the opposition upon electors and on union tickets for say, the People's nominee. This would not be for the Democratic nominee let us concede, but it would take at least thirty electoral votes from the Republican column, and secure the election through the Democratic House of the Democratic nominee had not we a majority of all the electors. This is an important consideration which must be borne in mind

31 George H. Knoles, *The Presidential Campaign and Election of 1892* (Stanford, Calif., 1942), p. 235.

from this time forth." Moreover, they argued, the Democrats had little to lose in the effort, for the "Democracy of Kansas is hopelessly gone," its strength in rural areas and among labor organizations having been absorbed by the People's party. Democrats should therefore seek to direct the new party's course. "So much has been accomplished in the defeat of Ingalls and a general smashing up of the old Republican machine," Moonlight told Cleveland in January 1891.

We Democrats could not as a party break up the huge machine by reason of the bitter prejudice attaching to the name "Democrat," but another organization with our indirect and almost silent help is doing the work, and I urge our men to aid and assist in the work, and when the smashing process is complete, we will gather up all the fragments, and strange as it may seem, they will all come to us. The Alliance in the meantime will *almost* destroy our party. . . . [In 1892] our western work must be to cause [Republicans] to lose four or five western Republican states through the power of the Alliance movement. . . . I confess a determination to use it for destructive purposes, and do not fear its future strength.[32]

Although Democratic leaders thus conspired to use the People's party in 1892 for their own purposes, they opposed the new party in 1891 for the same reason. National political considerations dictated fusion with the Republicans rather than the Populists, and within the state Democrats wanted to avoid being totally absorbed by the third-party movement. The state's Democratic editors, for example, announced in their annual convention that the party would not consider fusion with the Populists. For their part, the Populists saw no reason to fuse. John Davis retorted sharply to the announcement of the Democratic editors, "Who has asked them to [fuse]? Last fall they begged for fusion. . . . It was kindly but firmly declined by the People's Party. That has been the uniform policy of the People's Party toward both wings of the Wall Street party."[33]

After the election of 1891, however, Democrats began to maneuver toward a working agreement with the state's Populists for the election of 1892. John Martin, David Overmeyer, and other influ-

[32] George Glick to Grover Cleveland, November 27, 1890, A. N. Whittington to Cleveland, December 28, 1890, Thomas Moonlight to Cleveland, November 27, 1890, January 31, 1891, Cleveland Papers.
[33] John Davis Scrapbook, vol. "O," p. 44, KSHS.

ential Democrats immediately urged the creation of a coalition to defeat the Republicans, but on Democratic terms. The Topeka *Kansas Democrat* and the *Wichita Beacon* led the state's Democratic newspapers in reversing their earlier stand. Such spokesmen believed the 1891 election demonstrated that the Democratic party held the balance of power in Kansas and could take advantage of this position to advance Democratic interests. Together, the *Beacon* suggested, the Democrats and Populists could elect men to every office. The obvious course was fusion, with members of both parties on a joint ticket. Glick announced his willingness even to allow the Populists the major offices on such a ballot in order to insure tacit Populist assistance in national matters.[34]

These Democrats found support among a number of Populists who viewed the 1891 election as a warning to seek an accommodation with the Democratic party. With very few exceptions these fusion-minded Populists came from either the former Democrats or Union Laborites within the People's party. Both groups had traditionally regarded the Republican party as the enemy and had customarily fused against this common opponent in the past. Now they saw little reason to discontinue the procedure at a time when its success seemed assured. W. H. T. Wakefield corresponded with Moonlight on fusion arrangements, while such Populist newspapers as the *Pleasanton Herald,* edited by former Union Laborite J. E. Latimer, reprinted editorials from fusionist Democratic papers and strongly advocated cooperation with the Democrats on an abbreviated platform. Latimer suggested naming Glick, Martin, and two other Democrats to the ten-place state ticket and, as early as March, he placed his recommended ticket at the head of his editorial columns.[35]

Particularly influential among Populists in promoting fusion were members of the Citizens' Alliance. Organized within the urban areas of Kansas, the Citizens' Alliance had much higher proportions of former Democrats and Union Labor men among its members than did the Farmers' Alliance, and these men were more experi-

---

[34] *Girard Western Herald,* November 14, December 12, 1891; *Topeka Daily Capital,* November 14, 1891; *Wichita Weekly Beacon,* January 8, March 18, 1892.
[35] Moonlight to Wakefield, November 27, 1890, copy in Cleveland Papers; *Pleasanton Herald,* February 12, 19, March 18, 1892.

enced in the political deals and compromises of Kansas political life. Some Citizens' Alliances seem to have been established by Democrats in a direct effort to influence the People's party. In Hiawatha, for instance, a newly formed Citizens' Alliance listed among its ten officers seven Democrats and but one man who had previously affiliated with the People's party. Those who opposed fusion often directed their anger against such organizations, as did the Farmers' Alliance of Drywood Township, Bourbon County, in its June 1892 meeting, when all forty-eight alliancemen agreed that fusion with Democrats was incompatible with Populism and urged their representatives to "exert every possible means to defeat the fusion scheme of designing Democrats and characterless leaders of the Citizens' Alliance."[36]

Indeed, opposition to fusionist sentiment was strong in the People's party and especially among its major leaders of 1890. As the debate over fusion developed in early 1892, Peffer advanced the radical, morally based position of the anti-fusionists when he warned his followers from Washington: "I am opposed to any sort of fusion, coalition, or understanding of any kind with the Democrats. An arrangement of that kind means compromise. We are either right or we are wrong. If we are right, we should stick to it, and a compromise cannot help us." McLallin believed fusion meant "a sacrifice of principle and an ultimate sacrifice of strength," and he argued, "Better defeat than victory at such a sacrifice." Willits and Mrs. Lease raged at the mention of fusion, and of the five Populist congressmen only Simpson announced his support of the proposition.[37]

Simpson had already irritated many of his fellow Populist leaders. A Union Labor-Democratic fusion candidate in 1888, he had relied heavily upon continued Democratic backing for his 1890 election as a Populist, and he repeatedly made clear his intention to have such assistance in his reelection bid in 1892. His open concern for Democratic sensibilities annoyed Populists who viewed their party's very existence as a result of the treachery of both old parties.

[36] Grant Harrington, *Annals of Brown County* (Hiawatha, Kans., 1901), p. 261; *Topeka Daily Capital,* June 8, 1892.
[37] *Topeka Daily Capital,* February 21, 1892; *Topeka Advocate,* July 15, 1891, April 20, 1892.

Simpson's lobbying for the senatorial election of Democrat John Palmer of Illinois particularly upset Peffer; his initial resistance to the establishment of a national third party angered others, especially McGrath; and his abrasive personality alienated Clover and strained relations with Peffer in their first months together in Washington. By early 1892 Democratic newspapers were praising Simpson as "rapidly becoming an ultra Democrat" while denouncing Peffer and other Populists for "their unfavorable attitude towards the Democracy."[38]

Many party officials and political actives in the People's party inclined more toward Simpson's position than Peffer's. Concerned most immediately with organizing an election victory, they argued for "using a little political sense this year" and announced that the anti-fusionists "ought to know that three state tickets insures the election of the entire Republican ticket." Some like Latimer recommended placing Democrats directly on the Populist ticket while others such as Levi Dumbauld, chairman of the State Central Committee, merely favored the nomination of those Populists with Democratic backgrounds who would attract Democratic support. This second proposal was more popular and placed William A. Harris and John Ives in the forefront of speculation.[39]

These fusionists frequently met with Democratic politicians in early 1892 in hopes of reaching an agreement. The Democratic Tilden Club of Wichita, for example, invited fusion Populists to its meetings for discussion about possible joint action to defeat the common enemy. More important were the private meetings between leaders of the two parties on every level. In early January Populists of Democratic antecedents led by Van Prather, a founder of the National Citizens' Alliance, met straight Democrats in Kansas City and arranged to publicize fusion sentiment through Populist papers to be subsidized by Democrats. In March Glick and several Populist committeemen met in Atchison to divide offices between the two parties in order to construct a joint ticket. In April the Second Congressional District committees of the two parties met in Fort

---

[38] *Topeka Daily Capital*, May 23, 1891, January 6, February 21, 25, April 5, 1892; Karel D. Bicha, "Jerry Simpson: Populist without Principle," *Journal of American History* 54 (September 1967): 294-96, 304.

[39] *Pleasanton Herald*, March 11, 1892; *Wichita Weekly Beacon*, April 15, 1892.

Scott to choose a mutually acceptable candidate who could be placed before their actual nominating conventions in the summer. Party leaders of a number of counties likewise held private sessions in the spring in an effort to design local fusion tickets.[40]

At no time, however, did the Democrats indicate their agreement with the Populists on principles. Democrats based fusion proposals only on calculations of political bargaining and practical politics and not on ideological grounds. The same meeting of the Tilden Club that applauded fusion advocates heard a speaker recite the history of Democratic fusion maneuvers, each forged solely in response to the ambition and pride of Democratic candidates. Leading Democratic fusionist papers, moreover, argued that the tariff was the only issue in the coming campaign. Most importantly, Kansas Democrats stood as a unit behind Grover Cleveland in his quest for another presidential nomination. Glick, one of the leading Democratic fusionists, was Cleveland's best friend and advocate in Kansas and made frequent political trips in the former president's interest. In March the Democratic State Central Committee voted overwhelmingly for both fusion with the Populists and the nomination of Cleveland. The Democratic state convention in April selected a Cleveland delegation to the national convention with instructions to vote as a unit for him as long as his name was before the convention. The Kansas Democracy, Glick assured Cleveland afterwards, was "unanimous for you."[41]

As fusion arrangements between the two parties became more likely, Peffer repeatedly issued admonitions against the course. "Any bargain and sale of the offices which might be arranged by the Democrats and a few of the leaders of our party," he predicted in April, "would never be accepted by the thousands of alliancemen who went into the third party because they were done with the Democratic and Republican parties for all time. They did not

---

[40] *Wichita Weekly Beacon,* April 1, 1892; *Paola Times,* May 5, 1892; *Miami Republican* (Paola), May 6, 1892; *Topeka Daily Capital,* March 22, April 3, 5, 20, 26, 1892; Van Prather to Charles Robinson, January 10, 1892, Robinson Papers.

[41] *Wichita Weekly Beacon,* February 26, April 1, 1892; *Kansas Agitator* (Garnett), January 14, 1892; *Girard Western Herald,* April 16, 1892; *Topeka Daily Capital,* May 12, 1892; Glick to Cleveland, March 2, 10, 17, April 21, May 9, 1892, and Glick to Daniel Lamont, December 28, 1891, Cleveland Papers.

go into the People's party to assist by combination or coalition in the election of either Democrats or Republicans; they went into the new party as a matter of principle." A week later, after the Democratic House had voted down a silver bill, Peffer declared that Democratic duplicity as much as Republican injustice and corruption had caused the establishment of a People's party, and it was "now more apparent than ever that to fuse with either of the old parties simply because some politicians want office, would be to surrender principle for spoils and constitute a ridiculous blunder and one that would do great injury to the movement." Populism, he maintained, aimed "to benefit the whole people and not a few scheming . . . politicians who . . . spend their entire time in seeking to form combinations to get nominations and then devise ways and means to secure the office at the polls."[42]

The reaction of Populists to Peffer's pronouncements against fusion seemed to depend largely upon their attitude toward the movement in general. Those who viewed politics in broad, national terms and thus considered the national ramifications of Kansas action and who most strongly believed that the People's party would become a national force to remake society typically opposed any proposition to fuse with Democrats in Kansas. Clover, for example, agreed with Peffer that Democratic dissemblance in Congress, "if there was no other reason, ought to prevent any combination between the Democrats and alliancemen in Kansas or any other state."[43] With the exception of Simpson, other national figures among Kansas Populists also concurred with Peffer's antifusion views. Brought into prominence in 1890 by a mass movement which repudiated the old parties by its very existence, they saw no valid reason to retrogress. Furthermore, they were primarily responsible for launching the party into national politics. Editors like McLallin, who considered reform from a national perspective, or like W. C. Routzong who sought to preserve the ideological purity and idealistic fervor of the movement, provided effective public support for the middle-of-the-road position.

Rather than indicating a conservative policy, the term "middle of the road" had its origin in Peffer's admonition at the Cincinnati

---

[42] *Topeka Daily Capital*, April 5, 1892, *Kansas City Journal*, April 13, 1892.
[43] *Topeka Daily Capital*, April 5, 1892.

Conference to avoid the siren calls of the old parties, and thereafter it referred to those radical Populists who rejected fusion and its inevitable compromises of principles. Populism, these men and women logically argued, demanded national action to correct national abuses, and the party could not expect to create the necessary dissolution of the Solid South if it cooperated with the Democracy in Kansas. Moreover, Populism condemned both old parties, for they had combined, in the Populist viewpoint, to oppress the people through a confusion of real interests and plays on prejudice. The Populist intention, after all, was to destroy both old parties, which were corrupt in outlook and malevolent in operation, and cooperation with either would mean the betrayal of the promise of the people's movement; the adoption of the sordid practices of voter manipulation for offices and spoils that Populists believed they had abandoned with their former partisan allegiances; the admission that the motivating hope of a glorious political reformation in America was groundless, that the period of increasing acceptance of reform principles had ended, that the assistance of the unregenerate was necessary. The people's movement had developed as a political rebellion against the cynical methods as much as the callous objectives of the old parties, the mid-roaders remembered, and their political reformation could not with reason adopt the methods of the old parties without acknowledging failure of its objectives as well. "If it was merely to turn Republicans out of office, a fusion of the People's and Democratic parties would be both desirable and sensible," conceded mid-roader W. O. Champe. "[But] the offices are only a means to an end. To turn Republicans out of office, and then admit others not friendly to the reform movement, would be a piece of egregious folly. If the Democratic party believed in People's Party principles, or did the Republican party, then the organization of the People's Party was folly to begin with, and to fuse with either party is virtually an admission that the People's Party is not needed, has no distinct principles, and would stamp it as being merely a political excrescence."[44]

Fusion Populists, on the other hand, were usually politicians concerned with strictly local and state political matters. They had little or no regard for the wider consequences of their immediate

[44] *Kansas Agitator,* May 26, 1892.

actions, in respect to either national politics or party principles. They represented less the party's evangelistic, idealistic, and morally motivated wing, personified by Peffer, and more the pragmatic operators, long experienced in the hard politics of compromise and expediency. Indeed, while mid-roaders predominated within the Washington contingent and perhaps the inarticulate mass of the People's party, it was party officials and activists on state and county committees that usually adopted the fusionist rationale, thus making the fusion position stronger in the actual party organization than in either the highest leadership or the rank and file. To further consolidate their control over the party apparatus, fusionists attempted to isolate mid-roaders or undermine their influence. Willits claimed to have discovered "an organized effort by the People's Party fusion-fixers" to suppress him upon his return from his Alliance lectures in the South, and a mid-road member of the State Central Committee complained that the fusionist majority of the committee refused to notify the mid-roaders of committee meetings.[45] Fusionists liked to consider themselves as realists and mid-roaders as "cranks," devoid of political sense and hopelessly utopian. Their arguments for fusion with the Democratic party never considered subjects of political or doctrinal consistency but merely emphasized the probable Republican plurality in a three-sided contest. Indeed, fusionists claimed that those who were most concerned with the preservation of distinctive Populist principles were Republicans seeking only to prevent the fusion of their two dissimilar opponents. Populist hostility to such a coalition was proof to the fusionists of both the Democracy and the People's party that the mid-roaders were working in the interest of the GOP, either as traitors or as dupes.[46] This low allegation that anti-fusionists were crypto-Republicans proved perhaps the most effective weapon of these practical men.

Thoughtful mid-roaders objected to the fusionist appropriation and interpretation of the term "practical politics." A strict adherence to that conception of practical politics, after all, would have avoided the quixotic tactic of forming a third party in the first

---

[45] *Topeka Advocate*, May 26, 1892; *Washington Post*, May 27, 1892.

[46] *Pleasanton Herald*, January 15, March 18, April 1, 1892; *Paola Times*, May 5, 1892; *Wichita Weekly Beacon*, June 10, 17, 1892; *Topeka Daily Capital*, May 12, 1892; *Leavenworth Evening Standard*, July 11, 13, 16, 1892.

place. The anti-fusionists now argued that a truly practical policy, designed to achieve the complete objective, required total separation from the old parties: without traditional sources of support such as the old parties boasted, Populism must necessarily emphasize its distinctiveness. Mid-roaders in particular rejected the fusionist contention that political common sense dictated cooperation with the Democrats. The party's primary problem since its inception, they reminded all Populists, was to combat the idea that the People's party was "a Democratic aid society, or that it was in collusion with Democracy in any way." This fundamental necessity had forced them to establish a national third party and attempt to destroy the Democratic South in an effort to produce a partisan stability among their adherents who had only with difficulty broken the powerful emotional ties to the GOP. "In separating from the Republican party, Kansas farmers have had no intention of aligning themselves with the enemy whom they so long opposed and despised," declared one newspaper, and the ardently anti-fusion *Kincaid Kronicle* added that such Republican-Populists "look upon the Democrat party as being even worse than the party they left. It is folly to expect these men to vote to increase the power of a party they consider the worst that ever existed."[47]

Despite such strong resistance to their proposed course, fusionists of both parties evolved a plan for collaboration in a series of meetings in late spring. The details varied, but the main features were constant. Democrats would name candidates for a joint congressional ticket in two districts and receive two places on the state ticket, probably congressman-at-large and associate justice, in exchange for their endorsement of the remaining Populist candidates on congressional, state, and electoral tickets. Published reports generally accorded David Overmeyer and John Martin the Democratic spots on the state ticket, and while only the First and Second Congressional districts were to be given to Democratic candidates, the Democrats made it clear they would not support Clover or Otis in the Third and Fourth.[48] Simpson was more than

47 *Kansas City Journal,* April 12, 1892; *Kincaid Kronicle,* June 17, 1892.

48 *Kansas Democrat* (Topeka), July 18, 1892; *Leavenworth Evening Standard,* June 1, 1892; *Kansas City Star,* June 1, 2, 1892; *Topeka Daily Capital,* May 18, June 2, 1892; J. M. Jones to Charles Robinson, April 28, 1892, Robinson Papers; *National Economist,* June 25, 1892.

acceptable, and in the two remaining districts, represented by Davis and Baker, the Democrats did not even have the balance-of-power strength necessary to make demands, though they objected to both congressmen.

The party managers, both elected and self-constituted, had arranged for the disposition of Populist votes, but there remained doubt as to whether the rank and file would accede. Prather admitted that "the rub will be with the people's party in controlling the conventions." Glick expressed optimism but added, "Some crank though may spoil our plans." And another Democrat hopefully discussed fusion with Robinson: "Such an arrangement, I am assured the People's Party generally desire, (there are a few cranks in every party who have no practical sense) but the sensible element is now in control."[49]

The various Populist nominating conventions soon revealed that those anti-fusion "cranks" were stronger than either Democrats or fusion Populists had hoped, but also that in their inexperience and ignorance they were at the mercy of the fusionists, for whom politics was often a profession. The result was frequently the appearance of nonfusion coupled with the actuality of fusion. In May Populists began to hold county conventions and overwhelmingly instructed their delegates to the state convention to vote against fusion plans and candidates. Particularly averse to fusion propositions were the Populists of north-central and northwestern Kansas, where ex-Republicans greatly predominated in the party. There the Sixth Congressional District convention of the People's party renominated Baker on June 2 with strong expressions of anti-fusion sentiment and hostility to the possible gubernatorial nomination of Ives, whom it considered too Democratically inclined and weak on prohibition.[50] Such an outcome was expected, however, and the first test of the fusion scheme came in Holton the same day when the First Congressional District convention met.

The question of fusion immediately split the convention, with the mid-road faction led by former Republican Ezra Cary and the

---

49 *Kansas City Journal*, April 12, 1892; *Topeka Daily Capital*, May 24, 1892; Prather to Robinson, January 10, 1892, and Jones to Robinson, April 28, 1892, Robinson Papers; Glick to Cleveland, March 17, 1892, Cleveland Papers.

50 *Wichita Weekly Beacon*, April 15, 1892; *Topeka Daily Capital*, May 24, 1892; *Washington Post*, May 24, 1892; *Kansas City Star*, June 2, 11, 1892.

fusionists led by former Democrat J. W. Fitzgerald. Fitzgerald even declared he would not accept the convention's decision unless he thought it would attract Democratic support. Toward that end, Leavenworth Democratic leader S. F. Neely, arriving directly from a major conference in Kansas City between fusionist leaders of the two parties, intervened in the Populist convention to advocate the nomination of William A. Harris, promising that the Democrats would accept him as their own. But a division within the fusionist ranks among the supporters of Harris, Fitzgerald, and Everard Bierer, another former Democrat, led to the surprise nomination of Fred J. Close, a mild mid-roader and a stockholder with Peffer and McLallin on the anti-fusion *Advocate*. The swing to Close began when one Populist refused to "be a party to the Democratic scheme to nominate Colonel Harris," and added, "I have never been a Democrat and I pray to God I never will be a Democrat, and I don't propose to be led into the Democratic camp at this time."[51] The defeat of Harris disappointed fusionists of both parties and caused many to fear that no agreement at all would be reached. Charles Robinson more calmly observed that elsewhere fusionists would act less arrogantly and stupidly and the anti-fusionists would prove unable so easily to stampede conventions. Glick was also unperturbed, and he predicted that by October the Populists would honor the fusion arrangements by withdrawing their competing candidates. "This cannot be done in the convention," he was ready to concede, "but it will be done by the committees later in the campaign."[52]

Before the state convention, the Populists held three more congressional nominating conventions. As expected, the Fifth District in north-central Kansas made no concessions to Democratic sensibilities and unanimously renominated mid-roader John Davis. Congressman Otis was not so fortunate. Democrats were stronger in his district and Populists weaker, and his harsh anti-fusion statements had alienated the Democracy. The district's Democratic convention met in late May, resolved in favor of fusion, and then adjourned until June 14 at Emporia, the scheduled time and place of the Populist convention, thereby pressuring the People's party to nominate a Populist other than Otis. Overmeyer joined Martin as the guiding spirits of the convention in this attempt to force fusion upon the Populists. The Democrats signaled that while Otis was unacceptable they would support Levi Dumbauld, a former Democrat and, as chairman of the Populist State Central Committee, a leading fusionist.[53]

Dumbauld had already initiated a campaign to succeed Otis but had only succeeded in angering many Populists who then called a meeting in Emporia to demand an explanation. Dumbauld confessed to his critics that the Populist State Central Committee had met with the Democrats in hopes of arranging fusion and had agreed, among other things, to replace Otis with Dumbauld and nominate Overmeyer for congressman-at-large. The indignant Populists replied, one of them later wrote, "that the committee were either fools or traitors . . . , and that the people were able to make their own ticket without the help of the bosses, and further . . . that Otis had done his part by us and we would stand by him first, last, and all the time, and Overmeyer would have to bid good-by to the Democrats before we could support him."[54]

Though Populists were determined to reject Dumbauld and explicit Democratic dictation, many of their leaders remained ready to make some concession to attract Democratic support in the normally Republican Fourth District. The Populist convention consequently turned down both Otis and Dumbauld and selected E. V. Wharton, a Yates Center physician and a Democratic-Populist. The Democratic convention, which, as Otis later explained, had "hung around our convention all day, threatening to nominate a candidate twenty minutes after I was named," immediately applauded Wharton as "a good, sound Democrat," ratified the nomination, and "gleefully adjourned."[55]

Otis and the other mid-roaders bitterly condemned these proceedings. Otis warned that Populism was "jeopardized by this gang of unscrupulous office-hunting gluttons. Fusion means our ruin.

[53] *Kansas City Star,* June 6, 9, 1892; *Topeka Daily Capital,* May 17, 25, 26, 1892.

[54] U. C. Spencer to John G. Otis in *National Economist,* June 25, 1892.

[55] *Kansas City Star,* June 14, 1892; *Topeka Daily Capital,* June 15, 1892; *Emporia Tidings,* June 18, 1892; *National Economist,* June 25, 1892.

It is only the office-seeker who wants fusion and if our people allow themselves to be used in this way they will be pulling chestnuts out of the fire for others," he continued. "These fusion candidates won't come as near being elected as the candidates who made a straight fight on the Alliance platform and depend fully on the Alliance for support." Otis even hinted that he might run for Congress as an independent, for he believed that had the people still controlled the People's party he would have been renominated. Farmers particularly objected to the displacement of the "Milkman" by the nomination of Wharton, "who never farmed a day in his life, and probably never did a day's physical labor," and many supported a plan to defeat the fusionist politicians of the district by having an independent convention nominate Otis. Otis remained unreconciled, proud that "I was too much a middle-of-the-road man for the Democracy," but abandoned his plan of running independently.[56]

Others accepted the defeat of Otis more willingly. The Populist convention of the Seventh Congressional District, meeting in Wichita on June 14, cheered the news of Wharton's nomination. Former Democrats had more influence in the People's party of southwestern Kansas than generally elsewhere, and the district, represented by the agreeable Simpson, was strongly pro-fusion. Straight Democrats had promised to endorse Simpson if Populists outside the district cooperated with Democratic plans and candidates, and the rejection of Otis seemed to insure Simpson's dual nomination. Simpson had actively sought Democratic support, promised to encourage Populists to endorse Democratic candidates in other districts, and assured his Democratic backers that if Cleveland were elected they could control the district's patronage. Simpson easily won renomination at the Populist convention, and shortly thereafter the district's Democrats adopted him as their own candidate as well.[57]

The Populist state convention opened in Wichita on June 15, 1892, amidst intense discussion over fusion. The very selection of

56 *National Economist*, June 25, 1892; *Emporia Weekly Republican*, June 23, 1892; *Topeka Daily Capital*, June 18, August 20, 1892; *Washington Post*, June 17, 1892.

57 *Kansas City Star*, June 13, 14, 1892; *Wichita Weekly Beacon*, April 22, June 17, 1892; *Washington Post*, May 23, 1892; *Topeka Daily Capital*, June 5, 1892.

Wichita by the Populist State Central Committee, some believed, involved a bid for Democratic support, as did the choice of John Breidenthal for convention chairman. A former Union Laborite, Breidenthal provoked some opposition because a caucus of party officials had determined his nomination, but after seconding speeches by Wakefield and the popular Simpson he was elected. The issue of fusion entered into the consideration of candidates too, but as many fusionists had feared, the ungovernable convention apparently rejected their arrangements. The alleged fusionist candidate for governor, John Ives, had lost most of his backing because of his involvement as attorney general in reducing railroad taxation, and Lorenzo D. Lewelling, a Wichita produce dealer, received the nomination. Martin lost to Stephen H. Allen for associate justice, and W. A. Harris received the nomination for congressman-at-large instead of Overmeyer.[58]

The apparent defeat of the schemes for Democratic cooperation encouraged the mid-roaders and misled historians. Others were not deceived. If the Populists had rejected what would have been blatant examples of political manipulation in the proposed nominations of Martin and Overmeyer, they had allowed themselves to be led under Breidenthal's skillful direction into an unwitting implicit endorsement of fusion. The Populists' policy of letting the office seek the man, combined with their relative lack of access to the news media, resulted in the nomination of a number of surreptitious fusion candidates. Allen had been presented as the mid-road alternative to Democrat Martin and was elected easily; ten days previously he had been the unsuccessful straight Democratic candidate for Second District congressman in opposition to a Democrat who favored fusion with the Populists! Harris, who filled the other position promised to the Democrats, had been a Democrat, was perhaps the leading fusionist among the Populists, was very popular in his heavily Democratic home county of Leavenworth, and opposed the more radical elements of Populism while accepting little more than free silver from its financial program. Following his nomination, moreover, Harris declared that he was still "a good Democrat." Populists with Democratic backgrounds received other spots on the ticket as well, including Prather for state auditor.

58 *Kansas City Star,* June 13-16, 1892; *Wichita Daily Beacon,* June 15, 1892.

Even Lewelling, though a former Republican, represented a bid for Democratic support. Relatively new to Kansas, he had never worked with the GOP; promoted by Simpson, he was chairman of the fusionist Sedgwick County People's party and certain to receive the critical backing of Wichita Democrats. In addressing the convention, moreover, Lewelling clearly indicated his desire to cooperate with "honorable allies."[59]

Generally, the Democratic press expressed pleasure with the Populist ticket. "An investigation of the political antecedents of the men who were nominated by the People's Party convention" convinced the *Leavenworth Evening Standard* that the Populists were actively "bidding for Democratic success." It especially applauded the nomination of Harris. The *Wichita Beacon,* although disappointed that no Democrat qua Democrat was on the slate, described six of the nine candidates as former Democrats and urged Democratic support of the ticket, especially Lewelling. Moreover, the *Beacon* argued, such endorsement would place the People's party in the Democracy's debt from which Democrats might reap future benefits. The *Garnett Journal* likewise declared the majority of the Populist nominees "good Democrats," rejoiced that the "cranky element" of the People's party "has been relegated to the rear," and advocated Democratic fusion. Most Democratic politicians agreed. Martin praised the Populist ticket, and Glick promised that the Democrats would fulfill their part of the fusion agreement.[60]

In their own state convention in July, the Democrats divided into three groups, all for fusion but in varying degrees. One favored total fusion; one advocated electoral fusion and fusion on state candidates who were formerly Democrats; and the third favored only electoral fusion. Harris, Allen, John T. Little, the Populist candidate for attorney general, and other leading fusion Populists actively sought Democratic endorsement and repeatedly conferred with Martin, Glick, and Robinson. After a long debate, the convention declared for complete fusion and nominated the entire

59 *Lawrence Daily Journal and Evening Tribune,* June 7, 1892: *Topeka Daily Capital,* June 16, 17, 18, 1892; *Topeka Advocate,* June 22, 1892; *Topeka State Journal,* July 6, 1892.

60 *Leavenworth Evening Standard,* June 17, 1892; *Wichita Weekly Beacon,* June 24, 1892; *Garnett Journal,* July 15, 1892.

electoral and state ticket of the People's party. Democrats made no false statements of their motives for endorsing the Populist slate, and C. F. Diffenbach, the Democratic leader of Barton County, was remarkably candid: "The People's Party is fast becoming a part of the Democratic party and in two or three years we will have it all. Two years ago they would not have anything to do with us. Now they are glad to work with us, and the time is not very far ahead when the two parties will be one and the same, and it will be a Democratic party. That's why I favored the nomination of Jerry Simpson, and it is why I have favored fusion this year. It will eventually bring the new party into our camp."[61]

Elsewhere, Populists and Democrats attempted to complete fusion arrangements. In the Third District the issue was clear. Clover was unacceptable to the Democrats and the converse, and fusionists had agreed to replace him with a Democratic-Populist. At the convention only two candidates were presented: Clover and Thomas Jefferson Hudson, a lawyer and former Democrat. But Clover's feud with the popular Simpson, his publicized marital troubles, and his increasing passivity weakened his position, and the convention nominated Hudson with less contention than marked those struggles which were overt disputes over fusion. Hudson called himself a Populist in 1892, but Democratic papers still considered him a Democrat and praised him as the best candidate the Populists had ever nominated except for Harris. Subsequently, Third District Democrats gratefully nominated Hudson.[62]

Politics in the Second District proved more difficult and well illustrated the problems of the People's party. The district had been one of those specifically granted to a Democratic candidate by the fusionists, and the Democrats were determined to defeat the Republican incumbent, Edward H. "Farmer" Funston. As early as March the district committees of the Democratic and People's parties had conferred about naming a joint candidate, and fusion leaders constantly thereafter tried to restrain anti-fusion activities. Mid-roaders were increasingly vocal, however, and complained that their party officials had not been authorized to consult the Democrats or to usurp the rights of a nominating convention.[63]

61 *Topeka Daily Capital*, July 5, 7, August 19, 1892.
62 Ibid., May 18, June 4, 1892; *Wichita Weekly Beacon*, July 1, 1892.
63 J. B. Chapman to Robinson, March 26, 1892, Robinson Papers; *Topeka*

The Democrats forced the issue by rescheduling their convention to meet prior to the Populist convention and by nominating Horace L. Moore, a Lawrence banker. They then demanded Populist endorsement of the Democrat as the "only road to success" and denounced those who resisted as working in Funston's behalf. Populist indignation was intense. The *Kincaid Kronicle* censured the proposed "unholy alliance" and recited the past treachery of the old parties, specifically condemning the Democracy's deceitful practice of making platforms to gain votes with no intention of fulfilling its promises: "It is said that Moore is in favor of the reforms demanded by the people. If that is correct why is he not in the people's party?" W. O. Champe, veteran editor of the Garnett *Kansas Agitator* and one of Peffer's staunchest political friends, also implored Populists to keep in the middle of the road for the sake of principle and Southern support. Southern Democrats believed, he wrote, that fusion in Kansas would destroy the People's party in the South, and Champe declared he had received letters from Southern Populists urging Kansans not to fuse with the party that they were fighting to the death.[64]

The Populist congressional convention met in Garnett on June 22 amidst a crowd of lobbying politicians. Moore and Robinson arrived from Lawrence to plead the Democratic cause, and they were supported by Populist state candidates Allen and Little who hoped thereby to promote wider fusion. Willits, Champe, and other mid-roaders of the district argued against Moore. "If we go into the business of helping to elect Democrats to office," Willits told his listeners, "we might as well quit and go back into the old parties." Many Populists agreed with their formidable leader. One mid-road delegate, for example, declared, "These fusion delegates . . . come here in the interest of the Democratic party and have no right here. I will not stand it, and am going home to vote the Republican ticket." Willits rallied the mid-roaders to reject the fusionist arguments, and S. S. King of Kansas City received the nomination.[65]

Daily Capital, April 3, 5, June 8, 1892; *Leavenworth Evening Standard,* June 1, 1892; *Wichita Weekly Beacon,* May 6, 1892.

64 *Garnett Journal,* May 20, June 10, 1892; *Kincaid Kronicle,* June 17, 1892; *Kansas Agitator,* June 23, 1892.

65 *Topeka Daily Capital,* June 22, 23, 1892; *Kansas Agitator,* June 23, 1892; *Kincaid Kronicle,* June 24, 1892.

Democrats and fusion Populists complained vehemently. Robinson severely criticized Willits for preventing Populist endorsement of various Democratic candidates, especially Moore. Other Democrats, just returned from helping nominate Cleveland at their national convention, remaining willing to fuse on the electoral ticket in his behalf but announced their new opposition to endorsing other Populist candidates. Latimer, Little, and Allen continued to support Moore even though King had the Populist nomination, and they promised the Democrats of the district to have King removed from the race. Latimer's *Herald* announced that Populists needed votes and should therefore accept Moore to attract Democratic backing elsewhere in the state. Latimer denounced those who opposed this course as not possessing "the least particle of political sense" and as working in the interests of the GOP. In advocating fusion, he maintained, he was working for principles.[66]

Other Populists refused to accept these fusionist rationales. The *Kansas Agitator* condemned Latimer for helping arrange and defend the fusion agreement between Populist and Democratic committees. These actions by Populist leaders were not authorized by the rank and file, and "if anyone promised Moore an endorsement," added the *Kincaid Kronicle,* "they promised him something which was not theirs to give." The mid-roaders were especially harsh toward the fusionists who, "having failed to accomplish their nefarious designs," were "now trying to thwart the will of the people as expressed by their chosen delegates in convention assembled." The anti-fusionists ripped the reasoning of Latimer and his allies who argued for fusion as "anything to beat Funston." A banker who stood on a Democratic platform and supported Cleveland for president was no improvement over a Republican farmer, and his election would merely add to the Democratic majority in Congress which had already refused to aid the people. An honorable defeat would not injure Populism as much as such a victory. "To be consistent," one mid-roader charged, the fusionists who still intended to support Moore "should oppose Weaver because the Omaha convention did not endorse Cleveland."

66 *Washington Post,* June 27, 1892; *Wichita Weekly Beacon,* July 1, 1892; *Pleasanton Herald,* March 18, July 8, 22, 1892; *Topeka Daily Capital,* July 9, 1892.

The mid-road Populists were particularly annoyed that the assumptions and actions of the fusion leaders usurped the rights of the popularly chosen delegates. The fusionist attitude that votes were to be bartered by those who better understood the political situation ran directly counter to the original Populist demands that the people should participate directly in political decisions and that democracy should be effective within parties as much as within other elements of the social system. The dictatorial approach of the Democrats angered Populists as much as the arbitrary actions of their own leaders: "Who ever before heard of the politicians of one party trying to control the nomination of another party as was done at Garnett?" Moore's appearance before the Populist convention and his request for the nomination, they maintained, made him honor-bound by the convention's decision. Having failed to secure the nomination, however, he now attempted to subvert that decision. Fortunately for their party, they rejoiced, it was one thing to sell the Populists of the Second District, but quite another to deliver them. The unconditional Populist would resist illegitimate authority even when his leaders demanded obedience as necessary to the success of their schemes.[67]

Those who demanded fusion as "practical politics" further irritated the mid-roaders of the Second District. "If the convention had endorsed Col. Moore," Champe pointed out, "such action would have driven thousands of voters, formerly Republicans, back into the old party; and the failure to endorse him is being used to drive Democrats away from the Populists. It would seem that men of ordinary shrewdness could have foreseen this difficulty," he believed, "and have avoided it, by each party strictly minding its own affairs. The parties are certainly separate organizations, with principles and aims that widely differ; therefore, any attempt to fuse could only lead to a vast amount of friction, without advancing the cause of either party." Moreover, if the fusionists proved successful in removing King from the ticket, Champe predicted, Moore would not receive one-quarter of the district's Populist votes, for real Populists could not vote for a Democratic banker. Truly, he concluded, Funston could not have asked for a better situation than the expedient, practical, and sensible fusionists had created—

[67] *Kansas Agitator,* July 7, 14, 1892; *Kincaid Kronicle,* July 15, 1892.

that is, a sharply divided and bickering, quarreling opposition.[68]

The fusion Populists did not renounce their schemes. Democrats assisted them by promising to endorse Populist candidates elsewhere in Kansas if King were withdrawn. And Moore pointed out that he could finance a campaign himself while the Populists as a party were nearly penniless. Both groups pressured the Populist District Central Committee to replace King with Moore. The new Populist state chairman, John Breidenthal, an able exponent of "practical politics" and the separation of political principles from daily activities, also worked to remove King. Finally in July, the harried King grudgingly informed Breidenthal that he would withdraw if the party thought it best. Breidenthal immediately called a meeting of the Populist committee to accept King's offer. Although the Wyandotte County committeeman asserted that King's withdrawal would drive all former Republicans among his county's Populists back to their old party, the committee conferred with its Democratic counterpart and then substituted Moore for King on the Populist ticket. A Populist who had ably advocated his party's financial and social arguments in his book *Bondholders and Breadwinners* was thus replaced in a contest against a Republican farmer by a Democratic banker who insisted that the tariff was the real political issue.[69]

Disaffection among Populists was severe. The *Kincaid Kronicle* asserted that the committee had no authority to set aside the will of the people as expressed in their convention, and it refused to accept Moore as the party's nominee. Its editor arraigned the political managers of the People's party for being as arrogant and manipulative as any in the corrupt old parties and denounced the committee for actions traitorous to the people and the cause it claimed to represent. Others joined in the indictment of the machinations of Populist leaders. The *Agitator,* for example, declared the Populist bosses had deliberately usurped the rights of the people and subverted their wishes. Most dissident Populists

---

68 *Kansas Agitator,* July 14, 1892.

69 *Pleasanton Herald,* August 19, 1892; *Topeka Daily Capital,* March 16, August 16, 21, 1892; *Topeka Advocate,* August 24, 1892; *Kansas City Star,* August 16, 1892. For Breidenthal, see also James C. Malin, *A Concern about Humanity* (Lawrence, Kans., 1964), pp. 211-13; Walter T. K. Nugent, *The Tolerant Populists* (Chicago, 1963), pp. 137-38; *Kansas City Star,* January 26, 1891.

eventually though reluctantly accepted Moore as the Populist candidate because they saw no alternative, but they continued to censure the politicians of their own party. The *Kronicle,* however, proved unable to reconcile its campaign for political reform with the chicanery involved in this arrangement. Another expressed the paper's position well: "The great reformation movement for the purification of politics has fallen into the control of tricksters. Principles have been traded for expedients. The high moral plane has been abandoned." A Coffey County paper agreed: "What started out as a great uprising of the people for reform, a crusade against the evils of which both old parties were alike guilty, thus turns out to be a stupendous and perfectly shameless traffic for offices." The *Kronicle* suspended publication and expired.[70]

The transformation of the People's party evident in the differences between 1890 and 1892 was obvious to many. In 1890 idealistic and utopian-minded reformers had led discontented farmers in a movement to purge a corrupt society and political system as much as to reform financial legislation. In 1892 these men such as Peffer, Clover, Willits, McLallin, and Otis were either more involved in national politics or shunted aside on the state level. Technicians replaced ideologues as a mass movement was rationalized into an organized political party. Efficiency, expediency, and opportunism were adopted by "practical-minded" bureaucrats such as Breidenthal as either methods or objectives in their quest for immediate, tangible gains rather than the proposed reformation of society. Perhaps this was an inevitable process, but it might be argued that a reform movement demanded a clear vision of its purpose more than it required an efficient management of its adherents. Enveloped in the problems of organization, coordination, and administration of a political campaign, the professional activists succumbed to the ultimate enticement—victory at the polls—and concerned themselves little with the principles and ideas that originally had impelled the movement. These too often were merely obstacles in the path of fashioning a coalition that might prove successful. The tension between these two attitudes within the Populist coalition surfaced when such mid-roaders as Champe

70 *Kincaid Kronicle,* August 19, 26, 1892; *Kansas Agitator,* September 1, 1892; *Topeka Daily Capital,* June 26, August 18, 28, 1892.

spoke of the basic differences between *movement* and *party*. A. J. R. Smith, radical mid-road editor of the *Topeka Populist,* in fact, described the degeneration of Populism as a direct result of the transformation of the mass movement into a structured party, with its institutional imperatives diverting politicians from reform to deceitful manipulation.[71]

Although many Populists believed that their party officials subverted the ideals of Populism in their cynical disregard of the concept of popular control and their arrogant defiance of the limits of their proper authority, more immediately disturbing was the obvious Democratization of the party, stemming in part from the undemocratization of the movement. In 1890 Populists had spurned Democratic advances, and fusion had occurred only on Democratic initiative and through Democratic endorsement of Populist candidates. In 1892 Populist leaders had actively sought out Democratic leaders; proposed and agreed to fusion; repudiated movement figures such as Otis and Clover and replaced them with Democrats or Democratic-Populists; nominated others whose principal qualification was their ability to attract Democratic votes. The party of the people was now committed to support a middleman in farm produce against a prohibitionist farmer for governor and a banker against a farmer for Congress. It had refused congressional renominations to two ex-Republican farmers and named two former Democrats, one a lawyer and the other a physician. On the insistence of Democrats, it had removed from its ticket another Populist, duly nominated, and replaced him with a declared Democrat.

The *Mound City Progress* made the obvious conclusion: "Alliancemen would not believe Republicans two years ago when they told them that they were only playing into the Democracy's hands, but now the evidence is too plain to longer doubt it." The fusion policy in Kansas and other Western states, together with the increasingly apparent Southern intention to remain with the Democratic party, convinced many that they had indeed been playing the fool's part, and they rebelled against the dictation of their leaders. In some instances this took an organized form. In the Fourth Congressional District, many former Republicans denounced

[71] See especially *Kansas Agitator,* May 26, 1892, and *Topeka Populist,* March 3, 1893.

the deals made by the fusionists and asserted that "they did not leave the Republican party to go body and soul over to the Democracy; that if it has to be one of the old parties they will return to the one they naturally belong to." Many of these encouraged Otis to run as an independent candidate after Wharton received the Populist nomination. In the Third District, the discontented Populists did more than talk. They organized an Abraham Lincoln Republican party, a halfway house similar to the Jeffersonian Democrat factions organized in the South by others bound by partisan allegiance. Composed largely of Alliance farmers, the Abraham Lincoln Republicans objected to the nomination of the Democratic-Populist lawyer Hudson, but refused to rejoin the GOP to support his opponent, Governor (and banker) Humphrey. They proposed to nominate a straight Alliance farmer for Congress.[72]

Many individuals protested Democratic influence so strongly that they did not hesitate to return to full Republican fellowship. Most importantly, Frank McGrath disavowed the People's party after Harris's nomination and urged alliancemen to follow him back into the GOP. "The evidences are numerous in the conventions held this year," he announced, "that the middlemen, jackleg lawyers, and town loafers are more influential in directing and controlling the people's party than farmers. The success of the Democratic party seems to have become necessary with many leading People's Party leaders and to secure the defeat of the Republican party these leaders in the People's Party and the Democratic party are ready to lay aside their principles and by fusion secure the offices." This party emphasis upon politics rather than Populism drove many others back to the GOP, including John H. Rice, one of those most prominent in organizing the national People's party. Benjamin Matchett, Speaker pro tem of the 1891 legislature, also renounced the People's party and campaigned actively for the Republicans. He objected specifically to Populist support of middlemen like Lewelling in opposition to farmer candidates. The president of the Rawlins County Alliance similarly based his decision to return to the GOP upon the action of the Populist conventions in nominating, not farmers, but men of those classes

---

[72] *Pleasanton Herald,* July 22, 1892; *Topeka Daily Capital,* July 20, 1892; *Girard Western Herald,* July 15, 29, 1892.

alliancemen had condemned as parasitical. He also vigorously decried the Populist "truckling" to the Second District Democrats. "I was a Republican and from this time on hope to be." Many other Populists, from such prominent leaders as Judge W. S. Cade of Anthony to the twelve delegates in the 1892 Marion County Republican convention who had voted Populist in 1890, to those who had supported the party only with votes, followed the path back to the GOP, complaining of Democratic influence and elite manipulation.[73]

While the *Kincaid Kronicle* had discontinued rather than support a debased ticket, other Populist newspapers determined in their disillusionment to support the GOP directly once again. One Marion paper declared that the Populist party organization itself had repudiated Populism through its manipulations, bribery, and other tactics designed to arrange fusion. Methods condemned in the old parties, the paper continued, should not be adopted by the new one, and the Populist ticket formed by such methods should receive the support of "no man who is in the party for the honesty, principles, and purification of politics and the betterment of mankind." The Populist nomination of Harris, declared the *Goff Advance,* "settles it with us," and the *Advance* then revealed the tenuous success of the Populist conversion efforts among old Republicans steeped in years of partisan prejudice: "the people's party is [thus shown to be] hand in hand with and was created for the purpose of aiding the Southern brigadiers in fulfilling their threat of vengeance. Right here we foreswear all allegiance to the People's Party. We must be honest with ourselves. Hereafter we shall be found battling for square-toed, stalwart Republicanism. We would rather belong to the Republican plutocrats than the Southern brigadiers."[74]

Other Populists, watching events in the South, agreed with the *Advance*'s conclusion about the relative merits of Republicans and Confederates. Samuel Worthington, a Populist who had proposed in the state convention that all Union veterans present second

[73] *Topeka Daily Capital,* June 26, July 28, August 14, 27, 31, September 1, 4, and passim, 1892.

[74] *Marion Advance,* October 1, 8, 1892; *Goff Advance,* June 23, 1892; *Topeka Daily Capital,* September 29, 1892.

the nomination of Harris, decided after the Democratic victories in the Southern state elections to return to the GOP. He had supported Harris, he explained, "not because of any love for the ex-Confederate soldier, but because I wanted to show the South that we were willing to lay down the bloody shirt and ready to shake hands over the bloody chasm, but recent developments in Georgia show that they are not willing to do the same. It has been made perfectly clear to me," he added, "that the South is still solid, and that there is no possible show for the people's party in a single southern state." Therefore, he believed, "by voting with the people's party this year I would help to send Democrats to Congress, and help elect a Democratic president. The Democratic party is a party of negation and we can never hope to accomplish anything through it."[75]

D. G. Ollinger, chairman of the 1890 Populist First District Central Committee and chairman of the 1892 district convention, expressed even more clearly the persistent strength of sectional prejudice. In October 1892, reacting against the Southern violence toward Populists, he urged Republicans and Populists to unite their national committees and "consolidate the north against the solid south." Shortly thereafter he withdrew from the People's party to rejoin the GOP, explaining that "the people's party is only a Democratic sideshow, the principal object of which is to beat the Republican party out of the presidency." In a letter to Populist state headquarters, Ollinger commented further that a vote for Weaver represented a vote for Cleveland. Reform was still needed, he agreed, but without the South Weaver would be unable to win, and Cleveland as president would retard all good.[76]

Many other Populists announced in the autumn that election results in the South, Southern treatment of Weaver, Mrs. Lease, and other Populists, and the possibility of aiding the election of the monstrous Cleveland—all encouraged them to support the Republican ticket. There was no room for three parties in the North, they decided, when there was room for only one in the South.[77]

These apostates, however, largely involved only those superficially

[75] *Topeka Daily Capital,* November 2, 1892.
[76] Ibid., October 4, 5, 30, 1892.
[77] Ibid., October 20, 21, 25, 1892.

converted from the politics of prejudice and passion, and came from only the former-Republican faction of the People's party. The ex-Union Laborites, perhaps, entered the campaign with fewer illusions about politics; and the former Democrats had vociferously welcomed fusion with their erstwhile comrades and did not so strongly object to a national Democratic victory. Moreover, where the Populists had been strong enough in 1890 to elect their entire ticket, they often merely renominated their candidates by acclamation in 1892 and remained free from fusion politics. Especially in the heavily Populist Fifth and Sixth districts, where ex-Republicans formed the dominant faction of the party, did the Populists display the same cold attitude of 1890 toward the Democrats. If many Populists returned to the Republican party by 1892, many others did not yet believe the only choice was between "Southern brigadiers" and "Republican plutocrats"; that Populism involved no more principle than its leaders conceded; that choosing the lesser of evils was an adequate philosophy for political action; that the People's party was only "a great recruiting camp for the Democratic party."[78] They were prepared to wait for the South to register its decision against Cleveland in the national election, perhaps understanding the Southern reluctance to oppose the Democracy in strictly state elections. They were willing to give the People's party an opportunity to govern the state and trusted its declarations. They hoped that their radical ideals of 1890 would yet be fulfilled.

The actual campaign in Kansas in 1892 differed little from that of 1890. The issue of prohibition played only a minor role, though Republican gubernatorial nominee A. W. Smith's image among Democrats as "an intolerant and pernicious prohibitionist" encouraged their endorsement of Lewelling. Republicans tried to attract Republican-Populists, and except on financial issues their program was nearly as radical as that of the Populists, advocating government control of railroads and communications, mortgage redemption laws, taxation reform, abolition of child labor and labor blacklistings. The Topeka *Kansas Democrat,* in fact, believed the Republican platform "as wild and visionary as that of the People's Party." The Republicans awarded their nominations as the Populists had done in 1890 (and had conspicuously failed to

[78] Ibid., June 26, August 12, September 25, 1892.

do in 1892): Besides Smith, the leader of the agrarian reform faction within the GOP and Peffer's personal choice for governor four years earlier, the Republicans named a farmer for lieutenant governor, a black for auditor, and a laborer for state treasurer.[79]

Republicans continued to incite bloody-shirt prejudices against the Populists and Democrats as in 1890 and 1891: "Cleveland's substitute should be withdrawn. A vote for Weaver is a vote for the solid south." The Republican state chairman pressed his party's workers to emphasize "arguments on the political situation from a soldier standpoint." Republicans also sought to prevent former Confederates from voting.[80] In conjunction with such activity, they persistently stressed the increasingly plausible charge that the People's party served the interests of the Democracy. "If by any possibility the fusion ticket succeeds in Kansas and other Western states," warned one paper, "the effect will be to elect a Democrat president." Republican campaigners focused on convincing farmers that in state politics, too, the People's party "is rapidly degenerating into a tail to sail the Democratic kite." The *Newton Republican,* for example, saw in the policy of fusion the same course that Democrat C. F. Diffenbach anticipated: though apparently the People's party had swallowed the Democracy, in reality it was the reverse. "It has been very skillfully manipulated. To allow a handful of Democrats to control the great number that composed the people's party shows good generalship on the side of the Democrats. . . . In reality [the People's party] is the Democratic party under another name. . . . How do you [Populists] like it, you who were formerly Republicans?" Republicans also revived the old charge that agrarian radicalism injured the state's credit and economic development.[81] The calamity howls of Peffer-

---

[79] *Leavenworth Evening Standard,* July 1, 1892; James Smith to J. H. White, October 11, 1892, Humphrey Papers, KSHS; Raymond C. Miller, "The Populist Party in Kansas" (Ph.D. diss., University of Chicago, 1928), pp. 222-25.

[80] *Topeka Daily Capital,* September 17, October 19, 1892; J. M. Simpson to County Committeemen and Precinct Organizers, August 29, 1892, J. M. Humphrey to George Angle, February 20, 1893, and W. A. Owen to Angle, December 9, 1892, George C. Angle Papers, Spencer Research Library, University of Kansas; G. W. Shook to L. U. Humphrey, [1892], Lyman U. Humphrey Papers, Spencer Research Library, University of Kansas.

[81] *Topeka Daily Capital,* June 15, 17, 26, July 9, September 28, October 9, 25, 28, 30, 1892; Bishop W. Perkins to P. H. Coney, June 23, 1892, P. H. Coney Papers, KSHS.

ism infuriated the Republican press, but personal abuse of Populists remained the easiest and most popular response, with Peffer's beard, Simpson's feet, and Mrs. Lease's tongue attracting the most attention.

The Populists, too, largely duplicated their earlier campaign except in increasing organization by the party and less dependence upon the Alliance. Breidenthal established a Populist lecture bureau under his own direction in order to coordinate campaign speakers, and he arranged for Weaver and other party leaders from outside Kansas to address the state's Populists. The issues remained essentially unchanged, with emphasis upon governmental favoritism, economic depression, political corruption, and social alienation. Peffer was again among the speakers most in demand, and despite ill health and national speaking commitments, he conducted a grueling tour of Kansas after Congress adjourned. He consistently stood by the early Populist positions of 1890 on finance and social relations and, more than other leading Kansas Populists, provided their ideological justification. He again rejected free silver as a panacea and even denied the metallic basis of money; he restated Populist demands for government ownership of railroads and communications; he denounced Pinkertonism as one manifestation of legally sanctioned, class-directed violence while discussing the Homestead strike as an illustration of existing social inequalities.[82]

On the matter of politics, however, Peffer was less comfortable. He called upon Kansans to respond rationally to the issues raised and urged them to ignore the impulses of prejudice. He asked them to support Harris, not for what he had done, but for what he would do. And he implored them to avoid the abuse and vituperation that threatened harmonious action and to understand the peculiar nature of Southern politics. But Peffer refused to approve the fusion schemes, already in effect by the time of his return to Kansas, and he also declined to comment on questions about the actions and motivations of Populist fusion leaders. He publicly expressed regret that Otis had not been renominated and

[82] *Topeka Advocate,* July 22, September 7, 14, 21, 28, 1892; *Topeka Daily Capital,* July 22, September 4, 24, October 2, 12, 19, 21, 1892; *Garnett Journal,* September 23, 1892; Ruppenthal Scrapbooks, 3: 39.

pointedly had Otis accompany him on his campaign tour. He avoided endorsing Moore, even when Breidenthal billed them together in the fusionist stronghold of Pleasanton. Instead, appearing to a reporter to be "ill at ease," he discussed his role in the Senate. At least once, Peffer provoked criticism from politicians of both parties by attacking the policy of fusion from the stump; and he objected to Democratic participation, arranged by Breidenthal, in a grand Topeka rally on the eve of the election.[83]

By November, however, the Democrats had few objections to appearing with Populists. The adoption of the policy of fusion, so admirably suited to their needs and desires, had dissolved most of their opposition to the radical rhetoric of their allies. Even a group of conservative Democrats, who held an October convention to denounce fusion because it deprived them of the pleasure of voting directly for Cleveland, dropped their plans to name a separate ticket. Indeed, Peffer's staunch opponent, Edward Carroll, now Democratic candidate for Congress in the First District, withdrew in favor of the Populist nominee before the election, while Glick and Martin urged Democrats to vote for Populist candidates even where Democrats had a separate ticket.[84]

Both Populists and Republicans confidently predicted success before the polls opened. The day after the election, both parties believed their predictions had been fulfilled: "KANSAS REDEEMED" the *Topeka Capital* rejoiced, while the *Advocate* announced "CALAMITY OVERTAKES THE APOSTLES OF PLUTOCRACY." The confusion over the results indicated the closeness of the contest. When the full returns were in, the Populists emerged as the victor, but their margin over the GOP was slight. Weaver carried the state by fewer than 6,000 votes and Lewelling by only 4,432. Though Davis, Baker, Simpson, Harris, and Hudson were elected to Congress, Wharton lost Otis's Fourth District by a solid margin, and in the First and Second districts the Republicans made spectacular gains.

[83] *Garnett Journal*, September 23, 1892; *Topeka Daily Capital*, September 2, 4, 14, 15, 24, October 27, November 4, 1892; *Kansas City Star*, October 6, 1892; *Topeka Advocate*, October 26, November 16, 1892.

[84] *Wichita Weekly Beacon*, July 22, 1892; *Kansas City Star*, September 23, October 7, 8, 1892; Samuel Feller to Cleveland, September 21, 1892, Cleveland Papers; *Topeka Daily Capital*, October 8, 1892; *Topeka Advocate*, November 3, 1892.

Close was overwhelmed and Moore won election only after contesting the results. Moreover, control of the legislature was uncertain. Populists easily dominated the senate, but the house apparently had a slight Republican majority. In 1890 the opposition to the Republicans had received 59 percent of the state's votes; in 1892 the fusion ticket drew but 50 percent of the poll.[85]

Obviously the Republican appeals and the pressure of events in both Kansas and the South had driven many former Republicans from the People's party back into the GOP. The campaign and the election results dealt a serious blow to the grand Populist hopes. Enemies and transient allies alike heralded the death of Populism. "The disintegration which began long before it was in evidence that the South had not kept its bargain to help in bridging the bloody chasm will proceed more rapidly now," one Republican paper announced in reminding its readers that the *Advocate* itself had said only failure and defeat awaited the People's party without the South. The *Capital* surveyed the results of the national elections and decided "the people's party has reached the end of its rope. The man who rises majestically above the wreck is Senator Peffer." Democrat Glick predicted that "the People's Party will soon begin to fade and in four years it will contain only the cranks."[86]

Populists, of course, publicly interpreted the election returns differently and looked forward to the inauguration of "The First People's Party Government on Earth." But pure Populism in Kansas had clearly suffered severe blows from the twin impact of fusion in Kansas and rejection in the South. Though much of the effects of the first had been felt before the election, the full force of the second came only in November. Each reinforced the implications of the other and might be expected to encourage the drift of disappointed Republican-Populists back to the GOP. How the two administrations, Lewelling's in Topeka and Cleveland's in Washington, placed in office by these dual aspects of the campaign of 1892, used their power and for what ends would help to determine the future of the People's party.

---

85 *Washington Post*, November 7, 1892; *Report of the Secretary of State of Kansas* (Topeka, 1892).
86 *Topeka Daily Capital*, November 13, 15, 17, 1892.

CHAPTER SIX

That Iridescent Dream

THE CAMPAIGN and election of 1892 revealed serious weaknesses in the Populist strategy and grave disagreements over the direction the party should follow. Some Populists were tolerant of the infidelity of the South. Only the corrupt tactics and force of "the old bosses," they believed, had prevented the true voice of the South from registering itself. Other Kansas Populists were less charitable toward the South. The postelection discovery that Charles W. Macune and J. F. Tillman, both on the National Executive Committee of the Farmers' Alliance, had distributed Democratic campaign literature as official Alliance material in the South particularly incensed these Populists, who already considered that Southern alliancemen had betrayed them and their cause. At the annual national meeting of the Farmers' Alliance in Memphis in late November 1892, John Otis threw the delegates into an uproar by demanding that Macune be replaced or "we of the West will have to withdraw from the national order, for we have had enough of the purchased allies of the Southern Democracy."[1]

The election results also provoked disagreements as to the future of the People's party. Jerry Simpson, for one, believed with many commentators of the old parties that the "mission of the party is ended" and that Populists should follow him into the Democracy to enact the reforms they espoused. W. A. Peffer sharply contradicted Simpson and declared that Populists would stand by their party and its principles until success was achieved. Later, in 1893, Peffer advanced his own opinion on "The Mission of the Populist Party," one that neither Simpson nor any other Populist would ever be able to reconcile with the Democratic party. Writing in the *North American Review,* Peffer condemned as distractions the political debates like that of gold versus silver, describing a specie basis for money as a form of barbarism. The real issue was the existence of privileged arrangements like the national banking system. Populism, he maintained, meant that "the functions of government shall be exercised only for the mutual benefit of all the people. It asserts that government is useful only to the extent that it serves to advance the common weal," he continued, and "that the public good is paramount to private interests." The mission of the party, then, was to promote popular rights, encourage the aspirations of the common man, and provide for the equitable distribution of society's products. Populists distinctly did not advocate paternalism. "They only demand," he wrote, "that public functions shall be exercised by public agents, and that sovereign powers shall not be delegated to private persons or corporations having only private interests to serve."[2]

The divisions within the People's party since its formation, only partially papered over during the campaign, thus became more apparent again as the Populists debated their future. As the senatorial contest resulting in Peffer's election two years earlier had exposed Populist factionalism, the impending election by the new legislature to fill the remaining two years of the late Senator Preston B. Plumb's term further revealed the instability of the Populist coalition. Believing that the party had come to the end of its rope apparently did not frighten Simpson away from the scaffold, and he made a bold bid for the senatorial seat himself. Opposition to Simpson was strong, however, encouraged by both

1 *Girard Western Herald,* November 11, 1892; Mary E. Lease, "My Recent Trip through the South," *Frank Leslie's Illustrated Weekly* 76 (March 16, 1893): 161, 166-67; *Topeka Advocate,* November 23, 30, 1892; *National Economist,* November 26, 1892.

2 *Girard Western Herald,* November 25, 1892; *National Economist,* December 3, 1892; *Washington Post,* November 16, 1892; Peffer, "The Mission of the Populist Party," *North American Review* 157 (December 1893): 665-78.

those reluctant for the party to lose his congressional seat and those who objected to his Democratic and fusionist inclinations. Mary E. Lease, in particular, protested Simpson's candidacy, declaring that he had become a straight Democrat who merely used the unsuspecting Populists for his own interests. Simpson shortly withdrew from consideration but publicly advocated the election of a Democrat because, as he said, "they played fair with us this time, and we will need them in the future." Other Populists, including Governor-elect Lorenzo D. Lewelling, also supported Democratic claims to senatorial recognition, and Democrats naturally demanded the election of a fellow partisan. Anti-fusion Populists, of course, opposed any such candidates and were determined to have a senator from their own ranks. From Washington, Peffer urged Populists to shun Democratic assistance as they had in his election, so that the new senator would have no obligations to any party but his own.[3]

When the legislature convened on January 10, 1893, however, the issue of the senatorial nominee was distinctly secondary to that of the very organization of the house. Despite the election of their state ticket and their easy control of the senate, the Populists found themselves in the minority in the house according to the returns certified by the State Board of Canvassers. Populists believed that Republican officials had fraudulently given control of the house to their own partisans, and they presented a good case. A Haskell County Republican, for example, was awarded the election certificate from the 121st District because of the transposition of voting totals with his Populist opponent, a maneuver of the county clerk that the State Board of Canvassers acknowledged but refused to correct. Other Republicans declared elected included ineligible postmasters and nonresidents, and the Populists challenged still others on the basis of illegal votes, bribery, and miscount of ballots. The Populists wanted to bar from participating in the organization of the house all those whose seats were being contested, which would give the Populist representatives a majority; the Republicans demanded that the house ignore contests until organization had been completed and a special committee could be appointed to

[3] *Washington Post,* November 16, December 25, 1892; *Kansas Agitator,* December 29, 1892.

investigate. Under these circumstances, of course, the Republicans would control both the house and the special committee.[4]

In a tumultuous session, Republicans and Populists each organized the house, with conflicting leadership and membership, the Republicans swearing in all members whose seats were contested and the Populists enrolling their claimants to the contested seats. For a month this unprecedented situation continued amidst national publicity as "the legislative war." The state constitution gave the governor and the senate the power to determine the legality of the other house of the legislature, and Lewelling and the state senate recognized the Populist house. The Republicans refused to disband, and the Democratic members joined the Republican house. Thereafter the two groups alternated in Representative Hall, Republicans using it in the morning and Populists in the afternoon, as Lewelling tried to arrange a compromise. Finally on February 14 the Republicans forced matters by declaring the chief clerk of the Populist house in contempt of their body and attempting to arrest him. After a struggle, the Populists managed to free the clerk and retire to the capitol.

The situation then deteriorated rapidly. After their adjournment that evening, the Populists locked themselves into Representative Hall and asked the sheriff of Shawnee County to provide a force to protect the house and preserve the peace. The Republican sheriff refused, so Lewelling commanded the adjutant general to place guards in the capitol to maintain order. In the morning, however, the Republican legislators pushed their way past these guards and battered down the door to the legislative chamber with a sledge hammer. The Populists, frightened at such fierceness, retreated from the chamber, and the Republicans requested the Santa Fe railway company to send men from its railroad shops to defend the Republican house. Lewelling called out the militia to remove the entrenched Republicans, but the commanding officer, a strong Republican partisan, refused to obey the legal orders of the governor, and instead stationed soldiers and gatling guns on the capitol grounds to support more than a thousand armed Repub-

---

[4] *Topeka Advocate,* January 18, 1893; *House Journal* (Topeka, Kans., 1893), pp. 7, 69, 82, 125, 127, 175; William E. Parrish, "The Great Kansas Legislative Imbroglio of 1893," *Journal of the West* 7 (October 1968): 472.

lican "deputies" from the Republican stronghold of Topeka who were posted everywhere. Armed support for the Populists would be slower to arrive from outlying rural districts.[5]

The possibility of mass violence frightened none more than Lewelling, a sensitive man of Quaker background. On the snowy night of February 16, despite Peffer's advice to stand by the Populist house as the legal body, Lewelling made concessions to a committee of Republican legislators to end the conflict, concessions that guaranteed ultimate Republican victory: all militia, deputies, and assistant sergeants-at-arms were to be dismissed; Republicans were to retain possession of Representative Hall and the Populists find other quarters; and the decision as to the legal house would be made by the Republican-dominated state supreme court. The court made the expected decision, and on February 28 the Populists who met with Republican approval entered the Republican house.[6]

The legislative war was over, but only two weeks remained in the session, and little work had been accomplished. What the legislature thereafter achieved resulted naturally enough from Republican initiative and interests. The reform demands made in the Populist platform fell short of realization. The Populists had promised much and produced little and, after declaring theirs a righteous cause, had agreed to surrender to opponents whom they had characterized as evil and unprincipled. Moreover, with the assistance of the Republican-controlled news media, the Populists had given substance to the classic Republican charge that they were anarchistic cranks, not to be trusted with the responsibility of governing. Democrats agreed with Republicans that, as Thomas Moonlight wrote, the legislative war "is a fatal blow to the people's party."[7]

What the Populists had failed to accomplish discredited their movement, but something they had managed to finish hurt them even more. Before the legislative imbroglio was resolved, both houses and the senate met in joint session to elect a United States

5 Parrish, "Legislative Imbroglio," pp. 473-84; Joseph K. Hudson, *Letters to Governor Lewelling* (Topeka, Kans., 1893).

6 Parrish, "Legislative Imbroglio," pp. 484-87; *Washington Post,* February 17, 1893.

7 O. Gene Clanton, *Kansas Populism: Ideas and Men* (Lawrence, 1969), pp. 135-36; Thomas Moonlight to P. H. Coney, January 18, 1893, Coney Papers.

Senator. Although Populists had a clear majority of the legislators on joint ballot, the party was split over the fusion question. John Martin, the state's most prominent Democratic fusionist, actively sought the Populist nomination for senator and he received endorsements from many fusion Populists, including Lewelling. From Washington, Simpson maintained that it would be "good policy" to elect Martin, both as a reward for his fusionist role and because the Democratic majority in the United States Senate would seat Martin but might reject a Populist elected in the three-house legislature.[8]

Mid-road opposition to Martin was intense. Led by John Willits and Mary Lease, the anti-fusionists demanded that the Populists end their Democratic dalliance and name a straight Populist. Willits argued that it was better to lose with a Populist candidate than to win with a Democrat, and a Topeka mass rally agreed, resolving that the legislature should send no senator to Washington rather than a man committed to one of the corrupt old parties. The Populist caucus divided over Martin as the symbol of fusion, and gradually mid-road sentiment centered on former Republican Frank Doster. The caucus struggled for two days before Martin won a narrow decision when Breidenthal's supporters joined forces with the Democrats rather than the mid-roaders. Martin accepted the nomination with the announcement that he remained a Democrat and would enter the Democratic caucus in the Senate.[9]

On January 26, 1893, the Kansas Populists elected Democrat John Martin to the United States Senate. Eight Populists refused to accept Martin and scattered their votes. One representative explained his dissenting vote by noting that "he thought last night he was going to a Populist caucus, but found he had been entrapped into a Democratic stronghold." Populists outside the legislature were still more vocal against the party's choice. Peffer regretted Martin's election because his Democratic principles were in "direct antagonism" to all that true Populists considered "fundamental and vital" and because his adherence to the Democratic party militated against eventual reform. Mrs. Lease was more emphatic in dis-

[8] *Topeka Daily Capital,* January 22, 24, 1893.
[9] *Kansas City Star,* January 23-25, 1893; Michael Brodhead, *Persevering Populist: The Life of Frank Doster* (Reno, Nev., 1969), p. 79.

cussing the impact of Martin's election. "This is a death blow to the People's Party, both state and national. It will drive 100,000 Populists in the South back into the Democratic party, and in Kansas and in the North thousands will return to the Republican party. John Martin's election killed our party, and that is all there is to it." A Populist in the state of Washington testified to the wide impact of Martin's election when he lamented that it seemed to verify what Populists had been struggling to deny—the Republican assertion that the People's party was but an adjunct of the Democracy. The nation's Populists, he wrote, had watched Kansas for another senator like Peffer "only to have their fond hopes dashed to pieces." In the election of Martin, Kansas failed in its duty to stand firm and thus be an example for Populists elsewhere.[10]

Other Populists, of course, viewed Martin's election differently. Simpson announced, "I am so pleased I hardly know what to do." National fusionist sentiment was expressed by the party's 1892 presidential candidate, James B. Weaver, who had advocated fusion with the Democrats throughout his career as a third-party leader. The choice of Martin, declared Weaver, represented "the very best possible result" because, as he fatuously continued, Martin "has for years been openly in accord with the doctrines of the People's Party."[11]

The furor over Martin's selection and the legislature's failure to achieve any significant reforms encouraged the development of a vocal anti-fusion movement within the People's party in early 1893. That Democrats had sided with the Republican house at the same time that Populists elected a Democrat to the Senate intensified the anti-fusion sentiment. With the legislature still in session, protests began to rise against the fusionist rationale. "Beware of the man who says: 'Let us get power first. Then we can reform,'" warned one Populist. "The party that uses dishonest and corrupt practices to get into power, will be obliged to use the same means to retain power. Let us win our battles honestly or be defeated." Even

[10] *House Journal* [Populist] (Topeka, Kans., 1893), pp. 123-25; *Kansas City Star*, January 25, 26, 1893; *Chicago Tribune*, June 9, 1899; *National Economist*, February 11, 1893; *American Non-Conformist* (Indianapolis), February 23, 1893.
[11] *Kansas City Star*, January 26, 1893; Fred Haynes, *James Baird Weaver* (Iowa City, 1919), p. 346.

stronger mid-road statements came from Cyrus Corning in his newspaper, *The People.* The local fusionist Populist committee in Paola had repudiated his position during the 1892 campaign, and in 1893 he moved to Topeka where he continued his uncompromising editorials. He consistently distinguished between Populists and fusionists and maintained that "fighting fusion is not fighting the People's Party any more than fighting prostitution is opposing virtue." Through its fusion maneuvers, Corning believed, the People's party had "brought its worst elements to the front from Governor down the line. Its committees betrayed their trust. Its candidates, those who were privy to the infamous deal, sold out in advance of the election. Fraud has become the prominent ingredient in their make up."[12]

If these bitter words grated too harshly on sensitive Populist ears, anti-fusion sentiment was also conspicuous among more "responsible" papers such as the *Topeka Advocate,* which retained its respectability by refusing to believe the actualities of the fusion arrangements in Kansas. Fusion in 1892, for example, was, according to editor Stephen McLallin, "all on the Democratic side, and we [Populists] were in no way responsible for it." Nevertheless, Populists should avoid fusion in the future: "The People's Party stands for certain principles which will never be endorsed by those who are in control of either of the old parties, and if we would draw to our support the dissatisfied elements of both parties from the ranks of honest voters, we must keep clear of all entangling alliances. A straight-forward, middle-of-the-road course is the only rational course to pursue."[13]

In many local elections in 1893 anti-fusion Populists followed this advice and often ran tickets counter to the regular Populist slates, which reflected the fusionist domination. Others, however, announced their intention to support the Republican ticket, either in an effort to purge their party of the contaminating effects of fusion or as an end in itself. These intransigents defended this action as being more justifiable than joining "the political cesspool of ignorance and prejudice called Democracy" through fusion ar-

12 Ruppenthal Scrapbooks, 3: 87; *Topeka People,* March 25, 1893; *Topeka New Era,* April 8, October 21, 1893.
13 *Topeka Advocate,* April 26, 1893.

ranged by "the dangerous set of conspirators who are scheming to have us bound to the Democrats."[14]

The actions of the Kansas Democracy strengthened the mid-road determination to avoid any connection with it. The Democratic anti-fusion convention of October 1892 had resolved to reorganize the party on a conservative basis, and as the more reform-minded Democrats increasingly drifted into the People's party these stalwart Democrats came to dominate their party's machinery. Led by Balie P. Waggoner and Edward Carroll and their supporters among the railroad and banking circles of northeastern Kansas, they even opposed the election of Martin to the Senate and continued to fight his influence in the party. One stalwart expressed their dim view of Democratic fusionists: "They have prostituted the Democratic party in Kansas, and have brought the State into bad odor among the financiers of the country. They have done much to arrest our development, injure prosperity, and make times hard." The conservatism that characterized the anti-fusion Democrats was evident in their intention to establish a newspaper that would oppose "Populism, prohibition, woman suffrage, and all the communistic and latter-day fads that have run the State crazy. It will oppose any compromise with third partyites by which they are given control of affairs. It will advocate," this stalwart explained, "the development of the State's resources, better treatment of the railways . . . , the establishment of manufactories, the extension of a cordial invitation to capital. . . . It will support an honest dollar, and in this respect, as in respect to all other policies of national scope, will be a Grover Cleveland paper all the way through."[15]

By early spring 1893, representatives of this Democratic faction had gained control of the State Central Committee, and reorganization of the Kansas Democracy proceeded, with only stalwarts being placed in strategic positions on the various committees at all levels. Where the party organization was in strict control, the stalwart attitude prevailed among the Democracy's rank and file. Atchison County Democrats, for instance, resolved in October in

[14] *Kansas Commoner* (Wichita), June 15, August 24, 31, 1893; *Wichita Star,* September 2, 1893.
[15] *Kansas City Star,* October 8, 1892; *Washington Post,* May 2, 1893.

favor of the Cleveland administration and against prohibition, woman suffrage, and fusion. The Democrats of Norton County, however, where the party was considerably weaker and necessarily depended upon Populist cooperation to achieve any success in local politics, resolved "That we severely denounce the adjuncts to the Republican party known as 'Stalwart Democrats.' " Such dissension was but one sign that the votes which the Democratic party organization could deliver had decreased greatly. Indeed, while Populist leaders worried because so many ex-Republicans from their ranks were returning to the GOP, stalwart Democrats lamented the flow of fusionist Democrats to the People's party. The Sedgwick County stalwarts explained the process, naturally emphasizing Democratic maneuvers more than Populist concessions: "Through the machinations of so-called Democratic leaders with Populist tendencies, and the smooth, oily and deceptive utterances of John Martin of Topeka, many Kansas Democrats . . . have left the party and joined the Populists while others have gone over to the support of the Populists under the assumed name of Democrats."[16]

Democratic loss was Populist gain in only a limited sense, for the composition and direction of the People's party continued to change. This increasing Democratization of the party was but one part of a vicious circle in which the party found itself: The more the Democrats were attracted to the party by the concessions of the Populist leaders and the repugnant nature of the Cleveland Gold Democrats, the more the former Republicans withdrew from the organization, denouncing this Democratization of the party, the arbitrary actions of Populist officials, and the policy of fusion, which both contributed to Cleveland's election and furthered the Democratization of the Kansas People's party. And the more the former Republicans withdrew, the more willing and able were the remaining Populists to adopt the political tactics of fusion, and the more attractive the party became to Democrats.

Fusion with the residual, conservative Democracy was, at the least, ill-considered, but Lewelling, Breidenthal, and other Populist

---

[16] *Girard Western Herald,* February 10, June 16, October 6, 1893; *Washington Post,* April 11, 1893; *Norton Liberator,* April 14, 1893; *Kansas Commoner,* July 13, November 2, 1893.

leaders were determined to continue the policy. They believed that Democratic support was necessary if their administration were to stay in power and felt that through their policies they could attract more Democrats to their party than they would alienate former Republicans from their ranks. Consequently, they attempted to deemphasize Populist interest in prohibition and woman suffrage, issues anathema to Democrats and their immigrant followers but considered vital by most Populists of Republican antecedents, and they rewarded their Democratic allies with state patronage and cooperation on other matters.

The very success of the 1892 fusion arrangements and Lewelling's course in office created grave difficulties for the party, however. Democrats naturally expected and demanded patronage as payment for their assistance, and Lewelling's unhesitating distribution of offices to them angered Populists, who regarded the process as ignominious, without satisfying the Democrats, for they could never get as much as they wanted. Democratic leaders, in fact, warned Lewelling that unless he granted "our Democrats" more recognition, any future effort at fusion was doomed.[17] Factions in both parties to the fusionist coalition, then, became annoyed with the Populist fusion leaders.

Lewelling's appointments, moreover, were often ill advised, even apart from their partisan implications. His adjutant general, for example, had been disbarred by the Colorado Supreme Court after being accused of perjury and bribery. Lewelling finally removed him after an investigation revealed irregularities in his accounts. Some observers considered other appointees to be anti-labor, and Senator Peffer's son Douglas, as president of the Topeka Typographical Union, protested to Lewelling against at least one such appointment. The selection of municipal police commissioners eventually proved more damaging to the administration. These commissioners were charged with the enforcement of prohibition, and the natural instincts of the Lewelling fusionists were to relax regulation in an effort to please their wet Democratic allies. Some

17 For Lewelling's appointments and disappointments, see especially L. C. Uhl to Lewelling, April 17, 1893, V. W. May to Lewelling, April 12, 1893, W. H. T. Wakefield to Lewelling, April 13, 1893, and Lewelling to Mrs. E .S. Marshall, May 10, 1893, Lorenzo D. Lewelling Papers, KSHS.

evidence indicated that the administration had also taken money from Kansas City gamblers in return for naming acceptable police commissioners. Other scandals or charges of corruption tainted Lewelling's appointments to the state penitentiary, the School for the Deaf, and the State Board of Charities, while members of the governor's personal staff were implicated in questionable financial schemes.[18]

Another aspect of the fusionist program also caused discord and resentment. Fusion leaders in 1892 had arranged for the transfer of the Democratic *Fort Scott Daily Press* to Topeka to advocate fusion. After the election the Populist administration promised to reward this Democratic paper with the contract for the state printing. This brought protests from many Populists, who felt that Populist printing should go to the party's official paper, the *Topeka Advocate,* which had long struggled financially. Indeed, it depended upon Peffer's frequent assistance, as his senatorial salary made him a backer of many ventures among the poor Populists. After Martin's election, Lewelling and his associates concluded that further immediate major concessions to the Democrats, such as naming a state paper, would be a political mistake, for, as Lewelling conceded, "it would endanger the situation and drive away a great many supporters of our cause in return for what we might gain by this action." Although the *Advocate* secured the state printing, which provided enough income to keep the advertising-poor paper alive, Lewelling promised to contribute personally to the *Press* and suggested that in the future it might receive the state contract.[19]

Finally, the administration's opposition to woman suffrage and prohibition irritated many Populists. The two issues were long important in the reform movement and were inextricably linked in the minds of both their supporters and opponents. The People's party in 1890 had avoided an explicit demand for prohibition, but

18 Lewelling to H. H. Artz, February 23, 1894, Lewelling to D. M. Peffer, March 13, 1894, J. B. Welch to Lewelling, July 10, 1894, A. Clark to Lewelling, June 19, 1894, Lewelling Papers. See also *Topeka Advocate,* March 15, 29, 1893, February 28, 1894; *Topeka Daily Capital,* May 31, 1894; Walter T. K. Nugent, *The Tolerant Populists* (Chicago, 1963), p. 149.

19 Lewelling to G. W. Marble, April 18, 1893, Lewelling Papers; *Chicago Tribune,* June 9, 1899.

its leaders such as Peffer, Otis, and Willits were popularly connected with prohibition, and the party's state chairman in his official capacity had asked for a special session of the legislature to enact more effective prohibitory laws. Now woman suffrage appeared the more important. The 1893 legislature had drafted a constitutional amendment giving women the right to vote, and the measure would be the subject of a referendum in the 1894 general elections. Democrats strongly opposed equal suffrage, largely because it antagonized the immigrant groups that formed their base of strength. But woman suffrage had long been a favorite reform objective of most third-party members and of many Republicans, who had already achieved the triumph of prohibition. In the 1891 legislature, for example, the Populist house had approved a bill allowing women to vote and hold office. All Democrats opposed the bill and a majority of Republicans did likewise. Among the Populists, those of Republican antecedents favored the bill by thirty to seven, those of a traditional third-party background by twelve to one, and those formerly Democrats by only nine to six. The 1892 Populist state convention had apparently adopted by an overwhelming vote an endorsement of woman suffrage, but Breidenthal's parliamentary maneuvers resulted in merely announcing the party's support for a referendum on the question. This pleased suffragists while allowing Breidenthal and other politicians to contend that it did not strictly commit the party to equal suffrage. Thus, woman suffrage was not an issue alien to Populism in 1894 but was a logical demand of large sections of the party. Such Populists reminded those less zealous that if the party "ignored the rights of our sisters," it would be denying the essence of Populism and the meaning of a people's party. The *Norton Liberator,* for example, believed in 1894 that "thus far the cause of woman has been solely championed by Populism. We demanded the amendment [in 1892], we enacted the amendment [in 1893], now let us . . . ratify it."[20]

With the governor and party chairman against them, the suffragists looked hopefully to Senator Peffer for assistance. He had long

[20] S. W. Chase to L. U. Humphrey, October 20, 1890, Humphrey Papers, KSHS· *House Journal* (Topeka, Kans., 1891), pp. 490-91; *Legislative Blue Book* (Topeka, Kans., 1891); *Kansas City Star,* June 16, 1892; *Norton Liberator,* June 15, 1894.

advocated woman suffrage as a matter of simple justice, had worked with suffragists in Washington, and had supported the inclusion of an equal suffrage plank in the Omaha Platform. Unfortunately, as one suffragist lamented, Peffer was now involved in Senate work, politically unable to advance the cause of woman's rights in Kansas because Martin and Lewelling obstructed his efforts in their determination to promote fusion. Once again it seemed that politics precluded populism.[21]

Increasingly, then, some Populists began to fear that Lewelling and Breidenthal intended to prove the truth of Ingalls's contention that the "purification of politics is an iridescent dream." And most of those believed that the desire to continue the policy of fusion in the election of 1894 lay behind the sorry record the Populist administration was compiling. Perhaps the most important disaffection was that of Mary Lease. As chairwoman of the State Board of Charities she resented Lewelling's efforts to have Democrats named to positions nominally under her jurisdiction. She publicly attributed Populist losses in the 1893 elections to the policies of the Lewelling administration, seeing in the Populist defeat "a loud and effective protest against corrupt men and their measures and fusion with the Democrats." Shortly thereafter Lewelling attempted to remove Mrs. Lease from her job, but she countered with a suit against him, contending that his action was not based on her official performance but on her opposition to his political plans for fusion. In February 1894 the state supreme court ruled that Lewelling could not remove Mrs. Lease without cause, and the administration dropped the matter. Mrs. Lease, however, continued to arraign the fusionist course of Lewelling and Breidenthal, contributing to Corning's new mid-road paper, the *New Era,* and charging the administration with cooperating with Kansas City gamblers and accepting bribes from railroad companies. The administration retorted with questions as to her sanity, innuendos about her personal life, and claims that the GOP had bought her.[22]

Although the Lease-Lewelling contest seemed to be a mutually

21 *Topeka New Era,* April 14, 1894.
22 *Topeka Daily Capital,* November 11, 1893; *Kansas City Star,* January 2, 27, 1894; *Pleasanton Herald,* January 26, 1894; O. Gene Clanton, "Intolerant Populist? The Disaffection of Mary Elizabeth Lease," *Kansas Historical Quarterly* 34 (Summer 1968): 189-200.

damaging stalemate, other prominent Populists joined the mid-roaders like Corning in forming a People's party in exile. John Willits was an important addition after his criticism of the fusionists and their Democratic allies cost him his position on the State Board of Pardons. W. F. Rightmire and Noah Allen, another discharged officeholder, revived the Citizens' Alliance as an anti-administration organization. John Otis also became a supporter of the more uncompromising radicals among Lewelling's Populist opponents. By early 1894 these Populists had come to believe one of Corning's statements a year earlier: "By virtue of the unholy alliance [i.e., fusion] the elective officers have for the most part surrounded themselves with a set of political adventurers whose only claim to recognition is cheek and a willingness to barter away the rights of the people. Fusion means boodle, fraud and corruption."[23]

Corning's *New Era* led the radical mid-roaders against the Populist administration. In its first issue in 1894 the newspaper set forth their position: 1) The 1892 Populist campaign was based on fusion engineered by Breidenthal and others and implicitly endorsed by leading Populists; 2) Breidenthal excluded mid-road and female campaigners from the canvass so as not to antagonize Democrats; 3) the Lewelling administration rewarded Democrats and fusionists but harassed those who adhered to the Omaha Platform; 4) "the Populist campaign of 1892, in point of morals, bossism, and party lash driving, on account of the perfidy of trusted leaders, was the lowest ever made in the state of Kansas, ending in Democratic ascendancy." In attacking the elite dominance and political manipulation which he believed characterized the People's party more than the old parties, Corning invariably pointed to Breidenthal's role in the Second District in 1892, where the people's "sovereign right to name their candidates" had been denied. Lewelling's activities to promote continued fusion demonstrated to Corning that the governor's "sole aim has been to wreck the People's Party in the hopes of building up [the] Democracy. The *New Era* is right; Mrs. Lease is right; middle-of-the-road Populists are right; anti-administration Populists are right; the administration frauds must be turned under or Populism is forever doomed."[24]

23 *Topeka People,* March 25, 1893: Nugent, *Tolerant Populists,* pp. 156-57.
24 *Topeka New Era,* January 6, February 24, 1894.

There were other Populists in 1894 who also opposed fusion but who carefully disassociated themselves from the vociferous Corning and his condemnation of the Lewelling administration. Proud of having a people's government at least, they objected to any criticism that might endanger its reelection, yet remained in their own eyes steadfastly opposed to compromise and fusion. "I have always thought your administration wise and statesmanlike," wrote one such Populist to Lewelling. "Fusion, of course, is out of the question." The *Topeka Advocate* took a similar position. As the party's official paper, it loyally supported the administration against the charges of Corning and his associates while it asserted its opposition to any fusion whatever. Corning believed that McLallin decried fusion only under instructions from Peffer, backed by a threat to take control of the Advocate Publishing Company and secure direction of the paper's policy, but McLallin was a sincere mid-roader, mired in the impure quicksand of responsibility without authority and allegiance without commitment. He consistently placed the *Advocate* against compromise and fusion but blindly refused to believe Corning's indictment of the fusionist tendencies of the Lewelling-Breidenthal group. Other Populists made public their hostility to fusion through papers even less suspected of association with the radical mid-roaders and usually based their position on moral principles or national implications, for they emphasized adherence to the Omaha Platform.[25]

Despite such vocal anti-fusion sentiment, the People's party contained a more sizable group that prided itself on its alleged pragmatism and believed that fusion provided the only hope for the Lewelling administration to be reelected. Throughout 1893 Lewelling carefully expressed his appreciation for the Democratic support of the 1892 Populist ticket, which he believed had been crucial to his victory. Relying on "political wisdom," moreover, he renounced any suggestion that fusion and Populism were incompatible, and with Breidenthal sought to secure Democratic

25 George W. McKay to Lewelling, May 22, 1894, and J. D. Bradley to Fred Close, June 7, 1894, Lewelling Papers· *Topeka New Era*, March 31, June 2, 1894; *Topeka Advocate*, November 22, 1893, April 4, May 23, 1894· *Kansas Commoner*, March 22, May 31, 1894. For McLallin and the *Advocate*, see also *Topeka Populist*, May 19, 26, 1893; but for evidence of Peffer's increasing realization of the Populist predilection for fusion, see *Pittsburg Messenger*, March 16, 1894.

assistance in 1894. Early in the year, for example, Lewelling conferred with Democratic fusionist William H. Sears, son-in-law of Charles Robinson and confidant of W. A. Harris, as to prospects for Democratic support and received assurances that mutual compromises between the two parties would again insure fusion. Administration appointees canvassed other Democrats to gain backing for Populist officials, and administration Populists and Democrats alike advocated the manipulation of nominations to guarantee fusion, with a popular suggestion being to include Harris on the state ticket as the ultimate enticement to reluctant Democrats.[26]

By 1894, however, the question of fusion involved much more than the tactics of one campaign. At stake was the direction and commitment of the entire reform movement. Fusionists wanted to narrow the party's platform to the lowest common denominator, financial reform, and to avoid all other issues that might alienate various blocs of voters. The more determined the fusionist, the lower was his common denominator, and by 1894 it was clear that a demand for free silver even apart from considerations of national banks, irredeemable paper money, government loans, and other Populist demands within the entire issue of financial reform would receive the support of nearly everyone in a state in which all political parties had demanded free silver for more than a decade. Anti-fusionists, on the other hand, were committed to a wide range of demands across the whole spectrum of reform and argued that emphasis upon a single issue like the money question distorted the realities of America's problems and might prove counterproductive to the larger issue of the regeneration of society as a whole. Thus anti-fusionists advocated woman suffrage and prohibition; the democratization of the political system through expanded suffrage, direct election of senators and the president, and the adoption of the initiative and referendum; and the democratization of the economy through government ownership or control of the transportation system, communications, and natural monopolies and through the recognition of broad labor rights.

The party split not only over the principles which encouraged

---

[26] Lewelling to Dave Dale, June 6, 1893, William Wykes to Lewelling, May 11, 1894, and Harry Freese to Lewelling, [May or June 1894], Lewelling Papers; W. H. Sears to Lewelling, March 8, 1894, Sears Papers.

or prevented fusion but also over the expected consequences of the policy. Fusionists were concerned with strictly immediate results, the election of candidates to office. They argued that reforms came only with political power and that free silver would merely be the reform foot in the door of the status quo, a necessary first step in the march toward full enactment of the party's reform demands. Anti-fusionists considered that free silver alone meant nothing—indeed that it was the least important aspect of the party's demands for financial reform; that the achievement of such a minor reform might prevent acceptance of more thorough, radical, and necessary reforms; that the election of state officials through fusion had no bearing on national financial matters anyway; that cooperating with allies committed only to silver gave the party political power only to achieve silver coinage; that unconverted candidates, even or especially if elected, could injure the party; that the direction and ultimate success of the party could be compromised through concessions to gain short-run fusion.

On the most practical level, the argument over fusion was really an argument over the merits of the Democratic party.[27]   Mid-road Populists came overwhelmingly from the Republican-derived wing of the People's party and had an intense aversion to Democrats and the Democracy. Not surprisingly, considering the nature of American politics for the entire period in which they had lived, much of this animosity was based on emotional and blind prejudice. Mrs. Lease, for example, a Republican until she entered the reform movement, had lost two brothers in the Union Army during the Civil War, and her father had died at the infamous Andersonville prison. These cruel memories of her childhood shaped her whole

---

[27] Nugent, *Tolerant Populists,* p. 152, is quite mistaken in believing that fusion on the most pragmatic level was an argument over woman suffrage and prohibition—it was over the merits of the Democratic party. Suffrage and prohibition were but aspects of this, as was the silver issue; the first were sometimes instruments to frustrate fusion and the other an instrument to encourage fusion. Nugent's well-warranted determination to demonstrate that Populism was not nativistic leads him to interpret anything that might alienate immigrants as unessential to Populism and to assert that fusion (or, as he revealingly defines it on p. 153, "the presence of ethnic support") was the necessary, rational, and logical part of Populism. Such a view of fusion, in turn, leads him to deny the existence of differences between Populists and Democrats over other issues—an untenable position, particularly for the early years of Populism.

life, she insisted, and she was unable to forgive the Democratic party for its role in the sectional conflict—an inability on her part and millions of others' that the Republican party had encouraged as a matter of policy for all her adult life. "I respect and esteem Mr. Martin as a man, as a lawyer and as a gentleman," she announced in 1894, "but he is a Democrat, and you know I HATE DEMOCRATS. I AM DONE WITH DEMOCRATS AND FUSION."[28] By 1894, those Populists psychologically incapable of working with the Democracy had largely returned to the Republican party as Populism underwent Democratization, bitter that their hopes had been blighted by those who believed that cooperating with the malignant Democratic party would somehow result in a new and better political society.

Others based their objection to collaboration with the Democratic party on the realistic basis of concrete political proposals. Democrats opposed prohibition and woman suffrage, hoary issues with many Populists, and were committed to little beyond free silver in the Populist economic program. The subtreasury and government loans to farmers, the activating economic demands of original Populism, had already fallen victim to Democratization and fusion with the election of their bitter opponents Harris and Martin. Neither paper money nor government ownership of railroads attracted any support among Democrats. By 1894, moreover, Kansans who remained in the Democracy were, with notable exceptions, closely tied to the national administration and often hostile even to free silver. Fusion with such an organization could only be for office, not principle, even to the most flaccid Populist.

The most thoughtful Populists objected to the Democratic party because of its general attitude toward government and society. If parties had changed absolutely since the days of Jackson it was nevertheless true that the Democratic party remained relatively more committed to a strict construction of the responsibilities and possibilities of the national government than either the GOP or the People's party. As Peffer believed, "the foundation ideas" of Democracy and Populism were in direct contradiction. "Populists believe in the exercise of national authority in any and every case

28 *Pittsburg Messenger,* January 12, 1894; Clanton, "Intolerant Populist?" pp. 195-96, 200.

where the general welfare will be promoted thereby. The Democratic party is opposed to this." Too, he pointed out that many of the basic Populist ideas came from Republican antecedents, especially in financial legislation; Populists merely wanted the exercise of national government authority to be by and for the people rather than the manufacturing and financial classes. Prominent Democrats understood clearly this difference between the attitudes of the two parties. David Overmeyer, for example, argued that Populism was not the solution to the nation's problems, which he believed were the results of too much government. Other Democrats argued that Populism was merely Republicanism carried to its logical conclusion.[29] With such basic philosophical differences, any hope that a combination of the two parties for campaign purposes would further the cause of ultimate Populistic reform was seriously ill-founded.

Despite these major objections to cooperating with the Democracy, there were of course those within the People's party who favored fusion. Former Democrats, try as they might, could see little evil in the Democracy. Its traditions, principles, and attitudes were largely acceptable; at best, in the time-honored custom of politics, they denied that the Democracy of 1894 followed Democratic principles. Perhaps most had entered the new party only as part of an effort to create a political majority against the traditional enemy, the GOP; many others had joined the People's party only on the basis of its free silver advocacy following Cleveland's forced repeal of the Sherman Silver Purchase Act in 1893. They saw no reason not to limit the Populist appeal to free silver as that represented their total attachment to the new party. Many Populists of traditional third-party antecedents, while perhaps more in agreement with the former Republicans within their party as to goals and ideals, had consistently fused with Democrats in the past and for the most part were willing to continue the practice.

Still another factor complicated the issue of fusion in 1894. Fusionists such as Latimer, Harris, and Breidenthal continued to form a cohesive faction, but those opposed to fusion split into two groups. The first included those like McLallin, Peffer, and Doster, who rather blindly viewed fusion in 1892 as primarily a

<hr />

29 Brodhead, *Persevering Populist*, p. 67; *Chicago Tribune*, July 7, 9, 1899.

Democratic maneuver, achieved after the People's party had nominated straight Populist candidates, and who now believed that the Lewelling administration should be renominated but that further entanglement with Democrats should be strictly avoided. The second and far smaller group included those like Corning who believed that fusion in 1892 had been as much a Populist as a Democratic scheme; that the Lewelling-Breidenthal fusionists had so subverted the goals and ideals of the movement that in and of themselves they represented fusion and compromise, whether or not they secured the endorsement of the Democratic organization in 1894; and that therefore they must be defeated and purged from positions of power and influence within the party in order to save the movement. Corning and his uncompromising associates, then, would oppose not only Lewelling's renomination but also, if nominated, his reelection.

As the June 1894 Populist state convention approached, the radicals made final preparations. On May 31, Noah Allen, president of the National Citizens' Alliance, and W. F. Rightmire issued a circular calling on Populists to use every means possible to defeat the Populist administration. "We warn the members against the traitors in our camp," the circular read, "those who have control of the People's Party organization of this state, who for the sake of the emoluments of office have contracted to surrender the principles of the reform cause in this state to the British financial Hessians, the Democrats of Kansas, who endorsed and supported Cleveland and the gold standard." Breidenthal, Prather, and Lewelling had agreed with Democratic leaders, Allen charged, to name Democrats for secretary of state and associate justice of the supreme court and to renominate all other state officials in exchange for a Democratic endorsement of the entire ticket. Allen asked all alliancemen to meet and name a straight ticket if the Populist officials managed to produce such a fusion. Shortly after this appeal, the radical mid-roaders organized the Anti-Fusion People's Party League of Kansas, with Otis as chairman and Corning, Willits, and W. H. Bennington, another Populist prominent in 1890 as secretary of the original Citizens' Alliance, as lesser officials. In a last maneuver to prevent the administration from obtaining a fusionist convention, the People's party of Shawnee County, strongly anti-fusionist because of the influence of Peffer, Otis, Corning, McLallin, and their friends in Topeka, unsuccessfully demanded that the state convention be held under the "Omaha Ordinance for the Purification of Politics," which forbade all officeholders from participating in the party's conventions.[30]

The governor and his supporters countered with their own arrangements. Lewelling lieutenants worked in the local conventions preceding the state meeting to secure endorsements of the Populist administration and to discredit the mid-roaders as merely disappointed office-seekers trying to disrupt the party. The selection of the June date for the convention by the party leadership had already revealed that the fusionists were in control, for the Democrats had previously chosen July 3 for their convention and the earlier date gave the Populist politicians important leverage to promote a joint ticket.[31] Lewelling and Breidenthal wanted a platform limited to demands for economic reform, avoiding the issues of woman suffrage and prohibition. They also hoped to renominate the ticket that had been acceptable to the Democrats in 1892, made perhaps a little more attractive, and thus present the Democratic convention with both a platform and a slate it could embrace.

The Populist state convention opened in Topeka on June 12, 1894, with an immediate challenge to the administration's plans by the combined forces of the suffragists and the mid-roaders. The convention rejected the administration's choice for temporary chairman and elected Ben Henderson, a firm supporter of a suffrage plank. After urging the adoption of such a plank, Henderson then introduced a series of suffragettes, including Susan B. Anthony and Carrie Chapman-Catt, who pleaded with the delegates to support a cause essential to a people's movement. The committee on resolutions ignored the question, but a minority report placed it before the convention where it provoked a vociferous debate. Administration spokesmen argued against the inclusion of the

---

30 *Kansas Commoner*, June 7, 1894; *Topeka New Era*, June 9, 1894; *Topeka Advocate*, March 28, 1894.

31 *Topeka Daily Democrat*, March 14, 1894; *Kansas Commoner*, June 7, 1894; L. C. Clark to Fred Close, May 28, 1894, Lewelling Papers.

suffrage demand on the grounds that it would alienate the immigrant voters of the state and thus destroy the possibility of fusion. In short, it was politically expedient to avoid the subject. Henderson, an ex-Republican, retorted that the party was not making platforms for Democrats but for Populists; Doster, another ex-Republican, asserted that the foreign vote and the Democratic vote were not important but that principle was, and declared, "I stand against regarding this as a question of expediency." Otis announced that the question involved was merely, "Shall the people control the People's party or shall the politicians control it?" When Annie Diggs routed the ideological arguments of suffrage opponents, the convention accepted the plank.[32]

Although the radical anti-fusionists had won this battle against Breidenthal by uniting with those who supported equal suffrage regardless of their attitudes toward fusion, it was their only victory. The 1892 fusion ticket was renominated with two exceptions, Lieutenant Governor Percy Daniels and Secretary of State Russell Osborn, both former Republicans. Daniels had repeatedly disagreed with Lewelling's policies and then conditioned his candidacy on the party's adoption of his own graduated taxation proposals; Osborn declined renomination and was replaced by J. W. Amis, a former Democrat whose candidacy had Democratic backing. A new opening, for associate justice of the supreme court, was filled by the nomination of George Clark, "a sterling Democrat" according to the Democratic *Newton Journal*. Clark's nomination over former Republican W. C. Webb and M. B. Nicholson was another sign of the Populist willingness to fuse. Nicholson denounced the "schemes" of the Populist "manipulators" who had, he said, "predetermined to nominate Mr. Clark as a sop to the Democrats." Indeed, in these nominations, the convention largely followed the fusion line predicted by Noah Allen. Lewelling was renominated by acclamation, Breidenthal was easily reelected party chairman, and Mrs. Lease's bid to oppose Harris for congressman-at-large failed completely. Apart from the suffrage plank, which was not solely a fight over fusion, then, the convention stayed under

32 *Ottawa Journal and Triumph,* June 21, 1894; *Topeka Advocate,* June 20, 1894; *Kansas City Star,* June 12, 13, 1894; Nugent, *Tolerant Populists,* pp. 158-61.

Breidenthal's control and the few extreme mid-roaders had little influence.[33]

If Breidenthal expected Democratic endorsement he was to be surprised. And if the adoption of a suffrage plank did not represent an intentional repudiation of fusion by the Populists, neither did it alone inspire the Democratic state convention to field a straight ticket on July 3. Once again national considerations were important. In addressing the convention, the party state chairman described the 1892 fusion as simply a tactic to insure the election of the Democratic national ticket and pointedly added, "no such condition exists today." But not only were there no factors dictating fusion, there existed a need to defend the national Democratic administration from virulent Populist attack. As early as January the *Pittsburg Messenger* denounced the very suggestion of fusion as untimely wavering from support for Cleveland. Indeed, Democratic newspapers strongly condemned fusion throughout 1894. The *Topeka Democrat, Junction City Sentinel, Paola Western Spirit,* and other leading Democratic organs consistently opposed fusion. Democratic newspapers that had advocated the policy in 1892 were set determinedly against it in 1894. "Democrats today in Kansas," declared the *Wichita Beacon,* "have no sympathy with socialism. They do not believe in paternalism. They are not greenbackers. They oppose every form of government aid."[34]

In pointing out the characteristics of "Democrats today" the *Beacon* disclosed the party's conservatism in 1894. Most of the more liberal Democrats had already joined the People's party, a result the *Beacon* blamed on fusion, and remaining Democrats generally viewed the tumult of the 1890s with dismay. George Glick, who had advocated fusion in 1892 simply to advance Democratic political ambitions, complained in 1894 about the "isms that have injured the state" and declared that the party should campaign on tariff reform and sound money and avoid any connection with Populists. Glick also charged fusion with causing many Democrats to be

33 *Kansas City Star,* June 14, 17, 1894; M. B. Nicholson to Lewelling, June 23, 1894, Lewelling Papers; *Pittsburg Messenger,* June 22, 1894: *Fort Scott Daily Monitor,* June 16, 21, 1894; *Topeka Advocate,* June 20, 1894; Kansas Biographical Scrapbook, 3: 134, KSHS.
34 *Pittsburg Messenger,* January 12, 26, April 6, June 15, September 28, 1894; *Topeka Daily Capital,* July 4, 1894; *Topeka Daily Democrat,* March 13, 1894.

subsumed in the People's party. Even Overmeyer, who had opposed fusion in 1892 because of partisan loyalties and not political issues, believed that fusion in 1894 was out of the question, for it would mean Democratic endorsement of the anarchism and revolution revealed in Populism during the legislative war. The Coxey movement and Populist support for it in the spring of 1894 particularly alarmed Democrats and strengthened their opposition to fusion. Overmeyer declared, "Populism has now reached a stage where it is simply Coxeyism, and Coxeyism is incipient revolution superinduced by organized vagabondage and militant scoundrelism." With most party positions under the control of stalwart Democrats, it was clear that Democrats would reject fusion even before the Populist state convention endorsed woman suffrage.[35]

The suffrage plank, in fact, made little difference. Lewelling Populists reported to the governor that most Democrats took lightly the Populist declaration and that many immigrants favored endorsing the Populist ticket because they feared the Republican nominees would enforce prohibition stringently. S. W. Chase assured Lewelling that there was little complaint over the suffrage plank in heavily immigrant Leavenworth County and that the Populist convention's denunciation of the nativistic American Protective Association would attract more immigrant voters than would be alienated by the suffrage stand. Indeed, Friedrich W. Frasius, a prominent German Democratic politician, announced in late July that he had joined the People's party and would campaign for its ticket.[36]

If the action of the Populist convention on suffrage caused the defeat of fusion, as historians have charged, then there should have been Democrats who supported fusion before the Populist convention and opposed it afterwards. In reality there were few if any such political creatures. The Democratic *Atchison Patriot,* in fact, before the Populist convention, expected a non-fusion campaign, then ignored the Populist convention stand on woman suffrage, and finally became mildly fusionist before the Democratic state conven-

[35] *Marshall County Democrat* (Marysville), January 5, 1894; *Pittsburg Messenger,* January 26, 1894; *Fort Scott Daily Monitor,* July 1, 1894.

[36] Rufus Cone to Lewelling, June 22, 1894, S. W. Chase to Lewelling, June 20, 1894, and I. P. Campbell to Lewelling, June 9, 15, 1894, Lewelling Papers; *Kansas City Star,* July 25, 1894.

tion. The Democratic Central Committeemen of the Seventh Congressional District unanimously agreed in May that there would be no state level fusion—despite their simultaneous expectation that the Populists would dodge woman suffrage and prohibition. Less formal polls of Kansas Democrats before the Populist convention found them "well-nigh unanimous for a straight-out Democratic state ticket." Clearly, anti-fusion sentiment dominated the Democratic party, not the People's party, and regardless of Populist declarations on woman suffrage, a straight Democratic ticket was assured.[37]

The failure of fusion in 1894, unlike earlier years, lay with the Democrats and not the Populists. The middle-of-the-road Populists were more vocal than numerous by 1894, whereas the stalwart Democrats dominated their party. The Democratic state convention nominated a full ticket headed by Overmeyer and wrote a traditional platform emphasizing strict construction and the tariff while endorsing the Cleveland administration and denouncing the legislative war. Stalwart control failed only when the convention adopted a minority report favoring free silver. After his nomination, Overmeyer addressed the convention and argued for states' rights and limited government concepts. Many delegates regarded Prather "as a reasonably good Democrat notwithstanding his present party affiliation" and sought to have him endorsed. Even more favored accepting the Populist nominations of Harris and Clark. Several Democrats announced their opposition to cooperating with the People's party and still argued for the endorsement of Harris. The majority, however, rejected this "bait thrown out to Democratic suckers" and named a complete straight ticket.[38]

This rejection of fusion by the Democratic state convention did not end collaboration between Populists and Democrats in Kansas in 1894. Populists reaffirmed their intentions to gain Democratic support and eagerly made concessions for it. Lewelling and Breidenthal actively intervened in local Democratic conventions through Democratic-Populists to promote fusion arrangements, and the governor's Democratic appointees worked similarly to gain him Dem-

37 *Atchison Patriot,* June 2, 30, August 18, and passim, 1894; *Wichita Weekly Beacon,* May 25, 1894; *Topeka Daily Democrat,* May 11, 17, 31, 1894.

38 James Malin, *A Concern about Humanity* (Lawrence, Kans., 1964), p. 41; *Topeka Daily Capital,* July 3, 4, 1894; *Fort Scott Daily Monitor,* June 21, 1894; *Topeka Democrat,* June 15, 1894; *Pittsburg Messenger,* June 15, 22, 1894.

ocratic backing, a task apparently imposed on them as a condition of their original appointment. Lewelling also conferred privately with Democrats at their state convention in hopes of winning endorsement despite the unanimity of state Democratic leaders against fusion. Other Populists were less circumspect, and at least two state candidates, former Democrats Prather and Clark, lobbied openly at the convention for fusion, as did several of Harris's lieutenants. With the encouragement of the party leadership, Populists also took the initiative in proposing local fusion, and their county and legislative conventions carefully named Democrats directly to their own tickets in efforts to compel the Democrats to accept fusion. In one county this even resulted in the Populists placing on their five-man ticket four Democrats, including the chairman of the Democratic County Central Committee and a member of the Democratic State Central Committee. Even so, the Democratic county convention endorsed this "Populist" ticket only after "a hot fight."[39]

The conduct of the Populist congressional conventions of the First and Second districts indicated the change the party had undergone since 1892. In that year the First District Populists had refused to accept the fusion arrangements and rejected Harris for a mid-roader. In 1894 they attempted to force fusion upon the Democrats by nominating H. C. Solomon of Atchison. Solomon was described as "a genuine Democrat" and not "merely a Populist of Democratic antecedents." Indeed, stalwart Democrats had already declared Solomon their favorite for the nomination. The Democratic congressional convention subsequently praised the Populist capitulation as "prudent, wise, and sagacious" and then also nominated Solomon.[40]

In the Second District, where in 1892 the Populists had struggled so long to maintain the integrity of their party, the surrender was not so complete. Rather than forcing fusion on reluctant Democrats as in the First District, the Populist politicians merely sought joint

---

[39] R. B. Drury to Lewelling, July 3, 25, 1894, Joseph Pomeroy to Lewelling, June 21, 28, 1894, and A. Clark to Lewelling, June 19, 1894, Lewelling Papers; *Pittsburg Messenger*, July 13, 1894; *Kansas Commoner*, July 26, 1894; *Marshall County Democrat*, August 31, September 7, 1894.

[40] *Pittsburg Messenger*, April 27, 1894; *Atchison Weekly Patriot*, June 9, 30, July 7, 28, August 11, 1894.

consultations. The Populist convention met in June, well before the Democratic convention, but the chairman postponed the meeting until July in order to act in conjunction with the Democrats. A few mid-roaders introduced a bitter resolution censuring this arbitrary action, but most Populists were complaisant and refused to pass it. In July, however, the Populists were not yet ready to nominate an acknowledged Democrat like Horace L. Moore and instead named Frank Willard as their candidate. Nevertheless, the Populists expected fusion through Moore's withdrawal, and Willard attended the Democratic convention to obtain an endorsement. Although he had some support, the Democrats turned him down. Thus again the absence of fusion was largely the result of Democratic not Populist actions.[41]

This pattern held for the other districts as well. In each instance the Populist convention met first and the Democrats second, and in all but the Fourth District the Populists renominated a candidate that had been fused on by the Democrats previously. In each case in 1894 the Democrats refused the opportunity to enact the fusion they had welcomed earlier. They even declined to endorse Hudson and Simpson. Hudson's association with the despised Coxey movement, which he had served as a lawyer, was instrumental in alienating Democratic support. Simpson's rejection demonstrated the simple Democratic determination to avoid fusion in 1894, for, as one Democrat admitted, Simpson voted consistently with the Democrats in Congress and had strong political support from Democrats, both fusionist and stalwart. But like Willard, and unlike Solomon, he was a Populist not a Democrat.[42]

The relative absence of explicit fusion arrangements failed to mollify the radical mid-roaders. Unconcerned with Democratic reactions, they considered that the willingness of People's party leaders to compromise to achieve fusion represented compromise and fusion even if Democrats spurned the efforts. In 1890 the Democrats had sought fusion and had regularly been rebuffed; in 1894 it was the supplicant Populists who were rebuffed. To the mid-

---

41 *Atchison Weekly Patriot*, June 30, 1894; *Kansas City Star*, June 22, July 13, 1894; *Leavenworth Herald*, July 21, 1894; *Paola Times*, July 19, 1894; *Fort Scott Daily Monitor*, July 18, 19, 1894.

42 *Atchison Weekly Patriot*, August 18, 1894; *Emporia Tidings*, June 22, 1894; *Pittsburg Messenger*, August 24, 1894.

roaders this revealed the deterioration in the ideals and practices of Populism. Mid-road Populists objected to both Simpson and Hudson, regarding them as fusion candidates even with Democratic opposition. As in 1892, Populists in the Third District who could not accept anyone other than a straight nonfusion Populist formed an Abraham Lincoln Republican faction, which refused to support Hudson or the Republican nominee. These rigorous mid-roaders also believed that Lewelling himself personified fusion and had to be repudiated to cleanse the party. Corning responded readily to the question of the effect of mid-road opposition to Lewelling: "The answer is simple and easily given. The Populist ticket will be defeated and it ought to be." Willits agreed: "The Lewelling state ticket is unworthy of the countenance and support of the Populists of Kansas." Percy Daniels concurred, and from the vantage point of the administration itself: "The trouble with our present leaders is they want office more than they want to aid the masses."[43]

Defeat would have wholesome effects for the party, they concluded, for the reelection of the administration Populists would be counterproductive to substantive changes in the political system. The Democratic party ruled through Lewelling and Breidenthal, they charged, making true reform impossible while permitting political manipulations, corruption, and the deterioration of the party. "The membership of the People's Party is blinded by party zeal," announced Corning's *New Era*, "and in convention, this membership, through its delegates, endorsed all these infamies, and declared to the world that SUCH IS POPULISM. Defeat of the People's Party, therefore, is the only thing that will open the eyes of an honest membership and cause them to rise as men and patriots and rescue the principles of the party from the hands of incompetents and traitors." Freed from these debilitating influences, the People's party could carry out its mission. Defeat, Corning believed, would purify the party by driving out the expedient Democrats and "fusion pimps." Continued fusion would destroy the People's party.[44]

[43] *Kansas City Journal,* September 25, 1894; *Girard Western Herald,* September and October 1894, passim; *Topeka New Era,* June 30, 1894; *Pittsburg Messenger,* September 14, 1894.
[44] *Topeka New Era,* June 30, 1894.

These mid-roaders considered themselves the real Populists, committed to the entire Omaha Platform and the ideals that had ignited the Populist prairies in the beginning. They objected to Breidenthal's contention that they had left the party rather than the reverse. Ben Henderson, for example, long disturbed by evidences of fusion and its crippling effects, joined the mid-road element after the state convention but made clear that he remained a Populist and would support Populist nominees other than Lewelling, Little, and Breidenthal, whom he considered corrupt and detrimental to the interests of Populism. In October the anti-fusionists filed an independent, "Middle-of-the-Road Populist" ticket headed by Corning for governor. Breidenthal formally protested to the secretary of state, complaining that the Corning ticket had chosen its name to deceive People's party voters. A board composed of administration officials agreed and refused to allow the mid-roaders a place on the ballot. Many regular Populists saw in the actions of the mid-roaders evidence of Republican influence and money; even Mrs. Lease returned to Lewelling's side following Corning's ultimate defiance of the administration. Two weeks earlier she had denounced Breidenthal as "the man who betrayed the party that had elevated him to his position. They put him in charge to run the machinery of the People's Party and he acknowledged their kindness and regarded their confidence by selling the party out wholesale to the Democrats."[45]

Other anti-fusion Populists decided the proper road to take led back to the GOP rather than to the People's party of Chairman Breidenthal. Most prominent of these was former congressman and twice vice president of the National Farmers' Alliance, Benjamin Clover. Nationally and locally, he argued, Democrats opposed reform even while using Populists to secure political power for their own party. And the People's party, he believed, "has fallen into the hands of a dictator, whose power is absolute; who in practice of corrupt and disreputable political methods has out done all other political managers that have ever risen. . . . There is

---

45 *Kansas City Journal*, September 25, 1894; *Pittsburg Messenger*, September 21, 1894: Ben Henderson to Lewelling, April 12, 1893, and Lewelling to Henderson, April 18, 1893, Lewelling Papers; *Kansas Commoner*, October 25, 1894; Populist Party Clippings, 1: 332, KSHS; Walter T. K. Nugent, "How the Populists Lost in 1894," *Kansas Historical Quarterly* 31 (Autumn 1965): 254-55.

not a single idea that was advocated by us in 1889 and 1890, when we were laboring in the cause of reform, that is now adhered to by the populist party." Populism, Clover reminded Kansans, had declared for honesty and justice in politics, but Populists in power practiced the opposite. To retain his own self-respect, Clover concluded, he had to leave the People's party and return to the GOP, which he hoped had seen the error of its ways. Another important figure in original Populism, A. F. Allen of Vinland, the party's Second District congressional nominee in 1890, also returned to the Republican party, disgusted with the policies of the new leaders of the People's party.[46]

While the People's party thus continued to lose members to the GOP, it also became increasingly indebted to Democrats. During the course of the 1894 campaign Martin, Glick, and other Democratic politicians began to argue as Democrats for the election of Populist candidates, even over opposing Democratic nominees, in order to defeat the GOP. John Eaton, a Democratic chieftain, announced, "I will not be misled into the idea that either woman suffrage or prohibition are important issues in this campaign"; he agreed to canvass as a Democrat for the Populist ticket under Breidenthal's direction. Influential Democratic newspapers began also to urge support of Populists, while Populists in turn made special appeals to Democrats to "vote with friends." By late October a Populist paper believed that the Democratic voters were "rapidly concentrating on the Populist state ticket, and in addition . . . fusion has been effected in enough legislative districts to carry the legislature against the Republicans."[47]

Populists made their inroads into Democratic strength principally by emphasizing the issue of silver coinage. Free silver had been endorsed by all three Kansas parties, and Populists capitalized on the inconsistency of Democrats supporting Cleveland and silver and of Republicans favoring silver while adhering to a national party that clearly favored gold monometallism. In addition, the Republican candidate for governor, Edmund N. Morrill, was unsympathetic to silver, and Populists easily gained the backing of

[46] *Leavenworth Herald*, August 18, 1894; *Paola Western Spirit*, June 15, 1894.
[47] *Marshall County Democrat*, October 5, 12, November 2, 1894; *Kansas City Star*, October 20, 24, November 4, 1894; *Kansas Commoner*, October 11, 18, 25, November 1, 1894; *Girard Western Herald*, August 3, 1894.

silver Democrats for Lewelling. Even Senator Peffer, after he arrived in Kansas in September, stressed silver more than formerly, although he still was at pains to deny the intrinsic value of money and to demand paper money, government loans, and the destruction of the national banking system, while strongly advocating suffrage and equal rights for women. Most Populists in 1894 were not so conscientious and began to push silver as the panacea that the party had rejected earlier.[48]

While Populists thus attempted to focus on national issues, especially silver and secondarily labor and government during the depression, Republicans were content to attack the sorry record of the Lewelling administration. Morrill declared that he was "ashamed of Kansas" and urged voters to "redeem" the state from Populism. The scandals, alleged and real, of the Lewelling administration and the legislative war furnished all the campaign ammunition needed to shoot down Populist hopes. By late October Cy Leland, the Republican state chairman, stopped estimating his party's possible plurality and started to speak of an overall majority. Populists recognized the signs too. Mrs. Lease felt that the people were less interested in politics than during the earlier evangelistic campaigns; Breidenthal feared a sharp drop in turnout.[49]

The Republican victory was nearly complete. The entire state ticket was elected, the lower house of the legislature became overwhelmingly Republican, and every Populist congressional candidate but William Baker was defeated, and he retained office by fewer than 200 votes of more than 35,000 cast. The *Great Bend Democrat* gloated that "those Populists who told us that they could carry Kansas without the aid of the despised Democrats need not feel so sore about the results. They still have the state senate, and . . . Peffer."[50] But in truth the full Democratic vote delivered to the Populists would have made no difference: the GOP commanded once again a majority of Kansas voters. Indeed, explicit state fusion might have increased the margin of Republican victory by

48 *Marshall County Democrat*, October 5, 12, 1894; Raymond C. Miller, "The Populist Party in Kansas" (Ph.D. diss., University of Chicago, 1928), p. 267; *Topeka Advocate*, September 12, October 24, 31, 1894; *Girard Western Herald*, September 14, 1894.

49 *Topeka Daily Capital*, August 21, September 6, 1894; *Kansas City Star*, late October and early November 1894, passim.

50 Quoted by *Pittsburg Messenger*, November 30, 1894.

driving more Republican-Populists back to the GOP and, strangely but naturally, forcing stalwart Democrats to the same course.

Populists proposed a variety of reasons for the results. Jerry Simpson attributed Populist reverses to a large emigration from southern Kansas into the Cherokee Strip. Others blamed a large stay-at-home vote. Lewelling believed that he had lost the support of both "the prohibition element" and "the liquor element." Breidenthal argued that the depression injured the party in power, the Democrats nationally but the Populists in Kansas. Mrs. Lease charged the defeat to "the disgraceful compromise with Democracy two years ago and to the treachery perpetrated upon the people by the election of John Martin." These and other instances of "the bulldozing methods and treachery of state chairman Breidenthal" cost the party the support of many who formerly voted the Populist ticket.[51]

Other Populists looked for hopeful signs in the election. Peffer pointed to the large increase in the party's national vote as a sign of Populist vitality. Lewelling found even in the Kansas results some evidence that the party had not suffered an absolute loss in votes when he compared his return with that of Willits in 1890.[52] The weakness of this interpretation was that it depended upon analysis of the change in the poll for governor, from 106,000 for Willits when he ran behind his ticket because of Robinson's influence, to 118,000 for Lewelling when he ran well ahead of his ticket, apparently because of Morrill's reputed gold tendencies. A more accurate index of party strength, the vote for secretary of state, showed an actual decline, though slight, from 115,933 (or 39.42 percent) to 112,664 (or 38.19 percent).

The election results not only caused bravado or despair, they also served as a guide for future action. The mid-roaders hoped that the election made both the Democracy and fusion "beyond hope of resurrection." A more common attitude, expressed by the fusionists of both parties, was that the Republicans had triumphed "due to the fact that the Democrats and Populists would not

51 *Washington Post*, December 8, 1894; Lewelling to Davis Waite, December 19, 1894, Davis Waite Papers, Colorado State Archives and Public Records; *American Non-Conformist* (Indianapolis), November 15, 1894.

52 *American Non-Conformist*, November 15, 1894; *Washington Post*, December 8, 1894; Lewelling to Waite, December 19, 1894, Waite Papers.

combine against the common enemy. . . . In the future they will do so. They have learned a careful lesson, by which they will profit hereafter."[53]

The election returns also revealed a significant transformation of the People's party and raised questions concerning the ultimate efficacy of fusion and the nature of any future cooperation between Populists and Democrats. Most obviously, the maintenance of Populist strength had been accomplished by the virtual destruction of the Kansas Democracy. From 102,951 votes (31.19 percent) in 1888 the party shrank to 27,785 votes (9.42 percent) in 1894. Between 1890 and 1894, the Democrats lost 28,088 votes, the Republicans gained 28,432 votes, and the Populists remained relatively stable (a 3,269 vote decrease). The superficial conclusion, that Democrats left their party and voted with the Republicans, is highly improbable. Perhaps a few did, but there is little evidence to suggest that it was more than an isolated instance, especially with the traditional Democratic platform and ticket of 1894.

It is more likely that those who withdrew from the Kansas Democracy between 1890 and 1894 went overwhelmingly into the People's party and were counteracted by an approximately equal number of original Populists who returned to their old parties, predominantly to the GOP. It is perhaps as likely, in fact, that the state totals which erroneously suggest the direct transformation of Democrats into Republicans mask the very real possibility of a nearly direct, one-to-one, ratio of Democrats becoming Populists and original Populists turning Republican. Many prominent Populists made public returns to the Republican party during these years, while equally prominent Democrats made the trek to the new party. There is virtually no evidence that Democrats joined their traditional opponent, the GOP, or that Populists transferred to the Democracy, although a few scattered Republicans continued to join the People's party, their highly publicized explanations based on national events. Contemporary observers agreed that the People's party during these years underwent severe Democratization through this infusion of former Democrats and the departure of former Republicans.

[53] *American Non-Conformist*, November 15, 1894; *Washington Post*, December 2, 1894.

Analysis of election results confirms this interpretation.[54] Using county level data, the simple (Pearsonian) correlation between the decrease in the Democratic percentage point share of the vote from 1890 to 1894 and the increase in the Populist share of the vote for the same years is .724. Because Democrats lost support generally while Republicans gained, it is not surprising that the correlation between the Democratic decrease and the Republican increase is also positive, but it is a vastly weaker relationship (.219) than that with the Populist figure. The correlation between the Populist increase and the Republican increase for these years is —.510, indicating that those who left the People's party returned predominantly to the GOP. Further demonstrating Populist dependence upon Democratic recruits and Populist losses to the Republicans is an examination of those counties with a very stable but quite small Democratic vote during these years. These two qualifications make it likely that the Democrats included only those hard-core partisans who rejected all overtures to vote other than Democratic and clarify the relationship between the other parties. This is illustrated in Table 5.

TABLE 5

From Populist to Republican:
Changes in Party Support for Selected Counties, 1890-1894

County	Democratic % 1890	Democratic instability ± 1890-1894	Populist loss (points) 1890-1894	Republican gain (points) 1890-1894
Mitchell	6.34	0.40	10.81	9.04
Norton	6.43	0.84	9.59	8.86
Osborne	5.74	0.68	10.45	9.22
Ottawa	6.28	0.49	11.52	9.81
Rooks	4.63	0.31	13.43	10.74
Smith	5.45	0.98	6.23	5.91

Table 6 indicates the relationship between the Democratic and People's parties when the Republican vote of a county remained relatively stable.

---

[54] The same definitions and explanations of terms and variables developed in Chapter 3 are used in the following discussion.

TABLE 6

From Democrat to Populist:

Changes in Party Support for Selected Counties, 1890-1894

County	Republican instability ± 1890-1894	Democratic loss (points) 1890-1894	Populist gain (points) 1890-1894
Comanche	0.74	11.31	10.57
Edwards	0.10	5.49	4.70
Gove	0.29	8.28	7.70
Hodgman	0.29	21.59	19.36
Lane	0.28	5.92	4.00
Sherman	0.36	−1.16	−2.12
Stanton	0.79	−2.18	−3.99

Much more common than these two types of counties were those that exhibited the same misleading pattern that the state totals did: those that registered clear Democratic decreases and Republican gains with the Populists making minor shifts either way. As county level analysis reversed an apparent inference, however, so does inspection of local voting units reveal that impressionistic evidence was correct in predicting Democrat to Populist and Populist to Republican transformations. In Neosho County, for example, the Democrats decreased by 6.57 percentage points from 1890 to 1894 while the Republicans increased by 7.57 points. The Populists lost 1.43 points. Yet using rural township and urban ward voting districts as the level of analysis, correlations reveal that Democratic losses were not related to Republican gains. Rather, Republican gains and Populist losses were related as were Democratic losses and Populist gains. The rank-order correlation between Republican increases and Democratic decreases between 1890 and 1894 is −.031; between Republican increases and Populist decreases is .440; and between Democratic decreases and Populist increases is .862.

Similarly, analysis of local voting districts in Brown County, which experienced a major Democratic decrease (14.46 points), a sharp Republican increase (10.63 points), and only a slight Populist increase (2.99 points), reveals little connection between Republican gains and Democratic losses (rank-order correlation of .077) but significant association between Democratic losses and Populist gains (.767) and Populist losses and Republican gains (.482).[55] Further evidence of the Democratization of the Brown County People's party is in simple (Pearsonian) correlations which reveal that the Populists of 1894 were more related to the Democrats of 1888 than were the Democrats themselves in 1894 (.457 to .182).

By determining the differences between each party's actual vote in 1894 and its expected vote, given its 1890 vote and the voting turnout differential of the two years, one can estimate the changes in the absolute numbers of members of the three parties in the intervening years. A comparison of this estimate with the calculated composition of the People's party in 1890 by previous party affiliation reveals the extent to which Democratization had overtaken the party of the people. Considering that, as seems clear, the bulk of Democrats who departed the Democracy went into the People's party and that the bulk of the GOP's accessions came from its former partisans temporarily within the People's party, by 1894 the Kansas People's party was overwhelmingly of Democratic antecedents, with the possible composition shown in Table 7. Even conceding the most generous passage of "Democrats" of 1890 into the GOP of 1894, considering the influence of the Resubmission Republicans in particular, it seems unlikely that more than perhaps 2,500 would change in the Populist composition estimate from a

[55] Apparent indications that urban Democrats turned Republican are misleading. Leavenworth County is an example of such an instance, with but 15.50 percent Populist in 1890, a Populist gain of only 4.95 percentage points between 1890 and 1894, plus a Democratic loss of 32.43 points and a Republican gain of 26.49 points during those same years. Obviously if all 15.50 Populists of 1890 returned to the GOP in 1894 there would still have to be approximately eleven points from 1890 Democrats to produce the Republican gain. However, in 1890 many Republicans who favored Resubmission voted Democratic, and they were largely concentrated in areas (such as Leavenworth) that produced this pattern. In 1888 Leavenworth had but 49.09 percent Democrats; in 1890 11 percent more, 60.36 percent. In all probability these 11 percent were Resubmission Republicans who then returned to the Republican ticket (though not necessarily through the People's party) in 1894. This suggests either a total transformation of the Leavenworth People's party from Republican/Union Labor origins (the Leavenworth Republican vote dropped by 21.66 points between 1888 and 1890, which indicates that approximately 10.50 Republican points joined the Union Labor 1888 poll of 4.64 percent to create the 1890 Populist result) to an overwhelming Democratic composition; or that Populism was originally more dependent upon former Democrats than previously estimated (that more than eleven Republican points went Democratic in 1890 and that necessarily, then, Democrats voted Populist in 1890). In either case, however, the People's party in Leavenworth County in 1894 was composed overwhelmingly of former Democrats.

TABLE 7

Estimated Composition of People's Party in 1894
by Former Partisan Affiliation

Democrats	64,247	57.03%
Union Laborites	34,133	30.30%
Republicans	13,754	12.21%
Prohibitionists	530	0.47%

Democratic to a Republican heritage—far from challenging the majority position of ex-Democrats within the party (Table 8).[56] Combined with a relatively constant vote from the Union Labor wing, this Democratic-Populist strength made the People's party after 1894 highly susceptible to fusion or to party instability if the Democracy became even superficially committed to Populism.

The predilection of Populists to return to the Republican party seemed to depend upon the local strength of the Democracy, though correlation coefficients are not high because of the influence of those counties which experienced substantial Democratic votes from Resubmission Republicans in 1890. This naturally raised the index figure of Republican strength within the People's party for 1890, but since these wet Republicans probably returned largely to the GOP for the 1894 election the surface indication was a Republican exodus from a local People's party firmly in the control of former Republicans. Despite this complication there is a tetrachoric correlation of −.168 between the index of Republican strength within the 1890 People's party and the proportion of Republican strength lost between 1888 and 1890 that was regained by 1894. This suggests that, at least to a limited extent, the stronger were Populists of Republican antecedents in their county's People's party, the less likely they were to rejoin the GOP. By excluding only those four counties with indexes of Republican strength exceeding 100, this figure changes greatly to −.351. The return of Republican-Populists to the GOP apparently also depended upon

---

56 If fairly substantial parts of the Republican vote loss of 1888-1890 did indeed enter the Democratic party in 1890, then the People's party depended upon Democratic recruits to a slightly greater extent than estimated before, but the total number of Democrats among the Populists would not change significantly by the passage of Resubmission Republicans back to the GOP. See previous note.

TABLE 8

Alternative Estimation of the Composition of the
People's Party in 1894 by Former Partisan Affiliation

Democrats	61,750	54.84%
Union Laborites	34,100	30.28%
Republicans	16,250	14.43%
Prohibitionists	500	0.44%

the residual strength of local Democrats. The proportion of the Republican vote loss 1888–1890 regained by 1894 had tetrachoric correlations of .421, .393, and .206 with the Democratic votes of 1890, 1888, and 1894, respectively. The more likely, then, that Democrats could either carry the county as a separate party or gain control of the local People's party, the more likely it was for Republican-Populists to rejoin the GOP. Rank-order correlations suggest that this tendency was stronger in those regions less economically disturbed. Severe depression continued to drive disparate groups together in a demand for change.

Indeed, election results indicate a distinct difference in economic conditions between those counties that voted Populist in 1894 and those that voted for either old party. The transformation of a large part of the membership of the People's party because of political maneuvers and emotional appeals had removed many of the sharp differences evident in the 1890 figures, which in turn may again suggest the primacy of political motivation in the Populist experience. Nevertheless, on nearly every economic variable examined, the Populists were ranged on one side, the old parties on the other. This is demonstrated in Table 9. The old parties, in fact, were differentiated only on cultural variables.

The relative insignificance of the Democratic correlations with the economic variables in Table 9 reveals the Democratic dependence upon ethnic support. The Democratic vote correlated with the foreign-born population by .167, with Catholic population by .445, and with Protestants by −.318. Neither Populists nor Republicans correlated significantly with the variables reflecting Protestant or foreign-born populations, though Catholics were related to Populists by −.253. For all these variables, the sign of the Republican correlation was opposite that of the Democratic one.

TABLE 9

Correlation Coefficients between 1894 Party Votes
and Economic Variables

Populist	Economic variable	Republican	Democratic
.359	Mortgaged farm families	−.301	−.222
.123	Proportion of average acre-value under mortgage	−.107	−.051
.180	Interest rate	−.172	−.010
−.278	Average value of a farm acre	.300	.047
−.145	Average value of farm products per farm	.097	.054
−.192	Per capita assessed valuation	.156	.128

All this suggests that, generally, Populism remained the refuge of the economically distressed; that the greater were the economic difficulties the more the Populists held to their party and rejected the emotional appeals to return to the GOP; and that those who refrained from leaving the Democracy were either somewhat better off than their erstwhile fellow partisans or felt that religious or ethnic associations were more important.

What the voting statistics do not reveal was the nature of Populist dependence upon Democratic sources, within and without the party, and how that dependence circumscribed the direction the party would be able to take. Though the Democrats had an independent ticket, many Democrats voted Populist, still claiming to be, as one declared, "as good a Democrat as I ever was." Another silver Democrat vowed that "while I do not endorse some of the things of our Populists (and many of them will be dropped in time to come) I shall vote the [Populist] ticket." John Eaton, while campaigning for the People's party, announced, "I will advocate free silver but not fiat paper money."[57] Thus the People's party in 1894 depended upon straight Democrats as well as the superficial Democratic-Populists, who held little belief in anything other than silver in the Populist platform. Should the national Democratic party ever commit itself to silver (and Eaton declared his "faith and confidence in the national Democracy"), the People's party would be

[57] *Kansas Commoner,* October 18, November 1, 1894; *Marshall County Democrat,* October 26, 1894.

in danger of losing its remaining strength. By 1894, then, the People's party rested upon instability and depended upon a continuation of hostile attitudes toward the silver issue by the national Democratic party. No longer was Populism really a vital, positive, and aggressive reform force on its own; it had lost the initiative and could only react to the postures of others.

Republicans were perhaps more prescient. On November 13, 1894, they staged an elaborate public funeral in Topeka symbolizing the death of Populism. And indeed, Populism in its original form, creative nature, and radical motivation was dead. Populists may not have recognized it, and there would be some agonizing death throes, but Populism had failed to break the bonds of the American political system and had suffocated within. Dependent now upon those who cared little for it, Populism threatened to become only an adjunct of the Democratic party, united on an issue of little basic importance to the party's creed in order to sustain a political life. Populism, as Kansas had known it in the days of its pentecostal fervor to remake society, was no more. The Crusade had ended; Kansas was redeemed.[58]

58 See Miller, "Populist Party in Kansas," p. 280.

CHAPTER SEVEN

The Silver Panacea
Against Omaha Populism

As POPULISM underwent significant changes in the state of its birth, the national movement was also steadily transformed. There were some among the Populist national leadership, as in Kansas, who believed that the party could best succeed by suppressing the comprehensive reform aspirations expressed in its earlier days of enthusiasm and optimism and by then cooperating with those who were prepared to accept such limited objectives though they were hostile to the sense of the initial movement. Again as in Kansas, some of these accommodators were men of hoary reform credentials who thought they saw the main chance, but many others were recent converts to the People's party. Peffer remained among the most prominent Populist leaders, but he became increasingly less representative of the party as it drifted from its original intentions, his interests and desires opposing the process and its potential result.

Indeed, Peffer seemed to draw a distinction between Populism and politics. After 1891 he played a less active role within his party and rarely attended the frequent conferences of Populist politicians. Moreover, apart from campaigning for the Populist ticket each fall, he largely avoided direct intervention in Kansas political affairs except to issue his consistent warnings against fusion. He maintained that he gave "very little attention to the personnel of politics, as this thing of figuring how Jim, John or Jake would act in front of the enemy was very distasteful."[1] Instead, attending to the senatorial work for which, he always remarked, he had been elected, Peffer proved an indefatigable worker for Populist reform measures. Speaking of "the mass of Pefferian bills which daily fall into the hopper," one reporter commented in 1894 that "the fecundity of Senator Peffer in the matter of introducing bills has passed into a proverb." The conservative *Harper's Weekly* observed that Peffer "serves as a patient channel for the interjection into the Senate of impossible theories of legislation and barren ideas of finance." It added, however, that despite the visionary nature of his proposals, "he is sincere and honest in his views." Others agreed, and one observer noted that Peffer "seems to have won the respect and esteem of his colleagues, and to have convinced them that he represents a high standard of citizenship." Nor was his activity limited to the Senate chamber. He spent much of the summer of 1892 not campaigning but examining national bank failures. Immediately after the election he led a special committee from Chicago to Pittsburgh investigating the Pinkerton Agency and the Homestead riots. Most of the summer of 1893 he labored as the only active member of a Senate subcommittee inspecting agricultural conditions from coast to coast. This work resulted in his memorable report, *Agricultural Depression; Causes and Remedies.*[2]

The depression Peffer found in agriculture rapidly became a nationwide calamity of great magnitude in 1893. As banks closed their doors, businesses failed, and industries laid off workers, the nation turned to a fuller discussion of those economic issues that the destitute farmers of the West and South had already raised. In the Populist reform triad of land, money, and transportation, the issue of financial reform held clear priority. The subtreasury

1 *Kansas City Journal*, April 13, 1892.

2 *Washington Post*, January 17, 1893; December 5, 1894; *Harper's Weekly* 38 (March 10, 1894): 232; "The Populists in Congress," *Review of Reviews* 10 (July 1894): 11; L. B. Richardson, *William E. Chandler, Republican* (New York, 1940), p. 442; *Pittsburgh National Labor Tribune*, December 1, 1892; *Chicago Tribune*, November 17-22, 1892; *Topeka Advocate*, May 10, 1893; *Topeka State Journal*, February 28, 1896; W. A. Peffer, *Agricultural Depression; Causes and Remedies* (Washington, 1895).

and land-loan principles, after all, were the most prominent and peculiarly Populist of the movement's demands, and Peffer, Mc-Lallin, and other leading Populists had expected that the party would make the first fight primarily upon finance. But the money question to the early Populists distinctly did not mean free silver alone. They repeatedly emphasized that free silver was a minor, even insignificant reform, and none did so more than Peffer, who constantly denied altogether the metallic basis of money and the importance of silver coinage as a relief measure. Although regarded in the Senate as a staunch silverite, he often seemed to damn free silver with faint praise, declaring that "as long as we use metals for money I favor their unlimited use" and silver was as good as gold. Fiat paper money remained the ultimate objective. Peffer even bearded the silver lion in its own den when he spoke to the convention of silver men that organized the American Bimetallic League in Washington in May 1892. After warning them that free silver as a panacea was hopelessly inadequate to meet the requirements of the people, he asserted that the Omaha convention would not limit its demands to a one-plank silver platform.[3]

Although Populists considered silver as a minor reform, others viewed it as a major evil. Grover Cleveland and his financial advisers, in fact, even argued that the limited silver coinage provided for by the Sherman Silver Purchase Act of 1890 had largely caused the depression. The Treasury purchases of silver, they believed, encouraged gold hoarding, speculation, and the withdrawal of needed foreign capital and ultimately threatened the maintenance of the gold standard. Cleveland consequently decided that Congress had to repeal the Silver Purchase Act. Such an action, he was convinced, would restore the confidence of business leaders in the nation's monetary system and thereby end the depression. Cleveland's inaugural address in March 1893 emphasized the financial issue as paramount, and shortly thereafter he called a special session of Congress for August to repeal the Sherman Act.[4]

Populists determined to accept Cleveland's challenge, but not

---

3 *Topeka Daily Capital,* May 13, 1891, February 18, 1892; *Indianapolis Journal,* September 7, 1891; *Emporia Tidings,* June 18, 1892.

4 *National Watchman* (Washington, D.C.), April 13, 1893; J. Rogers Hollingsworth, *The Whirligig of Politics: The Democracy of Cleveland and Bryan* (Chicago, 1963), pp. 10-11.

all were careful to indicate that free silver alone did not represent the Populist commitment to financial reform. James B. Weaver, in fact, did not even wait for Cleveland to demand repeal before he accepted the primacy of silver. Free silver, he decided early in 1893, "is the line upon which the battle should be fought. It is the line of least resistance and we should hurl our forces against it at every point." Weaver was joined by Herman E. Taubeneck, the Populist national chairman, and together they took prominent parts in an August meeting of the American Bimetallic League. Taubeneck even accepted appointment to a committee instructed to act as a silver lobby during the congressional session. He optimistically believed that the People's party could benefit from the nonpartisan silver men and should work closely with the League.[5]

Other Populists were also ready to compromise their party and their principles in order to take advantage of the silver excitement. As always before, Jerry Simpson favored the easier course and urged Populists to join with silverites of the old parties and make the fight on silver alone. "I know that some will cry out against the apparent abandonment of other and greater reforms," he conceded, "but the people must remember that in reforming great national abuses, we cannot afford to be in haste." W. A. Harris was even more agreeable, being willing to approve as a compromise a devalued silver coinage ratio, perhaps 20 to 1 rather than 16 to 1, a proposal popular among Silver Democrats but anathema to most Populists.[6]

In contrast, Peffer denied silver's importance. He pointedly avoided the various meetings of the Bimetallic League and announced his intention to vote with the silverites against repeal of the Sherman Act only after stating his disagreement with "their premises and conclusions." Nevertheless, in the bitter struggle in the Senate, Peffer played a major role among the opponents of the administration. He led the counterattack when he offered unconditional free coinage as an amendment to the repeal measure.

[5] Fred E. Haynes, *James Baird Weaver* (Iowa City, 1919), p. 347; *Chicago Tribune,* August 1-4, 1893; Herman E. Taubeneck to Ignatius Donnelly, July 8, 1893, Donnelly Papers.

[6] *National Watchman,* July 27, 1893; *New York Herald,* August 8, 1893; L. D. Lewelling to W. A. Harris, August 25, 1893, Lewelling Papers.

Despite poor health, he also did his share in the desperate eighty-day filibuster, delivering what one newspaper termed "his 'three weeks' speech." Still, he did not restrict himself simply to silver; he spoke on other financial problems in the depression as well. As for the Harris ratio proposal, Peffer steadfastly rejected it as an unacceptable compromise of principle. "Though we be captured, we will not surrender," he declared, "and compromise is surrender."[7]

Cleveland likewise refused to compromise, though repeatedly urged to do so for the sake of party harmony. With ruthless use of patronage and other pressure he persuaded the Silver Democrats to stand aside. On October 30, the Senate finally voted for repeal, with only Peffer making more than a perfunctory protest. Cleveland's policies seriously disrupted his party without achieving the promised economic improvement and contributed to making silver the major political issue splitting the country. The vote on repeal had been largely sectional, not partisan, in nature, and thereafter Southern Democrats in particular recoiled from Cleveland, feeling that he had betrayed them. The South had been encouraged in 1892 to believe that in office Cleveland would accept free coinage and, as Peffer had predicted, the president's repudiation of it created "a rebellion among the farmers of the south." When the depression continued to deepen, the silver men of the South and West felt vindicated and aggressively moved to reinstitute silver coinage.[8]

The increased emphasis upon the importance of silver also threatened to disrupt the People's party. Weaver, Taubeneck, Kyle, and other Populist politicians continued to make clear their support for a reduction of the Omaha Platform to the single issue of silver and for a fusion with silver men within the old parties. The 1893 elections, which revealed a swing away from the Democratic party, further emboldened these men. They attended large bimetallic conferences during the fall and winter of 1893 to press

7 *Chicago Tribune,* August 3, 1893; *New York Times,* July 4, 1893; *Topeka Advocate,* July 5, September 20, October 25, 1893; *Kansas Commoner* (Wichita), August 31, 1893; W. A. Peffer to Davis Waite, October 25, 1893, Waite Papers.

8 Allan Nevins, *Grover Cleveland: A Study in Courage* (New York, 1932), p. 547; Elmer Ellis, *Henry Moore Teller* (Caldwell, Idaho, 1941), pp. 229-32; *Washington Post,* November 16, 1892.

the silver issue, and most of the congressional Populists signed a public address denouncing Cleveland's dictatorial actions and urging the American people to take up the cause of silver.[9] On the other hand, the *National Watchman,* founded by the Populist congressmen in 1892 in order to have a party organ in Washington, warned, "During all this excitement and discussion over the silver question it might be well to remember that the People's Party platform contains other, and we will add greater, principles than free coinage of silver." The *Watchman* also pointed out the lesson of the special session for Populists: the silverites were always prepared to compromise principle and cared for nothing but silver. "All they seem to want is free coinage with as little harm to the two old parties, and as little good for the Populist party as possible." It was therefore imperative, concluded the *Watchman,* for Populists to protect their party and "not suffer it to come under the domination of these so-called silver men." Peffer, John Davis, and other Populists joined in announcing their opposition to the silverite course, and even John Breidenthal expressed his disappointment "in the action of General Weaver in attempting to sidetrack the People's Party." Tom Watson implored the readers of his *People's Party Paper* to instruct every delegate they sent to any convention in order to keep the party in the middle of the road and prevent politicians from altering the party's platform or manipulating its voters, an intention that Watson recognized as "but too plan" on the part of some Populist leaders.[10]

This strong counterattack temporarily quieted the Populist clamor for a silver campaign, though the silver organizations continued the agitation. For his part, Peffer continued to press other issues during 1894. He agreed to introduce Jacob Coxey's proposals into the Senate and also advocated various relief measures of his own. After the administration used federal troops to suppress the Pullman strike during that summer, Peffer called for government con-

[9] *Topeka Advocate,* November 8, 15, 1893; *Washington Post,* February 23, 24, 1893; James Kyle to Waite, October 24, 1893, Waite Papers; John R. Morris, "Davis Hanson Waite: The Ideology of a Western Populist" (Ph.D. diss., University of Colorado, 1965), pp. 263-65.

[10] *National Watchman,* September 22, December 1, 1893; John Breidenthal to Waite, February 13, 1894, and Waite to James B. Weaver, February 28, 1894, Waite Papers; *Topeka Advocate,* November 22, December 6, 1893; *People's Party Paper* (Atlanta), January 12, 1894.

trol of railroads and coalfields, added his constant plea that all money be issued directly by the government, and concluded with the general position that all public functions should be performed by and through public agencies. Denounced as treasonous by frightened Eastern conservatives, this sensational speech castigated both old parties for precipitating the nation's troubles and promised eventual relief through the adoption of Populist policies. Without mentioning silver, Peffer presented a statement on the nature of Populism and the problems of America so compelling that hundreds of thousands of copies were ordered by labor unions and reform organizations. In speaking around the country after the Senate adjourned, Peffer continued to avoid an emphasis on silver. He received strong praise from the radical *Southern Mercury,* for example, when he spoke in Dallas on the eve of the election and stressed the old Populist triad of land, money, and transportation.[11]

If some Populists thus rejected the silver panacea, silver advocates gained strength in the other parties. Democrats like Ben Tillman, Richard P. Bland, and William Jennings Bryan and Republicans like John P. Jones, William Stewart, and Henry Moore Teller promoted the silver movement throughout the South and West. In 1894 such politicians began to gain greater prominence in silver organizations like the American Bimetallic League, where Populists had been conspicuous in 1893. The league held a major conference in Washington in August 1894, with Jones, Bland, and Bryan as primary speakers. The conference declared that silver repeal had failed to provide economic recovery, urged voters to make silver the decisive consideration in the fall elections, and recommended holding regional meetings to advance the bimetallic cause.[12]

Increasingly, too, these silver advocates began to put pressure upon the People's party. Senators Jones and Stewart did renounce the Republican party and declare themselves Populists, but most disdained any suggestion to break their party affiliations. They wanted silver and were willing to use the Populists while remaining

11 *American Non-Conformist* (Indianapolis), June 7, July 12, 19, 1894; *Topeka Advocate,* January 10, 24, March 21, 1894; *Southern Mercury* (Dallas), November 8, 1894; *Congressional Record,* 53d Cong., 2d sess., vol. 26, pp. 1176, 7231-37.

12 *Silver the Dominant Issue.* Report of the Action of the Bimetallic Conference . . . Washington, D.C., August 16-17, 1894 (pamphlet in the Lemuel H. Weller Papers, State Historical Society of Wisconsin).

within their own party. Some, like Eaton in Kansas, were ready to campaign for nominal Populist candidates on the sole issue of free silver while maintaining their devotion to the Democracy, but others wanted a Populist fusion on Democratic candidates.

There were Populists willing to be used too, though they believed the situation was different. As Breidenthal, Harris, and Simpson prepared to make concessions in Kansas, other Populists maneuvered to arrange fusion elsewhere. Chief among these was Weaver, whose entire career as a third-party advocate had been based on belief in the value of fusion. Admittedly ready to cooperate with the silver movement, Weaver directed Iowa Populists toward a fusion with Democrats and accepted for himself a fusionist nomination to Congress. Although he spoke of other issues, he based his own campaign on free silver. Perhaps more significantly, he corresponded with Nebraska's Silver Democratic leader, Bryan, in an effort to promote a wider fusion between the two parties. Criticizing anti-fusion Populists for "making the mistake of their lives," Weaver urged holding "a sort of interstate consultation over the situation in Neb, Dak & Iowa" to devise a silver fusion to prevent Republican success. He arranged speaking engagements for Bryan in Iowa while he helped campaign for the Democrat in Nebraska. Bryan himself actively advocated fusion between Populists and Democrats in Nebraska and found eager associates in Populist Senator William V. Allen, elected in 1893 with the help of Democratic votes, and Populist Congressman William McKeighan, a former Democrat elected on a fusion ticket in 1890 and 1892 and running as a fusion candidate in 1894.[13]

Bryan made no secret of his intentions and thereby provoked strong reaction from the nation's anti-fusion Populists. The *Topeka Advocate,* for example, repeatedly denounced Bryan as "an enemy to the People's Party and to all true financial reform," because of his silver monomania. If the Populists restricted their platform to

---

[13] Haynes, *Weaver,* pp. 346, 356-61; Herman C. Nixon, "The Populist Movement in Iowa," *Iowa Journal of History and Politics* 24 (January 1926): 25-26; Weaver to W. J. Bryan, September 1, 30, 1894, W. H. Lanning to Bryan, September 18, 22, 1894, M. B. Gearon to Bryan, October 3, 1894, C. J. Smyth to Bryan, October 13, 1894, C. D. Casper to Bryan, March 6, 1893, William Jennings Bryan Papers, Library of Congress: Paola E. Coletta, *William Jennings Bryan: Political Evangelist* (Lincoln, Nebr., 1964), pp. 99-103; *Non-Conformist,* August 2, 1894; *National Watchman,* June 15, 22, 1894.

silver, the *Advocate* believed, it "would be a backward step that would be absolutely fatal." Moreover, Bryan's additional proposition to attract Populist votes, the issuance of paper money, was nullified by his qualification, "redeemable in coin"—an attitude at total variance with the financial position of genuine Populists. The inequitable financial system had to be changed, argued the *Advocate;* it was futile merely to plate it with silver. Even Nelson A. Dunning of the *National Watchman,* much less hostile than Mc-Lallin to an emphasis upon the money question, condemned Bryan as "a Democrat and nothing else," who had never helped the People's party and whose plans for fusion involved the destruction of Populism. Perhaps even more the *Watchman* censured Weaver, Allen, and McKeighan for their "high-handed proceedings" in attempting to "force such schemes down the throats of square Populists." The Nebraska fusionists turned with such ferocity on Dunning that mid-roaders were astonished and Peffer, as president of the Watchman Company, felt it necessary to support Dunning publicly.[14]

Strangely, Dunning defended the fusion course of Southern Populists in 1894. Although theoretically, he conceded, fusion in the South with Republicans was no worse than fusion in the West with Democrats, extenuating circumstances made the first permissible. "Fusion in the West has for its object the one single purpose of gaining office," he explained, "while in the South it is not a fusion at all, but instead it is a uniting of all elements in favor of an honest ballot." Regardless of Dunning's tortuous reasoning, fusion was a popular tactic in the South. If often on Republican initiative, it had been virtually as widespread in the South in 1892 as in the West. In 1894 it was even more so. Dunning's defense of Southern fusion intimated that any Populist, given the nature of the struggle in the South, would endorse fusion, and indeed few Southern Populists rejected the plan. The most prominent fusionist was Marion Butler, a young North Carolinian who had succeeded to Polk's place in the state's Alliance and People's party. In 1892 Butler had proposed fusion with the Democrats despite Polk's objections; thereafter he maneuvered to secure fusion with the

14 *Topeka Advocate,* August 22, 1894; *National Watchman,* June 15, 22, July 20, August 3, 10, 1894; *Non-Conformist,* July 12, August 2, 1894; *Chicago Tribune,* June 22, 1899.

Republicans. In this he was successful, and the fusionist legislature elected in 1894 sent him to the United States Senate to continue his "adroit political leadership."[15] Some fusion arrangements were established between Populists and Republicans in at least North Carolina, Alabama, Georgia, Louisiana, and Arkansas. Tom Watson was one of the rare Southern Populists who vigorously opposed fusion, and even he profited from indirect fusion when Georgia Republicans failed to nominate a candidate against him. However few they were in either section by 1894, mid-road Populists in the West opposed fusion; too often Southern mid-roaders merely opposed fusion with Democrats.[16]

Following the 1894 elections, moreover, even fewer Populist leaders were inclined to stay in the middle of the road. Although the party attracted vastly more votes than in 1892, they were generally disappointed that not more was achieved. Despite substantial inroads made in the South, the region remained heavily Democratic; in the West the party lost congressmen and state officials if not votes. Particularly obvious to these Populists was the loss of the silver states of Nevada, Colorado, and Idaho, all of which had voted for the Populists in 1892. The only substantial results in the form of elected officers came from North Carolina, where Butler's fusion policy had placed a Populist and a Republican in the Senate and three Populists and two Republicans in the House. A policy of fusion beckoned thus more seductively, and silver seemed to be the logical basis for it.

Weaver spoke out freely after the election. He described the great national Democratic losses as a natural consequence of the revulsion against Cleveland's policies and the depression; but the resultant Republican triumph was unearned, for the GOP had no policies to solve the nation's problems. The People's party, he

15 *National Watchman*, August 17, 1894; Robert F. Durden, *The Climax of Populism: The Election of 1896* (Lexington, Ky., 1965), pp. 7-10; Abbott Swinson to L. L. Polk, June 1, 1892, and J. L. Ramsey to Polk, June 1, 1892, Polk Papers; Stuart Noblin, *Leonidas LaFayette Polk, Agrarian Crusader* (Chapel Hill, N.C., 1949), pp. 278, 289-90; Theodore Saloutos, *Farmer Movements in the South* (Berkeley, Calif., 1960), pp. 142-45.

16 *Pittsburg Messenger*, August 31, 1894; John D. Hicks, *The Populist Revolt* (Minneapolis, 1931), pp. 245-47, 329-33; William DuBose Sheldon, *Populism in the Old Dominion* (Princeton, N.J., 1935), pp. 109, 111; Fred E. Haynes, *Third Party Movements since the Civil War* (Iowa City, 1916), p. 280; C. Vann Woodward, *Origins of the New South* (Baton Rouge, La., 1951), pp. 275-76.

declared, represented the hope of the future. Yet he was prepared to restrict this party that had done so well. He urged Americans not to believe "the ill-considered utterances of some of its over-zealous, radical and unbalanced men. . . . All reform movements attract to their ranks men of radical and extreme views." Weaver then made clear his definition of radicalism when he urged a combination of men on the basis of silver. Privately, moreover, he expressed his willingness to meet with Bryan and Allen to "shape things properly."[17]

Herman E. Taubeneck, national chairman, was equally ready to check radicalism within the party. In mid-November he advanced his interpretation of the failure of Populism to sweep the nation in the past election and his determination for its future position. "I regret deeply that the people's party has been honeycombed and undermined by all sorts of schemes, fancies and abstractions. But for this unfortunate condition," he declared, "the people's party would have largely triumphed at the late election, but by rainbow chasing and endless freaks and foibles, we drove thousands upon thousands who are with us heart and soul on the money issue, into the ranks of the opposition." So believing, Taubeneck suggested that the party limit its platform to the single issue of silver. "No socialism nor anarchism," he added, sounding like an old party politician, "indeed no 'isms' of any nature or side issue, nothing but the fight for bimetallism against the single gold standard." Later in the month Taubeneck attended a conference of the American Bimetallic League in St. Louis to coordinate the activities of the silverites and Silver Populists in preparation for the 1896 election. At the conference Taubeneck denounced the "cranks, anarchists, and socialists" in the People's party and recommended that they be purged to create a "pure silver" party. Silver leaders such as Adoniram J. Warner, president of the league, praised Taubeneck's intentions but refused to tie silver to the People's party, which so many silverites found objectionable. That refusal merely encouraged some Populists to fashion a more conservative image for their party by subordinating all other issues to silver. As one declared, "If we are to carry this country in 1896 we must

---

[17] Haynes, *Weaver*, pp. 362-65; Weaver to Bryan, November 9, 1894, Bryan Papers.

satisfy the average man that we are reasonable and right." He therefore requested the party to suppress the impractical and visionary men within its ranks.[18]

Peffer was uncertain as to the course Populists should follow. He had always regarded the money question as the most important of the Populist economic demands. But he meant paper money, government issue, the abolition of national banks, the cessation of bond issues, and free silver when he spoke of the money question and he was unwilling to restrict it, even implicitly, to free silver alone, as Taubeneck, Weaver, and the silver leaders desired. He was prepared to accept Populist cooperation with such men, however, provided the coalition dissolved old names and organizations and first adopted a basic principle which "can be constantly applied to new phases of civilization as we advance. The central idea of Populism is that public functions should be exercised by public agents, and that basis is broad enough to include a discussion and a solution of every economical problem now in sight." That position, however, was no concession to Taubeneck and the silver men, who wanted to avoid just such broad principles. It represented Peffer's original position in the party, unchanged by the demands of the silver schemers. Moreover, only a week later Henry Demarest Lloyd, a leader of the most radical wing of the People's party, wrote Clarence Darrow of his plans to incorporate the nation's socialists into the Populistic movement: "If we will come out with a good budget of municipalizations and nationalizations in our platform, and a general principle like Peffer's—'Public ownership of public utilities'—or something similar, the Socialists will 'jine' as they say in Kentucky, and we will get up a head of steam possible in no other way."[19]

Lloyd, of course, already believed that "the People's Party platform is socialistic, as all democratic doctrine is," and it was to precisely this aspect of Populism that Taubeneck objected. Six months earlier, in fact, at the Illinois Populist state convention he

[18] *Southern Mercury,* November 29, 1894; *St. Louis Post-Dispatch,* November 27-29, 1894; P. W. Couzins to H. D. Lloyd, December 30, 1894, Henry D. Lloyd Papers, State Historical Society of Wisconsin; Joseph C. Sibley to Waite, December 13, 1894, Waite Papers; Morris, "Davis Waite," pp. 266-67; Martin Ridge, *Ignatius Donnelly: The Portrait of a Politician* (Chicago, 1962), pp. 337-40.

[19] *St. Louis Post-Dispatch,* November 14, 1894; Lloyd to Darrow, November 23, 1894, Lloyd Papers.

had sharply criticized Lloyd's Chicago Populists for their "socialism" and demanded that they leave the party. Now Taubeneck decided to hold a conference of Populist leaders in St. Louis in order that the party could "make known the fact that it has outgrown many of the 'isms' that characterized its birth and early growth, and take a stand on the financial question that will make it worthy of the support of those who . . . have not cared to support the party on account of its wild theories." He publicly hinted that the St. Louis meeting would entirely remove the subtreasury and related demands from the Populist platform, and he particularly urged "conservative" and "level-headed" Populists to attend this critical meeting in December.[20]

Virtually all the "Washington Populists" agreed with the decision to curtail the Omaha Platform. Except for Peffer, few original Populists remained in the nation's capital. Kansas had replaced men like Otis and Clover with men like Harris and Hudson; Southerners sent political opportunists like Butler rather than early, unswerving Populists like Watson. Those like Simpson and McKeighan who did remain from the first Populist contingent had always run on fusion tickets and were willing to grant concessions to the Silver Democrats in their states. Kyle, the only other senator besides Peffer chosen in the first Populist election, had been sent to Washington with Democratic votes and considered himself under some obligation to that party; furthermore he felt no commitment to Populism, either party or doctrine. Another new type of Populist was the far western Silver Populist like Lafe Pence of Colorado or Senators Jones and Stewart of Nevada, who joined the People's party in the first place only because of its silver declaration. Thus, products of direct fusion or inspired by silver zeal, Populist congressmen took a decided stand in support of Taubeneck's proposal. Pence agreed that "the time has come to drop all weak 'isms' " and Allen expressed his hope that the conference would "abandon all questionable doctrines and non-essentials." Dunning continued his erratic course on the *Watchman* by endorsing Taubeneck. "Leave the cranks at home. Leave the impracticables at home," he

[20] Lloyd to Darrow, November 23, 1894, and Taubeneck to Lloyd, December 10, 1894, Lloyd Papers; *National Watchman*, November 30, 1894; Chester McArthur Destler, *American Radicalism, 1865-1901* (Chicago, 1966), pp. 170, 228.

urged in reference to the St. Louis meeting. "Let us have no more sidetracks, no more three column platforms. . . . We can never expect to gain success when platforms are extended to take in the pet hobby or conciliate every crank in the nation. If the late election has taught us anything it is to push less issues with increased vigor."[21]

Peffer alone refused his consent. He was willing to emphasize the money question but unwilling to jettison "any proposition or principle which I have heretofore advocated." Although Butler, Allen, Stewart, and most of the other Washington Populists made plans to attend the conference, Peffer decided to stay in Washington. And in December, while others met in St. Louis to trim the Populist platform to silver, he introduced bills in the Senate to have the government control the railroads, to provide an increased and flexible currency, to relieve the destitute and dispossessed on public lands, to revoke the administration's authority to issue bonds.[22]

Other Populists outside Washington more directly moved against Taubeneck's scheme to purge the party of its distinctive character. The *Southern Mercury* even demanded that the national chairman resign if he refused to stand upon the party's platform. The *Topeka Advocate* denounced the "determination on the part of a few men who have identified themselves with the People's Party to narrow its platform to a single issue." Proclaiming its hostility to any such movement inspired by the Silver Populists, the *Advocate* declared that "Taubeneck can go with a free silver party if he chooses, but he will find that he cannot carry the People's Party with him." Davis Waite launched a letter campaign against the conference, asserting that only another regular national convention and not a group of self-appointed political managers had the authority to alter the party's platform. He received strong support from such mid-roaders as Ignatius Donnelly, Paul Van Dervoort, and George Washburn, who recognized that silver was too narrow a basis upon which to build the party and condemned the "self-constituted

21 *Non-Conformist,* December 6, 1894; *National Watchman,* November 30, December 7, 1894; Henry L. Loucks to Waite, July 30, 1895, Waite Papers; W. M. Stewart to H. E. Taubeneck, December 25, 1894, William M. Stewart Papers, Nevada State Historical Society.
22 *Non-Conformist,* December 6, 1894; *Topeka Advocate,* December 12, 1894; *Washington Post,* December 4, 1894.

crowd" for its short-sighted arrogance. Washburn also urged Donnelly to attend the meeting to counteract Weaver's influence. "General Weaver is credited with political discernment, and yet, Mr. Donnelly, I recall the fact that from the beginning of the Populist movement, whenever an emergency has arisen, he has been on the wrong side, while you have been on the right side . . . ; and in this coming meeting, I believe our past experience will be repeated."[23]

Lloyd was also concerned about the obvious determination of "some of our leaders . . . to take narrower ground and throw the radicals in the party overboard." He wrote of his anxiety that "revolutions never go backward. If the People's Party goes backward it will prove that it is not a revolution, and if it is not a revolution, it is nothing." From his friends, Lloyd received news that confirmed his fears. Henry Legate, a leading Bellamyite in Boston, wrote that the avowed purpose of the St. Louis conference was to eliminate the radical features of the Omaha Platform; and George H. Gibson, editor of the *Lincoln* (Nebraska) *Wealth Makers,* warned that Taubeneck had secured a large delegation of Silver Populists from the West and had avoided inviting the more steadfast Populists. Both pressed Lloyd to attend "to eloquently plead for the great truths and show up the folly of what the narrow minded leaders and politicians will insist on,"[24]

So encouraged, Lloyd, Van Dervoort, and other radical Populists went to St. Louis, determined to defend the entire Omaha Platform. On the first day the Silver Populists found, to their dismay, that they were in a minority. Weaver failed first to secure a secret meeting and second to grant Taubeneck the power to appoint the resolutions committee. The discussions revealed a strong distrust of the party leaders by many in attendance, culminating in a mid-road denunciation of a proposed national campaign committee as "a political monopoly, the worst of all monopolies, led by office-

23 *Southern Mercury,* November 29, 1894; *Topeka Advocate,* December 12, 19, 1894; Donnelly to Waite, December 14, 1894, Paul Van Dervoort to Waite, December 15, 1894, Waite to Robert Schilling, December 17, 1894, Waite Papers; Waite to Donnelly, December 11, 1894, George F. Washburn to Donnelly, December 22, 1894, Donnelly Papers.

24 Lloyd to C. A. Powers, December 16, 1894, George H. Gibson to Lloyd, December 19, 1894, Henry R. Legate to Lloyd, December 19, 1894, Lloyd Papers.

seeking men, who care more for politics than for principle and have office in view, and when that is had all that is wanted is at hand." Behind Lloyd's leadership, the conference rejected all attempts to shorten the Populist program and reaffirmed the party's adherence to the Omaha Platform.[25]

Staunch Populists everywhere welcomed the decision. Milton Park, editor of the *Southern Mercury*, happily reported that Taubeneck and Weaver left St. Louis wiser than they had arrived, and he trumpeted that "the effort of a few designing demagogues to sidetrack the Omaha demands in the interests of the bullionists at the St. Louis conference, proved a complete failure." Van Dervoort expressed his pleasure to Lloyd that they had been able to preserve the Omaha Platform. But he knew that Taubeneck and others still favored a one-plank platform; he cautioned, "We will have to meet this issue at the National Convention in 1896. It is not dead yet."[26]

Van Dervoort was more prescient than Park, for the conservative Populists refused to accept as binding the declarations of the St. Louis meeting and continued to advocate the overthrow of the original Populist principles. Senator Stewart regretted the St. Louis decision and voiced his fear that "it will be impossible for the People's Party or any party to succeed on the main issue unless it is made the sole issue." Dunning's *National Watchman* represented the opinion of most Washington Populists when it expressed disappointment in the St. Louis meeting and reproached "the overzealous and the crank," "the socialists and world savers," for their alleged lack of common political sense. The paper urged all the party's conservative members to attend future conventions to prevent another such folly, and it promised to campaign for the one-plank platform anyway. Later Dunning repeatedly complained of "the wicked and foolish surrender to the Chicago socialists by the St. Louis meeting" and called on Populists to set aside their idealism in favor of a commonsense approach to politics.[27]

25 Thomas F. Byron to Lloyd, April 8, 1895, Lloyd Papers; *Washington Post,* December 30, 1894; *St. Louis Post-Dispatch,* December 26-30, 1894; *Southern Mercury,* January 10, 1895.

26 Paul Van Dervoort to Lloyd, January 1895, Lloyd Papers; *Southern Mercury,* January 10, 1895.

27 *National Watchman,* January 11, 25, 1895.

The faithful Populists were astounded. How could a reaffirmation of the Populist creed be a surrender or a mistake? The *American Non-Conformist* was bewildered by Taubeneck's claim that the leading Populist papers had "committed an offense by urging the St. Louis conference to stand by the Omaha platform and not attempt to change it." The *Non-Conformist* wondered "when it became wrong for a Populist paper to uphold the Omaha platform," and editor Charles X. Matthews added, "We were always under the impression that the supreme test of Populism was the acceptance of that platform and that anyone who rejected it thereby proved that he was no Populist. But it seems that this notion is out of date." The charge that socialists had captured the St. Louis conference particularly irritated the straight Populists who replied that rather than being captured the mid-roaders at St. Louis had prevented others from seizing the party. The allegations about the "Socialist capture," Matthews explained, "originated with a small clique who went to the St. Louis conference for the purpose of running it and became disgruntled because they did not succeed." And having failed to transform the People's party into a silver party, they "have been wailing ever since. As usual the twelfth man on the jury is complaining that the other eleven are 'very contrary.' "[28]

The Silver Populists responded readily that the *Non-Conformist, Advocate,* and similar newspapers were themselves socialistic. The *Watchman,* in particular, viciously attacked McLallin and others who objected to Taubeneck's policy, declaring that their animus stemmed from Taubeneck's opposition to socialism and their own commitment to the disgusting doctrine. Fusionist papers such as the *Kansas Commoner* were less vitriolic but no less determined to defend Taubeneck, gently suggesting only that he and McLallin "honestly differ, somewhat, as to the best methods to pursue in accomplishing the same purpose."[29]

Taubeneck needed no assistance in defending himself or his plans. In two letters to W. Scott Morgan, an unswerving Arkansas Populist

---

28 *Non-Conformist,* February 7, 21, 1895; *Southern Mercury,* February 21, 1895; *Topeka Advocate,* January 23, 1895.

29 *National Watchman,* February 15, April 5, 1895; *Non-Conformist,* February 21, April 11, 1895; *Kansas Commoner,* February 14, 1895.

who edited the Populist readyprints, the national chairman provided a classic exposition of the attitudes of the compromising,
expedient, practical politician. On January 10, 1895, Taubeneck
responded to Morgan's questioning of the Silver Populist proposals
with the blunt assertion that "the party will either adopt my policy
or we will never succeed as a party." When Morgan complained
of his dictatorial tone and obvious indifference to Populist principles, Taubeneck replied on January 29:

The trouble, Mr. Morgan, is, that you are dealing with theories and abstract ideas which are as pliable as the paper upon which you write. I
have to deal with men and conditions. That is the difference between you
and I [*sic*]. Mine is a cold-blooded, practical politics, and yours is a dream-
land, living on theories and abstract ideas. I have never made a single
mistake, when I followed my own views, and I made none at St. Louis,
nor in calling a meeting of the committee. I have made mistakes in the
past, I admit, when I listened to the council [*sic*] of others.

Taubeneck then claimed that those who insisted upon strict adherence to the original Populist demands were ruining the party
by making it "impossible for Senator Stewart, Jones, and the silver
men in our party to remain with us." He specifically condemned
the *Wealth Makers,* the *Farmers' Tribune,* and the *People's Call*
for doing "us infinite harm." And then he lashed out again: "The
Topeka 'Advocate' is on the same line—you cannot tell whether
it is a single-tax organ, a socialist paper or a People's Party paper.
The 'Non-conformist' is gone. It has joined the socialists." Taubeneck finally concluded by repeating his charge "that our press
is drifting toward extreme socialism which the American people
will not endorse. I am not a socialist or communist in the remotest
sense, and I will fight it to the bitter end."[30]

Taubeneck's ideas of socialism may have been strange indeed,
but he clearly used the term not so much in a descriptive as
in a derogatory sense. The *Southern Mercury,* among the most
constant of Southern Populist papers, complained that Taubeneck
and the *Watchman* adopted the "old party howls of socialism"
against the straight Populists in an effort to discredit them, just
as reactionary leaders of the Democratic and Republican parties

[30] Taubeneck to W. S. Morgan, January 10, 29, 1895, Waite Papers.

employed smear tactics to undermine legitimate protest. The *Non-Conformist* responded sensibly to the fraudulent charges of the pseudo-Populists:

The Populist press is no more Socialistic now than it always has been. It is advocating precisely the same things it has been advocating all along. Neither is the Omaha platform any more Socialistic than when framed. How absurd, therefore, to say that because this press refused their consent to a change in their platform by an irresponsible conference of undelegated individuals, that it has gone over to extreme socialism. Clearly, it is not the Populist press . . . that has changed. It is those who thought it a brilliant stroke of statesmanship to swap horses while crossing the stream, to pull down their colors in the face of the enemy, to change front while the battle was in progress.

Itself thoughtfully critical of doctrinaire socialism, the *Non-Conformist* hoped that Populism would go forward, "without dictation either from extreme socialists or those who think they see socialists behind every bush that obstructs their way."[31]

In early January 1895 Weaver wrote privately of his dissatisfaction with the outcome of the St. Louis conference. He was convinced that Populists had to seize upon the currency question as their sole issue if they were to succeed. "One battle at a time is a universal law in the science of conflict," wrote the old soldier. "We can no more settle the three fold contention of the Omaha platform in a single struggle than we could fight three battles at one and the same time with a single body of troops." Weaver and Taubeneck then corresponded concerning the possibility of holding a private conference of those Populists willing to limit the party's platform to one issue ("our wisest heads," wrote Weaver). Such a conference could then publish a declaration favoring that course without facing the possibility of being outvoted on the issue again.[32]

As an apparent result of such discussions, Weaver went to Washington in late January with an address he had prepared for publication. This manifesto urged Populists to concentrate their energies on the financial question and to cooperate with all who opposed the gold standard, regardless of their attitudes on other issues. Weaver called a meeting of the Washington Populists to discuss

31 *Non-Conformist*, February 21, March 7, April 11, 1895.
32 Weaver to Donnelly, January 13, 1895, Donnelly Papers.

and sign the address. His arguments there satisfied all but Peffer, who objected that rank-and-file Populists would legitimately believe the address called for a concentration on silver alone, which, the senator noted, was but a small part even of just the financial question; that under existing circumstances, Populists would consider such advice as representing a move for Populist-Democratic cooperation; that such an address, especially after the St. Louis conference, would cause Populists to believe that their party leaders were attempting to dictate to them and manipulate their loyalties in an effort to arrange fusion.

Weaver replied that the Silver Democrats were preparing to raise the silver issue and it would be politically wise for the Populists to do so first. Peffer answered that the Populists already had raised the issue of free silver in the Omaha Platform in 1892, and that if the Democrats were so concerned about its importance they could join the People's party. After much discussion the meeting adjourned until the following day at Senator Allen's office. When Peffer arrived, he found only Weaver, but with the manifesto already signed by all the other congressional Populists plus the party officials like Taubeneck. Peffer spurned Weaver's entreaties and refused to sign, angrily protesting that Weaver's actions would lead to the destruction of the People's party through entanglement with Democrats over an unimportant issue.[33]

In publishing the address, the *National Watchman* confirmed Peffer's suspicions of Weaver's intentions. Sanctimoniously declaring its ignorance of why Peffer had not signed the document ("but presume it was through accident"), the *Watchman* announced its pleasure that its editorial position on the merits of a one-plank platform had been endorsed by the Populist leaders. Accordingly, it expected that "some of our papers . . . may raise objections to the proposed lines of this address," but it warned these mid-road papers not "to antagonize the propositions laid down in this manifesto." Denouncing faithful adherence to the full Populist program as "socialism," the *Watchman* argued for the repudiation of visionary schemes and for cooperation on one issue. "Let us be conser-

[33] *Topeka Daily Capital*, February 15, 1895; Kansas Biographical Scrapbook, vol. 137, p. 106; *Chicago Tribune*, June 15, 1899; *Non-Conformist*, June 27, 1895; *Topeka Advocate*, February 20, 1895; *Southern Mercury*, March 7, 1895.

vative and consistent in order to secure the support of the business men, the professional men, and the well to do."[34]

The *Watchman's* prediction of editorial objections to the policy proposed by the party officials was quickly fulfilled. The radicals voiced their complaints in the annual meeting of the National Reform Press Association (NRPA), which began in Kansas City, February 22, 1895, just one week after the publication of Weaver's address. Accusing Taubeneck of dishonesty, McLallin and other editors expressed their apprehension that the chairman and his associates planned to betray the People's party to the "Philistines." Morgan's reading from his correspondence with Taubeneck created an uproar at the editorial meeting. Taubeneck's bluntly stated intentions to abandon "the socialistic features" of the Omaha Platform and his arrogant assumption that those who disagreed with him had no recourse brought outraged cries for his resignation. But after extended discussion, the editors drew up resolutions designed to leave the public impression of harmony within Populist ranks. They declared that no authority existed to alter the Omaha Platform except another popularly elected national convention, and that while one question or another might seem most pressing "true Populists" should not ignore the other demands of the Omaha Platform. When many radical editors denounced these resolutions as a whitewash of Taubeneck and the National Committee, the NRPA appointed a committee to go to Washington to investigate Taubeneck's activities, determine the intentions of the party leaders, and warn them against trying to make silver the dominant issue. Even so, some Populists left the meeting disgusted that the NRPA had not openly condemned Taubeneck. "These editors," reported the *Kansas City Star,* "say that if the Populist Party abandons the Omaha platform now and makes free silver the only issue the party will be swallowed up by the Democratic party which is sure to declare for free silver in 1896."[35]

Taubeneck explained his views of the dispute between Populist politicians and editors to a Washington reporter. The NRPA, he

---

34 *National Watchman,* February 22, 1895.
35 *Kansas Commoner,* February 14, 1895; *Topeka Advocate,* February 20, 1895; *Non-Conformist,* March 14, 1895; *Kansas City Star,* February 22, 23, 1895; *Kansas City Gazette,* February 23, 1895.

declared, "is an advocate of the most radical socialistic ideas, government ownership of land, general paternalism, and all that sort of thing. The Populist party don't [*sic*] give a continental for socialism, don't [*sic*] want any of it in any shape, and that is where the trouble with the editors come [*sic*] in." Having cried thief as loud as he was able, the practical-minded national chairman then added of his party, "So far as there being any danger of its being absorbed by the Democratic party on account of its free silver plank, that is all nonsense."[36]

To the NRPA committee itself, however, Taubeneck proved less hostile. With the secretary of the National Committee, J. H. Turner, he agreed to sign a statement acknowledging that only a national delegate convention could revise the Omaha Platform, and he entertained the editors at national headquarters and convinced them that the People's party was prospering under his able direction. The committee also met with the Populist congressmen who had signed Weaver's address and secured their written pledge that they had no intentions of abandoning any of the Omaha Platform. The NRPA committee then publicly reported that all within Populist ranks was harmonious, that the Associated Press had misrepresented the position of the party leadership in an attempt to divide Populists, and that in fact the committee had not gone to Washington to investigate Taubeneck but to assure him that the Populist editors appreciated his efforts and stood by him.[37]

Yet this comforting report brought no end to the intraparty struggle over the direction Populism was to take. The Silver Populists continued their schemes to subvert the movement, and the mid-road editors persisted in their opposition to those who argued for a dilute Populism. Taubeneck's mouthpiece, the *National Watchman,* filled each issue with articles denouncing as invidious socialists not only Lloyd but anyone who opposed the plans of the Silver Populists, and it constantly ranted about "this socialistic conspiracy to obtain possession of the machinery of the People's Party." Furthermore, the *Watchman* continued to recommend

36 *Washington Post,* February 28, 1895.
37 *Topeka Advocate,* March 13, 1895; *Non-Conformist,* March 7, 1895; *Southern Mercury,* March 7, 1895; *Washington Post,* February 28, 1895.

trimming the Omaha Platform to one plank, as though neither the St. Louis conference nor the NRPA had ever met. McLallin described the degradation of Populism evident in the approach of the Silver Populist press: "The single-plank advocates have adopted the methods and the arguments of the old parties against Populists who insist that a broader and more comprehensive platform is necessary. . . . The *National Watchman* and Mr. Turner's new paper, the *Record Review,* week after week reiterate their non-sensical charge that socialism dominates the great body of Populists who still insist upon supporting other things besides financial reform. Not only this, they resort to the same unscrupulous methods of misrepresentation and deception that have ever characterized the plutocratic press." Taubeneck himself disregarded his pledges to the NRPA. In July, for example, he urged one Populist state convention to "build a platform making the 'money question' the great central idea, unencumbered with details or side issues." Moreover, he began a correspondence campaign to undermine the Omaha Platform.[38]

Weaver even more actively promoted the silver panacea among Populists. In a series of public letters in the spring of 1895 he advocated campaigning in 1896 on "the money question alone, unincumbered [*sic*] with any other contentions whatsoever." He traveled to Colorado to encourage a union of all silverites for the 1896 election, declaring that Populism on its own could never attain victory. In June he dominated a Des Moines conference designed to unite all silver men. He also attended an Iowa conference of Silver Democrats and tried to arrange a Democratic-Populist fusion for the state elections of 1895. Weaver later attempted to consign the Populist state convention to either fusing with the Democrats on a silver platform or supporting any ticket committed to silver, but he was thwarted by the straight Populists led by former Republican Thomas F. Byron.[39]

Most ominously, Weaver endeavored to stifle the opposition to

---

38 *Non-Conformist,* March 7, April 11, 1895; *National Watchman,* March 29, April 5, 12, 1895; *Topeka Advocate,* May 1, 1895; Thomas F. Byron to Lloyd, April 8, 1895, Lloyd Papers; *Southern Mercury,* July 11, 1895.

39 Haynes, *Weaver,* pp. 365-73; *Non-Conformist,* June 27, 1895; *Southern Mercury,* April 11, 1895; *Fort Scott Daily Monitor,* June 12, 1895; George Muller to J. B. Weaver, March 5, 1895, James B. Weaver Papers, Iowa Department of History and Archives.

his silver schemes. Publicly he unctuously refused to "quarrel with any person within the party, use hard names or hurl epithets at others who may differ with me." But privately he tried to oust Byron from his editor's position on the *Des Moines Farmers' Tribune,* a middle-of-the-road Populist paper opposed to "the one-plank clique (of alleged Populists)," as Byron described Weaver and Taubeneck. They in turn objected to Byron, not only because of his editorial hostility to their plans but also because at the St. Louis conference it was he who first saw through Weaver's parliamentary maneuvers to have the party endorse the silver panacea and began the successful counterattack of those who supported the retention of the Omaha Platform. With the assistance of other silverites, Weaver now used both financial and political pressure to have the *Tribune*'s owner forbid Byron to criticize "the single-plank shouters in the People's Party." At the same time, Byron wrote Lloyd, "while I am silent, Weaver is to advocate the 'stripping the platform to one plank,' as he lately put it, in letters to the *Tribune.* He has one going in this week, on which I am not allowed to comment." The Weaver Silver Populists then promised to pay the difference between Byron's salary and the salary necessary to attract a new editor acceptable to them. Finally, in May 1895, Byron was removed as editor and the *Farmers' Tribune* dropped its opposition to single-plank Populism.[40]

Among the Silver Populists, moreover, Weaver was one of the foremost supporters of the plans of the American Bimetallic League (ABL) to organize a silver party. Taubeneck apparently hoped to prevent the creation of an independent silver party by transforming the People's party into a silver party itself. He wrote to a protesting radical Populist in January, for example, that were a silver party organized, "no new recruits will come to the Populist ranks, except from the socialists and communists, and we will lose a great number of the best element in our party." But Weaver viewed a possible silver party with favor, anticipating that it would draw silver men who might object even to Silver Populism and that the two parties would fuse on a joint ticket in 1896 anyway. Weaver met with the silver men of the ABL in Washington in late

---

[40] Haynes, *Weaver,* p. 371; Thomas F. Byron to Lloyd, April 8, May 5, 28, 1895, Lloyd Papers.

February 1895 and at the same time also discussed with Bryan and other Silver Democrats the possibilities for a silver campaign. Out of these discussions came two important developments, though Weaver was publicly connected with neither. First, Silver Democrats in Congress, led by Bryan and Bland, issued a public address advocating free silver and the reorganization of the Democratic party to accomplish the restoration of silver coinage. Despite this indication that silver was regarded as an issue to be resolved within the Democratic party, the *Washington Post* reported that the Silver Populists were willing to enter a fusion campaign in 1896 with these Silver Democrats.[41]

The second development in Washington's winter of 1895 was the launching of the long-anticipated silver party, christened the American Bimetallic party. The silver leaders of the ABL after a conference on February 22, 1895, issued a public address declaring that neither the Democratic party nor the Republican party seemed likely to support silver and calling for all bimetallists to join in a new party with silver as the only issue. The conference suggested Joseph C. Sibley, a Pennsylvania Democratic congressman, for its tentative candidate for the new party's 1896 presidential nominee. Although the address made no mention of the People's party, the two Nevada senators, Jones and Stewart, nominal Populists both, signed the document and thereby demonstrated the extent of their commitment to Populism. Immediately after this conference, Sibley began to tour the country, campaigning more for silver than himself. Warner, Weaver, and other leading silverites and Silver Populists frequently accompanied him.[42]

The unswerving Populists strongly protested these developments. They had objected before to Taubeneck's warnings that a silver party would be formed if Populists did not restrict themselves to silver and they bitterly resented the attempts to make Populism palatable to those who might be expected to embrace this new

---

41 Taubeneck to Morgan, January 29, 1895, Waite Papers; William Jennings Bryan, *The First Battle* (Chicago, 1896), pp. 155-57; *Washington Post,* February 28, 1895; *Southern Mercury,* March 7, 1895.

42 Bryan, *First Battle,* pp. 154-55; *Washington Evening Star,* March 6, 1895; *Topeka Advocate,* March 13, 1895; William M. Stewart to Waite, September 19, 1895, Waite Papers; Stewart to [?] Julien, March 29, 1895, Stewart to Tom Watson, March 22, 1895, Stewart to G. S. Nixon, March 13, 1895, Stewart to L. C. Bateman, April 6, 1895, Stewart Papers.

party. "If these Republican and Democratic free silver men cannot stand on that [Omaha] platform," editorialized the *Southern Mercury,* "they are still in the bonds of iniquity, and have not given their whole heart to the reform cause." The *Advocate* sharply rebuked the silver party as a party of "ultimate redemption," which meant that in its only demand it accepted the theory of intrinsic value, anathema to original Populists. McLallin further flayed the "practical politicians" of the People's party for ignoring the fact that Populism was far more than free silver and for encouraging Populist connivance with the silver party. Mid-roader Gaspar C. Clemens of Topeka denounced the silver party as a plan of the silver mineowners, who had as much to lose as other monopolists if the Omaha Platform were successful, and he described it as "a fair-seeming hypocrite, pretending to succor when it means to destroy." "So long as there lives in this land a Henry D. Lloyd or a William A. Peffer," Clemens added, "the common people are not driven to take Sibley of Pennsylvania as their leader."[43]

The various positions of prominent Populists and silver leaders regarding the nature of the 1896 election campaign became clearer in March 1895. In response to questions from the *New York World* as to whether there would be a new party in 1896 and, if so, its basis and chances of success, Peffer, Watson, Weaver, Taubeneck, Butler, Warner, Sibley, and Alabama Populist Congressman Milford W. Howard replied for publication. Sibley and Warner alone argued that the new party already existed in the American Bimetallic party. They predicted that the silver issue would split the old parties and drive silver advocates into the new party rather than the People's party with its more comprehensive and radical platform. But Populists too would ignore all issues except financial reform, these silver leaders argued, and thus also join the new party.

Weaver, Taubeneck, and Butler represented a second position, differing only slightly from the first. They agreed that the money issue should be paramount and that Populists would disregard all other issues and join bimetallists of both old parties on a common ticket in 1896. "Those who desire to retard monetary reform by loading us down with other issues will, with the Socialists and

43 *Non-Conformist,* February 7, 1895; *Southern Mercury,* January 31, 1895; *Topeka Advocate,* March 6, 13, 1895.

Communists, go to the rear," Taubeneck announced. Butler specifically declared that the People's party would not be the agency of union because its "minor issues" would repel silverites of the old parties, but he believed Populists would leave their party to join bimetallists in a new party yet to be formed. Weaver and Taubeneck may not have seemed as ready as Butler to jettison the People's party, but the practical effect of their proposals was the same: fusion of bimetallists outside existing party lines.

Watson and Howard represented Southern Populism. They believed that no new party would be formed but that Populists and other bimetallists could form a united front against the financial policies advocated by the dominant leaders of both old parties. Howard carefully noted that Populists could not leave their party to join men who would be satisfied to return to the old parties after achieving silver coinage, but he declared his belief that Populists would freely emphasize the money question. The sincere bimetallists could then work with the Populists. Watson also expressed both his unwillingness to sacrifice any principle and his readiness to cooperate against Cleveland's financial policies.

Peffer provided the last position among those responding to the *World*. He wrote of his expectation that a new party would be organized, "but it will be built on a foundation deeper and broader than 'free silver' or 'bimetallism,' for those terms express nothing that reaches the core of the troubles which confront us." Free silver, he argued, would be useless if the prevailing system remained unchanged. Describing the miseries of depression America and the nature of corporate America, with the legal and extralegal force of the military and Pinkertons available to maintain the system and suppress the people, he scoffed at the suggestion that free silver would prove the salvation of the oppressed. "The new party," he declared, must be "founded on broad principles that will appeal to the public conscience, and its objects will be responsive to the people's wants. Anything short of this can only be preliminary to the work of organizing the great party that shall accomplish what we most need." Not free silver but that original Populist triad Peffer demanded: the destruction of the land monopoly, explained in its broadest sense; the abolition of the transportation monopolies through "public ownership and control of all means and facilities for the general movement of persons and property from place to place"; the overthrow of the money power through the destruction of banks of issue, the abolition of interests and rent, and the government issue of fiat paper money directly to the people.[44]

Two other positions held by opponents of the gold standard were not represented in the *World*. The first of these was that of the Silver Democrats such as Bland and Bryan who rejected the suggestion of leaving their party to achieve free silver and who trusted to their ability to reorganize Democracy on a silver basis. They wanted no formal fusion: all Populists and Silver Republicans were to enroll in the cause under the Democratic banner. Mid-road Populists such as McLallin and Park championed the final position. They differed little from Peffer, objecting primarily only to his declaration that a new party would be formed. McLallin praised Peffer, for example, for being the only one of the writers in the *World* with "a comprehensive view of the evils or the needs of the hour." Apart from his belief that a new party would be organized, "we find little else in his letter with which we cannot fully agree." On the other hand, McLallin criticized Taubeneck for stupidity in politics and blindness in principles. These mid-roaders believed that Populists should adhere strictly to the Omaha Platform and remain within their party, that Populism and not a new party, however based, provided hope of political reform. Peffer himself, however, considered that his *World* letter contained "not a single utterance . . . at variance with the Omaha demands" and added, "I have never at any time faltered in my allegiance to the cause of populism."[45]

Throughout the remainder of 1895 these various groups campaigned to gain acceptance of their viewpoints. Sibley, Warner, and the silver men traveled and spoke extensively and through their various organizations helped to subsidize a great outpouring of silver literature. In September the leading silver groups began discussions designed to bring about a merger for a joint silver effort in 1896. Such Silver Populists as Weaver and Stewart often cooperated in these activities. Weaver, for instance, traveled with

---

[44] *New York World*, March 24, 1895.

[45] Coletta, *Bryan*, pp. 96-97; *Topeka Advocate*, April 10, 1895; *Dallas Morning News*, August 8, 1895.

Sibley and Warner to Denver to boom the American Bimetallic party and even attempted to persuade recalcitrant Populists such as Davis Waite that the new party could be trusted. The silverites and Weaver had only mixed success, for Waite later told Donnelly, "Our populist dems [Democrats], whose populism never included anything but the free coinage of silver, are quite enthusiastic for the new party, but I think the populists proper will continue to stand on the Omaha platform." With even a closer view of Weaver's cooperation with the silver men, Byron commented that Weaver was "ruthlessly intriguing to turn over the Populist organization in this state, and also that in the nation, to the monopolistic Sibley outfit. . . . Weaver's view [is] that we should express ourselves as ready to unite with anything or anybody for silver."[46]

The Silver Democrats also actively canvassed in 1895. They called special conventions in several states to agitate the currency question and to resolve for free silver. In June they held a national convention in Memphis, attended by most prominent silver advocates. Although allegedly nonpartisan, the Memphis meeting was arranged, promoted, and controlled by Democrats. Much of the discussion centered upon the problem of keeping Democratic silver sentiment within the party and consequently also of attracting Populists to the Democratic party for a silver campaign in 1896. In August, many of the same Democrats met in Washington to establish a silver organization within their party, the Bimetallic Democratic National Committee. Declaring that the Democratic party was the traditional champion of bimetallism, they clearly revealed their intention to turn the silver movement into the Democratic party. Actually hostile to Populism, many of them favored a silver Democracy, for one reason, to undercut the People's party by enticing Democratic-Populists back to the Democratic party.[47]

Yet some Populist lambs were prepared to lie down with the Democratic lion. Butler, for one, attended the Memphis convention, described silver as more important than his party, and asserted

46 Marian Silveus, "The Antecedents of the Campaign of 1896" (Ph.D. diss., University of Wisconsin, 1932), pp. 13-15; Waite to Donnelly, April 22, 1895, Donnelly Papers; *Non-Conformist*, June 27, 1895; Byron to Lloyd, May 5, 1895, Lloyd Papers; Donnelly to Waite, August 28, 1895, Waite Papers.

47 Hollingsworth, *Whirligig of Politics*, pp. 35-41; *Washington Post*, August 14, 15, 1895; Bryan, *First Battle*, pp. 162-63; Stanley L. Jones, *The Presidential Election of 1896* (Madison, Wis., 1964), pp. 62-64.

his willingness "to sacrifice for the time all other policies of the Populist platform." Harry Skinner, a North Carolina Populist elected to Congress on a fusion ticket that Butler had helped arrange, also hoped that the convention would lead to a fusion of all silver forces in 1896. His candidate for president on such a ticket, he declared, was William Jennings Bryan. On the other hand, some Populists feared the increasing activity of the Silver Democrats as a threat to their party. Even Taubeneck began slowly to realize the possible results of his efforts to make silver the only issue for Populists. He attended the Illinois Silver Democratic Convention, for example, and protested that "the Democrats are trying to steal our platform, and I am here to object. The People's Party is the only simon-pure silver party."[48] But by 1895, free silver as a political issue had a dynamic all its own and no one could control it. Taubeneck forgot his fears and continued to advocate a silver-only Populism.

The genuine Populists also recognized the drift of events, but were not as complacent. One anti-fusion editor argued that "the thing for the Populist press to do now and henceforth, as it appears to me, is to gradually belittle silver from its unduly imagined dimensions of the national panacea . . . ; this course would tend to keep our voters from following the band-wagon of the free-silver fakirs." Such Populists ridiculed Taubeneck's claim that he only played practical politics by demanding a one-plank platform. Truly practical politics would suggest either emphasizing the distinctive features of Populism rather than that one issue held in common with other political groups, in order to maintain the party as a separate organization; or emphasizing substantive reforms or a general but significant demand as Peffer had suggested, to make a worthwhile contribution to the reformation of society should the party lose its independent identity in a larger movement. The policy of the Silver Populists, however, seemed to be that of stooping to be conquered. If an old party adopted a silver platform, after the Populists declared silver all important, the People's party

---

48 *Southern Mercury*, June 27, 1895; Woodward, *Origins of the New South*, p. 282; Harry Skinner to Bryan, June 10, 1895, Bryan Papers; J. U. Devine to Marion Butler, July 16, 1895, Marion Butler Papers, Southern Historical Collection, University of North Carolina Library; *St. Louis Post-Dispatch*, June 4, 1895.

would be doomed, either because it would have to consent to being subsumed in the larger organization, or because its adherents would naturally vote with the party most likely to be able to put that "essential" reform into practice. But since silver actually counted for little in Populism and represented no necessary part of the new order the Populists had promised, the party would have died without just reason or without adding anything to American political life—even if free silver were achieved. Thus, the course of the Silver Populists, argued the loyal Populists, was a suicidal move without practical purpose.[49]

Jerry Simpson attempted to ridicule those Populists unwilling to consent to a reduction of Populism to silver. "Now if I was starving for a square meal and some one should offer me a crust of bread I would deserve to die if I did not take it. So it is with the radical ones." The "radical ones," however, saw matters differently. They argued that if a crust of bread was all that they received, they would soon starve to death anyway—and those with whom Simpson proposed to fuse wanted to order no more from the Populist menu than the one silver crust of bread. Some such as McLallin even believed that the crust offered so generously by the enemies of Populism was poisoned: silver, he argued, "unaccompanied by other reforms which are more essential in themselves, would result in injury rather than benefit."[50] Such Populists were determined to hold out for the whole square meal, and they believed that it would be served soon after the people tired of begging for the thin crust and turned to demand their rights through Populism.

Senator Peffer was as active as any Populist in the defense of original Populism during 1895, campaigning once again extensively throughout the country. As McLallin anticipated, he had to explain his prediction of a new party. He clearly had not meant, Peffer answered, that he favored the creation of a silver-only party. Indeed, he was adamant that Populists should avoid the new silver party and he warned Dunning against the *Watchman*'s warm welcome for it. Nor did he favor the fusion of silver forces in 1896.

49 Thomas F. Byron to Lloyd, May 5, 1895, Lloyd Papers; *Topeka Advocate*, October 23, 1895; *Non-Conformist*, March 14, 1895; *Southern Mercury*, March 7, April 11, 1895; *Dallas Morning News*, August 8, 1895; *Girard Western Herald*, August 14, 1895.

50 *Girard Western Herald*, June 14, 1895; *Topeka Advocate*, April 10, 1895.

Rather, he foresaw that eventually there would be a political realignment from which Populists would emerge as dominant in the
principal party, which might have a new name for the sake of
political sensibilities but which would be formed about Populism.
He expected and would accept no major revision of Omaha Populism. "Our doctrines reach the disease from which the country
suffers; our declarations are responsive to the people's needs. Let
us stand by them, teach them, and vote them." He would accept,
Peffer repeated, an actual union of all political elements sincerely
in favor of reform—Populists, Socialists, and Prohibitionists surely,
plus those Republicans and Democrats who had heretofore resisted
Populism because of the strength of partisan ties rather than a
philosophical aversion—such as had happened when similar elements had combined to form the People's party itself; but he
strongly opposed a fusion of distinct organizations, each with its
own prejudices and incompatible traditions, and especially on the
sole basis of so insubstantial an issue as free silver. If some mid-road
Populists rejected the possibility that the nation's genuine reform
forces would have to coalesce once again into another party as had
happened so often before, they nevertheless were pleased to have
Peffer speak for them.[51]

Throughout the spring and summer Peffer toured the South and
Midwest, speaking at Populist camp meetings, county fairs, chau-
tauquas, and labor assemblies. Frequently he was billed together
with Governor Waite, and at least once in Texas Weaver and Peffer
appeared before the same audience. Weaver recommended substantial modification of the Omaha Platform, including the total
omission of the subtreasury plank, which he declared "should never
have been put in the platform at first." In contrast, Peffer advocated
strict adherence to Omaha Populism and predicted success for
faithful Populists in the future. Moreover, Peffer pointedly warned
Populists against trusting Weaver's proposed allies, the Silver
Democrats. Such politicians, Peffer noted, were precisely the men
the original Populists had debated in 1891 from the same platform,
and they still placed party above both principle and people; reform

51 *Non-Conformist,* September 19, 1895; *Topeka Advocate,* August 14, Septem-
ber 18, October 9, 30, 1895; *Washington Post,* March 8, October 12, 1895; *Dallas
Morning News,* August 8, 1895; *Kansas City Journal,* May 8, 1895; *National
Watchman,* April 26, 1895.

could come about only by getting into the middle of the road.[52]

Peffer explained the extent of his silver commitment to a Kansas City reporter in May. Silver, the senator contended, was only a temporary demand, necessary to redeem those government bonds which required payment in coin. Thorough Populists opposed silver as much as gold, for they denied the intrinsic value theory and the metallic basis of money altogether; free silver was acceptable only as a preliminary step toward an inflationary economy. He refused to comment on *Coin's Financial School,* the silver bible of Bryan and other bimetallists, but left the reporter with the impression that he considered it a superficial and inadequate account of financial problems. The journalist also recorded that Peffer "declares for the same old fiat system of paper currency upon which the Populist party was born." The editor headlined the story, "Opposed to Silver/Populists Are Not in Favor of the White Metal/Peffer Virtually Admits It."[53]

Such opaque reporting combined with either the partisan or the financial bias of much of the press often left the actual position of many Populists unclear.[54] In late summer, Peffer was reported first to have told a New York audience that silver no longer attracted attention in the West; to have told Kansans that he opposed free silver and favored a currency based only on land; to have announced his withdrawal from the People's party and the formation of a new party of his own. Peffer was kept busy denying all such absurd statements, attributing them to the partisan press, which he regarded as unreliable whenever reporting Populist opinions. Other Populists understood the situation. A Minneapolis Populist described the Associated Press stories of Peffer's conversions as "inventions of our diabolical enemies. They are equal to anything. The

52 *Dallas Morning News,* August 6, 8, 9, 1895; *Non-Conformist,* August 15, 1895; *Topeka Advocate,* August 7, 14, 1895; *Washington Post,* March 8, 1895.

53 *Kansas City Daily Journal,* May 8, 1895.

54 For this reason and because of sometimes careless research, historians have frequently misunderstood Peffer's attitude, depending, apparently, upon which issue of which newspaper they happened to read. Thus, Destler and Jones place Peffer among the Silver Populists, while Hicks and Woodward designate him a mid-roader. Martin Ridge resolved the problem by calling him both. Similarly, historians have misidentified other Populists, perhaps none more so than Jerry Simpson, whom Nugent and many others regard as a steadfast Populist ideologue. See Karel D. Bicha, "Jerry Simpson: Populist without Principle," *Journal of American History* 54 (September 1967): 291-306.

safe rule is not to believe a word they say." The *Non-Conformist* commented more calmly that "press dispatches concerning Populists must always be verified before they can be believed."[55]

Precisely because of this necessity to verify stories carried by the major news services, the NRPA attempted to establish a Populist news agency, centered in Kansas City. George C. Ward, a Kansas City mid-roader, was an able and popular writer for the "patent sides" that the Populists provided for their local newspapers. In September he wrote a long article which placed Peffer in the Populistic perspective. The various news stories had distressed Ward greatly, he wrote, for Peffer was "the leading exponent and advocate of populism and a commanding figure in the political arena." Ward therefore corresponded with the senator to investigate the reports of his apostasy. Peffer replied, "I am a Populist and approve the Omaha platform in its entirety, without mental reservation." The senator recited the planks of the platform as his own position, but provided a system of government banks as the "some better system" allowed to be substituted for the subtreasury plan, but designed to accomplish the same end of distributing money directly to the people at low interest rates. Ward gladly reported to his readers that "there is nothing uncertain or vacillating" about Peffer and urged them to support "the man who led the revolt . . . and first gave to populist principles a prominent position in national politics."[56]

Before Congress convened again in December, Peffer made two more forceful defenses of unconditional Populism. In early October, he took control of the Advocate Publishing Company and announced that, though McLallin would remain as active editor, he would henceforth direct the paper's editorial policy. He intended to include more miscellaneous matter, especially dealing with agriculture, but he would not change McLallin's middle-of-the-road political position. "In politics," Peffer declared, "the *Advocate* will be a broad-gauged Populist paper. Populism means a great deal more now—more than ever before," he added: this was no reduction of issues. Although he again expressed his willingness to cooperate with sincere reformers he reaffirmed his unalterable opposition to

55 *Non-Conformist*, August 5, 22, September 12, 1895.
56 *Kansas City Star*, February 22, 1895; *Topeka Advocate*, September 18, 1895.

surrendering the isms of Omaha and to accepting free silver as a panacea. Moreover, he would continue to direct the *Advocate* against fusion and the dictation of party managers. The *Advocate,* he wrote, would oppose "any and every sort of dickering or trading with enemies. . . . If the populist party would win and retain the respect of the people it must respect itself. What it denounces in other parties it must not tolerate within itself."[57]

Shortly after this announcement, Senator Stewart argued in his Washington paper, *The Silver Knight,* that Populists should discard all their reform demands except silver in order to create a coalition against the gold standard advocates. Any other planks might drive away silverites, Stewart contended. J. H. Turner, secretary of the Populist National Committee and a leading proponent of single-plank Populism, asked Peffer for his opinion of Stewart's editorial. Peffer replied in a widely reprinted letter, saying that he had no objection to "a union of the friends of monetary reform under the banner of the Populist party," but that he would never agree to an abridgement of Populist doctrine. Peffer conceded the Omaha Platform was not perfect, but he gave no encouragement to Turner or Stewart for he stood by his former position. Over the sub-treasury and government ownership of railroads, in particular, re-formers disagreed, Peffer wrote; but Populists believed in the principles behind those propositions and required the incorporation of those principles in the "some better system" allowed, such as his own proposal for a government banking system. Peffer, then, was willing to revise the Omaha Platform, but the Populist demands would have to be fully covered; indeed, he felt that Populism could not restrict its creed, for new subjects had developed since 1892 that the party should consider, including government by injunction, executive interference with Congress, the illegitimate use of federal troops to suppress labor strikes, the need to establish an income tax over the Supreme Court's obstructionism, and many more issues. Thus any acceptable revision of the Omaha demands would have to be on the basis of broad, general, and easily applicable principles, as Peffer had repeatedly maintained before, and not on one narrow and self-conclusive demand like free silver. Peffer then suggested

[57] *Topeka Advocate,* October 9, 1895.

that "the one great, basic principle underlying the movement which is culminating in the formation and growth of the Populist party is the *equality* of human rights—first, to the rights of the people as individual persons, and second, to the rights, powers, and duties of the people as a whole, when organized in communities, states, and nations." Such a general principle applied to the problems of the government, the economy, and the society at large would satisfy Peffer and the loyal Populists who followed him. To such a Populist vision he urged reformers to dedicate themselves, and he scorned the suggestion to make concessions and compromises to attract support from those committed only to the comparatively ignoble cause of free silver coinage.[58]

Despite Peffer's pronouncements, the silver issue continued to dominate political discussion when the Fifty-fourth Congress convened in December 1895. The 1894 election reversal left no party with a majority in the Senate, and six Populists held the balance of power. Silver Republicans Fred Dubois and Henry Teller were reported willing to organize the Senate on silver rather than partisan lines. Immediately Butler, Stewart, and Allen professed their readiness to combine with other silverites, while Peffer forlornly argued that the Populists should not align themselves with members of the old parties. The Populist caucus voted against Peffer's position and drew up a call inviting all alleged bimetallists in the Senate to a meeting to discuss organizing the Senate on silver lines. Committed to act with his fellow Populists, Peffer signed his name to the call, but insisted upon placing it last upon the document rather than first as usual.[59]

The possibility that elements favoring silver might unite to organize the Senate faded rapidly. Even Dubois declared that one thing he was "certain of, and that is neither party will enter into any combination with the Populists." In fact, Dubois suggested that perhaps Republicans and Democrats could come to an understanding on the Senate offices and patronage in order to eliminate Populist influence. Other indications of silverite antipathy to Populism came from a *Washington Post* interview with an Idaho silver advo-

---

58 Ibid., October 30, 1895.
59 *Washington Post,* October 13, 16, November 16, 1895; *Congressional Record,* 54th Cong., 1st sess., vol. 28, pp. 421-25.

cate. "Here in the East," he asserted, "you seem to think that we away out West, especially in the free silver states, all look to Populism as a savior, a last resort. Nothing of the sort. We indorse the free silver plank in the Populist party, but regard [Populism] . . . as empty theory, and hollow, dreamy Utopianism." Peffer was not disappointed with such reports. "As a matter of fact," he remarked, "the very thing I want to see, as a Populist, is a combination of the Democrats and the Republicans in the organization of the Senate. That will enable us to tell our people again, as we have told them in the past, that the two old parties are practically one."[60]

The silver meeting proved a failure. Of the fifty-two senators invited only four attended: the Democrat Benjamin Tillman and Silver Republicans Teller, Jeter Pritchard, and Lee Mantle. The Republicans simply indicated their refusal to break party lines and left at once. Tillman was only slightly more friendly and no more prepared to leave his party to act with the Populists. Peffer noted after the meeting that party ties were too strong to permit a silver caucus, but Allen maintained that something might yet come of this "preliminary meeting." And, indeed, in their action the Populists had finally agreed to come down to silver and work with members of the old parties on silver alone, without regard to party identity. But the Populist offer to cooperate outside party lines was not enough: surrender would have to be unconditional.[61]

For like the Alliance Democrats in the Fifty-second Congress, the silver men refused to place principles before party. The Republicans organized the Senate when the Populists would not vote on the issue at all, except for Kyle who sided with the Democrats. Following the vote, silverites of both parties gave their answer to Populism. Democratic Senator Isham Harris condemned the Populists for their abstention and asserted that he was as much an advocate of free silver as any Populist but that he would never break party lines to achieve it. Senator Dubois then declared that although the Silver Republicans favored bimetallism, they did not endorse an irredeemable currency as espoused by Peffer or the other Populist principles on land, money, and transportation.

60 *Washington Post,* November 4, 12, 16, 1895.
61 *Non-Conformist,* December 5, 1895; *Washington Post,* December 3, 1895.

Silver Republicans, he concluded, simply were not in sympathy with Populism and would never cooperate to advance any Populist proposal. Even on silver the two groups disagreed, for Republicans accepted it as basic money while the official Populist position accorded only expediency to silver and rejected the notion of ultimate redemption.[62]

Outside Congress too, as the election year of 1896 began, silver advocates had little use for Populists except for their votes, as Peffer caustically remarked. In Kansas, for instance, both old parties enthusiastically supported silver and yet recoiled from all other Populist reform proposals. Silver Republicans reacted bitterly to any suggestion that free silver was a Populist position and hastened to draw a definite line between themselves and the despised calamity howlers. Free silver was a reform to be accomplished within the Republican party. Only a few Silver Republicans threatened to bolt the party if it repudiated their position, and even these could not reconcile themselves to the "minor questions" of Populism.[63]

The silver craze affected Kansas Democrats perhaps even more than it did Republicans, yet they too were determined to stay within their party in advocating bimetallism, especially after silver men regained control of the party's state organization. The Fifth Congressional District's Democrats, heretofore dominated by stalwarts, illustrated this determination in their 1895 convention. They announced their support for free silver, demanded the reorganization of their party on a bimetallic basis, and asked for a state party conference to insure that Silver Democrats need not abandon their party. Democratic newspapers which had supported the Populist party in 1894 because of its silver advocacy now devoted themselves to silverplating the Democracy so that such a course would not be necessary in 1896. Their editors began by denying that Cleveland represented the party and promising the nomination of Silver Democrats only. Hence, there would be no need for a new silver party nor for a further dalliance with a Silver

62 *Congressional Record*, 54th Cong., 1st sess., vol. 28, pp. 421-29, 906-8; *Washington Post*, January 24, 1896.

63 A. L. Sponsler to P. H. Coney, May 20, August 8, 1895; William P. Hackney to Coney, March 2, 1895, Coney to William H. ("Coin") Harvey, August 9, 1895, Coney to C. V. Eskridge, August 10, 1895, J. W. Ady to Coney, February 8, 1895, Coney Papers.

Populism because true Democracy was a silver party. Besides, Populism had "too many side issues for us to grapple with."[64]

Democratic leaders scrambled onto the silver bandwagon. John Martin attempted to convince the party's officeholders, who largely owed their appointments to him, to repudiate Cleveland and follow him into the silver camp. After his senatorial term expired in 1895, he announced his candidacy for Peffer's Senate seat in 1897 and made clear his intention to create a silver Democratic party, "with a Populist annex." Even more significant in illustrating the relationship of Silver Democrats to Populism was the politician who became the state committeeman of the Bimetallic Democratic National Committee, the group Bryan accorded the most honor for transforming the party in 1895 and 1896: David Overmeyer. Inveterate foe of Populism, a seconder of Cleveland's 1892 nomination, opponent of active government, collaborator with Republicans, Overmeyer personified the Democratic antithesis of Populism.[65]

To restrict Populism to silver in an effort to gain such converts was to deny the very essence of the original movement; to agree to fuse with such politicians or to enter into their Democratic party for the sole purpose of achieving silver coinage would be to make of suicide a burlesque. Had Populism deteriorated so much since its days of pride and hope?

Both friends and enemies of Populism recognized the transformation of the movement, though they disagreed as to its nature and import. The severe changes wrought by the failure to convert the South and by the fusion and related policies of the party leadership from 1892 to 1894 were only accelerated by the increasing emphasis upon silver as a panacea. Taubeneck's determination to narrow the Populist program to silver found expression among Kansas Populists as well. State Senator Michael Senn, for instance, suggested that Populism could attract wider support by forgoing its comprehensive reform proposals to concentrate upon the single issue of free silver. The *Lyndon People's Herald* well symbolized the new Populism. Once a staunch organ for Populist radicalism, the *People's Herald* came under new editorial management in 1895. Rejecting the fervor

---

[64] *Marshall County Democrat* (Marysville), February 1, March 1, 8, May 17, July 5, September 20, 1895.

[65] *Washington Post*, November 13, 1895; *Non-Conformist*, April 18, 1895; Bryan, *First Battle*, pp. 162-63.

and goals of the early Populists, the new editor promptly renounced any intention "to set the world on fire" and advocated stressing free silver as "the fundamental issue" with all other Populist demands relegated to only "minor consideration." The *People's Herald* was no calamity howler, and even in the continuing depression it recommended Populist support for candidates it proudly described as a farmer "without a cent of debt whatsoever," a doctor who "is now enjoying a lucrative practice," another "successful and well-to-do farmer," and "a man of shrewd, keen and splendid business ability."[66]

There remained of course some original Populists who continued to reject the demand for Silver Populism and its accompanying predilection for fusion. These came predominantly from the dwindling number of Populists of Republican antecedents. Percy Daniels provided a comprehensive arraignment of the entire drift of the People's party in a public letter in July 1895. "The free coinage of silver will not right the wrongs of a plundered people," he declared; the party should not avoid the more vital issues it had promised to settle and which still demanded attention. Fusion he denounced as self-defeating, unprincipled, and unfurling "the banner of Populism that bears the hopes of the oppressed from sea to sea, on the wormy and crumbling stump of the Democratic flagship." Those Populists who promoted such a policy deserved censure for adopting "the reprehensible practices of the old parties,— bad habits which they promised to abandon when they joined the reformers. The party has halted to trade for votes when they should have pushed ahead on their march. In their success they have shown some of the same greed for spoils of office that they have so justly condemned in their adversaries." The 1894 Populist defeat, Daniels averred, had been a deserved repudiation of Populist leaders, not a condemnation of Populist principles. The party had been organized to purify political life, and Populists would "not deserve success until their leaders show they have resumed their allegiance to this purpose, and are governed by the same spirit of uprightness and candor as inspires the men in the ranks."

66 *Topeka Advocate,* December 12, 1894; O. Gene Clanton, *Kansas Populism: Ideas and Men* (Lawrence, 1969), pp. 182-83. Clanton provides a good discussion of Populist "metamorphosis" but one that leaves the inaccurate impression that this change came about largely after 1894.

The faithful Populists, he concluded, must reform their own party and rebuke those who had strayed from the straight path.[67]

Those Populists who agreed with Daniels were few indeed. As in the early days, the unconditional radical found expression in the Farmers' Alliance. With Willits and Otis as state officers, the Alliance condemned those who sought to discard its "trinity of principles" for silver alone. The anti-fusionist Kansas Populist League, composed largely of the same men, resolved in September 1895 that it opposed the stress on silver and stood by the entire Omaha Platform. But the Kansas Reform Press Association represented the more popular Populist position when it resolved in the same month to make free silver thenceforth the major political issue in Populist papers. The editors then discontinued their association with the Populist readyprint firm because its material, written by Taubeneck's mid-road adversary Morgan, "does not make the free silver idea prominent enough."[68]

Republicans delighted in pointing out the metamorphosis of Kansas Populists. After local Populists named six Democrats to their eight-place county ticket in 1895, the *Girard Press* commented that "the 'middle of the road' Populist seems to have departed from Crawford county. He was very vociferous a few years ago, but now calmly and smilingly wears the Democratic yoke." The Populist *Girard Western Herald* could only lamely reply that at least the candidates were not Republicans. Another editor took special aim at those Populists who were attempting to promote fusion on the basis of silver. "There is nothing of the old Alliance Puritan cry for reform in these men," observed William Allen White. "Has not the whole fabric of the reform party, its heroes, its aspirations, its ambitions, its lofty desires fallen among thieves on the Jerico road?" he asked. "Where is the Alliance man with the courage to deny that his party that was going to reform the world has made a 'deal' that would have been hissed out of the first farmers convention in the year of our Lord 1890?"[69]

To this there was no reply, and the Populists awaited 1896.

[67] *Girard Western Herald,* August 14, 1895.

[68] *Topeka Advocate,* February 6, October 2, 1895; *Kansas City Gazette,* February 23, 1895; *Topeka Daily Capital,* September 18, 1895.

[69] *Girard Western Herald,* September 20, 1895; Clanton, *Kansas Populism,* p. 178.

CHAPTER EIGHT

Reaping the Whirlwind

As THE POPULISTS prepared for the election of 1896, the first matter they had to consider was the place and date of the national convention. While such decisions of the old parties were based on financial promises and geographical location, that of the People's party held deep significance for the direction the party would take in the campaign, which both the Silver and the Omaha Populists recognized. As was clear from past experiences in state politics, a Populist convention held before either the Democrats or Republicans met would encourage an independent ticket or else cause any fusion to be on Populist conditions and candidates; a convention after those of the old parties would facilitate fusion on a silver candidate already selected or promote a silver-only campaign, as the party would be influenced by silver accessions from the old parties which rejected bimetallism. Middle-of-the-road Populist papers such as Peffer's *Advocate,* the *Chicago Express,* and the Dallas *Southern Mercury* all came out in October 1895 for an early convention. The *Express* explained that "an early convention will head off and give a quietus to the movements of the 'new silver party,' and will force into line or out of the party those ambitious populists who advocate leaving the middle of the road." Furthermore, an early convention would still the fears "that our party machinery is being manipulated in the interests of the enemy."

Radical Populists such as Davis Waite and Henry L. Loucks agreed that the convention should be held *"the sooner the better"* in order to prevent Silver Populists from determining the Populist course, certainly before the old parties met and perhaps even in late 1895.[1]

For opposite reasons, Silver Populists such as James Weaver, Herman Taubeneck, and Marion Butler favored a late convention. They believed that the Republican party would adopt a gold platform and that the Cleveland administration would control the Democratic convention, or at least prevent a strong silver man from receiving the presidential nomination because of the convention rule requiring a two-thirds vote to nominate. Nevertheless, to proceed even on that basis meant that they were willing to make the campaign on silver rather than Omaha Populism and were prepared to accept silverite influence upon the People's party. Those who argued for a late convention already had surrendered to silver as a panacea, either financial or political.

The Silver Populists worked closely with other silver advocates to force the People's party to adopt that course. The various silver groups had already scheduled a conference for Washington on January 22, 1896, to prepare for the campaign, and they urged the Populists to meet with them and agree to joint action and a late convention. Speaking for the Silver Democrats, William Jennings Bryan also pressed the Populists to delay their convention in order to assure a fusion silver campaign. Butler answered Bryan that he hoped to secure a fusion of all silver elements, and together with William M. Stewart he corresponded with the silverites toward that end. Weaver expressed his pleasure that Bryan's suggestions were "exactly in accord with the plan which Mr. Taubeneck and myself have been working to for some months past." The next step, as Stewart declared, was to have the Populist National Committee accept the plan at its meeting in St. Louis on January 17. The Silver Populists were determined, Weaver wrote privately, to achieve this objective. "We have had quite enough middle of the road nonsense, and some of us at least think it about time for the

---

1 *Topeka Advocate,* October 30, 1895; *Southern Mercury* (Dallas), October 10, 1895; Henry L. Loucks to Davis Waite, September 20, 1895, Waite Papers.

exhibition of a little synthetic force if we would accomplish any good purpose."[2]

The Washington Populists joined in this decision. Of the thirteen congressmen in the Populist caucus, eleven favored creating an alliance with the Silver Democrats for the 1896 campaign and consequently wanted a late convention. Only Peffer and Howard objected, arguing that such an arrangement with those essentially hostile to the spirit and greater demands of Populism would cause the destruction of their party and the suppression of more important issues and principles. Eventually Peffer agreed to sign his name to the caucus message advising a late convention, but he refused to place his name first on the document and glumly declared his belief that the People's party would soon be submerged into the Democratic party. Weaver's errand to Washington and his manifesto of the previous year, Peffer commented ruefully, had proved fruitful.[3]

At St. Louis the opposition to the schemes of the Silver Populists was just as ineffectual. Neither Washburn nor Lloyd attended, and Donnelly no longer opposed Taubeneck, but expressed his readiness to trim the Omaha Platform to emphasize silver. G. C. Clemens presented the most complete critique of the policy of the Silver Populists. Declaring that, "with the pertinacity of sordid men seeking selfish ends," Taubeneck and silver leaders had plotted for over a year to subvert the People's party, Clemens appealed to true Populists to "at once assert their supremacy over their party machine." A single-issue, fusion silver campaign, Clemens argued, would delay or destroy the triumph of the Omaha demands.

These traitors to the holy cause of the people would have us abandon, as they have already abandoned, every aim of our party, in order that we may secure the accession of old party politicians, who, we are coolly informed, are too ignorant or too capitalistic even to endure the mention of all our other reform demands. . . . About all these things we are to be

---

[2] W. J. Bryan to Waite, December 2, 1895, Waite Papers; Marion Butler to Bryan, January 8, 1896, and J. B. Weaver to Bryan, December 31, 1895, January 3, 1896, Bryan Papers; W. M. Stewart to Ignatius Donnelly, December 20, 1895, Stewart to H. E. Taubeneck, December 12, 16, 1895, Stewart to M. C. Rankin, December 26, 1895, Stewart and Butler to Joseph C. Sibley, January 6, 1896, Stewart Papers.

[3] *Washington Post*, January 18, 1896; *Chicago Tribune*, June 25, 1899.

silent, lest we hurt the feelings or shock the barbaric prejudices of our proposed allies. And what mighty achievement is to justify this sacrifice of principle? . . .

We can put silver back where it was in 1873, but we cannot put the world back there. And, in the world of today, with its gigantic trusts and combinations—none of which our proposed allies permit us to touch—would free silver restore the conditions of twenty-three years ago? What folly to even dream! Yet to demonstrate this folly and make a few men rich, we are to give up agitation of our really important principles. . . .

And why are we to do this wicked thing? Because . . . "The people are not ready for more radical reforms; and they are ready for free silver." Perhaps they are readier still for no reform at all, and so we had better all unite with the Republican party which seeks to prevent all change. . . .

What shall we do? The crisis is here. We are at the parting of the ways. . . . We are asked to turn back into the Valley of Desolation where bleach the bones of other parties which, tempted by sorid ambition, have been false to the hope they had inspired. Shall we submit and turn back? or rebel and push on?[4]

Clemens's plea fell on deaf ears. The Populists at St. Louis in 1896 were not those original Populists, filled with a revolutionary zeal to remake the world, ready to respond to the pentecostal appeals of such men as Clemens, Peffer, Willits, and Otis, and disdainful of suggestions that compromises might be the practical policy. Taubeneck spoke at the meeting of the necessity for a "new departure" in Populism, and the new Populists who listened were either those such as Taubeneck himself, who had long since forgotten why he had been named national chairman at the Cincinnati Conference in 1891, or those such as Thomas Patterson, who was participating in his first national Populist meeting. Patterson, editor of the Denver *Rocky Mountain News,* had been a prominent Democrat but turned Populist in 1893 on the sole basis of free silver. The Taubenecks and Pattersons were agreed that all isms should be dropped in favor of silver and that those Populists who objected—those true Populists to whom Clemens appealed—should be purged and forced "into the society of red anarchists and self-satisfied communists."[5]

Taubeneck, Weaver, and Butler had full control of the National

4 *St. Louis Post-Dispatch,* January 17, 1896; *Washington Post,* January 16, 1896; Gaspar C. Clemens, *An Appeal to True Populists* (Topeka, Kans., 1896).
5 *St. Louis Post-Dispatch,* January 16, 18, 19, 1896.

Committee. They had taken advantage of the poverty of most committee members and secured the proxies of those unable to attend, giving them fifty-one of the eighty-seven total votes. The compliant committee then followed their script exactly. It scheduled the party's convention after the dates already selected by the old parties and postponed a decision on the precise day until party leaders could meet with silverites at their Washington conference. It also obediently named Weaver, Butler, Patterson, and like-minded Populists to represent the party in those discussions. Finally, the committee adopted an astounding resolution for an allegedly independent political party with distinct principles. It urged all those favoring financial reform, "but who are not ready to become members of our organization," to hold a separate convention at the same time and place that the Populists would choose so that there could be a fusion on candidates. Taubeneck even hoped that the conventions themselves would meet together to name their candidates on a single platform. One prominent Silver Populist surveyed these actions and announced, "The one and vitally important thing we have done here is the determination arrived at to join forces with the silverites and ignore all side issues of whatever nature."[6]

So determined, the Silver Populists then left for Washington to help shape the silverites into a group with which they could combine in July. But the initiative the Populists had cherished as the vanguard of reform in the early 1890s was now completely gone, and the Silver Populists maneuvered into a rather subservient cooperation with the nonpartisan silver men. After consultation, both groups called their national conventions to meet on July 22, 1896, in St. Louis. Subsequently Stewart announced in his *Silver Knight* that union of all those who favored free silver was now assured. Similarly pleased, Taubeneck termed the Washington silver meeting "a grand success."[7]

[6] Paul Van Dervoort to Waite, January 20, 1896, Ralph Beaumont to Waite, January 19, 1896, E. I. Burdick to Waite, January 31, 1896, Waite Papers; *St. Louis Post-Dispatch*, January 16-20, 1896; *American Non-Conformist* (Indianapolis), January 23, 1896; *Southern Mercury*, January 30, 1896. See also Marion Butler to J. J. Mills, January 4, 1896, a form letter request for proxies, providing a blank form to return. Butler Papers.

[7] *People's Party Paper* (Atlanta), February 7, 1896; *Washington Post*, January

The measure of the change in Populism was evident in the comparatively mild protest against the actions of the Silver Populists in St. Louis and Washington. Those frustrated in their efforts at St. Louis to obtain an early convention and so preserve the independence of the party privately lamented afterwards that "the silver element ran things and we are to have our convention after the others have had theirs. We are to modify our principles so as not to hurt the sensitive feelings of the dissatisfied of the two old parties." Frequently they condemned as well the dictation of the Silver Populists and their manipulation of proxies. "As the situation is now," one wrote, "the so-called practical politician is in control. And principles are to be simply a foot ball to [be] tossed and kicked all about." From his experience, the old allianceman concluded, "I think I am too blunt for a politician and am simply an agitator." Peffer's *Advocate,* still opposed to the reduction of the Omaha Platform, reproved Taubeneck and the National Committee: "To be the successful head of a great party requires more ability than is necessary to fix up telegrams appointing proxies to suit the chairman, and more candor and truthfulness than has been exhibited by the chairman for the past two years. And it does not require any great ability or skill for a committee to wait and see what some other party is going to do." But the *Advocate* believed the committee had merely made an error in judgment and that Populists could only wait and hope for the best.[8]

Among major Populist newspapers, in fact, only the *Southern Mercury* stridently denounced the Silver Populists for deliberately planning to submerge Populism into the silver movement. Taubeneck and Patterson bore the brunt of the attack, but following the St. Louis meeting the *Mercury* wanted the whole committee revamped. Harry Tracy and Milton Park, publisher and editor of the Dallas newspaper, did not blame the silverites for intriguing with Populist leaders, "because that faction is composed of old party politicians who naturally cling to old party methods." They had a sharply different view, however, of Populists who favored

22, 23, 1896; Stanley L. Jones, *The Presidential Election of 1896* (Madison, Wis., 1964), p. 85; *Silver Knight-National Watchman,* January 30, 1896; H. E. Taubeneck to Ignatius Donnelly, February 18, 1896, Donnelly Papers.

8 Beaumont to Waite, January 19, 1896, Waite Papers; *Southern Mercury,* January 30, 1896; *Topeka Advocate,* January 22, 1896.

the same course. "As a reform party, seeking to deal honestly by the people and eradicate the abuses, corruption and rottenness that festers in the government, a result of old party rule, the people's party must pursue an open, honest course with the people, or it will fail in accomplishing the reforms it champions." Some local mid-road papers such as the *Kansas Agitator* similarly believed that the Populist politicians had betrayed Populism through their arrangements with the silver men, who, the *Agitator* pointed out, had declared their intention to nominate a silver candidate only if neither old party did so. "The leaders of this [Bimetallic] league have no sympathy with the demands of the Omaha platform . . . and the only use they have for our party is to pull their chestnuts out of the fire."[9]

The annual meeting of the NRPA in Dallas on February 22, 1896, vividly revealed how completely the Silver Populists had succeeded. Exactly one year earlier, the editors had held a tumultuous session, denouncing Taubeneck and his schemes, demanding his resignation, and appointing a committee to investigate him and his fellow one-plank Populists in Congress and on the National Committee. In 1896 Taubeneck attended the editorial meeting, expressed his preference for a silver campaign and fusion with other silver groups, and encountered no opposition. Pleasantries rather than diatribes and newspaper problems more than politics characterized the session. Taubeneck later wrote Donnelly of his success. "The Reform Press Association did good work," the chairman related. "Mr. Park and Tracey [*sic*] feel somewhat disappointed in not having things their way, but the sentiment for a union of forces was so strong that they could not stem the tide."[10]

While the mid-road papers were generally silent or moderate, moreover, the single-plank papers remained on the offensive. Perhaps most effective was Stewart's own *Silver Knight*, which he combined with the *National Watchman* after buying out Dunning in late 1895. Dunning himself continued to advocate Silver Populism in a weekly column published in many Populist papers. Just as vigorously, Dunning still denounced "socialists" and warned of

[9] *Southern Mercury,* January 30, 1896; *Kansas Agitator* (Garnett), January 24, 1896.
[10] *Dallas Morning News,* February 21-24, 1896; Taubeneck to Donnelly, February 29, 1896, Donnelly Papers.

the "secret organization which they have inside our party" which might gain control of the convention and insist on issues other than silver! Immediately after the National Committee meeting at St. Louis, Dunning even countered mid-road complaints by suggesting that socialists, being "well-supplied with money," might buy proxies to gain their ends. "For one," wrote Dunning, "I hope to see the time when 'short-haired' women and 'wild-eyed' men will no longer be a directing force in the reform movement."[11]

These views met an increasingly receptive audience. Not just in the West but throughout the South, Populists advocated a union with the silverites and declared their readiness to repudiate all reform demands save silver. Although the *Advocate, Southern Mercury,* and *Non-Conformist* continued to oppose Silver Populism, most politicians and papers submitted to the plans of Taubeneck, Weaver, and Stewart until an anguished Davis Waite could cry out against "Populist Paralysis" in late spring. "The paralysis that has befallen the People's Party," he complained, "—that has silenced every rostrum and halted all party progress in the most triumphant march ever made by a new political organization, is occasioned by a spirit of cowardly compromise and desertion of principle by those who were put in charge of party affairs on account of their presumed loyalty to the Omaha platform."[12]

In the meantime, Silver Populists worked to secure compliant delegations to the Populist national convention. In Texas in February, Taubeneck addressed the Populist State Committee, which then resolved in favor of a union of all silver advocates and praised him for his efforts. Taubeneck gloated to Donnelly that "the Delegation from Texas, in spite of the *Southern Mercury,* will be instructed for a union of forces. All the members of the State Committee including some fifty local papers have declared for it. The *Southern Mercury* does not represent the Populist Party of Texas." With Stewart he encouraged fusion in Oregon's early state election as another step toward an obedient delegation to the

11 *Southern Mercury,* February 20, 1896; *Silver Knight-National Watchman,* January 23, 30, 1896; Effie M. Mack, "Life and Letters of William Morris Stewart" (Ph.D. diss., University of California, 1930), pp. 277-78; *People's Party Paper,* January 3, February 7, 21, April 3, 1896.

12 W. M. Raymond to Henry Lloyd, February 28, 1896, Lloyd Papers; *People's Party Paper,* May 8, 1896.

national convention, and Weaver campaigned there in the interests of Silver Populism, warning mid-roader Jacob Coxey to withdraw. Elsewhere, one state after another instructed its delegates for silver fusion until Taubeneck exulted on February 29 that "everything now is facing in that direction." By early spring he estimated that 375 of the 400 delegates already chosen had been instructed for fusion "on a purely silver platform, in which other questions should be ignored." The Iowa Populist convention, under Weaver's and Taubeneck's personal management, was atypical only in its lack of pretense. After Taubeneck told the Iowans to "do nothing by word or action to offend the silver wings of the two older parties," they specifically voted down a minority report that called for a reaffirmation of the Omaha Platform, and instead enjoined their delegation to support silver fusion.[13] There would be no need to stampede the Populist national convention for silver and fusion; it was already so instructed.

In Kansas, the Populists met to select delegates on March 18, 1896. Taubeneck attended to urge Populists to cooperate with all silver elements, and he appeared before the resolutions committee and helped secure a weak platform, emphasizing financial reform and ignoring the old Populist demands. A few Populists warned that Taubeneck's course would destroy their movement, but under the direction of Breidenthal, Harris, Lewelling, and Simpson, the convention rejected mid-road proposals and adopted the platform, called for a union of all those opposed to the gold standard, and instructed the chosen delegates accordingly. The Silver Populists were delighted with these results. The *Silver Knight* was particularly pleased that the fusionist delegation to the national convention "will be headed by John W. Breidenthal, whose principle in politics is to get there if possible." This silver newspaper dismissed the radical challenge as easily as had the convention: "A few old style Alliance men who came to the convention are disgusted and disheartened, but they are no longer at the head of the organization, and they will be whipped into line." The con-

---

[13] *Southern Mercury*, February 27, May 14, 1896; Taubeneck to Donnelly, February 18, 29, May 15, 1896, Donnelly Papers; Stewart to Sylvester Pennoyer, March 13, 26, 1896, Stewart Papers; *Topeka Advocate*, April 29, 1896; *Des Moines Leader*, April 23, 1896.

vention's action further elated Taubeneck, Breidenthal, and Simpson, the paper reported, for it opened the way to state and national fusion.[14]

Indeed, a desire for fusion in Kansas to promote personal political ambitions was a major factor helping Taubeneck's position prevail. As early as February, one prominent politician remarked that if Taubeneck and his allies managed to control the national convention and nominate a silver-only candidate, then fusion on a state ticket would be forced upon the Populist and Democratic parties in Kansas. This promised consequence of national fusion was welcomed by those who believed it would assure their own political success. Harris and Lewelling both coveted the gubernatorial nomination; Simpson hoped to secure again joint nominations for Congress; and Breidenthal desired Peffer's seat in the Senate. Together these four men aided in shaping the convention to stress popular financial reform, slight other Populist issues, and appeal for a union of silver forces.[15]

The control of silver and fusion sentiment within the People's party was nowhere so evident as in the virtual absence of discussion as to the probable Populist presidential candidate. Though in comparison to the old parties, Populists had shown little interest in possible nominees in 1892, in 1896 they considered the question even less. Those men mentioned, moreover, revealed the bankrupt nature of the program of the Silver Populists, for they were overwhelmingly not Populists. Even Taubeneck, the party's chairman and foremost architect of the policy of capturing silver sentiment, responded to a reporter's question about possible candidates with three names: Sibley, Bland, and Bryan. Most Populists, whether consciously or not, were already playing a passive, defeatist role in national politics. Only the few isolated mid-roaders recommended Populists for the party's nomination in the spring of 1896. Peffer actually received more presidential endorsements in 1896 than in 1892 simply because of his loyal adherence to original Populism and because only mid-road papers were disposed to make sug-

14 *Kansas City Star*, March 18, 19, 1896; *Kansas Semi-Weekly Capital* (Topeka), March 20, 1896; W. Scott Morgan to Waite, April 1, 1896, Waite Papers; *Southern Mercury*, April 23, May 7, 1896.

15 *Kansas Semi-Weekly Capital*, February 18, March 20, 24, 1896; *Kansas Agitator*, January 17, 1896.

gestions. The *Ohio Populist,* for instance, proposed a ticket of Peffer and Eugene Debs. "Of all the populists who have figured prominently in public life," it declared, "none have 'wobbled' less than Senator Peffer. None have been more fearless and outspoken in defense of the whole principles laid down in the Omaha platform. Not once has he ever dodged, apologized, or 'flunked.' He has stood squarely on the whole populist platform, and has bravely defended it in its entirety."[16]

Such endorsements were only complimentary, however, for they ran distinctly counter to the drift of the party. Peffer continued to oppose a fusion of existing parties and the disavowal of any fundamental Populist principles. He particularly objected to the Populist surrender implicit in the suggestions of the Silver Populists that the party would accept a pure silverite as its candidate. Populists should determine their own course and nominate true Populists, not silverites, Peffer argued in his *Advocate.* He did not exclude converts, but he was adamant against those men who proposed to stand apart from Populism regardless of political developments. "The People's Party is in more danger from professed silver friends than from any other source," he wrote, "and if we will but look closely after our own beliefs and see that they are not bartered for promises of doubtful validity, we will retain our own self-respect and win the admiration of honest men of all parties."[17]

The Populist leadership, of course, did not recognize the wisdom of Peffer's statement, but the wily John Martin verified its accuracy with a perceptive comment of his own. "If the Democrats nominate the right kind of man on a proper platform," he declared in March, "the free silver Pops and free silver Republicans will vote with us. Those parties are not being conducted on logical plans and by proper action the Democrats will gain the support of thousands of the members of those parties."[18]

That the Democrats would take "proper action" and thus attempt to swallow the People's party without imbibing Populism seemed clear to Peffer by April 1896. In that month, as Democratic con-

16 *Southern Mercury,* January 30, July 2, 1896.
17 *Topeka Advocate,* March 25, April 22, 1896.
18 *Kansas Semi-Weekly Capital,* March 24, 1896.

ventions of state after state declared for silver, he asked in the *Advocate,* "If the Democratic National Convention Declares for Free Silver Coinage, then What of the People's Party?" Silver Democrats had no intention of bolting their party to join the People's party, he asserted; they proposed to control their own party. He believed, moreover, that they would be successful and name a silver candidate on a silver platform, thereby creating a crisis for the People's party. Criticizing those Populists who had helped bring on this difficulty by working with the Democrats, Peffer lamented that the Populist national convention should have been scheduled before those of the old parties. Nevertheless, he decided that Populists should make their own platform and name their own candidate as a distinct party, regardless of what the other parties did, and not "run away after false gods."[19]

Other Populists became similarly concerned over the possibility that the Democrats might declare for silver. L. D. Raynolds, mid-road editor of the *Chicago Express,* anticipated that "the charge will be that we are not consistent friends of silver if we refuse to fuse and if we do fuse it means death. The mistake I think is dawning on the minds of every true populist that was honest in the opinion that a late convention was best." Raynolds, however, did not consider Taubeneck or Weaver either true Populists or honest in their opinions. In fact, Taubeneck, writing over two weeks later, still expected that "the gold bugs" would control the Democratic as well as the Republican convention and believed the Populists would receive large numbers of Silver Democrats into the ranks. Weaver had come to realize the strength of the Silver Democrats, but a Democratic candidate on a silver platform held no fears for him. He did advise Bryan in late May to have the Democratic national convention make only provisional nominations but promised to do "all in my power" at the Populist convention to bring about fusion regardless. He had already expressed his willingness to have the Populists endorse Bryan if the latter received the Democratic nomination, and Weaver encouraged Iowa Populists to view favorably a Silver Democrat for president.[20]

19 *Topeka Advocate,* April 29, May 6, 1896.
20 L. D. Raynolds to Waite, April 30, 1896, Waite Papers; Taubeneck to Donnelly, May 15, 1896, Donnelly Papers; Weaver to Bryan, May 29, 1896, and L. W. Rissler to Bryan, May 16, 1896, Bryan Papers.

Throughout May and June, Peffer used the *Advocate* to fight the possibility that the Populists would be subsumed in a Silver Democracy. He repeatedly denied any connection other than silver between the two parties and instead linked the Democracy to the GOP as an avowed foe of Populism. The Populists should therefore keep in the middle of the road, he asserted, even if the Democrats declared for silver. Rather than ignoring issues other than silver, Peffer even announced that throughout July he would write a series of articles on "Government Ownership and Management of Railroads." The *Topeka Capital* acutely remarked, "Senator Peffer is too old-fashioned. He should come home, put his ear to the prairie and get in touch with the 'new Populism,' which long ago outgrew the government ownership fad."[21]

The party leadership moved to protect that new Populism from the attacks of the original Populists. In late May, Senator William V. Allen denied in the Senate that Populists had ever believed in irredeemable money. This capped a long series of Allen senatorial speeches designed to illustrate Populist conservatism and permit Populist-Democratic fusion on silver. Also in May, the National Committee established a news bureau to provide Populist readers with a stream of propaganda advocating one-plank silver Populism and fusion, supporting the decision for a late convention, and creating presidential booms for old party silverites. The *Cleveland* (Ohio) *Citizen* denounced this "alleged news agency" established by "Taubeneck and his satellites," and the *Missouri World* complained that its weekly newsletter represented "little less than a constant attack upon the proposition to adhere to the principles of our party." Taubeneck then renewed his attack on the antifusion Populist press and again hinted that the *Topeka Advocate* was a socialist, not a Populist, newspaper.[22]

Mid-roaders hastened to reply. One loyal Populist paper in Kansas defended the *Advocate* against Taubeneck with a bitter countercharge that the chairman was "a dickering, trading, self-seeking politician." Another censured "the double-dealing of our

[21] *Topeka Advocate,* May 13, 20, June 17, 24, 1896; *Topeka Daily Capital,* May 28, 1896.
[22] *Southern Mercury,* January 31, 1895, May 7, June 11, 1896; *Kansas Agitator,* May 15, 1896. See especially *Congressional Record,* 53d Cong., 3d sess., vol. 27, pp. 971-82.

national chairman, H. E. Taubeneck, and his little coterie of self-appointed leaders, Weaver, Turner, and others, who would willingly turn the People's Party over to the Democrats for the chance of a little political preferment and patronage." The *Kansas Agitator* recalled that "Judas betrayed Christ for thirty pieces of silver. Will those Judases who would betray the People's Party (for silver?) still further follow his example—go and hang themselves?"[23]

Thus, divided and bickering, the People's party awaited the first of the national conventions of 1896. But both factions knew which held the upper hand in the party. The Silver Populists not only controlled the party's organization but also included nearly all prominent Populists and a large majority of the convention delegates in their ranks. Not surprisingly, the Silver Populists expressed confidence. Raynolds spoke the fears of the mid-roaders when he wrote Waite, "I am afraid that matters will go badly astray" at the Populist national convention. Both groups, however, were in an awkward position because of the late convention. The party's Illinois state chairman expressed the Populist predicament best: "Of course we cannot say with any degree of certainty what the result will be but this I do know the present is fraught with great possibilities for our Party; However just at this time it is more or less subject to contingencies over which we have no control."[24]

The Republican national convention opened in St. Louis on June 16 under the complete domination of the political forces of William McKinley. Declaring itself "unreservedly for sound money," the convention nominated McKinley and jeered Senator Teller and other silverites out of the hall. The bolters then organized the Silver Republican party and publicly called all those who favored bimetallism to unite behind Teller as a joint presidential candidate.[25]

The Silver Populists at once recognized the barren nature of their policy, though they had long anticipated McKinley's nomination, the gold platform, and the Silver Republican bolt. If the

---

23 *Kansas Agitator*, May 15, 22, 1896; *Girard World*, May 21, 1896.

24 Raynolds to Waite, April 30, 1896, Waite Papers; A. L. Maxwell to Lloyd, May 13, 1896, Lloyd Papers.

25 *St. Louis Post-Dispatch*, June 17, 19, 1896; Jones, *Election of 1896*, pp. 169-73.

Democrats declared for silver, as now appeared likely, the People's party would be destroyed. In the far West, Populists had never been more than silverites with a few exceptions such as Waite, and now Patterson and Stewart led the region's Populists; they would vote with either major party that advocated silver. In the Midwest and Plains, the Populists by 1896 overwhelmingly depended upon former Democrats for their strength and were accustomed to fusion campaigns with the Democrats under the leadership of Weaver, Allen, Breidenthal, Harris, and others; these Populists too would prefer a Silver Democrat candidate to tenacious adherence to a Populist program and nominee. Even in the South, a Silver Democratic ticket would weaken Populism severely, for though Populists and Democrats held bitter feelings for each other, the silver education of the past three years would convince many Populists that their traditional party had returned to proper Democracy and so should they; moreover, the foremost Southern Populist, Butler, was completely committed to a free silver campaign, and much of the alleged Populist strength in the South was anticipatory only, dependent upon a Democratic rejection of silver which now seemed improbable.

The Silver Populist leadership seized upon Teller's projected candidacy as the only opportunity to redeem at least partially its position and retain some influence in the prospective silver union. Some conferences between Silver Republicans and Populists had already been held before the Republican convention, resulting in a tentative understanding that, suddenly, the interests of the two groups were similar and could be best met by concerted action to secure Teller's nomination first by the Democratic national convention and then by the Populists and the silverites. Taubeneck, Patterson, and other members of the Populist National Committee were in St. Louis to observe the Republican convention and, after conferring with the Republican silverites following their bolt, the Populist officials issued their own address urging Populists and all other silver groups to nominate Teller.[26]

Speaking of the impending Democratic convention, Taubeneck

[26] Elmer Ellis, "The Silver Republicans in the Election of 1896," *Mississippi Valley Historical Review* 18 (March 1932): 524-27; M. C. Rankin to Donnelly, June 9, 1896, and Taubeneck to Donnelly, June 20, 22, 1896, Donnelly Papers; *People's Party Paper*, June 26, 1896; *St. Louis Post-Dispatch*, June 20, 1896.

declared that the Democrats "must take Teller." Such a position was politically unrealistic. The Silver Democrats were the masters of the situation and would not waste their efforts of the past few years by nominating a Republican. This desperate maneuver of the Silver Populists only revealed more clearly how their own earlier unreasonable and perverted actions had trapped them. Deception had become self-deception.[27]

Unswerving Populists quickly denounced the Populist Teller address. Peffer declared that Teller deserved praise but not the Populist nomination for leaving the GOP. The party must have a Populist candidate, he asserted, and not merely a silver candidate. Moreover, Peffer objected to Taubeneck's continuing willingness to dictate to the party, especially on the eve of the national convention, and considered such action arrogant and "treacherous." Robert Schilling, the veteran Wisconsin Populist, also opposed Taubeneck's new scheme, declaring, "I am raising hell about the Teller address. They wanted me to sign it, but I refused point blank. These fellows run off after strange gods at every opportunity."[28]

Once again Clemens provided the most fitting mid-road critique of the policies of the Silver Populists. "I warned the People's Party that its managers were pursuing a dangerous course in giving undue prominence in their campaigns to free coinage," he wrote, "that, should the Democrats nominate free silver candidates on a free silver platform, our resolutions and papers would enable them to condemn us out of our own mouths for even keeping up our party organization instead of joining them." For, he continued, selfish politicians had proved faithless to Populism and had instead proclaimed "the paramount and pressing importance of a union of all in favor of free coinage." "But I was not heeded," Clemens reminded others. "I was 'an extremist.' I was not 'a practical politician.' "[29]

Clemens believed that the Populists had become the "dumb

---

[27] Taubeneck to Donnelly, June 20, 1896, Donnelly Papers; Jones, *Election of 1896*, p. 208; Paul W. Glad, *McKinley, Bryan, and the People* (Philadelphia, 1964), pp. 129-30.

[28] *Topeka Advocate*, June 24, 1896; *New York Times*, June 26, 1896; *Kansas Agitator*, July 3, 1896; Robert Schilling to Donnelly, June 22, 1896, Donnelly Papers.

[29] *Topeka Advocate*, June 17, 1896.

chattels" of autocratic leaders such as Taubeneck and Weaver, and indeed, the Silver Populists brushed aside criticism of their new course and offered to deliver Populist votes to a Republican candidate on a Democratic ticket. Taubeneck and Butler, in particular, insisted that the Democrats nominate Teller or be responsible for the disruption of the silver forces. Other Populists joined them in Chicago in early July to pressure the Democrats. Simpson promised Democrats that the People's party would ratify the Democratic nomination of Teller, while Taubeneck and Weaver issued a manifesto demanding that Democrats rise above partisanship and name Teller as a nonpartisan candidate upon whom the Populists and other silver elements could unite. A reporter for the *Chicago Tribune* aptly described the Populist maneuvers as "a grand game of bluff" and declared that "this is an evident case of the tail making strenuous efforts to swing the dog, but it not only will not work but is manifestly ridiculous."[30]

Teller must have agreed with the reporter, for from the start he never believed in the delusion to which the Silver Populists clung. Convinced that the Democrats would never nominate a Republican, Teller announced that the Silver Republicans would support a Silver Democrat and contended that his own nomination would be unwise. His announcement sent the short-sighted Silver Populists reeling again, for they finally recognized that their lavish praise of Teller would simply backfire if he supported a Democrat. Teller's slim chances in Chicago soon died altogether with the rise of William Jennings Bryan.[31]

Bryan had long worked assiduously if quietly toward the Democratic presidential nomination. No one in the Democracy had better silver credentials, and the Chicago convention was a silver convention. He received the nomination on the fifth ballot and an Eastern silverite, Arthur M. Sewall, a Maine banker and shipbuilder, balanced the ticket as the vice-presidential nominee. The platform unequivocally repudiated Cleveland in declaring not only

---

30 Taubeneck to Butler, July 2, 1896, Butler Papers; Butler to Stewart, June 24, July 6, 1896, and Stewart to A. J. Utley, July 2, 1896, Stewart Papers: *Chicago Tribune,* July 1, 2, 5, 7, 1896; *St. Louis Post-Dispatch,* July 8, 1896; Taubeneck to Donnelly, June 20, 1896, Donnelly Papers; Elmer Ellis, *Henry Moore Teller* (Caldwell, Idaho, 1941), p. 270.

31 Ellis, *Teller,* pp. 269-72: *Chicago Tribune,* July 1, 1896; Butler to Stewart, July 6, 1896, Stewart Papers.

for silver, but against bond issues and government by injunction and for an income tax and stricter federal regulation of railroads and trusts.[32]

Bryan's nomination on a silver platform threw the People's party into a turmoil. Some Southern Populists recoiled from the notion of cooperating with the Democrats, fearing that a Populist endorsement of Bryan would destroy their party and subject them to still further humiliation, discrimination, and violence at the hands of the Democrats. "Don't be deceived," warned the *Southern Mercury*. "Experience should teach us to 'fear the Greeks even when bearing gifts.'" Those "gift" planks, Southern mid-roaders argued, were inconsistent with the record of the Democratic party and were therefore designed only to attract Populist votes and eliminate the only important opposition to continued Democratic control of the South. And yet, with very few exceptions, Southern Populists were not opposed to fusion in theory. They had frequently fused with Republicans in the South and had eagerly cooperated with both Silver Republicans and the silver party; they had disproportionately supported Taubeneck's scheme to arrange a fusion on Teller and some still favored the Populist nomination of the Republican. The expedient Butler, moreover, was already considering plans for fusion with the Democrats in North Carolina before Bryan's nomination, and inclined toward the Populist acceptance of the Nebraskan after initial reluctance. Other prominent Southern Populists also urged Bryan's endorsement, including James G. Field of Virginia, the party's 1892 vice-presidential candidate, and Reuben Kolb, who as Alabama's foremost Populist had probably suffered as much from Democratic practices as any white Southerner. Truly less radical than the original Western Populists, moreover, Southerners had generally supported the scheme to narrow Populism to silver, particularly Butler and John H. McDowell but also such alleged mid-roaders as Cyclone Davis and Harry Skinner.[33]

[32] Glad, *McKinley, Bryan, and the People*, p. 130; William Jennings Bryan, *The First Battle* (Chicago, 1896), pp. 406-9.

[33] *Southern Mercury*, July 16, 1896; *St. Louis Post-Dispatch*, June 20, July 13, 1896; *New York Times*, July 21, 1896; Robert F. Durden, *The Climax of Populism: The Election of 1896* (Lexington, Ky., 1965), pp. 24-25; W. H. Kitchin to Butler, June 5, 1896, W. S. Bailey to Butler, June 8, 1896, Butler to C. A. Nash, January 6, 1895, Butler Papers; *Louisiana Populist* (Natchitoches), June 26, July 17, 1896.

The urban, radical Populists of the upper Midwest also opposed Bryan's endorsement, but again like the Southerners their opposition too often had no durable foundation. Many of them favored the nomination of either Eugene Debs or Jacob Coxey, but neither would consent to run against Bryan, and members of this faction slowly drifted to the Democrat. Even George Washburn, the Massachusetts Populist who had consistently fought Weaver and Taubeneck, decided that the Populists had no choice but to nominate Bryan. Henry D. Lloyd remained the sharpest critic of the Silver Populists and the Bryan boom. Even before Bryan's Democratic nomination, Lloyd complained that the delegates chosen by the Silver Populists for the national convention would never insist upon Populism, and he castigated Taubeneck for his misguided schemes.

The simple truth is Taubeneck has been flim-flammed. The politicians at Washington got hold of him, persuaded him that "free silver" was the supreme issue. . . . They got him to turn all the party maneuvers into building up this silver issue. Then they sweep in at Chicago, pocket the whole thing for themselves, and leave us at St. Louis only the Hobson's choice of sinking ourselves out of sight and resurrection in the Democracy; or, of beginning, de novo, within a few weeks of election, the task of making an issue and finding followers. The masses have been taught by us that "silver" is *the issue,* and they will of course have the common sense to give their votes to the most powerful of the parties promising it. If the management of the party had been in the hands of *really* practical politicians, instead of "Glaubenichts" like Taubeneck, the full Omaha platform could easily have been made the issue that would have held us together for a brilliant campaign, but now that cannot be done. If we fuse, we are sunk; if we don't fuse, all the silver men we have will leave us for the more powerful Democrats. And this is what Glaubenichts Taubeneck calls politics! Curious that the new party, the Reform party, the People's Party should be more boss-ridden, ring-ruled, gang-gangrened than the two old parties of monopoly. The party that makes itself the special champion of the Referendum and Initiative tricked out of its very life and soul by a permanent National Chairman—something no other party has! Our Initiative and Referendum had better begin, like Charity, at home.

Three days later, Lloyd again denounced the party officials and leaders for having diverted attention from real issues by emphasizing silver. Moreover, "the way in which the managers of the P. P. have schemed to deliver it first to the Republican Teller, then to the Democratic Bryan, is one of the most amazing exhibitions of 'politics' I ever heard of."[34]

The Populists of the Midwest and prairies generally felt no such qualms about either Bryan or the importance of silver. By 1896, these Populists were largely of Democratic antecedents, accustomed to fusion campaigns with the Democrats, and fully committed to Silver Populism; and they eagerly greeted Bryan's nomination and anticipated uniting behind him with the Democrats. Weaver announced for Bryan while still in Chicago seeking Teller's nomination! Senator Kyle strongly advocated the Populist nomination of Bryan. The Nebraska Populists, led by Bryan's friend Senator Allen, welcomed the new opportunity to work with the Democrat.[35]

Nearly all Kansas Populist leaders announced at once in favor of the Populist nomination of both Bryan and Sewall. Simpson, Harris, Breidenthal, and Lewelling, leaders of the state's delegation to the Populist national convention, all declared their intention to secure the nomination of both Democrats. Lewelling, eloquent as ever in the defense of compromise, declared that if the Democratic platform did not provide "all the measures which we have sought, we will by the election of Bryan, at least be able to strike a light by which we shall see our way clear to the ultimate triumph of the people over their oppressors." Breidenthal did not even regret the absence of Populist measures from the Democratic platform. He asserted that "the Populists could scarcely have done any better if they had been given full control of the Chicago convention," and he described the Democratic platform as "right in line with Populist principles and . . . acceptable to the great majority of Populists of the West." Even those such as John Davis who had recommended an early convention and a middle-of-the-road course reluctantly consented to fusion on Bryan, remarking that the position followed by the party leaders left the Populists with no choice. Populist county conventions throughout the state met hurriedly to endorse Bryan and instruct their delegates accordingly.[36]

34 Ray Ginger, *The Bending Cross: A Biography of Eugene Victor Debs* (New Brunswick, N.J., 1949), pp. 188-90; *New York Times,* July 21, 1896: Lloyd to R. I. Grimes, July 10, 1896, and Lloyd to Bayard Holmes, July 13, 1896, Lloyd Papers.

35 L. W. Rissler to Bryan, May 16, 1896, and Kyle to Bryan, July 11, 1896, Bryan Papers; *People's Party Paper,* July 31, 1896.

Strong support had existed among Kansas Populists for a fusion campaign even before Bryan's nomination. In fact, Breidenthal announced before the Republican convention that Populists would yield to Democrats and endorse their candidate if he subscribed to silver. Harris likewise hoped to arrange both national and state fusion on the sole issue of free silver. His lieutenant, William H. Sears, a former Democrat and now a nominal Populist, wrote Bryan before the Democratic national convention, advocating a fusion on the Democratic nominee and urging him to induce the Populists to accept such a course. Many Populists indicated their readiness in the numerous June conventions that resolved in favor of a national silver fusion with the Democrats. The July Democratic nomination of Bryan merely fired such Populists with more enthusiasm.[37]

Silver Populists of the Far West were just as unreservedly for Bryan. The state chairman of the Colorado People's party declared that the state's delegation to the Populist national convention would support Bryan, and other Colorado Populists such as Patterson and Pence similarly advocated his nomination. Teller urged Silver Republicans to endorse Bryan and assured the Democrat that Patterson would "do you much good at St. Louis." Even Waite was jubilant over Bryan's nomination and wrote Donnelly, "Of course I support him." Stewart, never more than a Silver Populist, saw Populism in the Silver Democracy. "The majority who controlled the [Democratic] convention," he wrote Butler, "were as emphatically Populistic in their sentiments and actions as you yourself. The platform is radical enough for you or me." Stewart would use his *Silver Knight* to promote the Populist nomination of both Bryan and Sewall.[38]

[36] *Kansas Semi-Weekly Capital*, July 14, 24, 1896; *St. Louis Post-Dispatch*, July 12, 1896; John Davis Scrapbook, vol. G, p. 50, KSHS; *Marshall County Democrat* (Marysville), July 24, 1896; *Topeka Daily Capital*, July 11, 1896; *Topeka Advocate*, July 22, 1896; *Kansas Agitator*, July 24, 1896; Ruppenthal Scrapbook, vol. 5, p. 29.

[37] *St. Louis Post-Dispatch*, June 11, 1896; *Kansas Semi-Weekly Capital*, June 23, 26, 1896; Sears to Bryan, June 23, 1896, Sears Papers.

[38] H. G. Clar to Bryan, July 10, 1896, and Teller to Bryan, July 15, 1896, Bryan Papers; *Topeka Daily Capital*, July 11, 1896; *St. Louis Post-Dispatch*, July 16, 1896; Waite to Donnelly, July 12, 1896, Donnelly Papers; Stewart to Butler, July 14, 1896, Stewart Papers.

Virtually alone among major Western Populists, Peffer did not immediately endorse Bryan or fusion. In early summer he had warned that fusion should not be considered inevitable if the Democrats adopted a silver platform, that the Populists could not consent to sacrifice their principles, that if the Democrats desired Populist assistance the time to seek it was before the Democratic convention. Peffer restated this position after the Republican convention in announcing his rejection of the Silver Populist scheme to nominate Teller. While he was convinced the Democrats would be for silver, he was equally confident that they would not commit themselves to other principles vital to Populism. "I had hoped," he repeated, "that there might be some amalgamation of Democrats, Populists, and silver men and others on a declaration of principles, and, if need be, a new name. But the time for that has gone by, and all that remains is for the Populist party to maintain its integrity by nominating its own candidates on its own platform."[39]

Peffer's defense of Populist integrity and independence met with stinging abuse among Kansas Populists. Surprised at the uniformity and pervasiveness of the opposition to his stand, Peffer retreated slightly but adhered to his long-expressed general position. Teller might be a good choice, he admitted, if the various reform elements joined to form a new and permanent party and then to nominate a candidate. But, he warned, Populists should not foolishly expect either a Democratic nomination of anyone other than a Democrat or a postponement of the Democratic convention in order to permit all reformers to participate equally and honestly in the formation of a new major party. Without such action, he believed, the People's party could not honorably do other than name its own candidate on its own platform. If cooperation with other silver elements was still thought necessary, a partial fusion could later be arranged on the electoral tickets in each state. The Democratic nomination of a Populist for vice president, he suggested, might be the best means to effect such limited cooperation as desirable.[40]

When the Democracy at Chicago performed according to Peffer's expectations rather than his hopes, he responded predictably.

[39] *New York Times,* June 11, 1896; *Southern Mercury,* July 9, 1896.
[40] *Topeka Advocate,* July 1, 1896; *Kansas Agitator,* July 3, 1896; *Kansas City Star,* July 14, 1896.

Praising Bryan as an able and honorable man, and commending the Democratic party for its generally progressive attitude, Peffer nevertheless told a reporter, "I think it would be improper for the Populist national convention to endorse Mr. Bryan. In fact, I think the Populists should adopt their own platform, name their own candidate for President, and maintain organization." Again, however, he expressed his belief that combinations on electoral tickets could insure a solid vote for financial reform while not compromising Populism or its ultimate triumph.[41]

Again Peffer was assaulted by Kansans as one who was out of touch with the new Populism. The totality and the fury of the condemnation made him once more explain his position. Though some accused him of "hedging" in a desire to gain reelection, and though obviously he continued to retreat from his solitary opposition to the course of the People's party, Peffer remained distinct from the flaccid Populists who urged total capitulation, and his position retained a basic consistency.[42]

Five days after Bryan's nomination, Peffer wrote an editorial entitled "Present Duty of Populists." "Events of the last four weeks," he declared, "have so changed the political situation that a grave responsibility has been suddenly thrust upon the Populist party." Instead of equivocating, the Republicans had "boldly and plainly espoused the cause of the money power," which portended "class rule, oppression of the poor—debt, poverty, perpetual enslavement of the masses." The Democrats, by contrast, had accepted the challenge and partially "espoused the people's side" by calling for an end to bond issues and national bank notes and for an income tax as well as free silver in their financial plank. The Populist responsibility was to defeat McKinley and what he represented, for the Populists had enough votes, Peffer maintained, when united with others demanding financial reform, "to win this battle for the people." Nevertheless, he asserted that the Populists should reaffirm the Omaha Platform and, though suggesting holding conferences with other financial reformers to arrange necessary cooperation, he did not advocate Bryan's nomination by Populists.[43]

41 *Topeka Daily Capital,* July 11, 1896.
42 *Kansas City Star,* July 14, 1896.
43 *Topeka Advocate,* July 15, 1896. See Norman Pollack, *The Populist Re-*

Peffer also wrote to the *Kansas Commoner* at the same time, revealing his modified stance. "The conversion of the Democracy," he wrote, made it "the wise and patriotic course" for Populists to unite against the oppression of the gold standard. But he emphasized, "We can do this and still maintain our organization for future use." The *Commoner* and other papers read this as an indication that Peffer had withdrawn his opposition to Bryan's nomination and would support the Nebraskan. "With the accession of Senator Peffer to the Bryan forces," the Associated Press reported, "the Populists of Kansas are practically a unit for the Democratic nominee."[44]

As the Populists descended upon St. Louis in mid-July, there seemed a strong possibility that the party might actually split over the question of nominating Bryan. Although historians have focused on the "extremist minority of mid-road Populists, who were ready to split the party rather than accept Bryan," Western Populists, with their solitary commitment to silver, were even more arrogant and determined to split the party if necessary to have Bryan. Stewart, for instance, declared that as Western Populists supported Bryan exclusively, "any attempt to run an opposition candidate by the Populists will be a failure and will destroy the Populist Party." Insisting that Populists approve Bryan, Stewart added that "the attitude of the Southern delegates will have no effect at all." Simpson proved just as imperious. "So far as Kansas is concerned," he remarked, "it matters not what this convention does. We will endorse Bryan and vote for silver." Waite, himself a radical who supported Bryan, commented, "The Southern delegates are not so radical as they were, but they are still sore enough to walk out of the convention if they are not given their own way. On the other hand, the silver men from the West are generally determined to have Bryan or walk out."[45]

In the face of the two antagonistic demands to accept totally and

---

sponse to Industrial America (Cambridge, Mass., 1962), pp. 107-10, for a discussion of the *Advocate's* course.

[44] *Kansas Semi-Weekly Capital,* July 17, 1896; *New York Times,* July 16, 1896.

[45] Durden, *Climax of Populism,* p. 28; Stewart to Butler, July 14, 1896, Stewart Papers; *Kansas Semi-Weekly Capital,* July 21, 1896; *St. Louis Post-Dispatch,* July 18, 1896; *Chicago Tribune,* July 22, 1896; Sears to W. A. Harris, July 24, 1896, Sears Papers.

to repudiate entirely the decision of the Chicago convention, a number of compromise proposals were presented to preserve the unity and identity of the People's party. Though each had its special champions at St. Louis and historians have debated the identity of their initial advocates, each major compromise measure eventually adopted in some form in 1896 had antecedents in Peffer's articles, letters, and interviews during the early summer in contemplation of possible reform alliances. It is, of course, impossible to determine his actual influence in formulating these compromises at the convention itself, for, as he was not a delegate, his public participation in the convention was confined to various honorary appearances. But he was quite visible in the activity surrounding the convention. As one reporter commented, "Senator Peffer, wise, whiskery, and wonderfully calm, in comparison with the intense, noisy, contentious throng of delegates, but just as cranky, extreme, and revolutionary in his way as any of them, sits about to give Senatorial advice."[46]

That advice was soon forthcoming. Arriving on July 18, four days before the convention opened, he refused to announce for Bryan as had been predicted. His editorials and letters had not endorsed Bryan and, as he told one reporter, they had been misconstrued. "There are only two points upon which I feel tenacious. The first is to maintain our party organization and the second is to combine the silver vote of the country." He urged the immediate reaffirmation of the Omaha Platform and the election of "a national executive committee to look after party affairs so as to preserve our party identity. There is no reason why we should abandon our doctrine or party." Second, he advocated the proportional representation of electors on a combined ticket with the selection of a common candidate to be made by them only after the election, either Bryan or the Populist nominee or, should the Populists make no nomination at all, from a group of Populist and Silver Democratic leaders. "That would allow all of us to vote according to party preferences, and it would relieve us of a great deal of friction that might otherwise occasion trouble."[47]

[46] *New York Times,* July 21, 1896.
[47] *Kansas City Star,* July 19, 1896; *St. Louis Post-Dispatch,* July 19, 1896; *New York Times,* July 21, 1896.

Peffer's proposal met with little favor at the divided convention. Mid-road leader Jacob Coxey did accept the basic plan and encouraged delegates to support it. The Kansas and Nebraska delegations, however, unanimously opposed Peffer's suggestions and argued for total endorsement of the Democratic ticket. Moreover, Bryan's representatives in St. Louis were reported as bitterly opposed to Peffer's plan as to that of the intransigents. Nevertheless, the proposal reemerged in the campaign in the policy of both Populists and Democrats in arranging fusion electoral tickets based on their respective strength in the various states, but with definite and specific commitments to candidates. It may also have influenced the decision of the convention to postpone the presidential nomination in order to achieve harmonious action.[48]

One surprising supporter of Peffer's plan was Taubeneck, who grasped it as the means to protect the independence of the People's party in the face of the demand for surrendering totally to the Democrats. Although other party officials such as J. H. Turner and Martin C. Rankin, secretary and treasurer of the Populist National Committee, had announced immediately for Bryan's endorsement—Turner even intimating that there was no further need of the People's party at all and that Populists should join the Democracy—Taubeneck reacted to Bryan's nomination with dismay. Initially favorable to Bryan, the chairman then decided that the People's party should avoid submersion in the Democratic campaign and nominate Teller after all. Teller, however, emphatically refused to be considered and urged all Populists to support Bryan. Taubeneck then declined to discuss publicly the question of Bryan's possible Populist nomination until the eve of the convention when he rejected it as representing "the surrender and destruction of the People's Party organization" and seized upon Peffer's plan as the party's salvation.[49]

Taubeneck's vacillation suggests that unlike such Silver Populists as Weaver and Stewart, who saw personal power and free silver as the only ultimate objectives, he had sincerely believed that his

48 *Kansas Semi-Weekly Capital*, July 21, 1896; *New York Times*, July 21, 1896; *St. Louis Post-Dispatch*, July 20, 1896.

49 *St. Louis Post-Dispatch*, July 15, 18, 19, 1896; Teller to Bryan, July 18, 1896, Bryan Papers; *New York Times*, July 21, 1896; *St. Louis Globe-Democrat*, July 20, 1896; John D. Hicks, *The Populist Revolt* (Minneapolis, 1931), p. 359.

schemes would deliver the nation's silver voters to the People's party. If so, however, it reveals at the same time that his "practical politics" were even more absurdly obtuse than the mid-roaders had earlier thought. In any event, the Western Populists doubted Taubeneck's sincerity, perhaps because they had worked closely with him before. They asserted that with his Teller manifesto he had tried to force upon the party a man who agreed with Populists only on silver but that he now opposed a man who agreed with them on many issues in addition to silver. Kansans particularly denounced Taubeneck for, they argued, he had formulated their state platform so that Democrats and silverites would accept his Populism; now the Democrats had adopted a stronger platform and fusion should be no less desirable. At St. Louis, Taubeneck soon reversed himself again and demanded the Populist endorsement of Bryan.[50] His political and, presumably, mental acrobatics so wearied all Populists by the end of the convention that he was not reelected national chairman and thereafter dropped out of Populist sight. Only the natural results of his misguided policies remained to torment the People's party.

The most immediate problem faced by the middle-of-the-road delegates was that of finding a candidate. Lloyd had hoped to focus the opposition on Debs, but Debs refused to be considered. Neither did Coxey desire to oppose Bryan. Some Southerners favored Charles Towne, a Minnesota Silver Republican, but Towne responded that all factions should support Bryan. On the eve of the convention, the Texas delegation, the largest and most determinedly anti-Bryan group, sent a committee to Peffer and promised to support him against Bryan. Peffer replied that Western Populists were so agreed upon Bryan that if he accepted the Populist nomination he would be unable to carry even a single county in his own state of Kansas. Josephus Daniels, an ardent Bryan Democrat reporting the Populist convention, explained the plight of the mid-road Populists on the day before the convention opened: "They cannot get a silver Republican or big Populist to accept the nomination."[51]

[50] *Kansas City Star,* July 17, 19, 1896; *St. Louis Post-Dispatch,* July 20, 1896.
[51] Eugene V. Debs to Lloyd, July 25, 1896, Lloyd Papers; *Abilene Monitor,* July 23, 1896; *Raleigh News and Observer,* July 22, 1896.

Accordingly, all but the most irreconcilable of the mid-road Populists agreed to accept Bryan's nomination provided the "plutocratic" Sewall were replaced with a Southern Populist. Peffer had suggested this, too, well before the Democratic convention as a possible means to consolidate the anti-gold forces, but Butler was the plan's leading advocate at the convention. Although fusion Populists Weaver, Harris, Lewelling, and Patterson rejected the scheme, it seemed to be the only answer to the plight of the convention, preserving the distinctiveness of the People's party and mollifying the unhappy Southerners while still substantially maintaining a unity of the silver forces. Only when most mid-roaders dropped their demand for an independent ticket—and even the Georgia, Tennessee, and Alabama delegations reported swings to Bryan—did Peffer finally agree to Bryan, convinced that a large majority favored his nomination in order to combine the opposition to the money power. Since the large Kansas delegation was vocally and unanimously for Bryan, some observers had been surprised at Peffer's obvious reluctance to support the Nebraskan. After his announcement, Peffer worked with other prominent Populists in the Bryan headquarters, but unlike them he approved the proposal to replace Sewall with a loyal Southern Populist.[52]

After hearing a long and conciliatory speech by Butler, as temporary chairman, the convention devoted most of the first day to committee meetings. On the second day, July 23, the delegates demonstrated their determination to consolidate political forces on Bryan and silver by electing Senator Allen as permanent chairman. Allen supported both candidates on the Democratic ticket and called for Populists not to "get into that stupid attitude where we are willing to stand so closely in the middle of the road that others will pass us in the race for success." Shortly thereafter the convention accepted the report of the resolutions committee, chaired by Weaver, and thus adopted a platform which stressed the financial question and invited the cooperation of all accordant groups. It seemed clear that Bryan would be nominated; those who opposed full capitulation to the Democracy would have to insist upon the

[52] *Topeka Advocate,* July 1, 1896; *St. Louis Post-Dispatch,* July 20, 22, 23, 1896; *Kansas City Star,* July 19, 23, 1896; *Kansas Semi-Weekly Capital,* July 21, 1896; *New York Journal,* July 23, 1896.

excision of Sewall from the ticket. The minority report of the committee on rules and procedures called for a reversal of the usual order of nominations and the selection of a vice-presidential nominee first, a maneuver designed to ensure the substitution of a Southern Populist for Sewall. The convention narrowly adopted this procedure.

Many Populists besides the mid-roaders believed the rumors that James K. Jones, Democratic national chairman, had promised to secure the withdrawal of Sewall for the Populist nominee if the Populists named Bryan to head their ticket. Thus hopeful, they nominated Tom Watson for the vice presidency, although Sewall received solid support from the Western states, including all but one of Kansas's ninety-two votes. Peffer was pleased with Watson's nomination, but Harris angrily refused to accept Sewall's defeat and the possible disruption of his own plans for fusion in Kansas. He promised that Western Populists would vote for Sewall in November anyway.[53]

Democrats Bryan and Jones also declined to countenance Sewall's defeat or his proposed replacement. In public telegrams, the two agreed that Bryan's name should be withdrawn if Sewall were not also nominated, and Bryan wired Allen privately his refusal to be a candidate if Sewall were rejected. Nevertheless, Weaver nominated Bryan, dismissed the candidate's views with the assertion that Bryan had no right to dictate to the convention, and Allen refused to release his telegram from Bryan. After seconding speeches by Taubeneck, Simpson, and others, the Populist convention agreed overwhelmingly with Weaver and nominated the Democrat for their party's highest honor.[54]

As the exhausted delegates left St. Louis, few Populists were pleased with the results of their convention. Most Western Populists intensely regretted the failure to nominate Sewall with Bryan and worried that the silver vote would be split after all. Southerners, including Watson, remained disappointed. Peffer had only reluctantly accepted Bryan and felt no great enthusiasm for the coming cam-

[53] Bryan, *First Battle*, p. 267; *St. Louis Post-Dispatch,* July 24, 25, 1896; *New York Times,* July 25, 1896; *Kansas City Star,* July 19, 25, 26, 1896; *Kansas Semi-Weekly Capital,* July 31, 1896; *Abilene Daily Reflector,* July 27, 1896.

[54] Hicks, *Populist Revolt,* pp. 364, 366; Bryan, *First Battle,* pp. 276-79; *St. Louis Post-Dispatch,* July 25, 26, 1896.

paign. Donnelly had seconded Bryan's nomination but bitterly believed that the Silver Populists and Democratic-Populists had betrayed the party; he intended to retire from politics after the election. Another Populist confessed a similar inclination after the convention: "I am sick and weary and tired of it all," wrote G. W. Everts. "I sometimes feel like never taking any further part in politics, not even to vote." He also belatedly recognized how the opportunistic course of party leaders had perverted the movement: "Somebody has blundered. Our convention should never have been postponed until after those of the old parties, with the object of catching the crumbs that might fall from their tables. Neither should it, harlot like, alluring with wanton smiles and beckonings," he continued, have asked "the lecherous and treacherous Democracy to come and occupy with us our bed. I admire the firmness of those middle of the road men. Their predictions are being fulfilled."[55]

Others also blamed Populist politicians for the debacle of 1896. Lloyd was disappointed in one group of Populist leaders and disgusted with a second. The first included those who reluctantly assented to Bryan and Democracy though they knew how inadequate free silver was to solve the nation's fundamental problems. Coxey made no resistance outside of the resolutions committee, he noted, and Waite accepted Bryan for the sake of harmony. "Senator Peffer, who has shown an ample courage in every emergency at Washington, sat silent, though he was bitterly opposed to the methods of the managers." Though disappointed, Lloyd could understand this group. He himself had been unable to summon the courage at St. Louis to deliver a prepared speech urging the delegates to reject Bryan. "The fear ruled that unless the reform forces united this time they would never again have the opportunity to unite," he explained. "If the radicals made a mistake, it was a patriotic mistake."[56]

Lloyd could not forgive the second group. Taubeneck, Weaver, and their associates, he claimed, had deliberately planned to subvert

---

[55] *People's Party Paper*, July 31, 1896; Martin Ridge, *Ignatius Donnelly: The Portrait of a Politician* (Chicago, 1962), p. 357; G. W. Everts to L. H. Weller, July 26, 1896, Weller Papers.

[56] Henry D. Lloyd, "The Populists at St. Louis," *Review of Reviews* 14 (September 1896): 303; C. Vann Woodward, *Tom Watson, Agrarian Rebel* (New York, 1938), p. 301.

the party for their own interests. There could have been no other result than the surrender at St. Louis "with managers whose sole occupation was to 'trim' off the principles of the party, and to seek for champions in all parties but their own." Lloyd then attempted to explain the Populist tragedy. "The leaders have never been men well grounded in reform principles, nor really desirous of effecting fundamental social and industrial changes. Their stock of radicalism consisted mainly in the no doubt very sincere belief," he continued, "that if they were 'in' and the others were 'out' the country would be saved. They went so far and only so far with their platforms as the pressure from the people compelled, and they were forever only too happy to respond to the voice of any siren of Fusion and slip out of the straight and narrow way of principle into the sweet fields of dalliance for office." Believing that the split between radicals and opportunists in the People's party would continue to widen, Lloyd soon rejected the party and turned to socialism, denouncing free silver as "the cow-bird of the Reform movement. It waited until the nest had been built by the sacrifices of others, and then it laid its eggs in it, pushing out the others which lie smashed on the ground. . . . The People's Party has been betrayed, and all that, but after all it is its own fault. No party that does not lead its leaders will ever succeed."[57]

In recent years historians have disputed Lloyd's charges as to the nature of the Populist leadership, the St. Louis convention, the importance of silver, and the desirability of fusion. One historian did little more than to argue that since the Populists fused on silver, fusion was ipso facto a "resounding affirmation of principle" and silver a radical issue. Another merely misread Lloyd's meaning and accepted the mouthings of Taubeneck in attempting to demonstrate that socialism and not silver tried to capture the Populist movement. The first, however, presented an intellectual history, with little consideration of political developments. Striving to explain a preeminently "practical" policy without recourse to specific events, the author accepted rationales. The other focused only on 1896, even then ignoring most of the preconvention period, and overlooked the nature of early Populism and the political develop-

[57] Lloyd to J. H. Ferriss, August 6, 1896, and Lloyd to A. B. Adair, October 10, 1896, Lloyd Papers.

ments within the party before 1896. There may indeed have been no "conspiracy" at the convention, as he asserts, nor were Populists at the convention tricked into naming Bryan.[58]

The "conspiracy" long preceded the St. Louis convention, and it had already triumphed in the January 1896 meeting of the Populist National Committee and in the state Populist conventions in the spring which sent Silver Populists to St. Louis. There was no reason to "trick" the delegates in the convention; they were well prepared to acknowledge silver and fusion as the only major goal and acceptable strategy of the party. The only significant objections arose over the question of with whom to fuse. Lloyd was indeed mistaken in believing that the genuine Populists at the convention could have "split the convention near the middle, if not . . . carried it." If Peffer or Coxey had accepted the leadership of the anti-Bryan Populists there would have been a more substantial protest than occurred behind the relatively obscure Seymour F. Norton, but one still far from defeating Bryan's nomination. Peffer was right about Kansas and the West. In his own state's delegation there were but two or three Populists who would have voted for his nomination. Lloyd was more realistic when he added that not only had Peffer, Coxey, and Waite not led the convention against silver and Bryan, but "their followers did not clamor to be led."[59]

But Lloyd was right about the preconvention conduct of Weaver and Taubeneck and about the cow-bird nature of silver. Silver had been among the demands of Populism from its earliest days, but it was a peripheral and unessential issue, even considered by most early Populists as almost a fraudulent issue. The opportunistic politicians within the party had seized upon it, as Weaver admitted, as "the line of least resistance," and systematically strove to remake Populism into a silver movement, forcing out of the party many of those who wanted to retain the sweeping reform commitment of early Populism and bringing into the party many more who regarded silver as the only issue. Separated by only five years, there should have been substantial duplication in the leadership of the Cincinnati Conference of 1891 and the St. Louis convention of

[58] Pollack, *Populist Response to Industrial America,* p. 103; Durden, *Climax of Populism,* p. ix.

[59] Lloyd, "Populists at St. Louis," p. 303.

1896. In fact there was not, testifying to the transformation of the party. Of those prominent in both, Peffer and Donnelly had represented the great majority in 1891 and accepted the 1896 results with grave reservations. Weaver and Simpson had almost alone countered the sentiment at Cincinnati but virtually dictated the St. Louis convention. Others influential at Cincinnati were nowhere to be found five years later: John Otis, Frank McGrath, Robert Schilling, John Rice, W. F. Rightmire, to name a few. Those ascendant at St. Louis had gained distinction either as a result of fusion maneuvers or as silver politicians: Butler, Allen, Harris, Stewart, Skinner, Patterson. Equally striking was that each of these was an officeholder explicitly forbidden by the Omaha Ordinance from participating in the party's deliberations. The Populists had failed in their attempt to assure popular control even over their own politicians. At the local and state level, the replacement of original Populists by conservative or Silver Populists had been even more marked, complicated further by partisan factors, particularly in the Midwest and West.

The People's party in 1896 was emphatically not the same as original Populism, but as Lloyd said, "It is its own fault." The Populists had agreed to compromise on issues and tickets and to deemphasize those radical measures they themselves had described as essential to the necessary reordering of America. Having done so, they lost the initiative to the Democrats, and yet could not truly claim to have converted the Democracy, for the Democrats of the South and West that nominated Bryan had advocated free silver before the birth of the People's party. Rather, the Populists capitulated to more clever Silver Democrats and then stumbled toward the inevitable destruction of their party. They agreed to subordinate party to principle at St. Louis, but they had already subordinated principle to politics. Populists had failed to heed Donnelly's earlier warning: "Let us subordinate everything to the success of the cause; but do not let us subordinate the cause to success."[60]

Moreover, subordination failed to bring that seductive and delusive success. The results of the St. Louis convention left the People's party in confusion not confidence. Would Populists notify

[60] Quoted in Ridge, *Donnelly*, p. 341.

Bryan of his nomination? Would he accept? How could he stand on two different platforms? Would Sewall or Watson be withdrawn? If neither withdrew how could the silver vote be united on Bryan? Without funds or an effective central organization, the Populists proved a distinctly junior partner to the Bryan Democracy in 1896. Watson and Butler, now the party's nominal leaders, argued bitterly throughout the campaign and each consistently sought to undermine the work of the other. As the new national chairman, Butler cooperated closely with the Democrats and everywhere tried to arrange fusion electoral tickets, some devoted to Watson, others to Sewall; Watson repeatedly denounced what he considered Butler's willingness to sacrifice the Populist half of their ticket to political expediency. Beyond this, they sharply disagreed over the propriety of fusion. And fusion continued to disrupt the party. The Populist candidate for governor of North Carolina illustrated the demoralization of the party when he wrote Butler, "I myself am 'befogged' at present, hardly know where to go, what to say when I speak, or 'where I am at.' " His perplexity resulted from Populist-Democratic fusion on the national ticket and a simultaneous Populist-Republican fusion on the state ticket. Was this what the original Populists had meant when they condemned both old parties as equal partners in oppressing the people? Watson thought not, and told Butler so: "Senator, a reform party has no right to exist if it has no valid complaint to make. Populists cannot denounce the sins of the two old parties, and yet go into political copartnership with them. The moment we make a treaty the war must cease . . . and when we cease our war upon the two old parties, we have no longer any excuse for living."[61]

The political situation in Kansas particularly irritated Watson. The Kansas delegates at St. Louis had overwhelmingly supported Sewall, and many proposed to stand by him despite Watson's nomination. They discounted the objections of Southern Populists because, they pointed out, Populist votes were not needed for Bryan to triumph in the Southern states. Both Harris and Lewelling immediately repudiated Watson. Lewelling argued that Watson

61 Jones, *Election of 1896*, pp. 321-26; Watson to Butler, September 27, 1896, Butler Papers; Hicks, *Populist Revolt*, pp. 368-79; Woodward, *Watson*, pp. 309-30; C. Vann Woodward, *Origins of the New South* (Baton Rouge, La., 1951), pp. 288-89.

should withdraw in favor of Sewall and declared Kansas Populists would remove the Georgian from their ticket. To facilitate fusion on the state level, Harris proposed that the Democrats could name the electors and the Populists the state ticket, and each endorse the others' nominees. In his comparable eagerness for Democratic support, Simpson promised the Democratic Seventh Congressional District convention that the Populists would replace Watson with Sewall, first in Kansas and then nationally.[62]

Only a few Kansas Populists defended Watson. Peffer praised him as "a Populist of the straightest sect," and he urged Kansans to "keep faith with the South" and stand by the Georgian. If Kansans repudiated the Populist national ticket at their state convention in Abilene in favor of Bryan and Sewall as Harris advocated, he declared, it would disrupt and disgrace the party. The smaller mid-road papers like the *Kansas Agitator* and *Girard World* also demanded support of Watson, but such Populists were clearly in the minority. When Breidenthal, now a member of the Populist National Executive Committee, perfunctorily remarked that Kansas Populists would uphold their party's national ticket, he provoked an outburst of complaint from both Populists and Democrats.[63]

Democrats proclaimed it the duty of Kansas Populists to endorse Sewall in order to consolidate silver sentiment. The *Atchison Patriot* warned Populists that if they nominated Watson electors, McKinley would receive the entire electoral vote of the state; therefore, those who demanded Watson electors were working in the interest of the gold-standard Republicans. Democrats, like Populists, had already made clear their intentions to have fusion. At the June Democratic state convention to select delegates to the party's national convention, the chairman again spoke of the 1892 fusion arrangements but unlike 1894 praised them. Once more fusion would aid the Democrats and opportunistically they clamored for it. Earlier some Democrats had proposed nominating Harris for governor in their August state convention. This, they believed, would assure a fusion ticket, if a nominally Populist one;

62 *St. Louis Post-Dispatch*, July 23, 1896; *Kansas Agitator*, July 31, 1896; *Abilene Daily Reflector*, July 27, 1896; John Breidenthal to Butler, August 2, 1896, Butler Papers; *Southern Mercury*, August 20, 1896; Durden, *Climax of Populism*, pp. 52-53, 76-78, 107-8, 119.

63 *Topeka Advocate*, July 29, August 5, 1896; *Kansas Agitator*, July 31, 1896; *Girard World*, July 29, 1896; *Kansas Semi-Weekly Capital*, July 31, 1896.

and many considered Harris as much a Democrat as a Populist anyway. In May and June, Democrats and Democratic-Populists, particularly Harris and Sears, had arranged a number of fusion nominations. Sears's major disappointment, in fact, was his inability to deliver one joint congressional nomination to a straight Democrat rather than a Democratic-Populist. By July the pattern was clear, and Kansas Democratic leaders assured a *Chicago Tribune* reporter at the national convention that there would be "a fusion between the Democratic and Populist parties, despite Senator Peffer's efforts to prevent it."[64]

Unlike 1890 when the Populist state convention repudiated all suggestions of fusion, or 1892 and 1894 when Populist managers denied fusionist intentions while scheming to fulfill them, the Populists at their 1896 state convention in Abilene made no effort to hide their determination to have Democratic fusion. They immediately named a committee to confer and arrange fusion with the Democrats, meeting simultaneously in Hutchinson. Concerned above all to assert the party's identity, Peffer argued futilely for the nomination of electors pledged to Watson, as the party's duly chosen nominee. Harris countered by describing Bryan, not Watson, as "the real choice of the St. Louis Populist convention," and he urged the delegates to endorse Democratic Sewall electors in exchange for Democratic endorsement of the Populist state ticket. The fusion committee accepted this proposal and the delegates dutifully agreed. The only concessions made to Peffer and the few other Populists who maintained that the party must recognize its own vice-presidential nominee were to permit the Populist ticket to list the Democratic electors under a Bryan-Watson heading and to promise that the electors would vote for Watson if he received more votes than Sewall outside Kansas.[65]

Having thus sacrificed Watson, the Populists next determined who would reap the reward of the Democratic recognition so secured. And as the Democrats praised the Populist agreement as a certain way to deliver Kansas to the Democratic national ticket,

[64] *Kansas Semi-Weekly Capital*, April 28, June 5, 16, 23, July 31, 1896; *Atchison Weekly Patriot*, August 1, 1896; *Marshall County Democrat*, July 24, 1896; Sears to J. B. Chapman, June 11, 1896, Sears to Enos Reed, June 1, 1896, and Sears to Daniel Mallison, June 2, 1896, Sears Papers; *Chicago Tribune*, July 4, 1896.

[65] *Abilene Daily Reflector*, August 5, 6, 1896; *Abilene Monitor*, August 6, 1896; *Topeka Advocate*, August 12, September 16, 1896.

they found the Populist state ticket to their liking too. "As rapidly as the Democratic convention received the names of the nominees of the Populist convention," reported one paper, "they were indorsed [*sic*]." No strong anti-fusion sentiment or candidates developed at Abilene. Peffer refused to endorse any candidate, perhaps reflecting this fact as much as a desire to avoid discord. Harris and Lewelling fought each other to a standstill, and John Leedy received the gubernatorial nomination. But Leedy had been a Democrat and a successful fusionist candidate for state senator in 1892, and he had arranged fusion in his own county in 1896 and favored fusion plans at Abilene. Former Democrats appeared frequently among the other nominees, and only the selection of Doster for the supreme court could have irritated the regular Democrats. Doster, however, was no longer averse to cooperating with Democrats, and most men distinguished between his rhetorical radicalism and his legal conservatism.[66]

Several days later the Republicans renominated Governor Morrill and prepared for the campaign. They were without enthusiasm, however; Morrill's administration had been marred by scandals and ineptness until he had lost the support even of many party regulars. The national gold plank, moreover, disrupted Republican ranks in Kansas, where silver had long been a tenet of party faith. Republicans were disproportionately represented in the silver meetings of the state after McKinley's nomination and in the delegation to the St. Louis convention of the silver party. Though most Republicans swallowed the golden pill, some did not. "I am afraid the once grand old party of this nation is going out of business this year," confessed one Republican before the Republican convention. "I do not believe that the State Ticket will win no matter who will be nominated."[67]

While the Republicans struggled into the campaign, the Populists also faced internal dissension. The protesters were few, however; by 1896 Populists largely numbered only those who favored the

66 *Abilene Monitor*, August 6, 1896; *Abilene Daily Reflector*, August 6, 1896; *Kansas Semi-Weekly Capital*, June 9, 1896; *Topeka Advocate*, August 12, 1896; Michael Brodhead, *Persevering Populist: The Life of Frank Doster* (Reno, Nev., 1969), pp. 92-102.

67 James C. Malin, *A Concern about Humanity* (Lawrence, Kans., 1964), pp. 202-3; *St. Louis Post-Dispatch*, July 17, 1896; Matt McDonald to P. H. Coney, July 16, August 4, 1896, Coney Papers.

fusion maneuvers of their leaders or who had become inured to the callous artifices of the reformers. Some such as Peffer and Clemens resigned themselves to the situation and tried to make the best of it, though Peffer devoted most of his time to the national campaign. Others such as Otis and Bennington turned, as Lloyd did, to socialism. Still other disillusioned Populists rejoined the Republican party, especially in local politics. As before, Willits, Corning, and Rightmire spearheaded the extreme mid-roaders who sought to repudiate the new Populism and remake the party according to its original intentions. Joined in 1896 by Abe Steinberger, vocal editor of the *Girard World,* these radicals had fought the dictation of Breidenthal and other party leaders throughout the year and had hoped to depose such specious Populists at Abilene but were themselves scarcely represented. Opposed even to Bryan's endorsement, they were determined to have at least one Populist on their national ticket and intensely contested the Abilene decision.[68]

The radical mid-roaders had three objections to the Populism of 1896. First, they opposed the political chicanery and arrogant assumptions of the fusionist managers, which betrayed the promise and ideals of an effective political democracy that they had found in original Populism. Second, they rejected the fraudulent silver issue and demanded adherence to Omaha Populism and the absolute independence of the party from the corrupt old politicians and parties. Finally, they despised the Democratic party, to which, moreover, they believed the fusionist Populists had delivered their party by their objectionable methods for narrow and selfish ends.

The *Girard World* provided the fullest illustration of this trilateral outlook. Denouncing the manipulations of fusionists for making politics a struggle for office and patronage rather than principles and reform, the paper wondered, "How long will scheming politicians think they can play the Populists for mere tools to use for their old party schemers and spoils hunters?" The ardent mid-road belief in the wisdom and justice of the individual voter prevented the radicals from fully grasping how completely the Pop-

68 *Topeka Advocate,* September 2, 23, 1896; Kansas Biographical Scrapbook, vol. 124, p. 122, KSHS; Minutes of the Republican Central Committee of Harper County, p. 113, KSHS; *Kansas Semi-Weekly Capital,* April 10, May 29, June 23, 1896; *Girard World,* January 30, March 12, July 16, 1896.

ulist rank and file had been educated to the acceptance of the fusionist rationale while it further caused them to expect optimistically that the Populists would yet reject their leaders. The *World* also arraigned the silver panacea. "Are the men who have been fighting the battle of humanity in this country for twenty years willing to acknowledge all they wanted was a change in basic money?" After Bryan's nomination, it declared, "The thoughtful Populist would just as soon be crucified upon a cross of gold as upon a cross of silver." At the same time, the *World* repudiated not only fusion but the intended partner to the fusion. Like virtually all the radical Populists, Steinberger had formerly been a Republican, and he constantly denied any connection between Populism and Democracy and scoffed at the notion of a new Democracy committed to sincere reform. "We confess that we are not ready to join the rotten and treacherous old Democratic party. . . . The Populist Party is not going to crawl into its grave to elect a Democratic president." The Abilene trade seemed to the *World* to involve all three offenses. "The delivery of the electoral ticket at Abilene last week to the same old Democracy which has been most bitter to Populistic teachings, was a cowardly act that cannot be condoned," the paper announced. "It was the trading of the national candidate for a mess of state pottage."[69]

Marion Butler asked Populist leaders to change the Abilene arrangement to guarantee Watson at least some of Kansas's electoral votes. Breidenthal replied that the matter was closed and the National Committee should not interfere lest it disturb the plan made to give the state government to the Populists. Steinberger, Willits, and Rightmire, hoping that Butler might recognize a straight Populist ticket committed to Bryan and Watson, conferred with Watson in September and then summoned a mid-road convention to nominate such a ticket. Willits and Rightmire pointedly revealed the changes in Populism by calling the mid-road convention as "your standard bearers in the campaign of 1890," and by denouncing the "office hunters who have secured control of the People's Party organization." At the same time, Willits explained to Butler that the Kansas Populist leaders had sold out the party to the Democrats and warned that "their wholesale slaughter of

[69] *Girard World,* July 16, August 6, 13, 1896.

the Party and our fearless leader of the South will be resented in a way that all may understand it."[70]

Most Populists angrily denounced the mid-roaders as working for Republican money and sought to drive them from the canvass. When Watson campaigned briefly in Kansas—over the objections of the regular Populist organization—Breidenthal kept him from the major cities, tried to censor his speeches, and declared that the Populist vice-presidential candidate campaigned "under the auspices and management of a Republican annex." Local party leaders tried to prevent Populists from attending mid-road meetings. And the regular Populists also attempted to prohibit the mid-road ticket from appearing on the ballot. For a "traitor," Steinberger had excellent credentials: president of the Kansas Reform Press Association, a member of the executive committee of the National Reform Press Association, secretary of the Populist Central Committee of the Third Congressional District, and a Populist central committeeman of Crawford County. Willits had been the first Populist gubernatorial candidate, the president of the Kansas State Farmers' Alliance, twice the national lecturer of the National Farmers' Alliance and Industrial Union, and that organization's national president in 1895–1896. Nevertheless, their determination to upset the fusion arrangements made them the verbal target for fusionists of both parties. Eventually, even those such as Peffer and Clemens, who had supported Watson and denounced the Abilene trade, came out against the radical anti-fusionists, fearful that their separate ticket would divide the reform forces and concerned about the scarcely disguised Republican approval of their actions.[71]

The mid-roaders failed completely. Butler refused to assist them, accepting Breidenthal's practical defense of the political deal as guaranteeing the election of Populists to state and congressional offices. In Kansas, Populists cooperated with Democrats as never

[70] Abe Steinberger to Butler, August 26, 1896, John Willits to Butler, September 9, 1896, H. W. Reed to Butler, September 10, 1896, Butler Papers; Durden, *Climax of Populism,* pp. 76-77, 93; *Girard World,* August 27, October 1, 1896; *Kansas Semi-Weekly Capital,* September 11, 15, 18, 1896.

[71] *Norton Liberator,* September 25, 1896; Sears to I. A. Stebbins, November 4, 1896, Sears Papers; *Abilene Monitor,* September 17, 1896; *Kansas Semi-Weekly Capital,* September 4, 15, October 13, 1896; M. J. Albright to Butler, September 23, 1896, Butler Papers; *Topeka Advocate,* September 16, October 7, 14, 28, 1896; *Kansas Agitator,* September 11, 18, October 2, 23, 30, 1896.

before. In carrying fusion principles to their logical end, members of each party participated in conventions of the other, and sometimes the conventions met together in one body. Where the conventions met separately but simultaneously, as in past years, there were few arguments over candidate and partisan recognition, and the delegates expected fusion as a matter of course and accepted it without discussion. Political trades, deals, and promises were openly arranged without the subterfuge of earlier fusion campaigns, and in some instances cooperation was remarkably cordial. In the congressional conventions of the Fourth District, Democrats expressed their trust in the judgment of Populists and did not even suggest any names for a fusion candidate. At other times, however, Democrats were more demanding, often encouraged by Martin who hoped to secure a Democratic balance of power in the next legislature in order to gain senatorial election in Peffer's place. Populist leaders, too, encouraged fusion arrangements for their own ends. In Leavenworth County, the Populists granted all county offices to Democrats in exchange for a fusion nomination to the state senate for Harris.[72]

Kansas Populists also rejected the mid-road appeal to avoid the artificial issue of free silver, and silver-tongued orators everywhere preached in the old pulpits of 1890 that had witnessed the Populist pentecostal tongues demanding a new society. Silver was the issue, however artificial, and it provided the means to wrest the state government from the Republicans at the polls. The fusionists elected their entire state ticket, a majority of members in both houses of the legislature, and six congressmen. Willits led the mid-road ticket with a mere 1,240 votes. But even in a state with a long nonpartisan tradition of silver advocacy, the margin of victory was surprisingly small. Bryan got a scant 51 percent of the vote and the state ticket even less. The "Popocrats"—with substantial Silver Republican help—had hardly overwhelmed an unpopular Republican administration. Significantly, nearly three-

---

[72] Breidenthal to Butler, September 21, 1896, Butler to Abe Steinberger, August 29, 1896, Butler to George Washburn, October 3, 1896, Butler Papers; *Kansas Semi-Weekly Capital,* August 4, September 1, 15, 1896; *Marshall County Democrat,* March 20, August 28, September 4, 1896; *Topeka Advocate,* August 19, October 21, 1896; *Leavenworth Times,* August 13, 1896; *Hays Free Press,* October 3, 1896.

quarters of the fusion votes were cast under the Democratic rather than the Populist heading.[73]

Nationally, Bryan and silver did even worse. With a record turnout, the country's voters rejected Bryan for the advance agent of prosperity. In addition to losing every state east of the Mississippi and north of the Potomac, Bryan even failed to carry five Western and four border states and lost the election decisively. The Democrats had suffered from the popular and just connection of the Democratic administration with the great depression, from traditional bloody-shirt appeals and prejudices, and from economic and social pressures of various kinds.

The Populists emerged from the Bryan campaign disorganized and confused. They had agreed to join the Democrats in a silver crusade as a practical move guaranteed to produce victory and reform, however minor; but their victory was lost in the nation's polling booths. The Bryan-Watson ticket received little more than 200,000 popular votes and Watson won only twenty-seven electoral votes. Although Populists achieved a share of victory in Kansas, Nebraska, and some other Western states, Republicans triumphed easily in North Dakota and Minnesota, and the Populists lost Colorado to a Democratic-Silver Republican fusion. Throughout the South, Populists fused with Republicans in state contests, achieving a great victory in North Carolina, but the effects of dual fusion maneuvers were demoralizing. Many Southern Populists refused to vote at all and some even voted for McKinley. And as fusion drove some Populists in Kansas back to the Republican party or into splinter Populist factions, fusion in the South encouraged some Populists to return to the Democrats. Under the influence of united efforts on the national ticket the People's party permanently lost many of its adherents to a partially revitalized Democracy. Major Populists placed a Bryan victory above party identity. Weaver, for instance, accepted a position on the Democratic national campaign committee, and even Donnelly campaigned in the Midwest for the Democratic National Committee after declining to canvass under the auspices of the Populist National Committee. On the other hand, Peffer campaigned extensively for the Populist National Committee and Waite broke with the fusionist Populist

[73] *Tenth Annual Report of the Secretary of State of Kansas* (Topeka, 1896).

party of Colorado, now under Patterson's control, to campaign on a middle-of-the-road ticket.[74]

Finally, compounding the original disaster it had inflicted upon Populism, the party organization had surrendered during the campaign much of the party's independence that its existence was designed to preserve. The National Committee worked closely with the Democratic committee, sought and received Democratic funds, failed to coordinate Populist state campaigns, urged Populist candidates to withdraw in favor of Democratic nominees, and accepted Sewall electors as an expedient policy. Watching these maneuvers, one Illinois Populist concluded that "the party organization [was] a disgrace to populism." Without waiting for the inevitable November defeat, G. L. McKean wrote Butler that he was renouncing all allegiance to such a party: "I shall remain a populist, but do not recognize the so-called People's Party as a political organization animated and directed by the spirit of true populism." It remained for Watson to pronounce the final words after the election. The party of the people, he declared, "does not exist any more."[75]

---

[74] Hicks, *Populist Revolt*, pp. 375-79; Roscoe C. Martin, *The People's Party in Texas* (Austin, 1933), pp. 243-44; Fred E. Haynes, *James Baird Weaver* (Iowa City, 1919), p. 382; Ridge, *Donnelly*, pp. 361, 364; John R. Morris, "Davis Hanson Waite: The Ideology of a Western Populist" (Ph.D. diss., University of Colorado, 1965), p. 280.

[75] Jones, *Election of 1896*, pp. 320-26; G. L. McKean to Butler, September 16, 1896, Butler Papers; *People's Party Paper*, November 13, 1896.

CHAPTER NINE

The Reward of the Faithful

AFTER THE election of 1896, the disintegration of the People's party accelerated. Having lost both its independence and its strength by being absorbed into the Bryan silver campaign, the party divided into quarreling factions that agreed only on the fact that Populism had changed greatly since its birth. Members of the mid-road group recognized this explicitly and demanded a return to early Populism and an avoidance of fusion and silver; the larger group implicitly recognized the transformation of Populism but believed the hope of the party lay in a continuation of the policies that had already destroyed its future. The latter position was absurd and myopic; the former attitude was no less self-deceptive for it was already obsolete. The American political system had broken its great challenger.

No episode in 1897 better illustrated the transformation of Populism than did the Kansas senatorial election. Populists totally ignored the old Alliance rule requiring the office to seek the man. No sooner had William A. Harris lost the gubernatorial nomination than he began to seek Peffer's Senate seat, with election to the state senate being the first step. John Breidenthal had supported the gubernatorial ambitions of Harris partially to clear the path to the Senate for himself, and he soon confirmed his candidacy as he had in 1891 and 1893, apparently limiting his personal goals to

a position awarded by politicians in the legislature rather than
an office determined by popular election. In November and December 1896, Lewelling and several other Populists also began to seek
the nomination openly. John Martin had announced his candidacy
in 1895 and reaffirmed it throughout 1896. Harris and Breidenthal
even set up official headquarters in Topeka by the first week in
January 1897. Harris was the most open in declaring his intentions.
He systematically gathered information about the legislators, and
his friend William H. Sears wrote individual legislators as early as
November to solicit their votes for him, promising that Harris never
forgot a favor and scarcely veiling a threat that he never forgot a
slight either. "I believe it would be a smart thing for you to tie
your fortunes to him," Sears wrote one legislator, "not only for
your present good but for future advancement."[1]

Peffer alone attempted to follow the old Alliance rule, though
eventually he also sought the party's nomination. In August he
replied to inquiries as to his possible candidacy for reelection by
declaring he had only one qualification that others lacked: senatorial experience. Without announcing a desire for reelection, he
would say only that he would regard it as a great honor. In early
November, moreover, Peffer returned to Washington to work on
senatorial matters, and he remained there until the session ended
in March, abstaining from personal appeals or the vigorous lobbying in which the other candidates engaged. In December, however,
he sent a circular letter to all Populist legislators, mentioning his
experience and knowledge gained in the previous years, summarizing his work in the Senate, and reminding them that "I have kept
faith with the people." This low-key bid for support was Peffer's
concession to playing politics, but it could hardly have been effective: an impersonal, formal letter, promising nothing more than
continued faithful service.[2]

More important, perhaps, for his reelection hopes was his control
of the *Advocate,* which defended him as the *Kansas Farmer* had in

[1] *Topeka Daily Capital,* November 25, 26, 1896; *Fort Scott Daily Monitor,*
January 5, 1897; W. H. Sears to D. M. Rothweiler, November 21, 1896, Sears to
W. B. Helm, November 20, 1896, and Sears to A. G. Forney, November 20, 1896,
Sears Papers.

[2] *Topeka Advocate,* August 5, November 4, 1896; *Topeka State Journal,*
December 11, 1896.

1891. But it was clearly defensive; Peffer simply no longer represented the People's party and had no definite base of support in the legislature. His opponents revived the old charges of his age and delicate health as well as new ones intimating that he had been less than generous to the state campaign in 1896. The *Advocate* accordingly printed long articles pointing out Peffer's present good health and noting that twenty-two senators were older. His alleged neglect of Kansas during the 1896 campaign, the *Advocate* explained, had been at the urgent request of the National Committee and with the permission of the State Committee. Even Breidenthal rebuked such criticism as unfair and joined others in pointing out that Peffer had long carried the party's financial burdens, especially in maintaining the *Advocate* at a heavy cost and campaigning in both state and nation at his own expense.[3] The *Advocate,* however, could not effectively rebut the major objection to Peffer. What he represented, most Populists wanted to avoid: anti-fusion politics, adherence to early Populism, and Republican antecedents. And if Breidenthal and others defended him for campaigning outside of Kansas in 1896, Peffer's opposition to fusion, the Abilene arrangement, and Leedy had only been too obvious.

The newspaper was not just a Pefferian *Advocate,* however. In the interest of the party, its columns were opened to all senatorial aspirants and the paper printed endorsements and articles supporting other candidates. Nor did Peffer attempt to persuade his rivals to withdraw. Breidenthal, for example, wrote privately to Peffer to inform him of his intended candidacy, and the senator, according to Breidenthal's friends, "assents and interposes not the slightest objection." Breidenthal, however, contended that Peffer's position had become hopeless and urged him to retire from the contest.[4]

Though Peffer refused to concede defeat, Breidenthal was correct in arguing that the Populist tide had turned against Peffer. Newspaper articles suggesting other candidates made this abundantly clear. The *LeRoy Reporter* perhaps best expressed the views of the new Populists: Peffer, the *Reporter* admitted, had done "very

<hr>

3 *Kansas Semi-Weekly Capital* (Topeka), December 29, 1896, January 8, 1897; *Topeka Advocate,* November 18, December 2, 9, 16, 1896; *Kansas City Journal,* November 14, 1896.

4 *Topeka Advocate,* December 2, 9, 23, 30, 1896, January 6, 1897; *Topeka Daily Capital,* November 25, 26, 1896.

well for a figure-head when the party was new and its members comparative strangers to one another. But things have changed," the paper continued. "Crazy and impractical notions have been dropped out of the profession of faith. Victory and a sense of responsibility have made the party more conservative and imbued its leaders" with different attitudes and goals. But Peffer remained committed to the original positions and therefore was unacceptable to most Populists in 1897. The *Reporter* concluded, then, it felt no surprise to see such men as Peffer gradually displaced by new and different men.[5]

Of course Peffer retained some support, but more among the rank and file than among the legislators, as straw votes invariably revealed. Some legislators, instructed for Peffer by their constituents, even announced their intention to vote for another candidate, mocking the original Populist emphasis upon popular participation and local control in politics. Most of Peffer's journalistic backing came from the moderate mid-road element, which emphasized his constancy to the principles of early Populism. The *Ness City Echo,* for instance, after announcing the results of a straw vote showing Peffer nearly three to one over his opposition and urging his re-election, declared, "Senator Peffer has gallantly and continuously fought for the principles espoused way back in the eighties." The *Kansas Agitator* remained one of Peffer's foremost advocates. In a poll of its readers, this mid-road paper found only one objector to Peffer's reelection, yet he could suggest no other acceptable candidate and based his protest simply on the belief that six years was long enough to serve. More characteristic was the assertion of one venerable reformer that he not only favored Peffer's reelection but that "if our senators and representatives go back on Peffer, they needn't expect the support of the old Greenbackers hereafter."[6]

The silver fusionists in the legislature, however, cared little for the old Greenbackers. They were more concerned about their Democratic antecedents and their Democratic allies. Democrats claimed that the legislature owed its election to their support and admitted that "the Democracy did not aid the Populists because it

5 Quoted in *Topeka Advocate*, January 6, 1897.
6 Ibid., November 25, December 2, 30, 1896, January 20, 1897; *Kansas Agitator* (Garnett), November 6, 20, 27, December 18, 1896.

loved that party more, but because it loved Republicanism less." Such self-interested action required a tangible reward, and future fusion, these partisans warned, was doomed unless a Democrat received the senatorial honors. Dangling fusion before the eager Populists, the *Newton Journal* announced that "the loss of Peffer is comparatively insignificant to the great gain that would surely result to the Populists from the election of a Democrat as senator."[7]

Faced with such demands, the Populist fusionists were all the more ready to drop Peffer, an anti-fusion ex-Republican, especially unacceptable to the Democrats, and to follow their usual practice: a covert surrender to Democratic demands while maintaining a semblance of integrity. In this instance, Democratic newspapers pointed the way by recommending the election of Harris. Harris was everything Peffer was not: a former Democrat, the state's foremost fusionist, an ardent Silver Populist, and a conservative who had always opposed the distinctive measures of early Populism. From the start, moreover, Sears had based his letter-writing campaign for Harris on the necessity of insuring future Democratic fusion. Peffer's defense only injured further his chances by emphasizing his faithful service and by defending his allegedly "visionary ideas" as strictly in accordance with party beliefs.[8] Populists in 1897 wanted to forget their origins as they had already repudiated their beliefs. Peffer was the spirit and representative of original Populism; Harris embodied the new Populism.

The politicians, reported one newspaper after another, had thus decided against Peffer. When the fusionist legislators caucused in Topeka on January 19, 1897, Peffer received but twenty-four of 102 votes; Harris won the nomination and, a week later, the election.[9]

The reaction to the election of Harris confirmed the expectations of the fusionist Populists and dramatically endorsed the transformation of Populism. Democrats were ecstatic. The *Newton Journal* described Harris as a Democrat and crowed that the Populists had

---

[7] *Kansas Semi-Weekly Capital,* January 12, 1897; *Newton Semi-Weekly Journal,* January 5, 12, 1897.

[8] *Marshall County Democrat* (Marysville), December 25, 1896; Sears to Helm, November 20, 1896, Sears to Jason Helmick, November 20, 1896, Sears to Rothweiler, November 21, 1896, Sears Papers; *Topeka Advocate,* January 6, 20, 1897.

[9] *Fort Scott Daily Monitor,* January 9, 1897; *Abilene Monitor,* December 10, 1896; *Topeka Advocate,* January 27, 1897.

answered the Democratic demand. Conservatives of all parties praised the decision. The *Topeka Capital* was pleased that, although nominally a Populist, Harris "has never been identified with the extreme element of that party and will not cause humiliation to his state by the introduction of sensational financial bills or by foolish political harangues." Most especially gratifying was the direct contrast to his predecessor. "His appearance in Senator Peffer's seat in the Senate will create a favorable impression and will be generally regarded outside of Kansas as an evidence that the more moderate counsels are in control of the Populist party in this state." Former Governor Thomas Osborn agreed. "There is a wide difference in the Populist party . . . from what that party was four years ago," he declared. "It has lost much of its former radicalism, and has virtually abandoned many of its impracticable schemes of governmental reform. I don't think its leaders will depart hereafter from a safe and conservative course." Only the few middle-of-the-road Populists complained. The *Kansas Agitator* deplored Peffer's defeat and added, "We do not admire Col. Harris and never did."[10] It was a tragic irony that opposition to Peffer in 1891 had rested primarily in the fear that he might prove less than completely committed to reform and might cooperate with one of the old parties, and that opposition to him in 1897 resulted principally from his steadfast adherence to those reform principles and his resistance to fusion.

Though the senatorial contest best represented the changes Populism had undergone since its birth, the performance of both the governor and the legislature further demonstrated the degradation of Populism and correctly questioned the wisdom of fusion politics. From the beginning the Leedy administration lacked the reformist zeal that had characterized early Populism or even the eloquent posturings of the Lewelling administration. Republicans praised Leedy's innocuous inaugural address for being devoid of that "sickly balderdash" that had formed the thrust of earlier Populist speeches, and the erstwhile calamity-howlers interrupted Governor Morrill's valedictory remarks with heavy applause when he spoke of the great prosperity and progress of the state and condemned those

10 *Newton Semi-Weekly Journal,* January 22, 1897: *Kansas Semi-Weekly Capital,* January 22, 29, 1897; *Kansas Agitator,* January 22, 1897.

who would criticize it. In office, Leedy blundered badly in working with the legislature and quarreled with other leading Populists.[11]

Leedy's patronage policies also disturbed the Populist ranks. He recalled that at their "early party conventions some one would invariably inquire, when a new candidate was brought forward, 'is he a Republican or a Democrat?' " Now, however, convinced that Populists no longer worried about former political affiliations, Leedy announced his intention to treat fusionists as members of a single party in distributing patronage. Leedy then ignored the recommendations of Peffer and other early Populists and awarded offices in a conscious attempt to consolidate Democrats and Populists permanently. Some Populists complained that Leedy slighted his own party while rewarding Democrats excessively. Radical anti-fusionists laughed at these myopic protesters "for not having intelligence enough to know the legitimate and inevitable consequences of political prostitution." The governor, they declared, "is simply trying to maintain and perpetuate that fusion which you . . . persisted in making in the face of . . . all our protests and admonitions."[12]

Leedy's attitudes toward prohibition and the metropolitan police law also disrupted party harmony. Leedy announced that he had not become a Populist "to hunt joints nor to fight resubmission," and like Lewelling he relaxed prohibition enforcement because of a desire to retain Democratic support. Prohibitionists in all parties criticized the governor, charged that he had made a deal with the liquor interests, and demanded the enforcement of the law.[13]

The legislature proved equally disappointing. For the first time, Republicans controlled neither house, and great results were anticipated. Instead, what the legislature of 1897 managed to achieve was merely to indicate that Populism had come full circle. In the original movement, the primary economic demands involved lower

[12] *Kansas Semi-Weekly Capital*, December 8, 1896, February 9, 1897; Peffer to Leedy, November 20, 1896, and accompanying letters to Leedy in John Davis Scrapbook, vol. L, KSHS.

[13] *Topeka Advocate and News*, February 9, 1898; *Topeka Daily Capital*, May 19, 1897, February 3, 1898.

[11] *Topeka Daily Capital*, January 12, March 10, 1897; Kansas Biographical Scrapbook "C," vol. 4, p. 255; John Dunsmore to Sears, July 28, 1898, Sears Papers.

interest rates and a maximum freight rate railroad law and were directed by Peffer in each instance. In 1897 the Populist legislature voted down bills designed to achieve these objectives and in each instance Harris directed the new Populism. Whereas the Republican legislature in 1889 had violated its reform pledges made in the campaign of 1888, thereby providing the real impetus to Populism, eight years later the People's party controlled the legislature and similarly repudiated its solemn pledges to the people made in the previous campaign. Those who argued that devotion to principles did not necessarily diminish when "practical politics" dictated the course of the party were proved disastrously wrong.[14]

Legislation to reduce the maximum legal interest rates had always been a major Populist goal. A bill designed to meet that demand failed in the senate when several Populists voted against it. These negative Populists were virtually coterminous with the party's non-farmer, middle-class element. Harris, still a state senator despite his elevation to the United States Senate, was the most vigorous opponent of reducing interest rates; he argued that higher interest rates would encourage Eastern capital to invest in Kansas and spur the state's economic development. These Populists were no calamity-howlers; Populism had become respectable—and perfidious.[15]

The Populist legislators also failed to enact a bill establishing a maximum freight rate for railroads, a perennial reform demand from at least the early 1880s, when Peffer strongly advocated it, and a Populist 1896 platform declaration as well. One legislator reminded his fellow Populists that such a law involved the "cardinal principle" of the state party. Nevertheless, the legislators sidetracked the designated bill for a weak substitute designed merely to revise the old and inadequate railroad commission. The senate unanimously passed this impotent bill and the house approved it by a 121–1 vote. The Republican support for the bill suggested its harmless nature and helped cause forty-four Populists to protest the bill formally because "it is not the measure we have promised

---

14 The phrasing comes from a Walter T. K. Nugent apologia for fusion in his *The Tolerant Populists* (Chicago, 1963), p. 187.

15 *Norton Liberator*, February 26, 1897; *Senate Journal* (Topeka, Kans., 1897), pp. 451-52, 525-27; O. Gene Clanton, *Kansas Populism: Ideas and Men* (Lawrence, 1969), p. 201.

the people." They also asserted that the bill had been promoted and approved by the railroad lobby. Though these Populists protested, they accepted the weak bill; Governor Leedy refused to do so and vetoed it. There was, however, no time left for the legislature to consider an appropriate measure, and the session ended without the promised railroad regulation. The architect of this disaster was none other than Harris, who had devised the objectionable bill and led the fight to defeat the inclusion of a maximum rate provision.[16]

The remainder of the legislative session provided no encouragement. Several Populists voted with Republicans to defeat a proposed initiative and referendum amendment, another prime Populist demand. A few minor reform laws were passed but the legislature rapidly dissolved into a contentious and vicious body with commonplace allegations of bribery and betrayal. The major quarrel occurred between Andrew J. Titus, a Populist of Republican antecedents already disgusted with fusionists in his district, and Lewelling, also a state senator. Titus charged the former governor with questionable lobbying and attempted bribery, and Lewelling retorted that Titus was involved in a conspiracy to destroy him politically. Jerry Simpson was also an active lobbyist, with at least as dubious intentions. His opposition to the maximum rate railroad bill and other distinctively Populist proposals provoked one observer to wonder, "Which is the real Simpson, the sockless ranter in Congress, or the conservative lobbyist in Topeka?" Finally the legislature appointed a committee to investigate the various charges of corruption, and for several months the bickering reformers denounced one another. No hard evidence ever appeared to prove the allegations, but when the legislature finally adjourned, the Populists were discredited, divided, and downcast.[17]

To many, the fruits of fusion were bitter. The old mid-road arguments against the election of H. L. Moore or John Martin seemed borne out again: if placed in power, those not wholly committed to reform could hurt the entire movement. The *Norton Liberator,* for example, condemned Harris and other fusionists

16 *Topeka Daily Capital,* February 24, 25, 1897; *Senate Journal,* p. 680; *House Journal* (Topeka, Kans., 1897), pp. 680, 908, 911.
17 *Topeka Daily Capital,* January 26, 30, April 6, 10, 11, 20, 1897.

who violated their platform pledges as the "Judases of Populism." The *Liberator* explained the lesson of the legislature: Populists should not replace the faithful who had definite and radical positions with newcomers who promised respectability and conservatism. "We were successful at the polls but defeated in the legislative halls. Thus our victory last fall became a more ignominious defeat, than if our candidates had failed of election." The *Kansas Agitator* agreed that the legislature weakened the party by voting against Populist measures promised to the people.[18]

After the legislature adjourned, the *Topeka Capital* justly commented that nothing remained of Populism. In the state the party had repudiated the essential features of Kansas Populism in the railroad and interest rate laws; in the nation the Populists had rejected the subtreasury and fiat money for silver. Populists in 1897 would jeer at Peffer's *The Way Out,* the paper continued. The new Populists simply refused to enact the Populist principles of the early 1890s. This pleased the *Capital* which saw the new behavior as more "sensible" and "responsible," but the paper also rightly pointed out that there was no need of a third party without distinct principles, that was guided by the same interests and objectives as the two major parties.[19]

Peffer, in active editorial charge of the *Advocate,* severely denounced the disloyal politicians as traitors to Populism. Sounding once again like an 1889 Republican disgusted with a Republican legislature, Peffer declared that platforms must be redeemed, not "made as a means of securing office," and he hoped that "in the future none but men who will be faithful to their constituents will be placed in power by Populist voters." He also struck out at Leedy's performance, especially on prohibition, appearing at mass rallies in Topeka to castigate the governor for refusing to perform his constitutional duty and for "abusing the temperance people" while cooperating with "the violators of the law." By June, Peffer's critical course continually "created consternation among the Populist politicians," one paper reported. One *Advocate* editorial, for example, made Leedy, according to a friend, "so mad when he

18 *Norton Liberator,* February 26, March 12, April 16, 1897; *Kansas Agitator,* April 2, 1897.
19 *Kansas Semi-Weekly Capital,* March 2, 5, 16, 1897.

read it that he tore the *Advocate* up and threw it into the waste-basket."[20]

Peffer's position also troubled the national party leaders. Even during the 1896 campaign he had insisted that the People's party and the Democracy were essentially different and that the fusion of 1896 was not a permanent union. Immediately after the election, Peffer declared that the reform forces must never again unite under Democratic leadership, and he repeated his old proposal for the creation of a new and permanent reform party under a new name free of the distracting prejudices associated with former partisan alignments. To organize such a party he favored calling a con-ference of reformers. This announcement met the same opposition of silence as his earlier proposals had. Moreover, many prominent Populists advocated a continued, even perpetual, fusion of the 1896 allies, and some were already prepared to follow Bryan into the Second Battle. Allen even offered to resign his Senate seat in favor of Bryan.[21]

Promptly after the election, Southern mid-roaders demanded the reorganization of the National Committee to end "the fusion heresy" and prepare for independent party action in the future. "Abolish the bargain counter, repudiate the fusion leaders, re-organize the party, oust the office-holders from our National Com-mittee," wrote Tom Watson, "—and Populism yet has a future." When his own suggestions were ignored, Peffer added his voice to those of the other mid-roaders. "I see there is a disposition on the part of some of our fellows to follow Bryan and his people," Peffer noted. "I, for one, am not in favor of a coalition of forces." The Populist predicament, as Peffer incisively explained, was that the party was composed of former members of the two old parties and was divided philosophically along approximately the same lines. The former Republicans believed in a strong and active national government, the former Democrats in a limited and negative government. "The radical or Republican element among the Pop-ulists," he declared, could not accept the theory behind the Dem-

<hr>

[20] *Topeka Advocate*, March 3, 10, June 2, July 14, 1897; *Kansas Semi-Weekly Capital*, May 11, 21, June 4, 1897.

[21] *Topeka Advocate*, July 29, October 21, November 11, 25, 1896; *Kansas Semi-Weekly Capital*, November 24, 1896; Fred E. Haynes, *James Baird Weaver* (Iowa City, 1919), pp. 383-85.

ocratic platform demands for state banks and redemption in coin, for example, "while the Democratic element does." Thus, one faction of the party eagerly sought the fusionist program that the other faction could never accept. And a reaffirmation of the original principles and purpose might cause the Democratic-Populists to withdraw from the party and thereby "leave us where we [were] in the beginning." Nevertheless, Peffer believed such a course was necessary if the Populists were ever to accomplish their initial objectives. "Principle before policy."[22]

Accordingly, Peffer joined other mid-roaders in urging that a conference be held to take steps to reverse the party's mistaken direction. The meeting was held in Memphis on February 22, 1897, to coincide with the annual gathering of the National Reform Press Association there. Paul Van Dervoort, president of the editorial association, believed that Weaver, Allen, Butler, and other Populist fusionists were planning to consign the party to the Democracy. He declared that it was therefore essential to devise a withdrawal from fusion and a return to original Populism. The conference agreed, and asked the Populist National Committee to arrange a delegate convention to decide the party's course.[23]

Butler saw no reason to accept this proposal of the mid-roaders. As chairman of the National Committee he approved his own policy and, if regretting his inability to coordinate the Populists in the country, saw fusion as an appropriate future strategy. Indeed, he believed he could best assist the party by isolating the extreme mid-road element in the party. He had not supported the Memphis meeting and he opposed a national convention to define the party's position because he feared that the radical elements would dominate such a meeting. In April, after consulting with Simpson, Harris, Allen, and other congressional Populists, Butler announced his refusal to convoke the requested conference and viciously denounced the mid-roaders. Peffer had urged Butler to call the convention and soon took angry exception to the chairman's course.

22 *People's Party Paper* (Atlanta), November 13, 1896; Tom Watson to Davis Waite, November 8, 1896, Waite Papers; *Southern Mercury* (Dallas), December 10, 1896; *Kansas Semi-Weekly Capital*, January 29, February 2, 1897; *Boston Herald*, January 11, 25, 1897.

23 *Boston Herald*, January 11, 1897; Paul Van Dervoort to Lemuel H. Weller, January 16, 1897, Weller Papers; *Southern Mercury*, February 25, March 11, 1897.

Peffer accused him and the congressional fusion Populists of misusing their power and criticized them for constantly harassing the mid-roaders. He reminded them that vital differences existed between Populism and Democracy. He harshly censured Butler and Simpson for their arguments that the mid-roaders were Republican tools, all the while they themselves accepted Republican assistance in North Carolina and worked with the Democrats. Simpson even listed himself in the *Congressional Directory* as a Democrat-Populist, provoking Peffer to designate him an "assistant Democrat."[24]

When Butler refused to call an official conference, a special committee of the NRPA did so, asking Populists to meet in Nashville on July 4, 1897. Peffer regretted that Butler's inaction made the conference unofficial and therefore incapable of resolving matters. It was necessary to maintain an independent, anti-fusion third party, he believed. Much of the Kansas Populist press immediately attacked Peffer for trying to create dissension in the fusion ranks and argued that the Democratic party was thoroughly reformed, thereby eliminating the need for an independent People's party. This duplicated the Democratic position, testifying to the virtual consolidation of the two parties. The Democratic *Manhattan Mercury,* for example, announced that the revitalization of the Democracy had removed the excuse for the existence of the People's party and that Populists should join the Democratic party. Even many Populist papers that nominally opposed Democratic absorption decried the mid-roaders as a disruptive factor financed and encouraged by the Republicans, demanded a boycott of the Nashville Conference, and apparently believed that Butler's policy of drift would somehow preserve the party's integrity.[25]

Despite the harsh criticism, Peffer continued to oppose the fusion Populists. He rebuked the National Committee for doing nothing to assure Populist autonomy, Weaver for working with the Democrats in Iowa, Allen for accepting money from Bryan ostensibly for Populist campaign purposes. He applauded the results of the

24 Marion Butler to Ignatius Donnelly, December 10, 1896, Donnelly Papers; *Southern Mercury,* March 25, 1897; *Topeka Advocate,* March 24, 31, April 14, 1897.

25 *Ottawa Weekly Times,* April 1, 22, 29, June 3, 1897; *Topeka Advocate,* April 7, 28, 1897; *Southern Mercury,* April 22, 1897; *Girard World,* May 13, 1897; *Kansas Semi-Weekly Capital,* June 11, 1897; *Norton Liberator,* May 21, July 9, 1897.

Nashville Conference, which condemned fusion and formed the National Organization Committee to keep the regular Populist Committee honest and to provide an organization within the party from which anti-fusion action could be launched. The object of the mid-road Populists, Peffer explained, "is not to destroy the party by declaring war against its regularly appointed officers, but to save the party by getting control, at the proper time and in the proper way, of the party machinery." Though Allen, Weaver, and other nominal Populists who accepted Democratic principles could become Democrats with little trauma, Peffer wrote, the mid-roaders were Populists who felt that serious differences existed between Populism and Democracy, who were not convinced that the Democracy was regenerated, and who believed that uniting with another party was equivalent to abandoning their own. Peffer declared that, if fusion was forced upon him again by the policies of Butler and his cohorts, he would probably feel "that it would be more manly, more honorable and more fitting every way to go as a volunteer Democrat or Republican than as a conscripted Populist. If our party is worth saving, let us fight for it under our own colors."[26]

So believing, Peffer accepted an invitation to campaign in Iowa against the Democratic-Populists. Weaver had led Iowa's Populists into the Democratic party after the legislature amended the state ballot law to prevent a candidate from being listed under more than one party. Desirous of fusion, Weaver did not hesitate to take the logical step and accepted the Democratic platform and name. He vacuously justified his action by claiming that it had gained 200,000 Iowa votes for the cause. Peffer retorted that it seemed a strange way to gain supporters: "That is the way Jonah captured the whale." When Stewart's *Silver Knight* made a claim similar to Weaver's, Peffer wondered publicly why, if the Democrats had really become Populists as the fusionists charged, "don't they take our name and adopt our platform?" Instead, Weaver's course showed clearly that the Populists had become Democrats, taking their name and platform. The few remaining Iowa Populists who rejected fusion rallied around A. W. C. Weeks and Lemuel H. Weller and determined to run a straight ticket. They called a

26 *Topeka Advocate,* April 28, June 30, July 14, 1897.

convention for August 19, 1897, and invited Peffer to address them.[27]

Anticipating criticism, Peffer carefully prepared his speech and read it rather than speaking extemporaneously. The People's party, he announced, had been organized when existing parties refused to face the harsh problems arising from industrialization that confronted the nation; they had become subservient to the nation's despoilers. Populism asserted "the equality of human rights" and demanded a fundamental restructuring of American life to place "paramount power and authority" in the hands of the people. The Democrats, Peffer charged, had never changed their opposition to this central thrust of Populism. They accepted in 1896 some peripheral demands of Populism—but not even these completely: they disavowed irredeemable paper money and were relatively unconcerned about the ratio to gold in silver coinage, thereby implicitly approving the gold standard. Peffer then outlined those matters which true Populists regarded as fundamental and balanced each with the Democratic position, concluding that Populists and Democrats remained distinctly opposed to each other. This being true, Peffer rejected the two propositions of the fusion Populists: first, that Populists limit themselves to silver, and second, that Populists ally themselves to the Democracy. The union of 1896, he declared, had been a temporary arrangement for one campaign, but the fusionists now wanted to make permanent the expediency of that year. Peffer assured his listeners, however, that as faithful Populists they need not accept the dictation or manipulation of politicians: we are "free to determine our own affairs in our own way as a party and as individual men."[28]

Abe Steinberger addressed the Iowa convention after Peffer and announced that the nation's discouraged Populists would be reinspired "when the news from Des Moines is wired over this country that you listen to these words from Senator Peffer of Kansas—and no man can assail his integrity; no man can question his

27 Ibid., July 14, August 25, 1897; *Silver Knight-National Watchman* (Washington, D.C.), July 1, 8, 1897; A. W. C. Weeks to Weller, July 5, 12, August 10, 1897, and J. Bellangee to Weller, July 25, 1897, Weller Papers; Herman C. Nixon, "The Populist Movement in Iowa," *Iowa Journal of History and Politics* 24 (January 1926): 101.

28 *Topeka Advocate*, August 25, 1897; *Girard World*, August 26, September 2, 1897.

honesty or the sincerity of his purpose, when he said to you: 'You are doing the right thing.' "[29]

Steinberger was greatly mistaken. National Populist leaders rebuked Peffer, and Kansas Populists exploded in bitter denunciation of their former senator. The *Ottawa Times* headlined its account of the speech, "Peffer Gone Wrong," and declared that as Democrats were Populists Peffer was promoting the election of Republicans. The *Topeka Independent* headed its critical account with "Unwise Leadership" and similarly asserted the congruity of the two parties. Others were less kind. The *Pleasanton Herald* described the former senator as "a consummate donkey," "an ingrate," and "despicable." Even Annie Diggs, an active fusionist by 1897, criticized Peffer from Iowa where she was campaigning for the Democratic ticket.[30]

Peffer sought to defend himself in the *Advocate*. He printed his speech to indicate that he had said nothing contrary to Populism and noted that his critics never reported what he said but only condemned the speech. Underlying his defense, however, was a bewilderment and incredulity. Nominal Populists were harshly arraigning him for defending the integrity of Populism and his party. Could not they understand what was happening? Peffer replied to his detractors that he was still a Populist—but were they?—and that he simply advocated remaining a Populist—but did they? He asked the critical *Eureka Union* if it could say "why Mr. Peffer should not be and remain a Populist if he so desires? . . . He is satisfied with the Populist party. Why should he be driven from it? Who has the authority to transfer his allegiance? Think a moment, Mr. Union, where are you drifting." He was less subtle in replying to Latimer's vicious charges in the *Pleasanton Herald:* "If the *Herald* wants to go into the Democratic party, why doesn't it go and stop its growling at Populists who prefer to remain in their own party?"[31]

Spurned by Kansas Populists, Peffer joined Davis Waite and Jacob Coxey in campaigning for the Iowa mid-roaders in September

[29] *Girard World,* October 28, 1897.

[30] *Silver Knight-National Watchman,* August 26, 1897; *Ottawa Weekly Times,* August 26, 1897; *Pleasanton Herald,* September 3, 1897; *Topeka Advocate,* September 1, 8, 1897.

[31] *Topeka Advocate,* August 25, September 1, 8, 15, 29, 1897.

and October. To his wife, Waite explained the hopes of these loyal Populists in their Iowa canvass. "We do not expect to carry the state," he wrote. "Weaver's cursed fusion has been too well arranged for that, but the Democrats, I think, cannot carry the election." Waite hoped that if fusion failed in Iowa, "the scheme will be seen to be impracticable, and our People's Party organization can be saved. . . . If we can only save the Populist organization and get rid of the traitors like Weaver, Butler, Allen, Taubeneck, Sockless Simpson, Cyclone Davis, and various other scoundrels too numerous to mention, who have more or less control of the party machinery," he continued, "—there is hope in the future, not in my time, but certainly in [Waite's young son] Frank's, and possibly people a good deal older." Though the Democrats failed in Iowa, the mid-road Populists could not claim the credit. The Populists polled fewer than 6,000 of the well over 400,000 votes—a showing that did not entitle the party to appear on any future ballot. Populism was dead in another state. "This is the result of General Weaver's suicidal policy of going into the Democrat party and voting the Democrat ticket," Peffer lamented.[32]

In Kansas, too, Peffer fought a losing battle against the fusion Populists. He insisted that the party return to original and independent Populism, adopt thorough and genuine Populist platforms, and nominate straight Populist tickets. James H. Ferriss, chairman of the executive committee of the NRPA, believed that Peffer stood alone in Kansas in supporting true Populism, but Steinberger, Willits, Clemens, and a few others still agreed with the former senator on the necessity of independent political action by Populists. Steinberger complained, "When the People's Party maintained its ground and stood for the people and its own creed it grew up and defied all opposition, but since tangling up with the Democracy for the offices and spoils, it has commenced to wane and dwindle away." Clemens taunted the fusionists by questioning the need to maintain the People's party between elections if they planned to fuse every time with the Democrats, as was their apparent intention. Willits provided another forceful moral condemnation of fusion Populism in an effort to defeat the policy in

<hr />

[32] Waite to Celia Waite, October 24, 1897, Waite Papers; *Girard World*, October 14, 1897; *Topeka Advocate*, November 10, 1897.

the 1897 elections. Fusion, he wrote, "is simply a compromise with wrong. It is an agreement with death and a covenant with hell. If our immortal declaration of principles is just and right, in the name of God let us stand by them and go down if need be, fighting for God, home, and humanity instead of disgracefully surrendering to the common enemy." Willits also presented the radical mid-road view of the People's party in 1897: "We have simply been sold and delivered to the Democracy by a gang of unprincipled office-seekers and self-constituted political bosses, who think more of self-interest than they do of the future of our country and the condition of our children and children's children for all time."[33]

There were a few local Populist struggles against fusion with the Democrats, but the party generally approved the policy without debate. Former Republicans continued to provide the base of anti-fusion sentiment, and the virtual absence of the first by 1897 made inevitable the absence of the second. Republican-Populists led by Andrew J. Titus fought the Simpson fusion machine in Harper and Barber counties. Simpson supported the regular Democratic nominees to defeat his Populist opponents and to prove the political necessity of Democratic fusion and his leadership. In Shawnee County, farmer and former-Republican John McIntosh objected to fusionist attempts to nominate Democrats ("Here, you _____ _____ _____, what are you doing? This is a Populist convention. We don't want no _____ Democrats nominated here."), but he was physically restrained until after the Populist fusionists had carried the day. Another Republican-Populist denounced Harris as the betrayer of the party because of his legislative performance. "But what else can we expect from a man who has all his life consorted with Democrats?" Harris "pretended to be a friend of the Populist cause. He mingled in our ranks, and finally he led the majority of the Populist Senators astray," declared Moses A. Householder. Harris "did all in his power to turn back the radical measures of his party."[34]

But Harris had become the Populist United States Senator, and

---

[33] *Topeka State Journal*, August 17, 1897; *Kansas Semi-Weekly Capital*, September 24, 1897; *Girard World*, October 21, November 11, 1897; *Topeka Advocate*, August 4, 1897; John F. Willits to B. F. Oldfield, July 20, 1897, Kansas Biographical Scrapbook, vol. 175, p. 27.

[34] *Kansas Semi-Weekly Capital*, July 20, October 7, 12, 29, December 7, 1897.

his policy dominated the party. Fusion was effected throughout Kansas in the 1897 elections, and both parties planned it again for the 1898 state election and the 1900 presidential election. Populist papers asserted the congruity of Populism and Democracy and advocated the permanent unification of the two parties. Even Peffer resignedly admitted to a Nebraskan interviewer, "I guess it will be fusion down there with us [Kansans] for a good many years to come," and he spoke of "the Demopops, as *they* are sometimes called."[35] Obviously, the meaning of fusion was changing. Once signifying a temporary alliance of individual parties for a single political campaign, fusion by 1897 was becoming a permanent policy, expected and accepted without discussion. Populists were truly losing their individual identities. The Democrats who had always hoped to capture the People's party for the benefit of the Democracy had succeeded. Common by 1897 were such statements as that of Populist state senator W. H. Ryan, a former Democrat, in which he advocated the complete abandonment of the People's party and the incorporation of Populists into the Democratic party. Mid-roaders complained that Ryan had merely masqueraded as a Populist and had constantly worked to subvert the People's party and force it into the Democracy.[36] Whatever the intentions, however, the results were convincing.

In this drift toward Democratic absorption of the People's party, Peffer's isolation became increasingly marked. Maine Populist leader L. C. Bateman believed that Peffer was the only Western Populist who understood the implications of fusion. "Peffer," declared Bateman, "towers above the pie-hunting mediocrities by whom he is surrounded, and who can appreciate neither his genius nor his patriotism." The object of continual criticism from the fusionists that dominated both parties, Peffer began to turn inward. After the 1897 election, he sold the *Advocate* and determined to retire from political life and devote himself to writing articles and to editing the "Farm Department" section of the *Advocate and News,* successor to his own paper. The *Norton Liberator* noticed

35 Emphasis added. *Girard World,* November 11, 1897; *Newton Semi-Weekly Journal,* June 22, November 16, 30, 1897; *Pleasanton Herald,* November 19, December 17, 1897; *Ottawa Weekly Times,* October 21, 1897; *Kansas Semi-Weekly Capital,* June 18, July 6, 1897.
36 *Girard World,* July 22, 1897.

his retirement with the comment, "Mr. Peffer, while a reformer, has considerable dislike for politics as now conducted, and felt somewhat restive in his position. It is a fact that the Populist party in its machinery and manipulations is patterning too much after the old parties to suit . . . [those] who have helped to build it up." J. W. Morphy, Peffer's friend and loyal assistant on the *Advocate,* also remarked that Peffer "is not a politician in the sense that the word is now used. He could not adapt himself to modern political methods, which is to his credit."[37]

In January 1898 Peffer published "The Passing of the People's Party" in the *North American Review.* "That the People's party is passing must be evident to all observers," he wrote. "*Why* it is going and *where,* are obviously questions of present public concern." Peffer assigned the dissolution of the party to the dissension over fusion. The split within the party, Peffer asserted, was decisive and fatal. Fusionists were already working with the Democrats in Kansas, Iowa, and Nebraska, for example, and were not even waiting to determine the position of the Democracy in 1900. The anti-fusionists refused to support a party with principles antagonistic to their own. The fusionists had rejected the repeated requests of the mid-roaders for a conference to adjust differences and decide upon the proper course for the party, and they had ignored Peffer's own suggestion, as an "individual anti-fusionist," to move toward the creation of a new party. The very readiness of the fusionists to accept Democratic direction, Peffer charged, prevented the formation of a new and unified party by causing Democrats to believe they could attract all reformers into their own party.

Obviously, fusion Populists would cooperate with Democracy in 1898 and 1900 while the anti-fusionists would not, Peffer continued. Therefore, the party was "passing." He was less sure of where the party was going but he hoped that eventually his desired political realignment would occur. In the meantime, while fusionists joined the Democrats, the anti-fusionists would in their own way continue the work for which the People's party was born. That work, Peffer conceded, would be delayed but it would come to fruition in time

37 *Topeka Advocate,* November 17, 1897; *Topeka Advocate and News,* November 24, 1897; *Norton Liberator,* November 19, 1897.

and the loyal Populists "shall have at last the reward of the faithful."[38]

This article plainly revealed Peffer's disenchantment with the evolution of the People's party. Nationally, the party organization was under fusionist control, and the mid-road opposition seemed both ineffectual and hopeless. In Kansas, fusionists completely dominated the party. Even the *Advocate and News* was no longer open to mid-road statements and urged Populists to nominate Democrats, while Simpson applied for a position on the Democratic National Congressional Committee, and Harris suggested a nationwide fusion of Democrats and Populists. Peffer avoided political activity, but kept busy. In January, for example, he addressed the state Farmers' Alliance annual meeting, was elected an officer of the Kansas State Historical Society, spoke to the annual convention of the Kansas State Temperance Union, and was elected to that organization's executive committee. He also wrote regularly for the *Advocate and News* on various general topics.[39] Clearly, Peffer was withdrawing from his political attitude of the 1890s and reverting to his agricultural and temperance interests of the 1880s and to a nominally nonpartisan attitude.

In the spring, Percy Daniels tried to draw Peffer back into political activity. In a public letter to Peffer, Daniels assured the former senator of his support in the face of the harsh criticism directed against him by the party leaders. Daniels also believed that the People's party had lost its opportunity to combine all reform elements under its own banner and that, as the Democracy was untrustworthy, a new party would have to be organized. Because the official Populist leadership, deceiving itself as to the true condition of the party, opposed the necessary realignment, Daniels urged that Peffer take the public lead in forming the new party by arranging meetings and calling a delegate convention of reformers.[40]

---

38 William A. Peffer, "The Passing of the People's Party," *North American Review* 166 (January 1898): 12-23.

39 *Topeka Advocate and News*, December 29, 1897, January 5, 12, 26, February 9, 1898; *Newton Semi-Weekly Journal*, January 7, March 22, 1898; F. C. Johnson to Jacob C. Ruppenthal, June 23, 1899, Jacob C. Ruppenthal Papers, KSHS; *Kansas Agitator*, January 21, 1898.

40 Percy Daniels to W. A. Peffer, supplement to *Girard Independent News*, April 14, 1898.

To Peffer, Daniels's plea must have sounded only too familiar, and only too futile. He ignored it. His public activity instead increasingly concentrated on prohibition, and he spoke regularly against Leedy's poor performance on the question. Prohibition had been imperfectly enforced throughout the decade, but under Leedy there was scarcely a pretense at enforcement. Democrats were delighted with Leedy's evident hostility toward prohibition, and some even expected that the People's party would declare for re-submission in its 1898 platform, but it was clear that the Pro-hibitionists would challenge the governor. Peffer's coolness toward Leedy fusionists plus his reputation as an ardent prohibitionist had encouraged speculation about his gubernatorial candidacy by May 1897. Peffer refused to countenance such talk and asserted his intention to avoid political office.[41]

By June 1898, however, opposition to Leedy was so intense among Prohibitionists that they determined to nominate Peffer, believing that he would attract both Populist and Republican support. After Samuel Dickey, the national chairman of the Prohibition party, visited him in Topeka, Peffer agreed to accept the nomina-tion provided the platform was confined to prohibition, and he accepted the nomination not as a Prohibitionist, but as a private citizen. Prohibitionists actually believed that Peffer could poll 100,000 votes and win, and many Populist officials, including Leedy and Breidenthal, feared his appeal. Indeed, anti-Leedy groups within the party threatened to support Peffer for the Populist gubernatorial nomination. Leedy accordingly sought to silence his opposition by suspending the metropolitan police system, which had provoked much of the prohibitionist resentment. Mrs. Diggs declared that this action left "no temperance Populist a shadow of excuse to give his vote to Senator Peffer." But Peffer's threat was short-lived for other reasons. He refused to discuss any question other than prohibition, made only nonpartisan speeches, and did not campaign actively. The Prohibitionist party had little official organization and depended on local ministers for strength and encouragement. And Peffer admitted that he did not expect to

41 *Topeka Advocate and News*, April 20, May 4, 1898; *Topeka Fulcrum*, April 8, 1898; *Kansas Semi-Weekly Capital*, December 31, 1897; *Norton Liberator*, May 28, 1897; *Topeka Advocate*, June 9, July 28, 1897.

be elected but that he only wanted to compel Leedy and Republican nominee William E. Stanley to promise enforcement of the Prohibitory law. If either would do so, Peffer said, he would end his campaign. By September Prohibitionists predicted that Peffer would receive but 10,000 votes and eventually he received fewer than that, though running far ahead of his ticket and nearly doubling the Prohibition vote of 1896.[42]

The Populists and Democrats joined in a complete campaign in 1898, even combining their party committees, few in either party objecting to the other any longer. But the fusionists had no chance. Discredited by their failures in the legislature, lacking the Silver Republican support of 1896, undermined by returning national prosperity, and opposed by a patriotic current to support a Republican president, they fell easily to the Republicans. The GOP elected its entire state ticket, a majority of the legislature, and all but one congressman.[43] Many Populists had predicted just such an outcome, and, perhaps in their frustration, they again lashed out at Peffer, a vivid symbol of their failure.

Peffer denied the charges that he had injured the cause of reform by his course. In his letter of acceptance, he had pointed out that the nomination came from "a party other than that to which I belong" and that his acceptance would not "affect my party relations, or change my party designation." His was a nonpartisan campaign. The Prohibitionists agreed. "He was not nominated as a party Prohib and does not claim to be one," the *Topeka Fulcrum* wrote of Peffer, "nor does the party claim him as a member. He claims to be a Populist, but it is a well known fact that he is . . . in reality a Populist without a party for the simple reason that the so-called Populist party are not populists, but fusionists first, last, and all the time." Peffer emphatically declared his own belief that the party had indeed left him, and not the reverse. His commitment to the original principles of the movement, he maintained, was undiminished, but "the present Populist party will inevitably

---

42 *Topeka Fulcrum,* June 10, July 1, August 12, 1898: *Emporia Daily Gazette,* June 8, 1898; *Anthony Weekly Bulletin,* June 10, 1898; *Kansas Semi-Weekly Capital,* July 2, 1898; *Topeka Advocate and News,* June 15, 22, August 31, September 21, 1898; *Newton Semi-Weekly Journal,* August 23, September 23, 1898; Kansas Biographical Scrapbook, "P," vol. 2, p. 61.

43 Nugent, *Tolerant Populists,* pp. 224-25; Clanton, *Kansas Populism,* p. 215.

be absorbed in the Democratic party. . . . I am not a Democrat and I cannot follow the Populist party into the Democratic ranks."[44]

Following the election, the fusionists speculated on their political future. J. Mack Love, Democratic state party chairman, announced that Populists no longer had any choice but to become Democrats fully and finally. A few scattered mid-roaders such as Clemens protested that "true Populists" would never accept the Democratic party, but most Populists seemed ready to acquiesce. There simply were not many original Populists left in the fusion coalition. "The trouble is," explained William Stryker, the thoughtful Populist state superintendent of public instruction, "that the People's Party has drifted away from the purposes for which it was created. The issues on which it was founded," he continued, "have been abandoned by self-styled leaders, and the party entered into league with the worst instead of the best element of the state. Much as I deplore [the recent] defeat," he concluded, "the party has brought it upon itself."[45]

Peffer also responded to Love's statement. Those Populists who had not objected to Democratic fusion, he believed, would join the Democracy as the People's party faded out of existence. But there were others who would not agree to such a course, Peffer warned. "As to the original Populist who remembers the Farmers' Alliance grip and pass word, he does not wish to be reorganized that way just now; he has no desire to be merged in a party that is not in sympathy with any of the ideas which he regards as vital." Peffer believed that "the original Populist clings to his first love," that, "in short, he believes in the people doing for themselves, through the agency of their government, everything that will tend to equalize benefits among the people, and that will in that way better than in any other serve the public interest." As the Democratic party opposed such an outlook, he expected that the original Populist would shun the Democracy. Indeed, "as between the Democratic and Republican parties, with respect to their foundation beliefs concerning the powers and duties of our government,

---

[44] *Topeka Fulcrum,* June 24, July 1, 1898; *Topeka Advocate and News,* June 15, 1898.

[45] *Topeka Advocate and News,* November 16, 1898; *Independence Star and Kansan,* November 18, December 9, 1898; *Kansas Agitator,* December 2, 1898.

the Republican idea is much broader than that of the Democratic, and may, therefore, be expected to advance faster in improving the agencies of public operations."[46]

The drift of Peffer's remarks was obvious. In the following spring, he declared that the vast increases in gold production, the increased use of commercial paper, and the return of prosperity had removed the financial question from politics and that he opposed the Democratic intention to make expansionism a partisan issue. "The Populist party has been eliminated nationally by the Democrats," he announced, "so those of us who don't want to flock by ourselves will have to vote our convictions as best we can." The principles of the Democratic party, Peffer believed, contravened those of the People's party, which centered about the need and desirability of a strong and active central government to promote the rights of the public. Fusion forced the Populists to choose between the Republicans and the Democrats, he maintained, and the Republicans favored the use of national power and had provided the antecedents of many Populist ideas. "The old simonpure Alliance man who left the Republican party," Peffer concluded, "never was headed for the Democracy, and he is not now." The press naturally reported that Peffer had "flopped" to the GOP. This Peffer strenuously denied, asserting that he had made but two points: first, that the People's party was dead and, second, that he was not a Democrat. "Now that the process of absorbing the Populist party is complete," he wrote, "and the fight is between Republican and Democrat, I respectfully ask leave to be against the Democrat and stop there."[47]

Peffer's distinction between being a Republican and being against Democrats in a political arena inhabited by only Democrats and Republicans was tenuous to say the least. Not surprisingly, the Populist press condemned him, continuing the harsh criticism heaped upon him for several years that, almost as much as anything else, drove him from the People's party. Peffer, however, tried to cling to this distinction. He repeated that he had neither left the

46 *Topeka Advocate and News,* November 23, 1898.

47 *Topeka State Journal,* May 18, 1899; Kansas Biographical Scrapbook, vol. 128, pp. 62-63; *Chicago Tribune,* July 9, 1899; Peffer to editor, *Topeka Daily Capital,* May 21, 1899.

People's party nor joined the GOP but merely that he believed that the political contests of the future would occur between the two old parties and "as between the Democratic and the Republican parties I have always been against the Democrats. . . . I expect to do all that I can honorably do to keep the Democratic party out of power in the nation." And in 1900, Peffer campaigned for McKinley and Roosevelt under the auspices of the Republican National Committee.[48] Regardless of his defensive reasoning, it was clear that the end had come. Populism had failed, and Peffer had returned home.

[48] *Kansas Agitator,* May 26, 1899; *Topeka Daily Capital,* June 23, 1899; Kansas Biographical Scrapbook, vol. 137, pp. 97-98.

CHAPTER TEN

Populism and Politics

WHATEVER their views on the merits of Populism, scholars have frequently agreed that it was ultimately successful if originally rejected. To list the Populist demands, declared one historian, "is to cite the chief political innovations made in the United States during recent times."[1] Many Populists in the first decade of the new century leaped eagerly and hopefully to the same conclusion. William Peffer expressed great pleasure that the principles which he had championed as a Populist and which were, he said, "laughed to death at that time are now considered respectable," and that in 1907 "the country now hotly demands legislation it abused me for advocating." He maintained that "today I do religiously believe in all the fundamental principles of the People's Party and have at no time cast them from me," and he continued to advocate reform in the social, political, and economic structure of the nation. But he accepted the hegemony of the GOP and eventually became an admitted Republican ("I'm an insurgent, though," he insisted). He had great praise for Theodore Roosevelt, believing that the president was "applying the principles of Populism."[2]

But Peffer must have known that this was a fiction. Roosevelt had regarded Peffer as an "anarchistic crank" in the 1890s and at one time urged that the Kansan be summarily executed. As president, Roosevelt's words remained more radical than his actions, and the transformation of American society promised in original Populism never occurred, despite the minor, palliative reforms of the twentieth century. The vaporings of Roosevelt became the triumph of Populist principles only through the cataracts of an old man's eyes and the mists of history.

Populism died because it failed to transcend the American political system. It was killed by those very factors of politics that its founders had intended to kill: prejudice, elite manipulation, corruption. Populists decried the divisive sectionalism still rampant in the 1890s and attempted to overcome it by promoting a union of sections based on generally shared interests; Populists arraigned partisan prejudices as destructive of the general good and urged the formation of a new grand union to surmount the obstacles provided by traditional and emotional party loyalties. Instead, the South rejected the Western yearnings in 1892 for the intertwined sectional and partisan appeals and stood as the Solid South for the Democratic party. Faced with this sectional and partisan rebuff of their good intentions, aggravated by the consequent election of a conservative Democratic administration, many Western Populists surrendered again to the intolerance and prejudices that had previously guided their political lives, reacting bitterly to the South and to Democrats. Thus, early, Populism underwent a significant change, with many former Republicans returning to the GOP, never to leave again, even in 1896. The People's party itself, too, became a sectional party, perhaps more so than either of its opponents, and yet it was unable to use effectively the possible advantages of

1 John D. Hicks, *The Populist Revolt* (Minneapolis, 1931), p. 407.

2 *Kansas City Star*, September 6, 1903; *Topeka State Journal*, June 27, 1907; *Topeka Daily Capital*, August 31, 1902; Kansas Biographical Scrapbooks, vol. 140, pp. 26-27, and "P," vol. 9, p. 107.

For Peffer's continued reform interests, see his following articles: "The Trust Problem and its Solution," *Forum* 27 (July 1899): 523-33; "The Trust in Politics," *North American Review* 170 (February 1900): 244-52; "Prohibition in Kansas," *Forum* 31 (April 1901): 209-12; "Fifty Years Ahead of Time: A Look Forward into the Political, Social, Industrial, and Labor Questions," Kansas Biographical Scrapbook, "P," vol. 14, p. 28; "Government Banking," *North American Review* 191 (January 1910): 12-17. The last mentioned involves nearly pure economic Populism minus silver: government banking, paper money, government loans directly to the people at low rates of interest, deemphasis of the tariff, abolition of note-issuing national banks.

sectionalism, which continued to be directed against it. In the West and in the South, the dominant party induced great instability in the Populist coalition by appealing to traditional loyalties and threatening the pending triumph of the despised minority party through the People's party. Ignatius Donnelly argued that popular prejudice against Democrats disrupted the People's party and destroyed the possibility of its success. "The Republican speakers claim[ed] that the People's Party men have all turned Democrats," he wrote, "and then they raked over the Democracy during the War, and drove our Republican friends back to their 'first love.'"[3] In the South, Republicans, especially black Republicans, served as the bête noire to keep party lines firm against Populism. Racial bigotry joined sectional provincialism and partisan prejudice in the triumphant assault on a Populism which, despite its rhetorical hyperbole, preached a realistic politics.

The struggle between partisans of different political traditions continued within the People's party. A Minnesota lawyer warned William Jennings Bryan against "the tyranny of political partisan-ship," which "is fundamental, all pervasive and permissive of all other political evils. As long as men regard the political instru-mentality through which a principle is to be obtained as of more moment than the principle itself, just so long will we have corrupt politics." That statement cogently explained the predicament of the third party, but Bryan already understood the problem and he knew that too often Populists themselves, despite their intentions, remained slaves to the same tyranny. In his own 1894 attempt to elect a fusionist legislature to send him to the Senate, he learned that "the Republican members of the Populist party voted almost to a man for the Republican candidate for their legislature." And, the Nebraska Democratic state chairman told him, "so it would be on every occasion when the issue is between a Democrat and a Republican."[4] Indeed, at least part of the fight over fusion involved simple distrust of Democrats, and Peffer's course during the 1890s typified that of the Populist who tried valiantly to overcome the partisan prejudice of his personal heritage and ultimately failed.

3 Ignatius Donnelly to W. A. Bentley, December 29, 1896, Donnelly Papers.
4 L. C. Harris to Bryan, October 21, 1895, and C. J. Smyth to Bryan, May 2, 1895, Bryan Papers.

The *Topeka Capital* had commented shortly after his senatorial election in 1891 that it was a "moral and physical impossibility for a man of Senator Peffer's antecedents and acquaintance with the differences between the Republican and Democratic parties to turn himself politically inside out at this late day." The issue was unsettled for nearly a decade, but perhaps never in doubt. Peffer was not the only major Populist who campaigned for Mc-Kinley in 1900; Mary Lease supported the GOP because "as I take it the issue has resolved itself into the old issue of copperheadism versus Republicanism, and as the daughter of an old Union soldier I feel that my place is with the Republican party." Thomas F. Byron, the anti-fusion editor whom Weaver forced from the *Des Moines Farmers' Tribune*, did not even wait till 1900. In 1896 he organized McKinley clubs in Iowa and supported the GOP rather than accept a national fusion with the Democrats.[5] The Populists had hoped to transform politics but had fallen under its dead weight; as the products of years of elite manipulation of passions and prejudices, they ultimately failed to escape from their past. But they had tried, something most Americans never considered doing.

Not just the trappings of the American political system, but the very nature of American politics also destroyed Populism. There were formal aspects to this: the bipolarizing effects of single-member legislative districts and other statutory features of the structure of American politics militated against third-party action. But the informal, though no less certain and decisive, features of politics proved eventually more destructive. The impulse of American politics was not toward a realistic appraisal of societal needs and a sincere attempt to solve the nation's basic problems. Rather, political parties were concerned with winning elections and more interested in votes than principles. Thus, the tariff, the bloody shirt, the Lost Cause, and white supremacy dominated political discussion before Populism: issues essentially irrelevant to the massive problems the nation confronted in industrialization, urban-

5 *Topeka Daily Capital*, April 3, 1891; *Leavenworth Times*, September 22, 1900; Kansas Biographical Scrapbook, "L," vol. 1, p. 130; Herman C. Nixon, "The Populist Movement in Iowa," *Iowa Journal of History and Politics* 24 (January 1926): 87.

ization, expansion, and immigration; but issues which would, because of their emotional content, mobilize electorates in state, section, and nation to maintain the dominance of self-seeking groups and parties. More than that, such sham issues often intensified national problems which continued to fester, unsolved, and diverted attention from real problems. Dependent upon traditional loyalties or ethnic-cultural cleavages for electoral support, old parties could not or would not formulate relevant policies for pressing economic, social, racial, and political difficulties. The two-party system did not meet the need to articulate constituent demands directly into the political framework.

What was significant about original Populism, after all, was that it developed outside the political system—and precisely because the system had proved incapable of responding to real needs. Yet in the transformation of Populism from a mass movement into the People's party, much of its democratic and directly responsive nature was lost. Populism became incorporated within the same system and the People's party became subject to the same influences that guided the other parties. The history of the People's party became one of a continuing struggle against the subversive tendencies of politics, undermining the original goals of Populism and substituting those of the old parties. The People's party, if originally for different reasons, became concerned with winning office and gradually accepted institutional objectives. Under the direction of professional politicians such as Taubeneck, Breidenthal, and Butler, Populist politics too became more of a struggle for office and power than for reform. The party became increasingly oligarchic and more easily dominated by its officials, and it became more and more difficult for the rank and file to influence policy. In Kansas, for example, as early as 1892 the party leadership rigged conventions, lied to its rank-and-file members, and overturned duly nominated candidates in the search for office.

In 1897 Davis Waite looked back at the Populist failure already evident and blamed the party organization. There had been no means to hold the party to principle, he lamented. It had adopted the same caucus system and the same party committees, used the "rotten delegates" and the "bossism" of the old parties. An "inside ring" had usurped the rights and circumvented the action of the rank and file, Waite asserted. "A few leading officials of the People's Party by as bald trickery in the way of bossism, bogus proxies, and paper delegates as ever distinguished 'Tammany Hall,' assumed supreme control of the party and exercised that control without consulting the popular will and without appeal." Henry Lloyd also complained about the increasing oligarchic control of his party. "When I see the selfishness, and stupidity, (synonymous terms) which appear in organizations, seeking to usurp the common sacrifice for personal advantage," he confessed to a friend, "I find it hard to keep my footing as a believer." Peffer similarly declared that local, independent action by autonomous popular groups would never interfere with the goals of Populism but that "the danger to Populism lies in the tendency of the party to go backward instead of forward."[6]

Annie Diggs recalled in 1901 that the true strength of Populism "never did lie in its party organization" and that in fact one of the roots of the movement was "a protest against the dangers and tyranny of permanent party organization." More important as a cause of Populism than economic distress, she argued, "was the discovery that the national machinery of both the Republican and the Democratic parties was set to the service of privileged classes and of commercial combinations." The people became furious when they understood "the humbuggery of the protective tariff. . . . the hypocrisy of the national party policies, the sham battle between Democracy and Republicanism over free-trade and protection." That vast mass movement of "the memorable revolt of 1890," she declared, was above narrowly "partisan politics." But "later, when success and official reward entered the minds of the people who came as recruits, the dominant spirit of the People's Party became less fraternal and unselfish."[7]

Percy Daniels saw the tragedy of the People's party. "It came. It saw," he wrote. "It has been conquered." Populism had repudiated "the methods of the old party machines" and denied "the celebrated theory of Mr. Ingalls that intrigue and corruption are essential to political success." But the party leaders set aside the

6 Davis Waite manuscript speech, 1897, Waite Papers; Lloyd to G. A. Gates, May 23, 1895, Lloyd Papers; Kansas Biographical Scrapbook, vol. 128, p. 60.
7 *Kansas City Star*, June 2, 1901.

original purpose of the movement, disobeyed the wishes of the rank and file, and adopted as legitimate tactics and appropriate goals what had been condemned. By 1898, Daniels denied that any party was controlled or directed in the interest of justice and declared that henceforth he would work outside the party system. "Parties as they exist today are bellowing imposters and organized frauds," he wrote, "sowing little but deception and garnering little but spoils and corruption. . . . They are either reliable machines of plutocracy and the corporations," he concluded, "or they are the handy tools of hypocrites and harlequins, and are as much responsible, through the deceptions they have practiced and the corruption they have defended, for the servitude of the masses to plutocratic usurpers, as are the lawless exactions of organized capital for their plundering."[8]

Those in control of the party machinery justified their manipulations in the name of "practical politics." Such machinations, however antithetical to the original professions of the movement, were necessary, argued Taubeneck, Weaver, Breidenthal, Butler, and Latimer, if the party were to secure election. Those who disagreed with such a policy were "impractical visionaries" and hopelessly utopian. It was not practical politics that the country needed, however; it had that in the Democratic and Republican parties. America needed realistic politics, a policy of ignoring facile prejudices, investigating the realities of problems, and formulating relevant programs without resorting to traditional and outmoded dogma. There were those who demanded just such a necessary radical reappraisal of American society, but they were precisely those damned as impractical visionaries. Gradually the Populist politicians succumbed to the same temptations affecting the old party leaders; too often converts to an elitist ideology, they proved as cynical as any of their opponents and certainly no more open and honest. But ultimately with less experience in dissembling, they lost to past masters. As much as the irrelevant tariff had served the old parties, the practical Populists used the issue of free silver as a political panacea. Essentially a minor reform, clearly of limited effectiveness, free silver nevertheless promised an electorate

[8] Daniels to Peffer, supplement to *Girard Independent News*, April 14, 1898; Percy Daniels in supplement to ibid., October 28, 1898.

to the People's party because as a panacea it was attractive to those who shrank from the requirements of realistic politics. Populist party leaders seized upon the issue to the exclusion of a consideration of vital problems and realistic reform proposals that the People's party had been created to advance. Silver and fusion, the tangible death instruments of Populism, did not dominate the People's party until its leaders subordinated the early demands of the movement in a practical grasp for power. Henry Lloyd wrote bitingly in 1896 of this Populist abdication of responsibility:

The men in the management of the P.P. who are specially and bitterly traitorously opposed to the real issues now before the public are the ones who have fanned this free silver back fire. All the railroad, telegraph, telephone, trust, bank, and other monopolists could ask nothing better than that the dangerous—to them—sentiment among the people be beguiled into believing that *the* principal cause of their woes was that the privilege of the silver owners to compel the people to accept their product as legal tender had been taken away. . . . [Demonetization, however, occurred long after the basis for the nation's social and industrial problems had been laid. But now] the poor people are throwing up their hats in the air for those who promise "to lead them out of the wilderness" by the currency route. It is awful. The people are to be kept wandering forty years in the currency labyrinth as they have for the last forty years . . . over the tariff bill.[9]

But the practical Populists suppressed the realistic Populists, and with the use of a prime old party technique. They condemned as "socialism" every suggestion that free silver coinage was not the primary and essential reform. Thus discredited in the eyes of those voters educated to the acceptance of panaceas, superficial solutions to nonexistent problems, and the avoidance of questioning the accepted myths which formed the bulwark of those in power, the radical Populists were pushed aside. Those such as John Willits who refused to acquiesce in the slightest to the demands of the party leadership were pursued with ever greater villification. A pariah in 1897, Willits explained his treatment as a mid-roader in 1896: "Because I refused to bolt our national convention, abandon the only Populist on the national ticket, and yell for the Democratic nominee and the Plutocratic Sewall, I was

[9] Lloyd to Bayard Holmes, July 13, 1896, Lloyd Papers.

denounced as a 'Hannacrat' by the whole gang of Democratic hirelings and cowardly, truckling, would-be Populists. You know too well the results," he continued. "Kansas went Democratic, the People's Party lost its identity, and the hands of time are turned back."[10]

Just as important as silver to the practical Populists was fusion, the policy of making concessions to other groups in hopes of finding a shortcut to political power. Fusion was a practical political maneuver in a political system that rewarded only one winner, but too often it required the betrayal of the promises of Populism (Peffer marveled at "how filthy the corruption of 'practical politics' among Reformers" became), and it gradually changed the composition, ideals, and objectives of the People's party.[11] Too, fusion was addictive and once taken it made the new party dependent and circumscribed its options.

Fusion and its requisite attendants of compromise, coercion, and constraint became the touchstone of Populism. Those who opposed fusion were interested in thorough, racial changes, focused on political reform which would provide a method to right any future abuses through establishing a responsive, realistic, and genuinely democratic political system. Fusionists were never as interested in political, or general, reform as in limited measures of economic reform. Lacking the great overall reformatory zeal, they were willing to refuse implementation of Populism where it was immediately possible—within the People's party—in futile hopes of achieving their own perverted program of personal power and a truncated economic Populism.[12]

In 1902 a Populist newspaper accused Peffer of being a traitor to Populism. Peffer replied that he had always stood for Populist principles, had demanded them in the Senate while Allen and others had denied them, had advocated them in party affairs, social positions, and all areas of life. He had resisted both compromise on Populist principles and fusion with other parties. "Had

10 John Willits to B. H. Oldfield in *Kansas Semi-Weekly Capital* (Topeka), July 27, 1897.

11 *Chicago Tribune*, June 29, 1899.

12 See William M. Stewart's comment upon Peffer in his *Silver Knight-National Watchman* (Washington, D.C.), August 26, 1897.

the party remained as it began," he added, "I would still be one of its faithful workers and earnest champions." But, he wrote to the editor, "you and others like you" wanted to compromise issues, restrict their application, emphasize free silver, adopt the unscrupulous methods of the unacceptable old parties, and fuse with the Democrats. Such a course Peffer had constantly opposed, he declared, "and advocated independent action on our own principles and policies. Who is the traitor—you or I?"[13]

13 Kansas Biographical Scrapbook, vol. 137, pp. 93-95, 97-98.

Essay on Sources

MANUSCRIPTS

Participants in a mass movement are rarely the type of people who possess or preserve personal papers, and lack of adequate manuscript sources has long hampered historians seeking to understand Populism. In the case of William A. Peffer, there is the additional disappointment that although he accumulated massive files of letters, scrapbooks, and diaries covering four decades and wished these papers to be given to the Kansas State Historical Society, his family divided the collection, nearly all of which was subsequently lost. The Kansas State Historical Society was able to acquire later several of the scrapbooks from Peffer's son, Douglas, but they largely contain only political cartoons. The Society also has a brief autobiographical sketch and several letters by Peffer, but most of his relatively few surviving letters must be found scattered in other collections.

The Kansas State Historical Society does have a number of other helpful manuscript holdings, especially the Lorenzo D. Lewelling Papers, which reveal the governor's problems in politics and patronage and provide a great deal of information on Kansas social conditions as well. The John Leedy Papers, from his term as governor, are fewer and disappointing. The Taylor Riddle Papers are also thin but should be consulted, for Riddle was Frank Doster's brother-in-law and the Populist state chairman in the late 1890s. The

Charles Robinson Papers and those of his son-in-law William H. Sears are valuable for the fusionist efforts of Democrats and Democratic-Populists. The collections of the following Republican leaders merit some attention: John J. Ingalls, M. M. Beck, Edmund N. Morrill, and Eugene F. Ware. The P. H. Coney Papers reflect the Silver Republican element. The Lyman U. Humphrey Papers are especially good for the Republican reaction to the rise of the Farmers' Alliance and the People's party entry into politics. Finally, the Society has two other collections, the Populist Party Manuscripts and the Republican Party Manuscripts, which should be surveyed.

The Kansas State Historical Society also has a number of relevant scrapbook collections, the most valuable of which are the John Davis Scrapbooks of the Populist editor and congressman; the Jacob C. Ruppenthal Scrapbooks of a local Populist official; the William H. Sears Scrapbooks; and the Farmers' Alliance Clippings, People's Party Clippings, and Kansas Biographical Scrapbooks, all assembled by the Society's staff from newspaper accounts.

The Spencer Research Library of the University of Kansas has several collections of interest. The George C. Angle Papers contain correspondence to a loyal local Republican party worker, with intriguing if incomplete references to the Farmers' Alliance; the J. B. Watkins Papers are a voluminous collection of the correspondence and records of a major land mortgage company, most immediately useful for viewing the moneylenders' political interests; the O. E. Learnard Papers throw light on the relations between Kansas politicians and railroads in the 1880s; the Lyman U. Humphrey Papers are much less full and more personal than those in the Kansas State Historical Society.

For Populism on the national level there are a few, widely scattered collections of considerable significance. The Ignatius Donnelly Papers at the Minnesota Historical Society are perhaps the most important, with correspondence both from major Populist figures and from local Populists, especially helpful for the early years of the movement. Virtually unknown and unused by historians are the Davis H. Waite Papers at the Colorado State Archives and Public Records. These include valuable information on the struggle against the Silver Populists' subversion of Omaha Populism as well as on the problems of Rocky Mountain Populism. The Henry D. Lloyd Papers at the State Historical Society of Wisconsin complement Waite's, for they contain much material on the radical Populists' efforts against the silver politicians. The Papers of Robert Schilling, first national secretary of the People's party, and of Lemuel H. Weller, both also at the State Historical Society of Wisconsin, similarly represent anti-fusion Populist views but are of little relative importance.

The fusionist Populists left little manuscript evidence of their activities. The James B. Weaver Papers at the Iowa Department of History and Archives are of small value, and it is necessary to examine Weaver's letters in other collections. The William M. Stewart Papers at the Nevada State Historical Society illuminate the labors of a major silverite who temporarily affiliated with the Populists. They are of special interest in revealing the early nature of silverite opposition to Omaha Populism and some of the maneuverings before the 1896 national convention. The Marion Butler Papers in the Southern Historical Collection of the University of North Carolina are particularly good for the campaign of 1896 and the problems the Populists then encountered in every part of the country but also have considerable information on the earlier activities of the Silver Populists.

Two other holdings in the Southern Historical Collection are of some value, the Leonidas L. Polk Papers and the Thomas E. Watson Papers. Most of Polk's Papers pertain to his varied activities before the 1890s, and Watson's Papers for the period are disappointing, limited mostly to business records and undated newspaper clippings.

Of the papers of non-Populists the most important are those of William Jennings Bryan in the Library of Congress. They contain considerable material on the fusion operations of Bryan Democrats and Nebraska and Iowa Populists before 1896 and valuable information on the actions of silverites of both parties leading to the 1896 Populist national convention. The Grover Cleveland Papers in the Library of Congress provide surprising glimpses into Democratic state politics, but the Benjamin Harrison Papers, also at the Library of Congress, offer little assistance.

NEWSPAPERS

The relative scarcity of manuscript material is partially compensated for by the wealth of newspapers available from a time of personal journalism. Most important, of course, were Peffer's own newspapers, the *Kansas Farmer* and the *Advocate,* both of Topeka. In Kansas, the most helpful papers of the mid-road persuasion were the *Kansas Agitator* (Garnett) of W. O. and Anna Champe, the *Kincaid Kronicle* for the campaign of 1892, and Cyrus Corning's *The People* and *New Era* (both of Topeka) with Abe Steinberger's *Girard World* for the extreme element thereafter. The fusion Populists were best represented in the *Kansas Commoner* (Wichita) and in the *Pleasanton Herald* of J. E. Latimer.

The *Topeka Capital* was the leading Republican newspaper and also provided the most extensive reporting of all state political developments. The *Atchison Champion* represented the more liberal Republicans, and the *Fort Scott Monitor* and *Emporia Republican* were other major GOP organs. The strange Democratic course is best followed in the *Wichita Beacon* and the *Kansas Democrat* (Topeka). More consistent was the conservative course of the Paola *Western Spirit* in opposing fusion with the Populists.

Over a hundred other Kansas newspapers were systematically read to cover all political positions within each of the three major parties, plus the Union Labor party and the Prohibitionists, and to cover every section of the state. They ranged from the *Valley Falls Farmers' Vindicator* and the *Norton Liberator* to the *Erie Republican-Record* and the *Marshall County Democrat* (Marysville). Citations of such journals can be found in the appropriate footnotes. Files of all these newspapers are in the splendid collection of the Kansas State Historical Society.

For national developments, the most important Populist newspapers were the *Topeka Advocate,* under both Stephen McLallin and Peffer; the *American Non-Conformist* (Indianapolis); and the *Southern Mercury* (Dallas). Balancing these mid-road papers were those of the Silver Populists, especially William Stewart's *Silver Knight* and N. A. Dunning's *National Watchman,* both published in Washington, D.C. Among others of major significance, the *People's Party Paper* (Atlanta) provided Tom Watson's point of view, and the *National Economist* (Washington) was valuable for the Farmers' Alliance in the early 1890s. Leading non-Populist newspapers consulted included the *Chicago Tribune,* the *Washington Post,* the *Dallas Morning-News,* the *Kansas City Star,* the *St. Louis Post-Dispatch,* the *Louisville Courier-Journal,* the *Cincinnati*

Commercial-Gazette, and the New York *Times* and *World.* Again, dozens of other journals, from every region and of every persuasion, were examined, and where appropriate they are cited in the footnotes.

Essential to the development of the statistical information pertaining to the demographic characteristics of Kansas partisans in the 1890s was the United States Bureau of the Census, *Eleventh Census of the United States, 1890* (Washington, 1891–1895). Also used were population and agricultural statistics derived from the *Biennial Reports of the* [Kansas] *State Board of Agriculture* (Topeka, Kans., 1887–1900) and election statistics recorded in the *Biennial Reports of the Secretary of State of the State of Kansas* (Topeka, Kans., 1885–1900). The *Congressional Record* and the *House Journal* and *Senate Journal* of the Kansas legislature contain considerable material apart from the legislative process itself and help indicate the changing objectives of Populists in office. Finally, specialized documents fully cited in the footnotes, such as the *Second Annual Report of the* [Kansas] *Bureau of Labor and Industrial Statistics* (Topeka, Kans., 1887) or Peffer's own Senate report, *Agricultural Depression; Causes and Remedies* (Washington, 1895), provide helpful information on their specific concerns.

Peffer was a prolific author, and I consulted all his published works. The most useful and important were *The Farmer's Side: His Troubles and Their Remedy* (New York, 1891), the primary expression of the early Populist positions on society, economics, and politics; *The Way Out* (Topeka, Kans., 1890), a proposed solution of agrarian economic problems similar to the more famous subtreasury scheme; "The Farmers' Defensive Movement," *Forum* 8 (December 1889): 464-73, which describes the various farm orders, their grievances, and their objectives preceding the 1889 St. Louis meeting that attempted to unite them; "Government Control of Money," in *The Farmers' Alliance History and Agricultural Digest,* ed. Nelson A. Dunning (Washington, D.C., 1891), pp. 262-71; and "The Mission of the Populist Party," *North American Review* 157 (December 1893): 665-78, which contains some general proposals to guide Populists. Peffer's attitudes toward the demise of Populism appear in his "The Passing of the People's Party," *North American Review* 166 (January 1898): 12-23; "Populism, Its Rise and Fall," published in the *Chicago Tribune*, 1899; and "The People's Party," in *Harper's Encyclopedia of United States History* (New York, 1902), 8: 130-37. His continued reform interests are obvious in "The Cure for a Vicious Monetary System," *Forum* 22 (February 1897): 722-30; "The Trust Problem and its Solution," *Forum* 27 (July 1899): 523-33; "The Trust in Politics," *North American Review* 170 (February 1900): 244-52; and "Government Banking," *North American Review* 191 (January 1910): 12-17, among other articles.

Other Populist publications of significant value include Gaspar C. Clemens, *An Appeal to True Populists* (Topeka, Kans., 1896), an anti-politics manifesto, opposing an early national convention in 1896 and insisting upon original, not Silver, Populism; a series of works by Percy Daniels which demonstrate his personal approach to reform, particularly *A Crisis for the Husbandman* (Girard, Kans., 1889), *A Lesson of Today and a Question of Tomorrow* (Girard, Kans., 1892), and *Cutting the Gordian Knot* (Pittsburg, Kans., 1896); John F. Willits and Abe Steinberger, *Populism* (n.p., n.d.), which in its simplicity of title as well as in its arguments conveys the feeling of change within the People's party as it defies the 1896 fusion plan; S. S. King, *Bondholders and Breadwinners* (Kansas City, Kans., 1892). The early positions of the Farmers' Alliance and People's party are well presented in W. Scott Morgan, *History of the Wheel and the Alliance, and the Impending Revolution* (Fort Scott, Kans., 1891), the official Southern Alliance history, and in Nelson A. Dunning, ed., *The Farmers' Alliance History and Agricultural Digest* (Washington, D.C., 1891). Populist campaign material is illustrated by Thomas E. Watson, *Not a Revolt, It is a Revolution: The People's Party Campaign Book* (Washington, D.C., 1892), and outlined by John Breidenthal, *Agitate; Educate; Organize* (Topeka, Kans., 1896).

A number of Populists described their leading associates, most notably Annie L. Diggs in two articles, "The Farmers' Alliance and Some of its Leaders," *Arena* 5 (April 1892): 590-604, and "The Women in the Alliance Movement," *Arena* 6 (July 1892): 160-79, and in a later eulogistic book, *The Story of Jerry Simpson* (Wichita, Kans., 1908). Hamlin Garland provided a classic description of Peffer, among others, in "The Alliance Wedge in Congress," *Arena* 5 (March 1892): 447-57. W. F. Rightmire supplied an insider's viewpoint in two reminiscent articles, "The Alliance Movement in Kansas—Origin of the People's Party," *Transactions of the Kansas State Historical Society* (Topeka, Kans., 1906), 9: 1-8; and "Organization of the National People's Party," *Collections of the Kansas State Historical Society* (Topeka, Kans., 1928), 17: 730-33. Henry D. Lloyd surveyed the Populist leaders and their actions at the 1896 national convention in "The Populists at St. Louis," *Review of Reviews* 14 (September 1896): 298-303.

William Jennings Bryan set forth his account of the 1896 election in *The First Battle: A Story of the Campaign of 1896* (Chicago, 1896), which is especially useful for its reprinted documents. Joseph K. Hudson, *Letters to Governor Lewelling* (Topeka, Kans., 1893), presents a Republican version of the infamous 1893 Kansas legislature. A Populist rejoinder is Edwin S. Waterbury, *The Legislative Conspiracy in Kansas. Court vs. Constitution. Who Are the Anarchists?* (Topeka, Kans., 1893).

SELECTED SECONDARY SOURCES

Populism has generated a great deal of scholarly work and a vigorous interpretive debate. Much of this is not directly relevant to this study, and for a proper introduction interested readers should consult Theodore Saloutos, "The Professors and the Populists," *Agricultural History* 40 (October 1966): 235-54, and C. Vann Woodward, "The Populist Heritage and the Intellectual," in *The Burden of Southern History* (New York, 1960), pp. 141-66.

For Populism itself, the most comprehensive history still remains John D. Hicks, *The Populist Revolt* (Minneapolis, Minn., 1931). Kansas Populism has received special attention from a number of authors. Elizabeth N. Barr, "The Populist Uprising," in *A Standard History of Kansas and Kansans,* ed. William E. Connelley

(Chicago, 1918), 2: 1113-95, is an early sympathetic account still extremely valuable; W. P. Harrington, a former Populist, produced a fine and informed master's thesis published as "The Populist Party in Kansas," *Collections of the Kansas State Historical Society* (Topeka, Kans., 1925), 16: 403-50; Raymond C. Miller overemphasizes the economic roots of agrarian politics in "The Populist Party in Kansas" (Ph.D. diss., University of Chicago, 1928). Of more recent studies, Walter T. K. Nugent, *The Tolerant Populists: Kansas Populism and Nativism* (Chicago, 1963), correctly maintains the Populist innocence of the indictment of nativism but sometimes is less accurate in discussing the political aspects of Populism. James C. Malin, *A Concern About Humanity: Notes on Reform, 1872–1912, at the National and Kansas Levels of Thought* (Lawrence, Kans., 1964), and *Confounded Rot About Napoleon: Reflections upon Science, Technology, Nationalism, World Depression of the Eighteen-Nineties and Afterwards* (Lawrence, Kans., 1961), imaginatively if arcanely pursue a variety of objectives dealing with reform traditions and methodology. A good synthesis, with particular emphasis upon major leaders, is O. Gene Clanton, *Kansas Populism: Ideas and Men* (Lawrence, Kans., 1969).

Specific aspects of the Kansas Populist experience have received coverage too. In an important article, "Some Parameters of Populism," *Agricultural History* 40 (October 1966): 255-70, Walter T. K. Nugent demonstrates the correspondence between Populist rhetoric and economic reality and proposes notable differences between members of the various political parties. In a more traditional way, Nugent also examines "How the Populists Lost in 1894" (*Kansas Historical Quarterly* 31 [Autumn 1965]: 245-55) but with results and interpretations much less satisfactory. William Parrish discusses the Legislative War in "The Great Kansas Legislative Imbroglio of 1893," *Journal of the West* 7 (October 1968): 471-90. William H. Chafe, "The Negro and Populism: A Kansas Case Study," *Journal of Southern History* 34 (August 1968): 402-19, argues that blacks were more concerned with practical than ideological factors in politics. Peter H. Argersinger, "Pentecostal Politics in Kansas: Religion, the Farmers' Alliance, and the Gospel of Populism," *Kansas Quarterly* 1 (Fall 1969): 24-35, suggests connections between economic conditions, religious activity, and political developments. Using Peffer's *Kansas Farmer* as one important example, Allan G. Bogue maintains that the "agrarian interpretation of the moneylender" needs significant revision in *Money at Interest: The Farm Mortgage on the Middle Border* (Ithaca, N.Y., 1955), a detailed study relevant to Nebraska as well as Kansas. Nebraska Populism itself has been fruitfully studied by Stanley B. Parsons. In a pioneering article, "Who Were the Nebraska Populists?" *Nebraska History* 44 (June 1963): 83-99, Parsons first used some of the techniques employed in this work to identify Populists by their socioeconomic characteristics. This he has developed and expanded, from a behavioral perspective, in his recent *The Populist Context: Rural versus Urban Power on a Great Plains Frontier* (Westport, Conn., 1973), which is especially valuable for its discussion of the structure of power in Nebraska. David S. Trask, "Formation and Failure: The Populist Party in Seward County, 1890-1892," *Nebraska History* 51 (Fall 1970): 281-301, is a study of a Nebraska county that rejected Populism for economic, ethnic, and political reasons.

Populism in other states in the Midwest and Plains has been treated more briefly by historians. Herman C. Nixon provides an admirable account of "The Populist Movement in Iowa" in the *Iowa Journal of History and Politics* 24 (January 1926): 3-107, while Fred E. Haynes examines Iowa Populism in the general context of *Third Party Movements since the Civil War* (Iowa City, 1916). Roy V. Scott, *The Agrarian Movement in Illinois, 1880-1896* (Urbana, Ill., 1962), demonstrates that Populism held little appeal for diversified, commercial farmers and suggests the weaknesses of agrarian political leadership as well. This should be supplemented by Chester McArthur Destler's useful and painstaking work, *American Radicalism, 1865-1901* (New London, Conn., 1946), which focuses on the labor side of Populist radicalism, particularly in Illinois. The Indiana experience earns direct treatment in Ernest Stewart, "The Populist Party in Indiana," *Indiana Magazine of History* 14 (December 1918): 332-67, and 15 (March 1919): 53-74, an early study that again indicates the vulnerability of Populism to political developments and provides a good account of 1896 fusion maneuvers. South Dakota receives limited consideration in Kenneth E. Hendrickson, Jr., "Some Political Aspects of Populism in South Dakota," *North Dakota History* 34 (Winter 1967): 77-92; and Terry Paul Wilson concludes that free silver and fusion caused "The Demise of Populism in Oklahoma Territory" (*Chronicles of Oklahoma* 43 [Autumn 1965]: 265-74). An imaginative and suggestive intellectual history of Populism focusing on the entire Midwest is Norman Pollack, *The Populist Response to Industrial America* (Cambridge, Mass., 1962), an impassioned defense of Populist radicalism and relevancy that is usually too quickly dismissed. Unfortunately, Pollack's determination to defend all who claimed to be Populists leads him into tortuous illogic when he defends fusion. A greater attention to political developments over time might have shown the wisdom of Cyrus Corning's statement that "fighting fusion is not fighting the People's Party any more than fighting prostitution is opposing virtue."

Despite its importance, Populism in the Rocky Mountain states is only recently the subject of historical examination, much of it emphasizing silverite politics. Thomas A. Clinch, *Urban Populism and Free Silver in Montana* (Helena, Mont., 1970), stresses the labor orientation of the movement in the West. Mary Ellen Glass, *Silver and Politics in Nevada: 1892-1902* (Reno, Nev., 1969), demonstrates that silverites were anything but reformers. G. Michael McCarthy, "The People's Party in Colorado: A Profile of Populist Leadership," *Agricultural History* 47 (April 1973): 146-55, refutes the view that Populists were "disillusioned old men who had experienced years of political failure and who had embraced numerous political philosophies before incorporating them into 'Populism.'" The most famous of the Colorado Populists is the subject of a valuable dissertation by John R. Morris, "Davis Hanson Waite: The Ideology of a Western Populist" (Ph.D. diss., University of Colorado, 1965), the first work to use the important Waite Papers. All studies of Far Western Populism should be superseded by a forthcoming book by James E. Wright.

The student of Southern Populism should begin with two general works, C. Vann Woodward's magnificent *Origins of the New South, 1877-1913* (Baton Rouge, La., 1951), and Theodore Saloutos, *Farmer Movements in the South, 1865-1933* (Berkeley, Calif., 1960). On the state level, Alabama has received the most thorough treatment. John B. Clark, *Populism in Alabama* (Auburn, Ala., 1927), is a competent study since surpassed by William Warren Rogers, *The One-Gallused Rebellion: Agrarianism in Alabama, 1865–1896* (Baton Rouge, La., 1970), and by Sheldon Hackney's very good *Populism to Progressivism in Alabama* (Princeton, N.J., 1969). Using social science concepts and quantitative techniques, Hackney more explicitly comes to conclusions similar to my own about the conflict between values and power in social movements, but his main concern is to demonstrate the discontinuity between Populism and Progressivism. Ironically, despite his approach, he fails to use the time dimension fully in his analysis or to take into complete account the factional nature of the Populist movement.

Three older but still valuable studies of Southern state Populism are Alex Arnett, *The Populist Movement in Georgia* (New York, 1922); Roscoe C. Martin, *The People's Party in Texas* (Austin, Texas, 1933); and William DuBose Sheldon, *Populism in the Old Dominion: Virginia Farm Politics, 1885–1900* (Princeton, N.J., 1935). A more general narrative of Mississippi politics is Albert D. Kirwan, *Revolt of the Rednecks: Mississippi Politics, 1876–1925* (Lexington, Ky., 1951). William Ivy Hair discusses this same traditional political struggle between conservative Democrats and discontented farmers but adds considerable social history as well in his *Bourbonism and Agrarian Protest: Louisiana Politics, 1877–1900* (Baton Rouge, La., 1969).

The historical record of much of Southern Populism has been shaped by C. Vann Woodward's superb biography, *Tom Watson, Agrarian Rebel* (New York, 1938), perhaps the single most compelling work on Populism. However, its influence has also helped lead to an unfortunate reversal of the earlier overemphasis upon Western Populism that neglected the South and to an inaccurate conclusion that "Southern Populism," as Richard Hofstadter became convinced in his critical *The Age of Reform: From Bryan to F.D.R.* (New York, 1955), "was at least as strong as the Western brand and contained the more radical wing of the agrarian revolt of the nineties." A more "typical" Southern Populist leader than Watson is described by Stuart Noblin in his biography of the president of the Farmers' Alliance, *Leonidas LaFayette Polk, Agrarian Crusader* (Chapel Hill, N.C., 1949). Southern political leaders who refused to break from the Democratic party are helpfully discussed in Francis B. Simkins, *Pitchfork Ben Tillman* (Baton Rouge, La., 1944), an examination of the leader of the South Carolina Alliance, and in Robert Cotner's biography of the Democratic governor of Texas *James Stephen Hogg* (Austin, Texas, 1959).

Martin Ridge, *Ignatius Donnelly: The Portrait of a Politician* (Chicago, 1962), is the best biography of a Western Populist, a careful, detailed study of a fascinating character. Fred E. Haynes, *James Baird Weaver* (Iowa City, 1919), is excessively kind to its subject. Ray Ginger, *The Bending Cross: A Biography of Eugene Victor Debs* (New Brunswick, N.J., 1949), and Chester McArthur Destler, *Henry Demarest Lloyd and the Empire of Reform* (Philadelphia, 1963), deal only briefly with the Populist activities of their admired subjects. Michael J. Brodhead, *Persevering Populist: The Life of Frank Doster* (Reno, Nev., 1969), is a fine biography of the Kansas Populist, though it deliberately avoids relating Doster to historiographical concerns. Brodhead further illuminates connections between the legal mind and the political man in an essay on another Kansas Populist Supreme Court Justice, "Populism and the Law: Some Notes on Stephen H. Allen," *Kansas Quarterly* 1 (Fall 1969): 76-84. Karel Bicha shows that there was even less connection between rhetoric and behavior for another Populist leader in "Jerry Simpson: Populist without Principle," *Journal of American History* 54 (September 1967): 291-306. One Populist whose behavior has always been suspect is the subject of a brief article by O. Gene Clanton, "Intolerant Populist? The Disaffection of Mary Elizabeth Lease," *Kansas Historical Quarterly* 34 (Summer 1968): 189-200.

Two biographies of leading Kansas Republicans throw little additional light on the topic of Populism: Burton J. Williams, *Senator John James Ingalls: Kansas' Iridescent Republican* (Lawrence, Kans., 1972), and Mark A. Plummer, *Frontier Governor: Samuel J. Crawford of Kansas* (Lawrence, Kans., 1971). A more important figure receives more detailed and valuable consideration in Paola E. Coletta, *William Jennings Bryan: Political Evangelist, 1860–1908* (Lincoln, Neb., 1964), Paul W. Glad, *The Trumpet Soundeth: William Jennings Bryan and His Democracy, 1896–1912* (Lincoln, Neb., 1960), and J. Rogers Hollingsworth, *The Whirligig of Politics:*

The Democracy of Cleveland and Bryan (Chicago, 1963), the last two particularly useful for understanding the convolutions of the Democratic party in the 1890s. Elmer Ellis has written the standard biography of the leading Silver Republican, *Henry Moore Teller: Defender of the West* (Caldwell, Idaho, 1941). Stanley P. Hirshson traces one important element in Republican politics of the period in *Farewell to the Bloody Shirt: Northern Republicans and the Southern Negro, 1877–1893* (Bloomington, Ind., 1962), but declining concern for Southern blacks did not necessarily mean an end to bloody shirt politics, and Hirshson overlooks the continuing strength of sectional prejudices in the electorate.

Paul W. Glad surveys personalities and issues of both parties and the role of attitudes and emotions as well in his excellent and underrated study of the election of 1896, *McKinley, Bryan, and the People* (Philadelphia, 1964). The fullest discussion of that critical election is Stanley L. Jones, *The Presidential Election of 1896* (Madison, Wis., 1964). The Populist role in the campaign is described by Robert Durden in *The Climax of Populism: The Election of 1896* (Lexington, Ky., 1965), a useful book marred by the author's too complete reliance on the Marion Butler Papers and his failure to investigate Populist actions before 1896 that helped determine the direction and development of the campaign he details. In their books cited above, Clanton, Hackney, Hicks, and Woodward examine aspects of the post-1896 Populist experience, but none is fully satisfying, which perhaps the Populists would have found appropriate.

Index

42-44, 62, 79, 89, 100, 130, 146, 159-61,
162-63, 167, 175, 176, 297-98
Prohibitionists, 100, 223, 282, 285,
297-98; as a faction within the
People's party, 39, 49, 73, 74n,
187, 188

railroad regulation, 2, 7, 283-84, 285;
in farmers' program, 6, 9, 15, 25
Rankin, Martin C., 258
Raynolds, L. D., 244, 246
Record Review, 214
Republican party: effect of the
People's party on, 88, 89, 95, 97, 110,
111; attitude of, toward the People's
party in 1891 elections, 99-100, 116;
and sectional ploy, 100, 115, 117-18;
fuses with Populists in the South,
113-14, 200-201, 250, 266, 274; and
silver, 216, 246; 1896 national
convention of, 246, 247; Peffer's
attitude toward, 255, 299-301, 302,
305; National Committee of, 301; in
Kansas (*see* Kansas Republican
party); mentioned, *passim*
Republican-Populists, 49, 50, 84, 85,
94, 115, 117, 173; and Populist
factionalism, 54-56, 78, 161, 170, 293;
voting behavior of, 72-79, 184-89;
and fusion, 79, 129, 130, 139, 168-69,
231, 293; return of, to the
Republican party, 140, 142-46, 150,
160, 183, 184-89, 303-4; attitudes of,
toward government, 286-87, 299-300
resubmission, 40, 44, 297
Resubmission Republicans, 40, 74-75,
76, 187, 187n, 188n
Rice, John H., 81, 143, 265
Rightmire, William F.: helps organize
the People's party nationally, 81-82,
85, 99, 100, 265; opposes the
Lewelling administration, 165, 171;
and 1896 campaign, 270-71
Robinson, Charles, 44, 46, 48, 49, 167,
183; and gubernatorial nomination,
36-40, fusion plans of, 130, 131, 135,
137, 138
Roosevelt, Theodore, 301, 302, 303
Routzong, W. C.: editor of *Kincaid
Kronicle,* 126
Ryan, W. H., 294

St. Louis conference of 1892, 84, 86,
109-10
St. Louis conference of 1894, 204-8,

210, 211, 214, 215
St. Louis convention of 1889, 24-25, 93;
demands of, 35, 39
St. Louis meeting of the People's
party National Committee (1896),
234-38, 240
Saloutos, Theodore, 60
Schilling, Robert, 248, 265
Sears, William H.: fusion activities of,
167, 253, 268, 280; promotes Harris's
senatorial election, 277, 280
Second District, campaign of 1892 in,
124-25, 129, 136-41, 144, 165;
campaign of 1894 in, 177-78
sectionalism: in politics, 3, 28, 44-45,
56, 80, 88-91, 95-98, 100, 101, 110,
112-13, 114-20, 144-46, 147; effect of,
on the People's party, 83-85, 97,
103, 112-13, 114-20, 144-45, 147, 150,
303-4
Sedgwick County, 66, 74, 135, 160
Senn, Michael, 230
Seventh District, 40, 133, 175-76, 267
Sewall, Arthur M., 249, 252, 253, 260,
261, 265, 266-68, 309
Seward County, 63
Shawnee County, 45, 65, 66, 84, 171-72,
293
Sherman, John, 99
Sherman Silver Purchase Act, 170,
194, 195-96
Sibley, Joseph C., 216, 217, 219-20, 242
Silver Democrats, 195, 196, 265;
activities of, 198, 211, 216, 220-21;
cooperate with the Silver Populists,
199, 204, 214, 220-21, 223, 234-35,
244; attitudes of, toward fusion, 219,
220, 228; attitudes of, toward
Populism, 220; in Kansas, 229-30;
control Democratic party, 248, 249
Silverites: oppose Populism, 197, 202,
217; organize silver party, 216; and
Silver Populists, 216, 234, 237, 238,
240, 245, 259
Silver Knight (Washington, D.C.), 226,
237, 239, 241, 253, 289
silver party, 216-17, 250, 269
Silver Populists: attempt to subvert
Populism, 202, 204-7, 209-11, 213-16,
221-22, 234-39, 245; support fusion,
202, 214, 215-16, 219-21, 234, 237,
239-42; attack their Populist
opponents as socialists, 203-4, 207-9,
211, 213-14, 239-40; displace original
Populists, 204, 265; advocate late